TRAITORS
OR
PATRIOTS?

TRAITORS OR PATRIOTS?

A STORY OF THE GERMAN ANTI-NAZI RESISTANCE

Louis R. Eltscher

Published by McNidder & Grace
21 Bridge Street
Carmarthen
SA31 3JS
United Kingdom
www.mcnidderandgrace.co.uk

Original paperback first published 2020
US hardback edition first published 2018

© Louis R. Eltscher 2020

All rights reserved. No part of this work may be reproduced or transmitted in any form or by any means, electronic or mechanical, including photocopy, recording, or any information storage or retrieval system, without permission in writing from the publisher.

Louis R. Eltscher has asserted his right to be identified as the author of this work in accordance with the Copyright, Designs and Patents Act 1988.

A catalogue record for this work is available from the British Library.

ISBN: 9780857162038
Ebook: 9780857162045

Cover design by Lara Peralta
Designed by JS Typesetting Ltd, Porthcawl

Printed and bound in the United Kingdom by Short Run Press, Exeter

In memory of Carolyn, who cared

"Treason" had become true patriotism, and what was normally "patriotism" had become treason.

– Eberhard Bethge

Contents

Acknowledgments ix

Preface xi

Introduction xiii

Chapter 1 The Burden of History 1

    Leaders and Assassins 4
    The Legacy of the Great War 7
    The Doomed Republic 8
    Right-Wing Extremism 10
    Enter the Nazis 12

Chapter 2 The Nazis in Power 19

    The People React 20
    The People's Community 28
    Conformity, Dissent, and Terror 32
    Racial Warfare 42

Chapter 3 An Emergent Resistance 45

    Constraints 45
    Conception and Gestation 51
    The Conservatives 55
    Nazi Distortions 65
    The Churches 68
    The Socialists 85
    Two Resistance Groups 95
    Individuals and Small Groups 105

Chapter 4 An Organized Resistance 115

    The Blood Purge 115
    An Oath of Allegiance 118
    Rearmament and the Rhineland 125
    1938: A Pivotal Year 133
    Treason 136
    Anschluss and Sudetenland 141

Chapter 5 The Army – Four Rounds of Resistance 148

    Round I: The Oster Conspiracy, July to September 1938 149
    Round II, Part 1: The Abwehr, September to November 5,
    1939 175
    Round II, Part 2: The Abwehr, November 6, 1939 to
    May 1940 203
    Round III: Army Group Center, August 1942 to October
    1943 214
    Round IV: Operation Valkyrie, March to July 1944 240

Chapter 6 The Last Act 264

    Retribution and Martyrdom 265
    Finale 282

Appendix A Glossary 290

Appendix B Dramatis Personae 295

Appendix C The Sources of Nazi Racism 300

Notes 306

Bibliography 351

Index 357

Acknowledgments

Traitors or Patriots? is the outgrowth of a course that I have offered periodically in a national adult education program known as OASIS. As I first began to present the story of the resistance, I quickly realized that many of those in my class, though well educated, were not necessarily well versed in either German or modern European history. I also realized that a grasp of this broader context was essential to a proper understanding of the resistance story. Therefore, I began to write an essay that ultimately grew into this book. I extend my thanks to all who were part of that course for their interest and inspiration.

Many other people provided invaluable help as the work proceeded, and I wish to thank them as well. Several good friends encouraged me to pursue the project to completion – friends such as Lou Andolino, Larry Britt, Jim Fleming, and the late George Aberle. They all read earlier versions of the manuscript and offered invaluable criticisms and insights. Ingeborg Oberdoerster, my German-language teacher, kindly read the manuscript to ensure that my use of the German language was correct. Special thanks go to David Ferrell, professor emeritus of theater arts at Nazareth College in Rochester, New York. Because of him, the final product reads much better than earlier drafts. Special thanks also go to Martha McNeill, who is a former copyeditor. Her reading of the earlier draft also resulted in a greatly improved manuscript. In addition, I must cite the invaluable help supplied by my "computer guru," Louis Sabo, in preparing the manuscript for publication.

Finally, and most importantly, I want to thank all my family for their continued love and support. Special thanks go to my daughter, Judy Malloy, for her help in preparing the manuscript, and to her husband, Nicholas Down. Nicholas, an artist, who designed the cover for the US edition of *Traitors or Patriots?* Sue Warrick, my elder daughter, donated her editorial expertise to the preparation of the revisions to this book. Sadly, my dear wife, Carolyn, passed away as I was working on this revised edition. Her love and support are greatly missed.

Preface

The inspiration for *Traitors or Patriots?* can be found in the experiences that I had as a young teenager growing up in the United States during World War II. I knew that my ethnicity/ancestry was almost completely German. My paternal grandfather was born and raised in Dobschau, Austria (now Dobsina, Slovakia), and my paternal grandmother's place of birth was Zwiesel, Bavaria. Both migrated to the United States at the end of the nineteenth century. They met in Pennsylvania. My mother's family had come to the United States much earlier, probably near the beginning of the eighteenth century. Circumstantial evidence suggests that the original homeland was the Breisgau region of southwest Germany.

The knowledge of my family origins became the source of many troubling thoughts as I absorbed the news of the day, along with the war propaganda that accompanied the news. Germany was drawn in the darkest-possible shades. Allegedly, the entire German nation gave wholehearted support to Adolf Hitler and his minions and to their racist ideology. A small but typical example of the widespread animus toward Germany and the Germans can be found in a book published in 1944, *Not Nazis but Germans*, by Dimitri J. Tosevic, who is identified as a "Yugoslav political journalist." Speaking of World War II, he makes the following comments:

> The Germans are not sinning for the first time. The Germans have, during the last eighty years, thrown Europe into five bloody wars.

And:

> The German nation must be punished. It must be reeducated from its very foundations ... Let us not forget that the German has remained the Hun and the aggressor for centuries. He must not again plunge us into barbarism and the blood bath of the

Dark Ages. (Dimitri J. Tosevic, *Not Nazis but Germans* [Toronto: The Ryerson Press, 1944])

Was there something unique about my almost exclusively German heritage? Was there something in my blood that would predispose me to this sort of antisocial and murderous behavior? These questions ultimately led me into a lifetime study of German history as my profession. They also led me to write this book, which is directed to a general audience that may not be particularly well versed in Modern European – especially German – history.

Introduction

The story of the German anti-Nazi resistance, 1933–1945, can be seen as a classic morality tale. It speaks of a modern, well-educated, and highly sophisticated society that descended into the hell of what may well have been the most evil regime in all of recorded history. It also speaks of a determined few who attempted to decapitate the Nazi Party by assassinating its leader, Adolf Hitler. These determined few fully understood the high probability of failure, but they nevertheless persevered, not counting the cost of that failure. They were Germany's conscience during the nightmare years of the Third Reich.

The history of the resistance movement begins with an account of the conditions prevailing in Germany during the years preceding the Nazi accession to power in 1933. It was a time when the nation and its people had been traumatized by over a decade of war, defeat, political revolution, social upheaval, and economic distress, all of which rendered Germany extremely susceptible to the blandishments of a false messiah promising an escape from this torment. Included in this promise was a utopian vision of a Germany restored to its prewar greatness. It would be a Volksgemeinschaft, or "people's community," reclaiming the "traditional values" that many Germans believed had been trampled underfoot by a new postwar world that was completely foreign to them. In reality, Hitler despised the masses; he cared nothing about the German people and nation. His goal was self-aggrandizement, and Germany and its people were the means to that end. Rather than creating a true and inclusive national community, his people's community was intended to be a nation comprised of completely isolated and atomized individuals whose minds and actions he would totally control. Once in power, he made skillful use of his superb propaganda machine to manipulate public opinion. Anger, fear, and ignorance were his weapons. Consequently, few saw the absolute nihilism that was at the heart of this so-called "movement," and many, including some who ultimately became active participants in the anti-Nazi conspiracy, initially allowed themselves to be deceived by what they thought was a message of hope and renewal.

Others, however, were not beguiled by this false messiah, but they were powerless to resist the man and his minions. Most Germans went along simply because they had no choice. A very few acted entirely alone or in very small groups to demonstrate their anti-Nazi convictions. Others – most of them army officers, plus a few civilians connected to the military establishment – formed an active conspiracy to eliminate Adolf Hitler. They knew that war was inevitable so long as he remained in power and that the war's ultimate result would be catastrophic for Germany and Europe. The war itself only spurred them to further action. They knew that the longer the conflict continued, the greater the disaster would be at the end.

Ultimately the conspirators realized that defeat and disaster could not be avoided. Nonetheless, they persisted in their determination to eliminate the archfiend. These men, many of them motivated by deeply held religious convictions, became convinced that they were engaged in a struggle for Germany's soul. Although several attempts were made on Hitler's life, they all failed, even though some came tantalizingly close to success. Arrested, tortured, tried, convicted, and executed, these resisters remain exemplars of true patriotism for all time.

What follows is the story of a Germany unknown to many. It is a story of incredible courage and conviction that transcends time and place – a story for our own time and for all time.

CHAPTER 1

The Burden of History

On the night of November 8, 1939, Adolf Hitler traveled to Munich to deliver a speech to the Nazi Party faithful at a beer cellar in the heart of the city. Known as the Bürgerbräukeller, it was the site of an episode known to history as the Beer Hall Putsch, which occurred on November 8, 1923. Led by Hitler and his newly created Nazi Party, the speech delivered at this gathering was to be the first step in a planned coup d'état (putsch) against the Weimar Republic, which had replaced the imperial government at the end of World War I. Although it failed miserably, Hitler commemorated the event each year with a rally at the cellar. He customarily began speaking about eight thirty in the evening, concluding around ten o'clock. On this particular night, however, he altered his schedule.

Hitler had flown to Munich from Berlin, but because of frequently foggy conditions and the exigencies of war – Germany had just launched its military campaign against Poland that precipitated World War II the previous September – he decided to take his personal train back to Berlin; it was scheduled to leave at 9:31. Consequently, after beginning to speak at about 8:10, he concluded at 9:07. Normally he stayed around after the speech to chat with the "old fighters" who had been with him from the beginning of his political career. This time, however, he left the cellar immediately. Almost exactly thirteen minutes later, a massive explosion ripped through the beer cellar, killing eight people and injuring sixty-three. Had Hitler been on the speaker's dais at that moment, he most probably would have died, irrevocably changing the course of twentieth-century history.[1]

The immediate question on everyone's mind when they learned of the incident was "Who did it? Who is the culprit?" Various scenarios were offered as explanations, such as a story that the British Secret Service had planned the assault, which was not an unreasonable assumption. Other theories had some disgruntled members of the Nazi Party plotting Hitler's death. For example, SS chief Heinrich Himmler tried unsuccessfully to link the episode with a dissident, left-wing Nazi faction known as the Black Front, the leader of which was Otto Strasser, who had been expelled from the Nazi Party and now was living in exile.[2] Within the army was the suspicion that one or more inside their own ranks were responsible, whereas still others thought that Communists had set the bomb.[3]

The truth was both simpler and more startling, given that the perpetrator actually was a mere carpenter working entirely on his own. His name was Georg Elser. His journey from the quiet, conventional life of a skilled craftsman living in Königsbrünn, a small town in southwest Germany, to the position of a would-be assassin of his country's head of state provides insight into the moral issues facing all of those who participated in the anti-Nazi resistance.

Born in 1903 in southwest Germany in what now is the German state (Land) of Baden-Württemberg to a family of modest means – his father reportedly was a farmer and lumber dealer – the young Georg attended the local school and subsequently became an apprentice carpenter. He also worked for a time in a watch factory in the nearby city of Konstanz. There he learned the skills that enabled him to construct the intricate clock mechanism that armed the Bürgerbräukeller bomb. He was remembered as a rather quiet but sociable man who had a limited circle of friends and who participated in various cultural organizations, especially those connected with music. He played both the zither and double bass. A Protestant, he was a regular churchgoer, whose religion has been described as "simple, non-intellectual and traditional."[4] One of his favorite activities was hiking with friends. Although he fathered a son out of wedlock, he never married.

To the extent that Elser had political views, they were decidedly leftist. He tended to vote Communist, not for ideological reasons but because out of all the many political parties in the Weimar Republic, he believed the Communist Party served the workers' interests most completely. At the behest of a friend, he joined the militant Red Front Fighters' League (Roter Frontkämpferbund) of the Communist Party, although he never was an active participant in its political activities and had little interest in theoretical issues such as Marxism. He "was no thug and no hard-nosed ideologue."[5]

He did, however, hold a passionate hatred of Nazism and what it represented. His loathing of the Nazis was obvious from the onset of Nazi rule. He ostentatiously refused to participate in the obligatory Nazi rituals, such as the "Heil Hitler" greeting and the straight-arm Nazi salute. On more than one occasion, he refused to listen to Hitler's speeches that were broadcast over the radio. He resented the encroaching power of the state over individual activity, most particularly, the suppression of civil liberties. He especially detested the policy of "coordination" (Gleichschaltung) and its demands for absolute conformity to the Nazi ethos.

His decision to make an attempt on Hitler's life evidently was made in the fall of 1938, when he concluded that the Führer was plotting war and the only way to stop him was "the 'elimination' (Beseitigung) of the regime's leadership," which for him included not only Hitler but also Minister of Propaganda Joseph Paul Goebbels and Luftwaffe chief Reichsmarschall Hermann Göring.[6] At that point, he "methodically and without hesitation"[7] began making his plans. During the following months, he visited the Bürgerbräukeller several times, taking measurements and making detailed sketches of the large hall, which could accommodate upward of three thousand people. Additionally, he began the construction of the devices to arm and activate the bomb, such as a clock mechanism with which he could set the precise detonation time. He also stole explosives and fuses from two places where he worked, an armaments factory and, later, a quarry.

By September 1939, he began work in the beer cellar itself. He labored for thirty-five nights hollowing out a main support column located near the speaker's dais.[8] Each evening, he entered the cellar. As it closed for the night, he hid until everyone had left, and then he went to work throughout the hours of darkness until morning light, carefully removing all traces of his presence before he left. Obviously unemployed at this point, he was living off his savings, which amounted to approximately 350 to 400 marks, a not inconsiderable sum for that day. By November 6, the bomb was in place and armed. He returned the next night to make sure that all was functioning correctly. It was. He left Munich the following morning, November 8, for Konstanz, and then traveled to Switzerland and safety, or so he hoped.[9] In April 1939, before the outbreak of war, he had reconnoitered the Swiss border with Germany and decided that he could escape to Switzerland under cover of darkness.

With World War II now in progress, however, the borders were much more heavily guarded, and a German border patrol apprehended him before he could make it to safety.[10] Suspecting that he was a smuggler, the guards searched him for contraband, such as cigarettes. Instead, they found suspicious-looking metal parts, pliers, a postcard of the Bürgerbräukeller, and most incriminating of all, notes on making explosives.[11] Later that evening, the border guards received news of the explosion, and Elser's fate was sealed. He was taken to Munich and thence to Berlin, where he was subjected to severe beatings, including being repeatedly kicked by SS leader Himmler, in order to extract further information from him. Himmler and Hitler both believed that Elser somehow was linked to the British Secret Service or the aforementioned Black Front.[12] Ultimately, however, the Nazi leadership accepted his story that he had acted entirely alone.

He subsequently was sent to the Sachsenhausen concentration camp, where he languished for five years. Remarkably, he was well treated, probably because Hitler wanted to use him in a show trial after the war in order to "prove" that he was a British agent. Shortly before the end of hostilities, he was taken to Dachau concentration camp, where he was executed during an air raid, making his death appear to have been caused by a bomb.[13]

Leaders and Assassins

The story of Georg Elser and his attempt to assassinate Adolf Hitler encapsulates the wider story of the anti-Nazi German resistance almost perfectly. All the moral and ethical issues and all of the practical problems that the resisters faced are found here. In sum, it is a microcosm of the larger story. Elser personified the entire resistance movement. Was this man a hero or villain, a traitor or a patriot? What motivated him to make an assassination attempt on the life of Adolf Hitler? Answers to these and similar questions lie at the center of the resistance story.

Human history is replete with stories of assassination plots, and the motives run the gamut from derangement, personal animosity, and a desire for revenge to hate, anger, and ideology, or a combination thereof. Many assassins, such as those who murdered, or attempted to murder, presidents of the United States, were at the very least mentally unbalanced. Others, such as Gavrilo Princip, were motivated by ideology, in this case, extreme nationalism.

Princip was the assassin of the Archduke Franz Ferdinand, heir apparent to the Habsburg throne of Austria-Hungary. The archduke's death provided the spark that in the summer of 1914 plunged Europe into four ghastly years of war. Like many other assassins, Princip and his coconspirators thought they were serving a greater cause, in this case, Slavic nationalism and independence from Austria-Hungary. His southern Slav compatriots regarded him as a hero. To commemorate the event, they placed a paving stone at the spot in Sarajevo, Bosnia, where he'd stood when he fired the fatal shot. Many of the inhabitants of that region still regard him as a hero.[14]

The moral issues surrounding the question of assassination are very complex. Is it ever moral – the "right thing to do" – to kill a person in the pursuit of a moral cause? This question tormented the anti-Nazi resistance movement throughout the entire twelve-year life of the Third Reich. Four men who became active members of the organized army resistance personified the conflicts of conscience that many members of the resistance, military officers and civilians alike, experienced in their efforts to eliminate the Führer. Three were soldiers, and one was a clergyman, a civilian who was attached to the counterintelligence section (Abwehr) of the military establishment.

All three soldiers were career military officers who gave Adolf Hitler a degree of support before he assumed political power in 1933. The reasons are not difficult to discern. These men were steeped in the ethos of the Prussian military tradition and had absorbed the social and military values of Imperial Germany – that is, they were monarchists committed to authoritarian rule and to a society based upon a rigid class structure. They believed that Western liberal democracy and its values had no place in the Germany they loved. They also believed that obedience to orders issued by their superiors in the military hierarchy was a sacred duty. Their sense of honor dismissed as abhorrent any behavior that would give even a hint of mutiny. They were traditionalists but not extremists. They were conservatives in the best sense of that often-misused term. Their names were Hans Oster, Henning von Tresckow, and Claus Schenk von Stauffenberg. As with Elser, each one of these men came within the proverbial hair's breadth – within hours or even minutes – of eliminating their nemesis. They also were the leaders of four phases, or rounds, of the anti-Hitler conspiracy that existed within the military establishment.

The fourth man of this group was the clergyman Dietrich Bonhoeffer. Unlike the three soldiers, he opposed the Nazis openly and passionately well before they assumed power. He was among the very few public figures in Weimar Germany who fully recognized the nihilism that was at the core of Nazism and its beliefs. However, he had to overcome the constraints of a four-hundred-year tradition within the Lutheran Church that taught the importance of submission to civil authority. During the religious and political chaos of the sixteenth century, the Protestant German princes protected the Lutheran Church from its enemies, ensuring Lutheranism's survival. The long-term result of this connection was the emergence of a close relationship between government and religion that has survived into the modern era.

Martin Luther's doctrine of the two kingdoms provided the basis for this relationship. The civil authorities had the responsibility of upholding law and order in the "kingdom of this world," and the mission of the church was "to proclaim the kingdom of God." Neither authority was to interfere in the affairs of the other. Despite the strictures imposed by this doctrine, however, Bonhoeffer recognized early on that Hitler had to be removed from power by whatever means available if Germany were to be saved from war and disaster.[15] He experienced no "prolonged inner struggle. For him the Hitler dictatorship had always been inherently and ineradicably evil; his opposition to it was based on deep-rooted spiritual conviction rather than compelling national interest."[16] Thus, when the opportunity arose, he joined the Abwehr – the counterintelligence section of the Armed Forces Supreme Command (Oberkommando der Wehrmacht, or OKW) – ostensibly as a "confidential agent" (Verbindungsmann, or V-Mann).[17] In fact, he was a courier for the resistance. He became the conscience of the conspiracy to kill Hitler.

All of these men – Oster, Tresckow, Stauffenberg, and Bonhoeffer – faced the same issue: Is assassination ever justified? They reached the same conclusion: in certain extraordinary circumstances, it is. And extraordinary circumstances definitely prevailed in Nazi Germany. These four men were absolutely convinced that Adolf Hitler was the personification of evil and had to be eliminated – killed. This was the only way to exterminate the Nazi pestilence that was ravaging their fatherland. This shared conviction separates these men from other assassins of history. They were neither deranged nor ideological fanatics. Rather, they had an unsurpassed clarity of moral conviction and perception.

They knew that under normal circumstances, assassination was an immoral act. They also recognized that at times a lesser evil, murder, must be perpetrated in order to overcome a greater evil – in this case, continued Nazi rule. Even the clergyman Dietrich Bonhoeffer understood this. In a lecture he delivered in 1929, he spoke the following words: "There are no acts that are bad in and of themselves; even murder can be sanctified. There is only faithfulness to or deviation from God's will." In commenting on this statement, his biographer, Ferdinand Schlingensiepen, wrote:

> This sentence might make us think of his involvement in the conspiracy to assassinate Hitler, and at least be amazed that … Bonhoeffer already was not only thinking of such a thing as possible, but even saying it out loud – with, as yet, no idea of the weight such words could carry.[18]

The three soldiers and the clergyman pursued their goals with unremitting determination, even though they knew toward the end that they most likely would fail and they would forfeit their lives in that failure.

The Legacy of the Great War

A major theme of this story is the continuity of history. History does not repeat itself, but knowledge of the past is essential for an understanding of the present. And so it is with the German anti-Nazi resistance movement. A complete understanding of this story requires a journey into Germany's past. It is an arduous, circuitous, complex, at times painful, but essential journey. Questions abound. Why did the German people and their leaders act as they did? What motivated them? To answer, we must examine the Nazi phenomenon itself. What were its origins? What were the conditions inside early twentieth-century Germany that allowed the Nazi movement to arise and flourish? How did the Nazis secure power? What was their ultimate goal? Finally, we have what is probably the most important question of all: Just who was this man Adolf Hitler, and how did he acquire almost complete control over the German nation?

* * * *

This part of the story begins with the year 1918 and the conclusion of World War I, also remembered as the Great War. This conflict was a truly pivotal event, arguably the most significant in twentieth-century history. By every measure, it was a European catastrophe. It not only produced enormous destruction and material loss; it also shattered the myth of Western superiority and set into motion the process of decline that brought European world dominance to an end. Moreover, the Great War and its aftermath set the stage for an even more catastrophic war that would bring Europe to its knees a generation later.

The human cost was unprecedented. Although French per capita losses were greater, total German losses were the greatest of all the belligerent states, with 1.8 million dead and 4.2 million wounded. No significant military action had occurred on German soil, but the nation experienced a complete military, political, social, and economic collapse at war's end. The empire was gone, society was in chaos, the people were struggling to survive, the specter of starvation hovered everywhere, and the nation was on the edge of civil war.

Even though conditions improved somewhat the following summer, Germany's position remained precarious. Unfortunately, the Treaty of

Versailles, which officially concluded hostilities between Germany and its erstwhile enemies, served only to prolong the animosities that the war had generated. This was a harsh and vindictive peace settlement imposed upon a defeated enemy. Germany was now a pariah. More than the other Allied powers, France especially was determined to exact its last full measure of revenge from its neighbor. Thus Germany suffered significant territorial losses, was saddled with an onerous reparations burden, was required to reduce its military establishment to a token force, and worst of all, was obliged to accept the infamous "war guilt clause" (Article 231). In the words of the treaty, the "aggression of Germany and her allies" had "imposed" the conflict upon the Allied powers.[19]

All of this produced animosities within Germany that bore bitter fruit twenty years later. The period between the two world wars was, in fact, more of a truce than actual peace. Significantly, these were the years of conception, gestation, and birth for the Nazi state. The poisonous atmosphere generated by the Treaty of Versailles continued unabated right up to the outbreak of hostilities in 1939.

The Doomed Republic

In addition to the Treaty of Versailles, the year 1919 brought the Weimar Republic to Germany. Technically it came into existence on the afternoon of November 9, 1918, when Phillip Scheidemann, a member of the German Social Democratic Party and a delegate to the Reichstag – the lower house of the imperial parliament – spoke to a group of demonstrators outside the Reichstag building in Berlin and announced that the kaiser had abdicated the imperial throne. He concluded his speech with the words "Long live the great German Republic."[20] The imperial government had collapsed unceremoniously as a consequence of military defeat. Not wishing to be associated with the armistice and the uncertain peace that would inevitably follow, those who had exercised the powers of government for many years simply departed the scene.

The provisional government that followed – comprised largely of the Social Democrats – faced a series of almost insuperable issues. Essentially it had to stabilize a country wracked by social and political chaos, bring a disastrous war to an official conclusion, and lay the foundations for the infant republic. This required a new constitution, which went into effect on August 14, 1919.[21] For the first time in its history, Germany was a liberal democratic republic. Unfortunately, long-term chances for this infant's survival were very limited, largely because it was the child of military defeat, a fact that its detractors never allowed its defenders to forget. In retrospect, Germany's first experiment in liberal democracy was doomed from the start. It was too closely associated with the traumatic events of the then recent past, most particularly the despised Treaty of Versailles.

Beneath the facade of republican government lay the bureaucracy of the ancien régime, which had little or no commitment or loyalty to the new system that was now in place. The law courts, the civil administration, and the educational system remained unchanged. The so-called "revolution" at the end of the war that brought about the dramatic change in government was, in fact, no revolution at all. The sympathies of those who still occupied the offices of the republican government lay with the displaced empire. Consequently, a double standard of justice prevailed. Right-wing extremism was not merely tolerated but was actively supported in many instances, whereas left-wing extremism was violently suppressed.

As if the political and social conditions within Germany were not bad enough, the economy suffered a complete meltdown in 1923. The war had produced an inflationary spiral that grew with increasing ferocity in the years of peace immediately following the conclusion of hostilities. Inflation reached gargantuan proportions on November 15, 1923, when the exchange rate for the reichsmark stood at RM 4,200,000,000,000 to one US dollar![22] International intervention ultimately brought the crisis to an end, but the political damage was done. Whatever reserves of confidence and trust that the German people may have had for the Weimar Republic were now all but gone. Many Germans across the social and political spectrum believed that the republican government would not last, largely because it did not reflect the historic traditions and values of the German nation. Rather, it was a foreign system imposed upon a defeated nation by the victorious enemy; it was believed to be only a "temporary phenomenon."[23] Thus, the broad base of support that a democracy requires if it is to function effectively did not exist in Germany in the 1920s. The Weimar Republic lacked legitimacy.

Nevertheless, Germany did enjoy a short-lived period of political, social, and economic stability from 1924 to 1929, thanks in large measure to financial help provided by American loans. These years witnessed an effulgence of artistic endeavor that was almost unprecedented in German history, especially within such a short time frame. The collapse of the old order unleashed a torrent of creative genius unconstrained by the taboos and prejudices of Imperial Germany. The "political and social imagination" was freed to experiment with new ideas and new forms of expression.[24]

Those five years are remembered as a golden age of the republic, and Berlin was its mecca. A burgeoning new art form, the cinema, was a predominant part of the artistic scene. Just a few names associated with German cinema during the years of the Weimar Republic will suffice to provide a hint of its brilliance: film directors and producers such as Max Reinhardt, Billy Wilder, and Fritz Lang, along with the actors Peter Lorre, Erich von Stroheim, and Marlene Dietrich.

These artists and writers were exploring the new twentieth-century world and all of its implications. They observed the emergence of an:

> ... urban, industrial society, the mélange of sights, sounds, and thoughts connected with the city, with science and technology and layers of bureaucracy, with rational modes of thinking, with complex, social hierarchies, the world of the bourgeoisie and proletariat uncomfortably situated amid the old nobility and a still-substantial peasantry, an urban demimonde of gamblers, thieves, cops, and prostitutes and an educated middle class desperately trying to maintain its stature and status.[25]

These features of the Weimar culture also were the source of the animus held by the republic's enemies toward the republic itself and its supporters.

This clash between tradition and modernity was the source of the right-wing extremism that became Germany's curse between 1919 and 1933, and ultimately through to 1945. Its hallmarks were extremist nationalism, a total rejection of liberal democracy, and violence. Though not extremists in any sense of the word, many of the men who would become leaders of the anti-Nazi resistance joined in the chorus denouncing the republic. They had been schooled in the traditions and values of an age that was passing into history; they wanted to restore it. Their wishes eventually brought them into contact with an unscrupulous politician who manipulated them with false promises of a restoration of that world. Their disillusionment would prove to be very costly.

Right-Wing Extremism

Throughout the twelve-year history of the Weimar Republic, the sinister influence of right-wing extremism cast its shadow over the entire German nation. Symptomatic of this condition was the appearance of several extremist nationalist and racist political parties devoted to the overthrow of the Weimar Republic. One of these was the Nazi Party. The nation's southernmost state, Bavaria, where many within the state government shared the views of these parties, quickly became a boiling cauldron of racist (völkisch) extremism. Those in power "turned [Bavaria] into a haven for right-wing extremists from all over Germany."[26] This fact alone helps to explain Adolf Hitler's rise to power.

Bavaria, especially its capital city, Munich, gave Hitler a safe haven within which he could build his "movement" for transforming Germany into his image of a racially pure state that would become the dominant world power. He had lived in Munich before the war, and when hostilities began, he joined a Bavarian unit of the imperial army. He saw combat as a dispatch runner, and returned to Munich after his discharge from military service in 1919. In September of that year, he joined the German Workers Party, one of the many small, anti-Semitic, and militantly nationalist political parties that were proliferating in Bavaria. The name subsequently was changed to National Socialist German Workers Party (or Nazi, the acronym for the German, Nationalsozialistsche Deutsche Arbeiter Partei), and he became its leader (Führer) in 1921.

The terrible inflationary crisis of 1923 and ensuing social and political unrest provided Hitler with the opportunity to make a bid for power. For some time, he had been in contact with the minister-president of Bavaria, Gustav von Kahr, under whose governance right-wing extremism found its Bavarian home. Although both men wanted to bring down the Weimar Republic, they could not agree on the means to accomplish this end. Each man was trying to use the other for his own purposes, and no deal was struck.[27] Nonetheless, Hitler was determined to move ahead with his plans for a coup d'état against Berlin.

When Hitler learned that Kahr had scheduled a rally to promote his own ambitions, he decided that the time had come to make his move. He would hijack the meeting. Thus, on the night of November 8–9, 1923, Hitler, together with a detachment of his storm troopers (SA), disrupted Kahr's rally at the Bürgerbräukeller, the aforementioned beer cellar in the heart of Munich. Seizing control of the meeting, Hitler announced that the "German revolution" had begun. He planned to march on the city hall, take over the city government and then the state government of Bavaria, and finally go to Berlin and depose the national government.[28]

Naturally, Kahr and his associates resented Hitler's actions and were able to inform the authorities of what was going on in the Bürgerbräukeller. Consequently the putsch failed. Hitler was arrested, tried, convicted of high treason (Hochverrat), and sent to prison, but he served only nine months of a five-year term. Thanks to a Bavarian judicial system that was sympathetic to Hitler's goals, if not his methods, the man was released, and he immediately set about rebuilding his divided and demoralized party. The annual commemoration of this "Beer Hall Putsch" episode provided the backdrop for Georg Elser's assassination attempt in 1939.

Although the Weimar Republic's golden age began shortly after Hitler's putsch attempt, disquieting signs of future trouble persisted. An underlying sense of anomie and uncertainty lay beneath a relatively placid surface. These conditions allowed Hitler to rebuild his shattered party and construct an effective political organization. The Nazis successfully created a self-image as something more than a mere political party. They characterized themselves as a "movement" (Bewegung) that would bring a "national revival" to Germany and restore the nation to its true greatness and power.[29] This was the feature of the Nazi message that appealed to many of the men and women who would provide the foundation of the anti-Nazi resistance movement just a few years hence.

The golden age of the Weimar Republic came to an abrupt end in October 1929 with the collapse of the international financial market. The crisis began in the United States and quickly spread to the entire world, ushering in the economic crisis known to history as the Great Depression. Once again and within a decade, Germany experienced severe economic reverses that threatened to plunge the nation into complete chaos. Unemployment skyrocketed and brought with it all of the attendant social problems. By 1932, the unemployment figure had reached some six million. Including the dependents of those who were unemployed, the total of those directly affected by the loss of work was some thirteen million people, which represented approximately one-fifth of the entire German population.[30] This calamity provided the Nazis with an opportunity to take control of the German government. As in the past, the threat of complete social disintegration provided the essential ingredient for Nazi success.

Enter the Nazis

By 1932, the much-maligned Weimar Republic was on its deathbed, and the Nazis – as well as others – were preparing to dance on its grave. For the Nazis, the moment for a coup seemed to have arrived, but Adolf Hitler was determined to come to power legally, that is, through the electoral process. He would not repeat his mistake of November 8–9, 1923. Indeed, a series of elections brought the Nazis to the portals of political power, although elections never took them through those portals. The Nazis did not stage a coup, nor did they ever secure a majority of seats within the Reichstag. Instead, the path to power led through a series of political bargains that Hitler struck with three men who wished to manipulate matters to serve their own interests. Hitler would become their puppet in an authoritarian government of their own design. Instead, the puppet became the puppeteer.

These three men were the aged president of the Weimar Republic, former field marshal Paul von Hindenburg; Minister of Defense General Kurt von Schleicher; and Franz von Papen, a former military officer and politician who had served as a very ineffective chancellor during this deepening crisis. They were representative of that class of people categorized as conservatives. They hoped desperately to replace the detested republic and all it represented with an authoritarian government that would restore those so-called "uniquely German" values that the forces of liberal democracy, in their eyes at least, had crushed. Nonetheless, they recognized the need for a popular politician capable of building the mass support that they knew they needed in order to reach their goal. Hitler and his Nazi Party appeared to provide the means to this end.

* * * *

Hitler's first electoral attempt came in the spring of 1932, when he ran for the presidency and lost. Nevertheless, he did secure the more important political office of chancellor the following winter on January 30, when an act of political chicanery gave him the power he craved, thereby consigning the Weimar Republic to the rubbish heap of history.

How did this happen? Just how did Hitler and the Nazis secure power? The answer is as simple as it is tragic. The tipping point of January 30, 1933, came when these three men and their supporters, thinking they could control Hitler, named him chancellor. This decision was an incredibly foolish move and had catastrophic consequences. The Nazis actually had lost seats in Reichstag elections held in November 1932. The high-water mark for their electoral success had come the previous July, when 13.1 million Germans cast votes for the Nazis, giving them 37.4 percent of the vote and 230 seats in the Reichstag. Those numbers fell to 33.1 percent and 196 seats in November. Within four months, the Nazis had lost some 2 million votes. To all appearances, they had peaked in their popularity; this is the judgment of history as well. Thus, Hitler secured political power after suffering a significant electoral defeat.

Contrary to Nazi mythology, there was no seizure of power (Machtergreifung). Rather, people who should have known better simply gave Hitler the chancellor's office, planning to use his popularity to manipulate the masses for their own purposes. Ironically, they had denied him power after that spectacular electoral victory in the summer of 1932, but they gave him power just as Nazi popularity was waning.[31] Thanks, however, to Papen and Schleicher's scheming with others and to Hindenburg's reluctant assent, Hitler was able to cobble together a government, even though only three members of his eleven-man cabinet were Nazis and even though the Nazi Party held only 196 seats in the 584-member Reichstag. For all practical purposes, however, the Reichstag already had ceased to function. It had been moribund for well over a year, as a succession of chancellors had bypassed it, ruling instead through emergency decree powers granted by the president and authorized by the constitution.

Through the skillful manipulation of the modern media – namely, radio and film – Adolf Hitler "had engineered the appearance of a mandate."[32] Hitler and his hooligans were now in power, and the Nazis were ecstatic. Schleicher and Papen, along with many who shared their interests and ideals, were well pleased and believed that Germany's return to greatness was now assured.[33] Papen especially was confident that Hitler and his Nazis would do his bidding. To those who voiced their skepticism about the appointment, Papen said, "We've engaged him for ourselves" and "within two months, we will have pushed Hitler so far into a corner that he'll squeak."[34] Alfred Hugenberg, an extreme nationalist, press baron, and leader of the small and extremist right-wing German National People's Party, said, "We're boxing Hitler in."[35]

Other conservatives were less sanguine. President von Hindenburg had his doubts as well. He had always held the "Bohemian corporal" – the name he'd given to Hitler – in contempt, but he nevertheless gave his reluctant support to Hitler's appointment, believing that this was the only way to save Germany from total collapse. Together with Hindenburg, General Erich Ludendorff had formed a duumvirate that ruled Germany during the last years of the Great War. He was totally dismayed by this turn of events and wrote the following words to his former comrade in arms: "I solemnly prophesy that this accursed man will cast our Reich into the abyss and bring our nation to inconceivable misery. Future generations will damn you in your grave for what you have done."[36] He could not have known just how prescient his comments were. Ironically, he had given Hitler his wholehearted support as an active participant in the 1923 Beer Hall Putsch attempt.

Nonetheless, pessimism such as this definitely was a minority view, especially within the military establishment. Many army officers, including future anti-Nazi conspirators such as Hans Oster, Henning von Tresckow, Claus Schenk von Stauffenberg, and future chief of staff Ludwig Beck, gave enthusiastic support to the new regime – at first.[37] Ultimately, however, they all had to answer a simple question: Was the goal of this revival worth the risk of a Nazi-led Germany? The initial answer was yes. Unfortunately, they failed to see the long-term consequences of that answer. Thus, the immediate issues surrounding Hitler's accession to power encapsulate the contradictions that were part of the larger issue of resistance to Nazism when it first came into sharp focus within the next twelve months.

* * * *

Although Hitler had secured the long-coveted position of chancellor on January 30, 1933, his position was tenuous, and he knew it. A revolving-door pattern of ministries had been the norm throughout the fourteen-year history of the republic, and there was no guarantee that this pattern would not continue. Hitler and his party might well be out of office in a matter of months or even weeks. Consequently, he took several immediate steps to consolidate his hold on the instruments of government. Most importantly, he needed legitimacy, and that required a mandate from the German electorate. Thus, he set a date for new elections to the Reichstag to be held on March 5, 1933. In the interim, the Nazis set about ensuring that those elections would achieve the desired result, namely, a solid Nazi majority. This would give the Nazis the legitimacy to force the passage of legislation that would enable them to turn Germany into a totalitarian dictatorship.

Therefore, a carefully orchestrated political campaign was set into motion that included not only a program of fear but also a massive propaganda effort designed to ensure success for the Nazis. Joseph Paul Goebbels, the propaganda minister, proclaimed March 5 to be the "Day of the Awakening Nation," with "mass demonstrations and parades, processions and carefully staged appearances." For example:

> On the eve of the election Hitler appeared in the city of Königsberg. Just as he was ending his rapt appeal to the German people – "Hold thy head high and proud once more! Now thou art free once again, with the help of God" – a hymn could be heard swelling in the background, and the bells of the Königsberg

cathedral pealed during the final stanza. Meanwhile, on the hills and mountains along Germany's borders, "bonfires of freedom" were lit.[38]

In addition to the propaganda campaign, these March 5 elections "were held in an atmosphere of palpable terror."[39] Episodes of violence and brutality, such as beatings, torture, and street battles – especially between Communist and Nazi factions – together with bullying, intimidation, and death threats, had all become a feature of Nazi rule with Hitler's accession to power. They were greatly intensified with the approach of the March 5 election. The political parties "were subjected to every kind of sabotage and disruption, while the police sat idly by in accordance with their instructions. By election day fifty-one anti-Nazis lay dead and hundreds had been injured. The Nazis themselves counted eighteen dead."[40]

The volatile political atmosphere was further intensified by an episode that occurred a mere seven days before the election, when the Reichstag building was mysteriously gutted by fire. The culprit was a young Dutch Communist, Marius van der Lubbe, who was apprehended, tried, convicted, and executed for his deed. This incident provided an excellent opportunity for the Nazis to further consolidate their power and enhance their prospects of victory in the forthcoming elections. The day following the fire, Hitler secured the passage of an emergency decree, drafted by the cabinet and signed by President von Hindenburg, ostensibly for the purpose of suppressing "Communist acts of violence endangering the state."[41] In fact, this decree gave Hitler carte blanche to suspend virtually all the civil liberties guaranteed by the Weimar constitution.

Many German citizens, holding an almost morbid fear of and hatred for Communism, gave wholehearted support to Hitler and the Nazi Party to take whatever action the Nazis deemed essential to deal with the "Communist threat." A cloak of secrecy, together with whispered rumors, heightened the fear. An eyewitness account of these events relates that people warned, "Be careful, my friend! Do you know what happened to X?"[42] People knew that something was going on, but no one seemed to know just what it was. Only enough information was released to intensify the terror. "Communists," who might be lurking "anywhere," allegedly were perpetrating acts of violence, such as the Reichstag fire. Some individuals purportedly "died while resisting arrest," while others had "committed suicide." "Others," it was said, "just vanished. One did not know whether they were dead, incarcerated or gone abroad – they were just missing."[43] Police records indicate that by October 1933, some twenty-six thousand persons had been arrested. Many others disappeared "without legal formalities into the hastily constructed concentration camps that were spreading across the land."[44] In fact, a silent reign of terror was descending on Germany that would remain in place for twelve years.

* * * *

The results of these elections provide a clear insight into the actual mood of the German people in early 1933 – a window, as it were, into the soul of the nation. Paul Bonart was a young worker in the Carl Zeiss optical company, located in the city of Jena, and was also a member of the anti-Nazi underground. He described the election process as he experienced it:

> We had hopes that the outcome [of the election] might bring at least a few changes in our present government. But when we saw what was happening at the voting place, we realized that our voting franchise was finished.
>
> The regular closed voting booths were gone. They were replaced by a very long table with a curtain. Hanging from the ceiling, it divided the table lengthwise ... kind of, because it did not come down completely but stopped short about a foot from the tabletop. You cast your ballot on one side, while on the opposite side three SA men watched whom you were voting for. There were Nazi uniforms all over, two guarding the doors, others milling around behind you.
>
> The walls were "decorated" with slogans like: "A true German is no coward! He casts his vote openly." Fortunately, I had prepared my voting list before arriving. I smiled at the SA men, raised my arm, shouted, "Heil Hitler!" and slipped the ballot in the envelope. An elderly SA man, who had been standing at my side, took the envelope out of my hand, and placed it in the box. Friends related that their voting places looked about the same.[45]

Such was Nazi democracy in the Third Reich. Given these voting conditions and given the Nazis' massive effort to ensure the "proper" outcome of the elections, one could logically assume that they would win a resounding victory. But that assumption would be wrong.

Only 43.9 percent of the German electorate voted for the Nazi Party. Despite the propaganda and terror, 56.1 percent of the Germans who participated in that carefully controlled election voted against the Nazis. Although the party leaders had gone to great lengths to ensure an absolute electoral majority, they fell well short of their goal. The German nation was still not ready to embrace Hitler and Nazism wholeheartedly and completely.[46] Hence, a nascent source of anti-Nazi activity existed from the beginning of Nazi rule, but it lacked two elements: organization and leadership.

Germany never had a political leader capable of challenging Hitler's almost magical – one might say it was black magic – ability to dominate public life. There was no way an anti-Nazi movement could effectively neutralize the Nazi propaganda machine, partly because a police state descended upon the nation almost immediately, effectively preventing an opposition movement from developing. Hitler's so-called "wilderness years" from 1925 to 1930 were spent in creating an extensive and tightly controlled political organization in the form of the Nazi Party, and he had done his work well. Moreover, the one institution within Germany that might have effectively challenged Hitler's rule – the army – was itself hopelessly divided over what could be described as the Nazi question. Even those members of the officer corps who eventually provided the leadership for an active resistance were, at this time, still willing to give the man a chance to rechart the course upon which the ship of state had embarked in 1919. By the time they reconsidered their own position, it was too late.

Yet the question remains: Just how did Hitler assume office? Those March 5 elections had denied him the Reichstag majority essential to his assumption of power as chancellor, the chief political officer of Germany. Under normal parliamentary practice, he either would have to undergo still another election or find a political party willing to enter his proposed government, thereby giving him that essential majority. He found a willing partner in Albert Hugenberg and the latter's German National People's Party. This created what officially was a coalition government that preserved the facade of legitimacy. In truth, parliamentary government was dead. A Nazi dictatorship was already taking control of Germany.

CHAPTER 2

The Nazis in Power

The Nazi accession to power in 1933 brought with it a new terminology. Familiar words acquired new connotations not completely understood at first. There were, for example, the terms "law and order" and the "people's community," plus words such as "dissent," "resistance," "criminal," and "treason." What did they signify in the Nazi lexicon? How did the Nazis use them in practice? Only the passage of time brought clarity to the way in which the Nazi authorities applied them. In order to fully grasp the relationship of the Third Reich to the people it ruled, words such as these require closer examination.

"Dissent" normally refers to nonconformity and protest. In Nazi usage, it was applied to individual activities that were forbidden (verboten), such as listening to foreign radio broadcasts like the British Broadcasting Corporation (BBC) – especially during the war years – telling antigovernment and anti-Nazi jokes, and giving clandestine support to repressed individuals and groups. Soon, criminal activity included mere verbal criticism of the government.[1]

"Resistance," on the other hand, pertained to activities designed to actually overthrow the Third Reich.[2] The Nazis melded these two distinct terms into one concept, however. All nuances were blurred. There was no distinction between "dissent" and "resistance." Everyone on the spectrum from passive dissident to active conspirator was by definition an enemy of the Reich. Opposition of any sort was ipso facto treasonous. Nazi Germany, one of history's most complete totalitarian states, politicized the entire society.[3]

Here was a system that sought to exercise – and in many cases succeeded in exercising – control over both mind and body. Unlike a simple police state that represses dissident behavior but generally ignores one's thoughts so long as those thoughts do not produce actions detrimental to its power and control, a totalitarian state such as the Third Reich wished to control what people thought as well as what they did. Moreover, the Reich achieved this goal while maintaining a "veneer of legality."[4] The Nazi use of language was an important part of this process.

The People React

Unsurprisingly, a wide range of reactions among the German people greeted the momentous events of early 1933, from wild enthusiasm to sullen or fatalistic acceptance to determined opposition. For many – perhaps most – there was fear and apprehension. Events completely beyond their control threatened to overwhelm them completely. These years marked the depth of the Depression, with the fear of unemployment and the prospect of financial catastrophe an ever-present reality. In such insecure circumstances, "not to have gone along with the Nazis would have meant risking one's livelihood and prospects, [and] to have resisted could mean risking one's life."[5] People from all walks of life accommodated themselves to the new as best they could. In such circumstances, often the safest option is to say nothing, and many concealed their true feelings about Nazism behind a wall of silence. Rudolf Steiner, a Jewish Berliner, examined the overall reaction to the abrupt changes that took place after January 30, commenting as follows:

> People have transformed themselves ... they put on masks. No one knows what the individual thinks [or] ... what he feels, whether he hopes for the fall of this regime ... because even the loudest spokesmen for the Nazis do not prove with their cheers that they believe in the ideology ... What do the masses think? You can hardly guess ... The masses, as well as individuals who are not Nazis, are silent and wait.[6]

Many Germans doubtlessly shared the attitude recorded by a diarist who said that a friend and colleague who was "anything but a Nazi" was seen wearing a "discreet swastika lapel pin." When the diarist asked why, his colleague responded, "Well why not? I'm no risk taker." Many such people were labeled "Beefsteak Nazis" – brown on the outside, red on the inside.[7]

Many joined the party out of conviction. They sincerely believed in what they thought was a positive message of hope for the restoration of a lost world. The Führer and his Nazi Party were the harbingers of a new day that was dawning, or so they believed. The naïveté of these early supporters concealed the dark shadows already being cast by this self-described renewal movement. Many of the future resisters were part of this group.

Pure opportunism motivated others. For them, supporting the Nazi Party was a means of achieving status and respectability. This was especially true of the lower middle class. For the first time in German history, this group had a path of upward social mobility to positions of power and prestige. Those with limited education, or even limited abilities, now had a way of climbing the socioeconomic ladder. Party loyalty was more important than capability and competence.[8] Thus, they became loyal Nazis, continuing a trend that had been a hallmark of the Nazi Party from its earliest days. Although Nazism appealed to all social and economic classes, its center of gravity had always been the lower middle class.

* * * *

Despite the combination of opportunism and sincerity reflected in the large numbers who joined the Nazi Party, an overall sense of hopelessness and foreboding permeated much of German society. Sebastian Haffner, a celebrated German writer and historical journalist, wrote of his reaction to the Nazis' accession to power in 1933: "We were in the Nazis' hands for good or ill. All lines of defence had fallen, and collective resistance had become impossible. Individual resistance was only a form of suicide." Regardless of attitudes and feelings toward the Nazis, everyone had to conform. Each one "had to make his or her own compromise with the regime."[9]

For the opponents of the Nazis, there were two choices: leave and go into exile or stay in Germany. Many chose exile. Thus began the flight of talent, often to the United States of America, that continued until World War II. Germany's loss was America's gain. This flight produced a significant brain drain by the end of the decade. Artists, writers, and musicians, especially those who were considered left wing or too avant-garde for Hitler's tastes, realized that it was time to go. As true artists, they had a clear insight into Germany's future under National Socialism, and they knew that there was no place for them in that future. The list of their names reads like a Who's Who of the German intellectual and artistic community: conductors Bruno Walter and Otto Klemperer; composer Paul Hindemith; writer and Nobel laureate Thomas Mann; playwright, poet, and theater director Bertolt Brecht; modernist painters Paul Klee and Wassily Kandinsky; composer Kurt Weill and his wife, singer Lotte Lenya; actress Marlene Dietrich; the distinguished architect Walter Gropius, whose Bauhaus school of modernist architecture and design was a special target of Hitler's obloquy – these are just a few of the some two thousand individuals connected with the arts who left Germany in 1933 and after.[10] Those from other walks of life who fled Germany included Paul Tillich, one of the most prominent theologians of the twentieth century, and Albert Einstein, perhaps the greatest physicist of all time.

Those whose political activities and convictions represented a potential challenge to Hitler's rule were special targets of his wrath. For example, former chancellor Heinrich Brüning's name was on an execution list at the time of an episode known as the Night of the Long Knives, which took place on June 30, 1934, when a large number of people on Hitler's enemies list were murdered. However, Brüning had been warned of impending danger and went to London that night, thus escaping death.[11] Others forced into exile included leaders of the German Social Democratic Party (Sozialdemokratische Partei Deutschlands, or SPD), many of whom left almost immediately after the Nazis came to power. They went to Prague and set up the German Social Democratic Party in Exile (Die Sozialdemokratische Partei Deutschlands im Exil, or SOPADE), which established a secret correspondence with SPD members remaining in Germany. These documents are a valuable source of information on life in the Third Reich.

Hitler had a particular hatred for the SPD. It was the only political party that consistently opposed his ultimately successful attempt to destroy the Reichstag as a true legislative body. Moreover, the Nazis and their supporters considered the SPD to be a special enemy, partly because the latter had vigorously defended the Weimar Republic and its democratic values, and partly because the SPD was paradoxically seen to be at one with the Communists as the harbingers of world revolution. Thus, Nazis and all of the extremist parties on the right, as well as more moderate conservatives – even some who eventually became active in the resistance – viewed the SPD with great suspicion. Some even saw them as a mortal threat to the German nation.

This charge was a complete fabrication. In truth, Social Democrats were both patriotic nationalists and bitter enemies of the Communists. Nevertheless, the conviction that the members of the SPD were the enemy lay at the heart of conservative thought and proved to be a tragic barrier to the creation of an effective anti-Nazi mass movement. This barrier helped to cripple resistance efforts. Ideology trumped reality and rationality. In truth, the political left had a much-clearer picture of the true nature of Nazism than did the conservatives. The "earliest organized resistance to National Socialism came from the left."[12]

A Jewish exodus also began immediately. Hitler's virulent anti-Semitism, though tempered and somewhat nuanced before and immediately after his accession to power, was never far below the surface. In the meantime, the Nazi Party army, the brown-shirted thugs known as the SA

(Sturm Abteilung, or storm troopers), accentuated the party's anti-Semitism through its accelerating street violence. The message was simple and clear: Jews were not welcome in the Third Reich. Seeing the proverbial handwriting on the wall, Germans of the Jewish faith began to leave their homeland. In the first year of Nazi rule, 1933, an estimated 37,000 Jews departed Germany. By 1938, approximately one-fourth of Germany's total Jewish population of 550,000 had fled.[13]

Those anti-Nazi Germans who chose to stay had two additional choices. The first was to try to undermine and ultimately bring about the demise of the system from within. This choice was available only to those who had previously occupied positions of power and influence in government and society and who still retained a degree of authority, especially within the military establishment. The problems these people faced were monumental. Organized resistance from the inside carried a significant risk of detection. These people would be working alongside their enemies, and a careless remark or a misstep of any sort would immediately arouse suspicion. Moreover, two ever-present questions remained unanswered. Where was the leader able to command a clandestine organization that could not only overthrow the Nazi state but also create a functioning provisional government? This became an especially critical issue after war began in 1939. Secondly, the issue of mass support remained unresolved. With all of the social, political, and economic divisions that had helped to destroy the republic still in existence, how could an organized resistance movement build a solid base of mass support when the members could not agree on methods and goals among themselves?

The mistrust and animosity that the conservatives held against the SPD highlighted this problem. Had these two groups been able to form a well-organized anti-Nazi coalition, Germany's subsequent history may well have followed a different, more sanguine course. Thus:

> The deep enmity between the various political camps toward the end of the republic left the budding resistance fractured into small circles and cells, which often had no contact with one another despite physical proximity. They all agreed that it was essential to resist but most were reluctant to join forces.[14]

It was one thing for those on the outside to make an assassination attempt, either individually, as in the case of Georg Elser, or in very small groups, as dangerous as that was. It was something else to work on the inside, especially with the unanswered questions of leadership and organized mass support hanging over the heads of the resisters. Moreover, the Third Reich was an absolute police state, operating a terror machine of consummate ferocity that would retaliate against its self-defined enemies without the slightest compunction. Those who opposed the Nazis in whatever way faced that supreme reality.

The second option for the anti-Nazi Germans who either chose to stay or could not leave was to retreat into a kind of internal exile, that is, to withdraw into one's self and live a life of total detachment from the outside world. Theirs would be a world of "social exclusion" and "personal isolation."[15] A significant number of people from the intellectual community, including scholars, writers, and those who were members of the various professions, made this choice.

* * * *

Acquiescence did not translate into enthusiasm, however. Although the masses had no alternative but to accept what was occurring in German society, "a very large section of the electorate, over half of the population which played any part in political life, had not been beguiled by Hitler and National Socialism."[16] A telling example of this was a second election (of sorts) that was held on November 12, 1933. It consisted of two parts. The first part was an "election" to choose deputies to the now emasculated Reichstag. This "election" was much more effectively controlled than the March 5 election. For example, no opposition candidates were allowed, because all political parties except the Nazi Party were outlawed, meaning, naturally, that only Nazis were permitted to stand for election. The second part was a referendum to legitimize the decision of the German government to withdraw from the League of Nations.

The results of this "election" spoke much about the German people and their feelings toward the Nazi Party. As anticipated, some 93 percent of the electorate expressed approval of the decision to withdraw from the League, and 92 percent voted for the Nazi list of candidates. However, at least three million voters cast deliberately invalid ballots.[17] Paul Bonart recalls that the actual percentage of no votes in his polling place – a small town in the Thuringian Forest – was 78 percent "yes" and 22 percent "no," which caused great consternation among the Nazi officials, one of whom was the mayor of the village. These men presided over the openly conducted counting process, presumably to preserve the pretense of legitimacy. But the actual results came as a profound shock to everyone in the room. A 22 percent negative vote was entirely unacceptable. "The mayor thought it would be a disservice to his beloved city to accept and publish such numbers." After several telephone calls and much private discussion among the officials, the mayor made the following statement: "The national average of yes votes appears to be between 92 and 93 percent. That's what we are going to show for our city as well." Not all Germans were enthusiastic supporters of the Third Reich.[18]

Enthusiastic or not, average German citizens could do nothing about the emerging Nazi dictatorship, either individually or collectively. They were completely powerless under Nazi rule. Therefore, most people simply hunkered down and hoped for the best. And indeed, on the surface at least, things did seem to improve. At this point, the darker side of Nazi rule was effectively hidden from public view, thanks largely to Joseph Paul Goebbels's Ministry of Propaganda. Despite the omnipresence of the party and secret police, most Germans doubtlessly lived in reasonably secure and stable conditions during the first part of the Nazi era, 1933 to 1939.[19] The chaotic years of the unlamented Weimar Republic were behind them; the street fighting, assassinations, and political murders that had punctuated life during the fourteen years of republican government had come to an end. Political and social unrest, turmoil, and conflict were a fading memory. Initially, the Third Reich brought with it "a new sense of purpose and direction [and] a new feeling of hopefulness and confidence" for the future.[20] It was a time of security and prosperity that contrasted significantly with the previous fourteen years of uncertainty and strife. For most people, the most important feature of this period doubtlessly was the stabilized economy. Employment conditions improved steadily. Years later, many had a fond recollection of these times. They remembered "the guaranteed pay packet ... adequate nourishment ... and the absence of disarray in political life."[21]

And yet, much of those "good times," especially economic prosperity, was based on an illusion. For example, there was very little real capital growth given that the nation had been put on a war economy from the very beginning of Nazi rule. Because production emphasized weapons manufacturing, few economic resources were devoted to improving the economy's capital base. The consequence of all this was inflation. By 1939, Nazi Germany was beginning to experience a fundamental economic reality: that no modern industrial society can achieve complete autarky, or total economic independence. The inevitable clash between consumer wants and military needs was producing the classic symptoms of a serious inflationary spiral. Ultimately and inevitably, the "good times" experienced over the short run would not last. The economic future – the "long run" – was much more clouded than generally understood. People tend to disregard the long run. They see only the immediate situation.

Therefore, the period during which the Nazis enjoyed the "most solid and consistent popular support" was the midthirties. It has been described as the "high noon" of the Nazi years. Economic prosperity undoubtedly contributed significantly to this public support.[22] "The ease of the Nazi takeover and the emergence of a pro-Hitler and pro-Nazi consensus suggests that the majority had abandoned any hopes they might have had for democracy. And especially with the recovery from the Great Depression, they found it easy to support an authoritarian dictatorship."[23] By the end of the decade, however, the gathering war clouds on the far horizon brought a shudder of apprehension to all Europeans – Germans included – as they recalled the Great War and its horrors. Yet all of this was several years in the future and could not be comprehended in 1933. For the short run, the Germans were content to accommodate themselves to the realities of the Third Reich. After all, they couldn't do anything about it anyway!

An important element in the acceptance of the Nazi state was the overweening fear of the so-called "Bolshevik menace," which lay to the east in the Soviet Union. The Nazis exploited this fear masterfully. The "international Communist conspiracy" had been the bogeyman of Western Europe and the United States since 1918. Many saw it as a mortal threat to the very survival of Western civilization, and this fear was nowhere more evident than in post–World War I Germany. Although the actual threat was far less than the fear, there was sufficient circumstantial evidence to support the belief that the nation had to close ranks against the Communists. The short-lived Communist uprising in 1919 known as the Spartacist Rebellion appeared to confirm the danger from the political left.

The social and political turmoil that characterized the early years of the Weimar Republic provided effective grist for the Nazi propaganda mill as the party, now in control, moved to suppress all political opposition through the effective manipulation of fear. They knew the connection between fear and dependency; they knew that "fearful people are ... more easily manipulated and controlled, more susceptible to deceptively simple, strong tough measures and hard line postures ... They may accept and even welcome repression if it promises to relieve their insecurities."[24] Thus, the Nazi message was simple: "Be afraid; be very afraid!" This message, coupled with the assurances that only the Nazis could save Germany from the Communist menace, proved to be an effective technique for consolidating Nazi rule over the entire nation. Hence, for many Germans, Nazism represented a welcome return to "law and order" after the chaos of the preceding fourteen years.[25]

The carefully controlled press reinforced this attitude. For example, the concentration camps that were becoming a well-established fixture in the Nazi state were described as correctional facilities for asocial elements within German society. Understandably, only those whom the Nazis declared as asocials were candidates for incarceration in these camps: people such as "Communists and the social rabble and misfits," namely, alcoholics, homosexuals, sex offenders, habitual criminals, beggars, and the chronically unemployed. These camps supposedly had many "virtues." They provided "military discipline, punctuality, scrupulously observed cleanliness, and the work ethic." They had an "educative purpose" that provided a "correction and a warning" to those "deviants" who failed to conform to the norms of good citizenship.[26] Hence, concentration camps were proclaimed to be a great benefit to society, and the Nazi-defined good Germans had nothing to worry about – not yet, at least! A good citizen, after all, does not complain or protest!

The dark side to all of this was not readily apparent to most people. They did not yet realize that once initiated, arbitrary arrest, incarceration, and punishment are hard to stop. They did not yet realize that law and order without justice is tyranny. Therefore, a common belief during the early years of Nazi rule held that perhaps things would not be so bad after all. And indeed, the conditions of life for many Germans from 1933 to 1938 seemed to confirm that belief, so long as one was not a Communist, socialist, Gypsy, Jew, liberal, Jehovah's Witness, or anyone officially deemed unfit.

The system of terror that was the foundation of the Nazi state remained in place, however. Though usually unseen, and often rationalized as an attribute of "law and order" when it was seen, it began almost immediately, and continued with increasing ferocity throughout the life of the Third Reich. Reliable sources estimate that some three million German citizens were incarcerated for "political crimes" during the Nazi era, 1933–1945.[27] Some were held for a few weeks, some for the entire twelve years. Of those incarcerated, "approximately 800,000 were held for active resistance."[28] In the year 1933 alone, about one hundred thousand people spent time in a concentration camp, of whom some five hundred to six hundred were killed.[29] All of this clearly shows that the first victims of the Nazis were the Germans themselves.

The People's Community

One of Adolf Hitler's primary goals was the creation of a "racially pure" and thoroughly regimented Volksgemeinschaft – a "people's community" – that he would completely dominate as its leader, Der Führer. The ideological foundation of Nazism was racism. Hitler had absorbed the social Darwinist worldview that dominated so much of Western thought in the early twentieth century. In the social Darwinist paradigm, all of life was a struggle for the fittest to survive. For humanity, it was a struggle for racial supremacy. For the Nazis, it was a conflict between the most superior of the "races," namely, the "Nordic" or "Aryan" peoples and all other "races," especially the Jews and Slavs.[30] The Nazis saw this conflict as the only way to create a true "master race," which then would populate the Volksgemeinschaft. It would be a Nazi utopia, a brave new world of complete perfection. It was a classic ideological model. It also was the dark side of the Nazi message that followers – including future resistance activists – failed to comprehend at the beginning of the so-called Nazi "movement." Once Nazi rule commenced, the German nation was subjected to an increasingly intense propaganda campaign, with subliminal messages promoting a program of "racial hygiene." Though not outwardly anti-Semitic at first, this program was carefully contrived to convey the idea that racial purity was essential to the creation of a true Volksgemeinschaft.

Through the use of film, together with the printed and spoken word, Nazi propaganda skillfully manipulated public opinion, and in so doing laid the groundwork for what was to become an increasingly overt campaign against Germans of the Jewish faith. This Nazi obsession with racial purity was the logical expression of Hitler's belief that biology, that is, race, was the sole determinant of history; this belief in turn produced the obsessive concern for the creation of an exclusive Volksgemeinschaft and the use of police power to ensure its realization. "Anything that did not fit the normative standards of the people's community or could be construed as an agent of social dissolution theoretically fell under the purview of the police."[31] Thus, two groups populated the Nazi world, "the 'ins' and the 'outs.'" The former, the "racially pure" who were totally committed to the Nazi ideology, would comprise the Volksgemeinschaft. All others, namely, the racially impure and the "deviants" – those who dissented in any way from Nazi norms – were excluded.[32]

Later, during World War II, this obsession with racial purity became the justification for the hideous behavior of the "operations groups" (Einsatzgruppen) within the SS (Schutzstaffel, or Security Staff). These actions would be played out across the killing fields of Eastern Europe just a few years hence. As German troops conquered more and more territory, the Einsatzgruppen began to carry out their orders to literally eradicate the so-called "lesser peoples" through a designated program of racial extermination. At the beginning of the Russian campaign, Reichsmarschall Hermann Göring declared, "This war is not the Second World War. This is the great racial war. In the final analysis it is about whether the German and Aryan prevails here, or whether the Jew rules the world, and that is what we are fighting for out there."[33]

This statement reflected a kind of Nazi morality that was based on the concept of racial purity. "Biological cleansing" required "radical surgery,"[34] namely, the systematic elimination of the Untermenschen (subhuman creatures of the human species, such as Slavs and Jews). Only the death of these Untermenschen could excise the racial bacillus that was infecting the Volksgemeinschaft. Nazi morality thus demanded the murder of untold millions. The depraved behavior of the Einsatzgruppen became a moral crusade.

Alfred Rosenberg, who was the official "philosopher" of Nazism, declared in 1943 that the Nazis were liberating Europe from the "Jewish leprosy" and that their actions in Eastern Europe were "not brutality, but rather clean, biological humanitarianism. Better eight million Jews disappeared than eighty million Germans. The bridges have been broken behind us, and there is no way back anymore."[35] The Nazis thus admitted to their heinous crimes but claimed that they had been committed to the service of a higher good. This was the Nazi conscience at work. The ends justify the means. So it is with any ideology.

Means and ends were not foreseen in 1935, however. The logical consequences of the Nazi ideology lay in a clouded future. Few people then could foretell that the path from the Nuremberg Laws would lead to Auschwitz. These laws, proclaimed in 1935, were a series of decrees defining the legal status of Jews living in Germany; they effectively removed "German citizenship from persons of 'non-German blood.'"[36] Thus, the monstrous work of building a Nazi Volksgemeinschaft continued. It reached an unprecedented level of barbarity on November 9, 1938, when a vicious pogrom remembered as the "Crystal Night" (Kristallnacht) was launched against Germany's Jews.[37]

A minor incident precipitated the pogrom. Two nights earlier, a Polish teenager of the Jewish faith had shot and fatally wounded a German diplomat when the young man learned that his parents – with whom he had lived in Germany – had been deported to Poland. The episode took place in Paris. When Joseph Paul Goebbels learned about it, he decided to elevate it into a "major propaganda exercise." He put his Minisry of Propaganda to work and manufactured a story declaring that this was an attack on the Third Reich by "world Jewry," and that Germany's Jewish population would pay a heavy price for this dastardly act.[38] Thus encouraged, Nazi thugs – the brown-shirted SA storm troopers, the Gestapo (Geheime Staatspolitzei, or Secret State Police), and the SS – went to work. They unleashed a "carnival of bestial passions." Synagogues and homes, together with some seventy-five hundred Jewish business establishments, were either damaged or destroyed in an orgy of obscene violence that raged throughout the night of November 9–10. Ninety-one Jews were murdered, and thirty thousand were rounded up and sent to concentration camps.[39]

Kristallnacht produced a storm of protest, both national and international. A wave of disgust, embarrassment, revulsion, and shame swept across Germany, and the international community erupted with outrage. This episode became a turning point in the lives of several men who subsequently became active in the resistance movement. Helmuth Groscurth, a young army officer, expressed his "repugnance and outrage" in his diary with the following words: "One has to feel ashamed of still being a German."[40] Groscurth is recognized as one of the first of the army officers to join the resistance. He also played a critical role in the conspiracy to assassinate Hitler. He and Hans Oster have been described as the "soul of the resistance" within the Abwehr, the counterintelligence section of the armed forces, or Wehrmacht. The Abwehr would soon become a major center of resistance activity.[41]

Others who shared Groscurth's revulsion were galvanized to action as well, including the conservative career diplomat Ulrich von Hassell and Claus Schenk von Stauffenberg. Peter Yorck von Wartenburg, a lawyer, reserve military officer, and cousin of Stauffenberg, reacted to the brutal excesses with disgust and outrage. The episode transformed him from a "lukewarm supporter to an ardent opponent" of Hitler. He denounced the Nazis' genocidal racism "unreservedly and unequivocally," and ultimately became an active participant in the civilian resistance group known as the Kreisau Circle. He has been described as the "heart" of that group.[42]

Hans Bernd von Haeften was another individual whose reaction to Kristallnacht became a life-altering experience. He became part of a resistance group within the foreign office that had contact with army conspirators.[43] A man of deep religious conviction – he was a boyhood friend of Dietrich Bonhoeffer and a member of Bonhoeffer's Confessing Church[44] – he was greatly disturbed by the German clergy's failure to give what he considered to be an adequate response to Kristallnacht. He wrote to a friend who was a Protestant clergyman, expressing his "bitter disappointment" over the clergy's failure to adequately condemn the pogrom. "Haeften could not understand how those who were supposedly the moral leaders of society could remain silent in the face of such a blatant violation of morality." Later, at the time of his treason trial in 1944 after the failure of Operation Valkyrie, Haeften unrepentantly declared, "Adolf Hitler was the incarnation of evil."[45]

Kristallnacht was a major step in the escalation of Nazi anti-Semitism.[46] For the first time, Nazi Germany experienced both government-sponsored and government-sanctioned anti-Semitic violence. The inhumanity that lay at the core of Nazism had revealed itself in its full fury for all who wished to see. Many saw and – like Helmuth Groscurth, Peter Yorck von Wartenburg, and Hans Bernd von Haeften – responded by taking an active role in the nascent resistance movement. But the Nazis had acted with impunity. There was no way to call them to account for their behavior. Kristallnacht was but a foretaste of what was to follow.

* * * *

The general acceptance of Nazi racial policies reflected a craving for stability, security, and survival in an unstable and insecure world. If the price for achieving these goals included regimentation, subservience, and the use of force against "the other" or the "asocials," so be it. Terror directed against these "community aliens" was acceptable if it served the purpose of restoring "order."[47] Inexorably and inevitably, the individual was subsumed into the mass totalitarian police state. Omnipresent and omnipotent, this state tolerated no dissent of any sort. Although not necessarily overt, the threat of violence and punitive action was ever present. Positive expressions of support were essential if one wanted to avoid becoming a "community alien." Certain norms of behavior were expected of all national comrades (Volksgenossen), such as active and enthusiastic participation in party functions, including attendance at all party rallies and flying the Nazi flag with its swastika (Hakenkreuz) on appropriate occasions.

Gradually, the distinction between politics and private life disappeared. "The air in Germany had rapidly become suffocating [and] daily life had become hollow and mechanical."[48] Individuals were expected to surrender their autonomy and become merely an extension of the group personality, the features of which were determined by the Nazi Party. All values – cultural, social, political, artistic, ethical, moral, religious – had to conform to the norms of the state. Ideology dominated everything. Life became totally politicized. The realization of the Nazi-inspired Volksgemeinschaft required the creation of a "system of thought control and surveillance that penetrated right into the family."[49] This in turn meant that every form of criticism or dissent, every petty complaint, was at least potentially tantamount to treasonous behavior. Thus, the Nazis "transported a large portion of everyday conflict into the realm of anti-Nazism,"[50] whether or not such action was even intended to be anti-Nazi.

Conformity, Dissent, and Terror

A close examination of life in the Third Reich reveals that the well-worn images of the masses enthusiastically expressing their unalterable support for Hitler and his minions, while certainly not false, fail to convey the reality of dissent, dissatisfaction, and nonconformity that lay behind those images and the methods that those in power employed to command that support. A variety of contradictory elements became the sum and substance of everyday life in Nazi Germany. In order to maintain control, the Nazis combined terror and repression with various conciliatory gestures, declarations of moral purpose, and concessions. An example of this last was the Strength through Joy (Kraft durch Freude) program that began in 1933.

Ostensibly designed to provide travel opportunities and cultural enrichment for those on the lower rungs of the socioeconomic ladder and to break down class barriers, it in fact was a means of further extending control over the private lives of citizens by subsuming them into the mass. The program closely regulated leisure-time activities in order to isolate individuals and bring them under tight surveillance. This was all part of a process of atomization, whereby individuals were progressively isolated from one another. Individual autonomy gradually disintegrated and was replaced by the Nazi-inspired Volksgemeinschaft. The Strength through Joy program was a typical example of a Nazi policy that, in another context, has been described as a combination of "flattering words and oppressive deeds."[51] The Nazis produced an "intellectual construct" of this Volksgemeinschaft, comprised of "national comrades" (Volksgenossen), except for "a few fragments at the margin."[52] The Ministry of Propaganda worked assiduously to present an image of total unity committed to a single purpose: creating their Volksgemeinschaft. It was a self-portrait of "a closed, harmonious national community."[53]

This community was based not upon consensus and genuine mass support, however. The operative principles were propaganda and terror, both of which were required for effective manipulation and control of German citizens. One of the most effective instruments for presenting the Nazi message was the cinema. Generations of viewers have seen films of adoring crowds in a state of almost orgasmic ecstasy welcoming the Führer as his motorcade passed by. In truth, many – perhaps most – of these images are false. They were carefully posed, edited, or censored in order to convey the message of absolute unity. They were fabricated out of whole cloth. It was pure myth. And "Unity that is not based on truth is a sham."[54] Nazi Germany certainly was not based upon truth.[55]

As this process of "coordination" (Gleichschaltung) unfolded, one of the many ironies of Nazism gradually appeared. Here was modern technology, such as the radio and cinema, being put to the service of an anachronistic and reactionary state that was rejecting the very foundations of Western civilization. A corrupt and brutal regime was corrupting and brutalizing the German people. Ultimately, National Socialism brought about the destruction of German society. The war that the Nazis precipitated became, at the end, the proverbial war of all against all, with each individual left alone in a world that was collapsing into nothingness. Thus, the artificial Volksgemeinschaft created a totally atomized world completely devoid of genuine community ties.

*   *   *   *

The unspoken reality that lay behind these many expressions of apparent unity was the pervasive, ubiquitous, and persistent system of terror. People were obliged to give at least the appearance of being fired with enthusiasm for the new regime. Party block leaders (Blockleitern), who stood at the base of the Nazi Party pyramid and who engaged in surveillance at the most local level, took special note of any nonconformist activity. An example of unacceptable behavior that could lead to serious trouble for the perpetrator was failure to participate in the Eintopf, or "one-pot [Sunday] meal." The Nazis gave this traditional German stew a political connotation, thus demonstrating how they corrupted even the German language. Every German family in the Third Reich was expected to serve only one meal on one Sunday a month – the Eintopf – and the money saved was to be donated to social service projects. The Eintopf was advertised as "the meal of sacrifice for the Reich."[56]

A similar program was the Winter Help (Winterhilfe), an annual fund created to help finance the National Socialist People's Welfare Organization, a supposedly private agency that was intended to promote solidarity among the socioeconomic classes. This presumably would strengthen the Volksgemeinschaft. Everyone was expected to participate in this annual fund drive, and anyone who refused to contribute was denounced as a narrow-minded bourgeois or philistine (Spiesser).[57]

High on the list of proscribed activities was giving shelter and support to victims of persecution, although many dared to assist these victims despite threats and intimidation. Family members were encouraged to report deviant activity among their relatives – children against parents, spouses and siblings against each other.[58] The war only intensified this activity. "The participation of ordinary citizens as informers who would tip off the authorities was recognized as essential to safeguard the home front." Additionally, "the Gestapo was ordered to suppress 'every attempt to subvert the determination and will to fight of the German people.' Anyone who voiced doubts about victory or questioned the justification for the war was to be arrested."[59]

Thus disputes, disagreements, and conflicts of any sort, and however petty, were often reported to the Gestapo; many had little or nothing to do with denunciations of actual illegal activity. Instead, personal motives that "ran from seeking material advantage to gaining emotional revenge" lay behind most of this behavior.[60] Paradoxically, these actions undermined the image of a harmonious and properly functioning people's community. The Gestapo policy of encouraging informants to spy on neighbors – or even family – unwittingly opened the floodgates to a torrent of information, most of it of minimal value.

Reinforcing the Gestapo and its spies was the Nazi Party itself. It was ubiquitous, with party functionaries literally everywhere. Beginning in the "wilderness years" of the 1920s, Hitler had built a vast and elaborate structure that spread throughout the entire German nation and permeated every level of society, down to the smallest of the local communities. At the top of the structure was the administrative district (Gau), of which there ultimately were forty-two. Below each Gau was a series of further subdivisions, from the largest, a circuit or circle (Kreis), down to local groups (Ortsgruppen) encompassing fifteen hundred to three thousand households. Within the cities there were additional subdivisions into street cells (Zellen) of four to eight city blocks each. The smallest unit was the block (Block) of some forty to sixty households. Each of these districts and subdistricts had its leaders (Gauleiter, Kreisleiter, Ortsgruppenleiter, Zellenleiter, Blockleiter) who formed the hard core of the Nazi civil administrative structure and who were the most dedicated and fanatical members of the party.[61]

Hence, the tentacles of the Nazi Party spread to almost every nook and cranny of the German nation. No one was free from observation by party functionaries. Every sort of activity was observed, and any deviation from the official norms of behavior was duly noted. Persons entering or leaving an apartment or house were closely monitored. Nothing and no one escaped from the party's pervasiveness. A careless word, a chance remark, or an indiscreet comment could bring disaster to the person or persons making it. Everyone and everything was under close surveillance. Under such conditions, any activity that could be construed as serious dissent – whether individual or collective – was all but impossible. The Nazis took advantage of every opportunity to enforce conformity and suppress dissent.

The Elser bomb plot is such an example. It gave the Nazis the chance to take measures to suppress any perceived opposition to the Nazis. In an atmosphere heavily charged with fear and suspicion, many completely innocent people fell victim to anonymous charges of disloyalty. Such denunciations led to severe repression. Suspects were subjected to a sequence of events that by now had become commonplace: arrest, interrogation, and imprisonment. Within a week of the Elser episode, guidelines were established for the interrogators, such as "Did the suspect display a special interest in Hitler's Munich speech? Did the suspect express surprise that the speech had concluded without incident? And had the suspect remarked recently that the Nazi government's days were numbered?"[62] Even individuals whose behavior years earlier had exhibited a lack of enthusiasm for Hitler were apprehended and in some cases imprisoned. Hence, these events provided the Nazis with an excuse to tighten the noose around the necks of the German people even more. Examples of specific action at this time included seventy arrests in Düsseldorf, plus the execution of an unknown number of Jews in the Buchenwald concentration camp. Forty Bavarian monarchists were apprehended as well.[63]

Thus reality gave the lie to the image of a perfect people's community. Nazi Germany, in truth, was a society replete with conflict and contentiousness, although much of it was inconsequential. There was considerable criticism and complaint about the little things – living and working conditions, food shortages, and so on – that were part of everyday life in Nazi Germany and which wartime conditions only exacerbated. Dealing with these issues became a burdensome problem for the Gestapo. Much time was consumed responding to petty complaints of this sort. Repression and retaliation existed alongside dissent and nonconformity, much of the latter taking place just "below the threshold" of police invervention.[64]

National Socialism projected itself in utopian terms as a modern technological society possessing the requisite institutions capable of operating and managing social life in a proper manner. The Nazi utopia came at a high price, however.

> It pushed the utopian belief in all-embracing "scientific" final solutions of social problems to the ultimate logical extreme, encompassing the entire population in a bureaucratic racial-biological design and eradicating all sources of nonconformity and friction. It demonstrated the destructive power of modern technology by waging world war; in everyday life it offered a foretaste of a depressing, atomized form of society abjuring social, political and moral responsibilities and deriving its coherence solely from bureaucratic procedures and institutions of incorporation and from the vapid, specious charms of mass consumption.[65]

Nazi Germany was a modern technological society completely devoid of moral content. It had no soul, but it did have overweening power to suppress even the hint of dissident behavior. In such a world, a well-organized and broad-based resistance movement could not exist without strong charismatic leadership and a high degree of unity. And the German resistance movement had neither.

* * * *

The march toward an expected war over Czechoslovakia in the summer of 1938 revealed yet another crack in the facade of the perfect people's community. Premonitions of war deepened, and the German people – like European people everywhere – reacted in a manner far different from the wild enthusiasm with which they had greeted military confrontation twenty-five years earlier.

The American journalist William Shirer, who spent many years reporting the exploits of the Nazis, observed the reaction of Berliners to a military parade through the city streets on September 27, 1938. The parade, designed to whip up popular enthusiasm for the anticipated invasion of

Czechoslovakia, was scheduled to take place as the workers were leaving their offices at the end of the day. The response to this display of military bravado gives some indication of how the German people, in this case the Berliners, really felt about impending hostilities. It was, observed Shirer, a "terrible fiasco ... The good people of Berlin simply did not want to be reminded of war." He goes on: "They ducked into the subways, refused to look on, and the handful that did stood at the curb in utter silence ... [It was] the most striking demonstration against war I've ever seen."[66]

Shirer subsequently walked from his initial vantage point on Unter den Linden, one of the main thoroughfares in Berlin, to the Reich's Chancellery, where Hitler was reviewing the troops from a balcony. "There weren't two hundred people there. Hitler looked grim, then angry, and soon went inside ... What I've seen tonight almost rekindles a little faith in the German people. They are dead set against war." As he went back inside, Hitler reputedly said to Goebbels, who had accompanied him, "With people like that, you could never carry on a war."[67]

The comments of General Erwin von Witzleben provide an insight into his attitude toward the Czech crisis. As commander of the military forces of the Third Military District (Wehrkreis III) around Berlin, he also commanded the troops marching in the parade. Moreover, he was one of the very few generals who were determined opponents of Hitler from the beginning of Nazi rule. He was an active participant in the conspiracy against Hitler, and reputedly said of the parade that "he was tempted to unlimber his guns right there and then go in and lock 'that fellow' up." Witzleben eventually became one of the central figures in the army conspiracy against Hitler.[68]

In 1940, Shirer recorded the same sense of apathy among the Berliners when they learned that the German Army had occupied Paris. "Berlin has taken the news of the capture of Paris as phlegmatically as it has taken everything else in this war."[69] One can reasonably assume that the Berliners shared this attitude with many, if not most, of their fellow countrymen. But the question remained: How could an effective resistance movement mobilize this apathy and inertia to bring an end to Nazi rule? The question went unanswered.

The little organized dissent that did occur in the Third Reich before and during the war went on within the working class, the members of which "kept up an attitude of sullen refusal [to cooperate with the Nazis], which on many occasions led to positive acts of opposition."[70] The German historian Detlev Peukert has written, "Resistance by workers formed the most significant component of the German resistance movement."⁷¹ Consequently, former members of the now outlawed trade unions and political parties on the left were special targets of Nazi efforts to eradicate all opposition – real, potential, or imagined. In pure numbers, these people comprised the largest group of those who suffered political persecution. Although the majority of the working-class population was politically inert "out of necessity," most workers stubbornly refused reconciliation with the Nazis.⁷² Despite displays of nonconformity and dissent, however, there was virtually no active resistance.

"Hans Q. Public" definitely was not part of any national mass resistance movement. Hence, unlike occupied Europe during World War II, where the underground resistance had a high degree of legitimacy, no secret national resistance movement ever developed within Germany. Instead, there was a gradual evolution of attitudes toward the Nazi state: apprehension at the beginning in 1933, then euphoria as conditions appeared to improve in the midthirties, and finally disillusionment and ultimate despair as total war eventually engulfed the entire nation. For example, a secret SD (Sicherheitsdienst, or Security Service of the SS) report of May 1943 declared, "The mood of the national comrades (Volksgenossen) is at present calm. There is not, however, the necessary conviction and belief in final victory."⁷³

* * * *

As the system of terror suppressed potential opposition to Nazi policy, the propaganda machine continued to manipulate public opinion and to generate support for the regime even as defeat loomed ever larger. Throughout the twelve-year Reich, Goebbels and his Minisry of Propaganda had adjusted its message to the need of the hour. The initial propaganda line in World War II had been triumphalist, as the spectacular military successes of 1939 to 1941 trumpeted a message of inevitable victory. The Wehrmacht was portrayed as the "vanguard of a greater German Empire."⁷⁴ After the defeat at Stalingrad, however, Germans became the "defenders of European culture against communist tyranny."⁷⁵ No longer were the Germans the masters of the world. Now they were the underdogs, fighting against an implacable and monstrous foe. With their backs to the wall, the choice was either victory or annihilation, and the growing realization of impending defeat brought with it the "call to total sacrifice."⁷⁶

Goebbels gave a speech before a "specially selected" audience of ten thousand party loyalists at the Berlin Sports Palace (Sportspalast) on

February 18, 1943, that was broadcast to the entire nation. It was a call for total war. Describing the consequences of a German defeat in lurid terms, he declared that it "could be avoided only by sheer force of will and the complete mobilization of society." The nation, he said, must adopt a more "spartan way of life." He went on: "We are all children of our people, forged together." "Do you agree?" "Are you prepared?" In response to each question, the crowd, its emotions raised to a fever pitch, screamed its fanatical response: "*Ja!*"[77]

Subsequently, fourteen million copies of a pamphlet entitled *Do You Want Total War?* were distributed to party offices. Shortly after the speech, what has been described as a "barrage of 'appeals, instructions, decrees, speeches, conferences and publications'" descended upon the nation.[78] Unsurprisingly, these appeals were portrayed in anti-Allied, anti-Semitic, and anti-Bolshevik settings. Typical of this last was a placard that appeared on the walls of buildings in all of the major cities: "Victory or Bolshevik Chaos!"[79]

All of this was clearly seen for what it was: a government-inspired propaganda ploy. Nonetheless, Goebbels and his minions had skillfully conflated the fear of what could accompany a defeat with recollections of the Great War and its aftermath. The awful memories of 1918 to 1919 were recalled: a total social, political, and economic collapse of the nation, coupled with fears of an even greater catastrophe should this second war be lost. Most importantly, the message resonated with many Germans. Others, more realistic, recognized that defeat was inevitable. The increasing war-weariness was reflected in an anonymous rhyme that appeared in the Ruhr district with its many coal mines shortly after the infamous "Do You Want War?" speech. It was addressed to the aircrews – the "Tommies" – of the British bombers that were now making their almost nightly visits to German cities: "Lieber Tommy, fliege weiter; wir sind alle Bergarbeiter; fliege weiter nach Berlin; die haben alle ja geschrien" (Dear Tommy, fly farther. We are all miners. Fly farther to Berlin. They all have screamed yes). Not everyone accepted the message of total war and ultimate victory.[80]

In another clever move designed to build popular support for total war, the Ministry of Propaganda implicated the German people themselves in the horrific Nazi crimes being perpetrated in Eastern Europe. The Nazis not only admitted to certain war crimes but also declared that the crimes had been committed in the name of the German people; "they produced the intimacy of complicity, not the distance of ignorance."[81] Rather than conceal, the Nazis attempted to manipulate and manage "the facts of the

Holocaust."[82] They were in effect saying, *Now you know. You are in this with us, like it or not; you are as guilty as we. Therefore, you had better fight to the bitter end.* Like Rosenberg, Goebbels used the metaphor of the burned bridges. He declared, "We've [*i.e.*, the Nazis] burned our bridges behind us. We can't go back, and don't want to anymore. We will either go down in history as the greatest statesmen of all time, or the greatest criminals."[83]

An indication of the success of Nazi propaganda in identifying the public with the regime and the Führer is seen in the popular attitude toward the conspirators at the time of the attempt on Hitler's life on July 20, 1944. These men were almost universally condemned as traitors.[84] By then, this propaganda campaign was so successful that for most Germans, a future without Hitler was beyond their ability to comprehend. Nation and Führer had indeed become one.

Ironically, Great Britain's Royal Air Force and the US Eighth Air Force inadvertently aided this propaganda effort. From 1943 to the end of the war, these air armies pummeled Germany with a round-the-clock bombing campaign. German cities literally were subjected to twenty-four hours of continual air raids. Pre–World War II airpower theorists had predicted that such bombing would destroy civilian morale and force the government of the country so attacked to capitulate. In most instances, however, just the opposite happened. The air war not only failed to destroy German morale but also actually drew the people closer to their Nazi leaders and reinforced their determination to persevere against insurmountable odds. The events unfolding all around the German people confirmed for most of them the Nazi claim that the Allies intended to utterly destroy Germany.[85]

Nonetheless, this reaction was not universal. In at least one instance, the civilian response to the continuous bombing was quite different. In late July 1943, the city of Hamburg was subjected to a series of four bombing raids that produced death and destruction of unprecedented proportions. For all practical purposes, Hamburg was destroyed. "In the four great raids taken all together, Allied bombers had flown more than 2,500 missions over the city, dropping over 8,300 tons of incendiaries and high explosives on their target." The civilian population suffered 40,000 deaths and 125,000 injuries sufficiently serious to require medical attention. Those who suffered the loss of their homes numbered 900,000. Some 56 percent of civilian homes were destroyed.[86]

This bombing had a significant impact on civilian morale, but not to the Nazis' benefit. Like many major German cities, Hamburg consistently gave what at best could be described as lukewarm support to the Third

Reich. "Discontent [thus] came easily to the surface here because belief in the Nazi system had never gone very deep into the masses." The citizens of Hamburg did not hesitate to express their dismay and disgust with the Third Reich. "Popular anger was directed not against the British for their 'terror raids' ... but against Göring and the German air force, which had patently failed to defend the homeland, and against the Nazi Party, which had brought this destruction on Germany."[87]

Many – doubtlessly most – German civilians saw themselves as innocent victims of this air war, which essentially was true. However, their government had sowed the wind, and they were now reaping the whirlwind. Thus, by late 1944, the nation was tied to its leadership for good or ill. The war indeed had become an apocalyptic struggle, and the brutalization of the German nation, which had begun in 1933, continued relentlessly. Propaganda and police power ensured that the Nazis remained firmly in control. Regardless of the people's reaction to the air raids, the Nazi Volksgemeinschaft was approaching completion and fulfillment.[88]

As mentioned earlier, many Germans chose a kind of "internal exile" in reaction to Nazi control of their homeland. Rather than participating in the public life of the Third Reich, they retreated into their own private world, which consisted only of immediate family and close friends. This passivity was reinforced by the continued presence of the Nazi apparatus of terror, which grew more effective, efficient, and fanatical with the passage of time. It was not always overt, but it was always there. It reached its apogee under the conditions of total war now devastating the nation from the air. Under the pressure of incessant bombing, social relations fragmented in the struggle for mere survival. A "climate of resignation" prompted people to just "wait passively for the war to be over."[89] Actual working conditions only contributed further to this climate. Overwork was an ever-present problem; ten- to twelve-hour shifts had become common. People were physically as well as emotionally worn out. Thus, the Nazi terror machine, the emotional and physical exhaustion that accompanied the conditions of total war – especially total aerial war – and the reality of living in a repressive totalitarian police state effectively suppressed any thought of mounting a serious resistance movement.[90]

Consequently, the German people became increasingly isolated from one another, whether out of personal choice or necessity. This isolation had a significant impact upon the anti-Nazi resistance. As society became increasingly atomized under Nazi rule, so the potential for collective action against that rule declined even further. Hence, no truly organized mass resistance movement would or could emerge under these conditions. As they withdrew from the outside world, people found their interest in their individual survival increasing and their concern for the excesses of the regime decreasing. Because of this, potential resistance activity was further crippled. The SOPADE Report for November 1935 had commented prophetically: "The essence of fascist control of the masses is compulsory organization on the one hand and atomisation on the other."[91] Therefore, the Nazi attempt to create its unique Volksgemeinschaft reached its ultimate expression at the war's end. Its paradox is obvious. The ultimate artificial Nazi "community" became a state consisting of a totally isolated, atomized, and controlled population. This community could be achieved only through total war, thus confirming its nihilistic implications.

Ironically, these conditions served to further stabilize the Third Reich. As the process of atomization became more complete, the Nazi system became more secure domestically, even as it was disintegrating from military collapse outside the boundaries of the fatherland. The implications for the resistance are readily apparent. There was no mass support for an organized mass resistance and no popular uprising against the Nazis, simply because the "structural preconditions for 'mass resistance' did not exist." These conditions produced a fatal weakness for the resistance movement. Its leaders were completely isolated.[92]

Racial Warfare

As the Volksgemeinschaft was reaching its dénouement in Germany, the full force of the Nazi racist ideology was approaching complete fulfillment in Eastern Europe. Consequently, there appeared a supposedly unique type of combat soldier, one who reflected the Nazi ethos, who projected "a new kind of brutal heroism," and who "increasingly assumed the virtues of unsparing and ruthless strength."[93] All of this was part of the process of physical and psychological brutalization that had been an integral part of the Nazi state from the beginning. Since 1933, the entire German nation – especially the military establishment – had been subjected to an increasingly intense and virulent propaganda campaign that portrayed the Jewish people as "the other," the enemy within, who had to be removed by whatever means possible and necessary. This campaign reached its apogee with the war in the east. Commented one soldier in a letter written in July 1941, "Any sign of humanity seems to have disappeared from deeds, hearts and minds."[94] The nihilistic nature of this racial war accentuated the savagery of military conflict in that it subjected the German soldiers on the Eastern Front to a virtually unprecedented series of mind- and soul-numbing experiences. One SS man, writing to a relative in November 1941, "reported that he had had to shoot down 500 Jews, including women and children, in Poland, that many were not dead, but others were just thrown on top, and that he could not take it anymore."[95] The experience of this soldier was not unique. Whereas some SS men became desensitized to the slaughter occurring all around them, many others suffered severe psychological trauma. "By November 1941 at least one psychiatric hospital specialised in treating SS men 'who have broken down while executing women and children.'"[96] Not all members of the SS had become totally soulless beasts.

With obscene irony, the Nazis portrayed their spectacular victories in the summer of 1941 as part of a great crusade to rescue European civilization from the clutches of godless, materialistic, atheistic communism. This is a reminder of the social milieu prevailing in Germany in the years before the Nazis achieved power. Many contemporary Germans, it will be remembered, viewed the Weimar Republic as a cesspool of moral degradation that the "un-German" forces of mass democracy, liberalism, and socialism had created. These people believed as well that Bolshevism lay just over the horizon, ready to seize power at the opportune moment. Operation Barbarossa – the code name for the Nazi invasion of the Soviet Union – which was portrayed as a "just war to defend the fundamental values of the Western world,"[97] would end this threat for all time. If the deaths of millions of people were the price to be paid for victory in this struggle, so be it. This war was nothing less than a mortal Manichaean struggle, an "apocalyptic conflict between the forces of good and evil."[98] As one considers the true nature of Nazism, the difficulty of viewing it in these terms becomes readily apparent. Such, however, are the ways of ideology; in this netherworld, up is down and down is up. The corrupting work of Nazism continued unabated, and most of the Wehrmacht generals stood by, scarcely raising their voices against these outrages. The moral deterioration of the army leadership that had begun as early as 1934 continued without surcease. The term "moral cowardice" does not seem to be an inappropriate description of their behavior.[99]

The ideological indoctrination imposed upon the frontline soldiers during Barbarossa only reinforced the dehumanization that inevitably accompanies any war experience. Nazi propaganda constantly reminded these soldiers that the German Army was on a "crusade against Bolshevism,"[100] fighting a racial war against a barbaric, merciless, and ruthless foe.[101] This would be a war of annihilation, of total destruction, and it was planned as such from the outset. German soldiers had a moral obligation to participate in the grim work of racial purification, including the murder of women and children, so that the world could enjoy peace and their own children would "have a better future."[102] It was gruesome but necessary work. History demanded it. Nazi ideology demanded it. The survival of Western civilization was at stake. Racial warfare had reached its apogee in Eastern Europe.

CHAPTER 3

An Emergent Resistance

The first few years of Nazi rule witnessed a complete absence of anti-Nazi activity. There was no active individual or group resistance whatsoever. The traumas associated with the Weimar Republic, especially its last years, had taken their toll on the German people and nation. Fear, discouragement, and apprehension, together with hope, promise, and optimism, aptly described the mind-set of the German people as the Nazi Party began its rule. Germany was exhausted. Whatever opposition had existed before January 30, 1933, had melted away, and any thought of resistance, organized or unorganized, could be dismissed as fanciful or absurd. Across the political spectrum, all signs of political resistance, real or potential, evaporated. For all practical purposes, the Nazis had carte blanche to thoroughly purge the entire nation of any organization or activity that could be remotely construed as anti-Nazi.

Thus began the program of Gleichschaltung, or coordination, whereby every organization and institution was "Nazified," that is, brought under the purview of the Nazi Party. Intimidation, repression, and persecution, along with outright violence, increased dramatically.[1] This marked the beginning of the process that turned Germany into a totalitarian state. "Prohibitions, seizure of buildings, and confiscations of property that a short time before would have brought Germany to the verge of civil war now elicited only shrugs."[2] The writer Sebastian Haffner describes the dismay felt by many Germans with the following words: "There was not one single example of energetic defence, of courage or principle. There was only panic, flight, and desertion. In March 1933 millions were ready to fight the Nazis. Overnight they found themselves without leaders ... [This reflected] a 'terrible moral bankruptcy of the opposition leadership.'"[3]

Constraints

Too many Germans in positions of power and authority did not yet recognize the truly depraved nature of the Nazi system. "The problem was ... not solely the lack of will to resist but equally [the] lack of comprehension of the nature of Nazism."[4] Two men in particular come to mind in this regard, namely, General Kurt von Schleicher and Franz von Papen. These men and others chose to look aside, to ignore the evil that was beginning to engulf them. They chose to believe Hitler's lies because they wanted to believe them. His promise of a restored world of imperial greatness held a fatal attraction for them. They failed to accept the fact that the past can never be recovered in its completeness, and they were indulging in a dangerous delusion that would bring them and their nation to absolute calamity. They displayed an appalling lack of judgment.[5]

Many of the future resistance leaders shared this delusion. One such man was Carl Goerdeler, a highly regarded politician who had repudiated the Weimar Republic and all it represented. He was convinced that Anglo-Saxon parliamentarianism, with its political party system and its emphasis upon mass [*i.e.,* democratic] politics, had brought his country nothing but grief, and that the only way out of the Weimar quagmire was a return to a more traditional form of government, such as a monarchy. Years later, after he had become an active member of the resistance, he described his vision of a post-Nazi Germany that was a reflection of his earlier convictions. That vision was based upon his belief that an authoritarian form of government best represented the German ethos. This Germany would be founded on "Christianity as the basis of society, [and would be accompanied by] the rule of law [and] freedom of belief and conscience."[6] Goerdeler, like many of his social class and temperament, initially chose to support the Nazis, believing that the Third Reich represented the solution to Germany's governance problem. They believed that it held out "the promise of a civic and spiritual revival." All of "the weaknesses of mass rule, party politics, military ineffectualness, and crass materialism" would end with Hitler in power.[7]

Carl Goerdeler was born in Schneidemühl, Germany (now Piła, Poland), in 1884 into – according to historian Gerhard Ritter, who also was a friend – "a large, loving middle-class family that was cultured, devoutly Lutheran, nationalist, and conservative."[8] It also was a family committed to public service. Goerdeler's father had been a district judge and a member of the Prussian legislature. The young Carl followed in this tradition. As a member of the Great War generation, he served in the imperial army on the Eastern Front and rose to the rank of captain. After graduation from Tübingen University, where he studied law and economics, he was elected mayor of Königsberg (now Kaliningrad, Russia) and was highly regarded as "a hard-working and outstanding municipal politician" during the era of the Weimar Republic.⁹ Subsequently he became Reich price commissioner both in the Republic, from 1931 to 1932, and in the Third Reich, from 1934 to 1935. He also served as mayor of Leipzig from 1930 to 1937. Like many of his socioeconomic class and political persuasion, he initially supported Hitler and tried to offer constructive criticism, naïvely believing that the Nazis – especially Hitler – were amenable to rational argument. He sent numerous memoranda to the Führer offering advice on economic policy; all, naturally, were totally ignored. Hitler persisted with his own economic and financial programs that Goerdeler "regarded as highly irresponsible."[10] All of this contributed to Goerdeler's growing disillusionment with the Third Reich, which by 1937 was almost complete.

The turning point for him had come in November 1936, when the English conductor Sir Thomas Beecham brought the London Philharmonic Orchestra to Leipzig for a concert to be given at the famous Gewandhaus concert hall. The great German composer Felix Mendelssohn had served as conductor for the Gewandhaus orchestra and had been instrumental in establishing close relations between Germany and Great Britain in their musical endeavors. Beecham wished to lay a wreath at a statue of Mendelssohn that was located at the entrance to the Gewandhaus. Goerdeler gave his permission, and the ceremony took place. The following morning, the wreath and statue were gone.

The local Nazi Party boss had removed both the wreath and the statue during the night and had destroyed the statue. Goerdeler, who had been away on a trip to Finland when the episode occurred, was infuriated. As a result, he resigned from his position as mayor. This incident was the last straw in a series of confrontations that had taken place between Goerdeler and Nazi authorities over the preceding two or more years. Goerdeler was one of the first civilians to awaken from a self-induced somnolence with regard to the Third Reich and its pretensions. Ultimately, he became one of the most important participants in the civilian opposition movement. The German journalist and historian Joachim Fest describes him as the "central figure in the civilian opposition."[11]

A true resistance movement was some two years away, however. The "high noon" of Nazi popularity was still in place, thanks largely to Hitler's dominating personality, as well as to the success of Nazi policies such as those that had revived the economy. This fact alone highlighted the most serious problem that a future resistance movement would face: the Nazis had a leader, whereas the resisters had none. The resisters had no national figure capable of challenging Hitler or of uniting the diverse factions that comprised what would become the resistance. There was no one who could bridge the divide between conservatives on the one hand and the SPD on the other. Thus, the two interrelated problems remained: a lack of leadership plus disunity among those who wished to free Germany from Hitler's tyranny. Moreover, the menacing Nazi police state remained an ever-present reality.

This contributed to an even more formidable barrier to effective action, namely, the constraints of public opinion. The resistance movement never had the public behind it in any organized manner. Consequently, it lacked the power to influence the course of events. Mass opinion, which Goebbels and his unscrupulous Ministry of Popaganda manipulated with great virtuosity, effectively tied the resisters' hands. As the diplomatic and military successes accumulated between 1936 and 1940, the Nazi state appeared to be invincible. German prestige and power had been restored after years of humiliation, and with all of these successes came mass support. In this triumphalist atmosphere, any thought of a successful coup was patently absurd. Furthermore, the reversal of fortune that eventually brought ghastly suffering and catastrophic defeat to the German nation produced a perverse kind of support that demanded unwavering allegiance and dedication to the state in its hour of deepest need. Anything less than this kind of wholehearted and fanatic devotion was denounced as treason. The Nazi Party controlled the masses, and the resistance did not; in the modern world, successful political movements must have mass support, especially during wartime.[12] The relentless nationalism of the Nazi state hamstrung the resisters, both in victory and defeat.

* * * *

Mass support for political action is a distinctly modern concept; it did not exist in the preindustrial world. In the eighteenth century, for example, rulers such as the famous Prussian king Frederick the Great (Friedrich der Grosse) could completely ignore the masses, because their participation in the political process was unwanted and unnecessary. With the coming of the industrial age, however, large numbers of people were needed to produce the goods necessary for successful governmental action, especially in the conduct of war. Large armies increasingly became the order of the day, and large numbers of the general population were required to produce the weapons of war, as well as the uniforms, the foodstuffs, and all the other accouterments essential to the proper functioning of a large military establishment.

The French Revolution first demonstrated the need for mass mobilization. The year 1793 introduced the levée en masse, a true citizen army, but the inevitable sacrifices that accompanied such warfare required a cause to sustain the mass support essential to success. That cause became the survival and victory of the French nation itself. Significantly the French national anthem, "La Marseillaise," contains the phrase "Aux arms, citoyennes" (To arms, citizens!).

As we fast-forward 150 years, we see the same dual process of inspiration and intimidation taking place in Nazi Germany. The Nazi system co-opted the entire German nation to support its expansionist warlike policy. Thus, viewed as a political movement, the resistance was doomed practically from the start. To repeat, no modern political movement – especially one that proposes dramatic change – can succeed without a broad base of organized popular support, and the resistance did not have one.

Ironically, many of the resisters who became a part of the conspiracy against Hitler mistrusted, disliked, and even feared both the masses and democracy. Consequently, these people not only were unable to build that broad base of support for their goals but also had no desire to do so. This attitude contributed further to the isolation of these individuals from the masses, such as those of the working classes who had supported the socialist movement. It would be a continuing, ongoing problem for the conspirators during the entire twelve-year history of the Third Reich, severely hindering their activities.

Nonetheless, attempts were made to bridge the gap, and contacts were made between various groups in an effort to form alliances. The Kreisau Circle, for example, was able to attract several "devoted but undogmatic socialists" to their group. One such man was Adolf Reichwein, an educator with socialist leanings. He actually joined the Kreisau Circle in 1940.[13] Former trade union leader Wilhelm Leuschner held conversations in the fall of 1939 with retired army chief of staff General Ludwig Beck, a major figure in the resistance, about a general strike to coincide with an officers' revolt, although nothing came of the plan. Carl Goerdeler succeeded in forming ties and friendships with Wilhelm Leuschner and another trade union leader, Jakob Kaiser. However, other conservative members of Goerdeler's civilian group of resisters condemned these efforts, believing that they went "too far toward restoring democratic 'Weimar' conditions."[14] Sadly, this attitude proved to be the rule throughout the history of the resistance movement.

All of these elements – diversity, disunity, and insufficiently organized mass support – continued to frustrate efforts to create an effective anti-Nazi movement. Simply stated, the resistance was never unified.[15] Although contacts between and among the various groups existed, "it was less by virtue of an overarching organization or plan of action than by an overlapping membership." There was no "real common denominator or unifying idea, not even a collective name." In fact, the term "resistance" did not come into usage until well into the post–World War II years. Instead, there was a wide range of diverse groups, various autonomous "cell groups," not an overall umbrella organization. This autonomy and decentralization existed for one primary reason: it served as a protective measure against the ever-present danger of Gestapo infiltration, which became increasingly acute with the passage of time.[16]

There was, however, one institution that might well have made a difference in 1933 had its leadership been more politically astute. That institution was the German Army. Only the army could have stopped Hitler and the Nazis, but tragically, it failed. As will be seen, a determined anti-Nazi resistance movement eventually did develop within the ranks of the military leadership after several agonizing years of soul-searching over the morality of resistance and tyrannicide, and it came tantalizingly close to success on several occasions, only to be ultimately thwarted in achieving its goal of eliminating Hitler.

Despite the differences, a unity of purpose among the disparate groups did exist, namely, an unshakable opposition to the Nazi state. By 1938, there was a growing realization that "National Socialism was not simply a party like any other; with its total acceptance of criminality it was an incarnation of evil; so that all those whose minds were attuned to democracy, Christianity, freedom, humanity or even mere legality found themselves forced into alliance."[17] Additionally:

> The opposition in prewar Germany was far greater than the Nazi proclamations of unity indicated. Tens of thousands of political enemies were and remained in prison; thousands were executed for active opposition [which] was far more prevalent than Nazi propaganda would admit; the secret surveillance reports of the Gestapo give an entirely different picture.[18]

Thus, what has been described as a "few fundamental maxims" united the resistance, namely, "a refusal to participate in the violence, mindlessness, and injustice on all sides; a strong sense of right and wrong; and ... a desire 'somehow simply to survive with a sense of decency.'"[19]

Therefore, a common bond united all opponents of the Nazis, whether or not they were an active part of the resistance, and those who did play an active role were exceptionally tenacious in their attempts to bring Hitler and his henchmen down.

Conception and Gestation

As the year 1938 dawned, a resistance movement was in its beginning stages, even though the totalitarian police state that Germany had become was now ensconced. Any sort of opposition, when discovered, was dealt with in typical Nazi fashion – that is, with extreme brutality. Nevertheless, many were becoming increasingly apprehensive about Nazi rule and were beginning to think of ways to do something about it. Two developments in particular were causing growing consternation among many who initially had greeted the coming of the Third Reich with considerable enthusiasm. The first was a significant escalation of anti-Semitic activity. The second was an increasingly adventurous foreign policy.

* * * *

Central to Nazi ideology was the obsession with what the Nazis considered to be the Jewish "menace" and their determination to eradicate it completely. The Nazi mind saw the Jews as "the repositories of an alien, un-German spirit, and their removal as part of a cultural revolution that would restore 'Germanness' to Germany." This "cultural revolution" led to the dismissal of many who were an integral part of German cultural, educational, and artistic life. Although the implications of Nazi racist policy would not be fully realized until the war years, life was becoming increasingly difficult for the German Jewish community. First, there was the thinly disguised anti-Jewish propaganda campaign that began almost immediately after January 30, 1933. Additionally, a boycott of Jewish shops and small business establishments took place on April 1, with SA storm troopers standing guard outside the stores warning people not to enter. The boycott met with very limited success. Many non-Jewish Germans completely ignored the intimidating presence of the storm troopers and continued to patronize their favorite Jewish business establishments. For the German Jews, however, this one-day experience marked a turning point. State-sponsored persecution had replaced routine discrimination.[20] In the meantime, SA thugs continued their anti-Jewish rampage against individuals and property unconstrained by the government, and even though Hitler himself was downplaying his own racism at this point.

In 1935 came three decrees that are known to history as the Nuremberg Laws, which effectively "disenfranchised all those citizens 'not of German blood.'"[21] The term "not of German blood" obviously referred to Germans of the Jewish faith. These decrees provided for the legalization of "biological-racist anti-Semitism."[22] This prewar anti-Semitic activity culminated in the abhorrent Kristallnacht of November 9, 1938. The worst was yet to come, but enough violent racist activity had already taken place to suggest where the Nazis were headed with their anti-Semitism, although virtually no one could comprehend the program of annihilation that the Nazis would perpetrate in Eastern Europe in the near future.

The problem of Nazi anti-Semitism placed many future resistance leaders in a quandary. Anti-Semitism had been a part of European culture for hundreds of years, and Germany was no exception. Many members of Germany's upper classes – including members of the officer corps in the military establishment who themselves came from the traditional landed aristocracy – sincerely believed that Jews could never be truly assimilated into the mainstream of German culture. It was said of these traditionalists that:

> They typically displayed the fashionable bigotry of the exclusive drawing room or the elite gentlemen's club. They looked down with condescension on the Jewish parvenu who might have acquired a great deal of money but could never attain the social status that only family and tradition bestowed.[23]

This attitude reflected a class consciousness with roots that were embedded in the tradition-bound feudal society of medieval Europe. To these people, "the Jews were an alien element incapable of being fully assimilated into German society."[24] Carl Goerdeler was an almost perfect example of such an individual. An examination of the many letters, memoranda, reports, and so on that he produced over his lifetime definitely shows that he never held any hatred of the Jews.[25] While mayor of Leipzig, he did all he could to protect the Jewish population of his city from the depredations of the SA storm troopers. As with most of those of his social class who would become active in the resistance, he abhorred the events associated with Kristallnacht and its aftermath. Nonetheless, he – and they – accepted without question the assumptions that provided the foundation for the racism that was an intrinsic part of the Western world of their day, namely that the "races" could not coexist harmoniously as a single, multiracial community.[26] In the instance of Germany, Goerdeler believed that the differences between the Jewish and Christian communities were irreconcilable. The solution, therefore, lay in "separation, not assimilation or coexistence."[27] He wrote that "Jews living amongst other peoples would always, again and again, become victims of persecution."[28] Beliefs such as these were not too dissimilar from the mind-set that lay behind the laws, attitudes, and beliefs that permeated American society during the years of racial segregation in the United States and which regrettably remain part of its ethos to this day.

Another future member of the resistance who shared Goerdeler's conservative sentiments was Ulrich von Hassell. Described as a "sophisticated, cosmopolitan aristocrat,"[29] Hassell, unlike his father and other members of this aristocratic Prussian family who had served in the Prussian Army, chose a career in diplomacy, and he distinguished himself in the German Foreign Office, serving as ambassador in several postings. He had been an early supporter of Hitler and the Nazis, but he became increasingly disillusioned with them as the passage of time progressively revealed the true nature of Nazism. He also had a brief dalliance with anti-Semitism early in his career, but he thoroughly rejected the crude racism of the National Socialists. By the late thirties, his initially favorable view of the Nazis had undergone a significant transformation. As with so many of the eventual resisters, Goerdeler's turning point came with Kristallnacht. He was outraged by the episode and wrote of the "bestial barbarity" displayed on November 9, 1938, declaring that the "moral credit of the Third Reich" was deteriorating. The Nazis, he wrote, had become an instrument of corruption.[30] Addressing the core issue of National Socialism, he declared, "What must be the inner nature of an ideology that requires such methods in order to prevail!"[31] The citizens of the German nation themselves, he went on, were the primary victims of Nazi rule.

Members of the military establishment were experiencing a similar epiphany. Repelled by the Nazi racial violence, some officers and soldiers had a growing sense that Kristallnacht represented a turning point for Nazi anti-Semitism. No longer content with mere discrimination or even expropriation, Nazis displayed a racism that had become murderous. The door was opening to the monstrous behavior that would become the norm in a few years hence. This was a new kind of racism that would lead to annihilation.

Many of the men in the officer corps of the German Army shared the anti-Semitic prejudices of their civilian counterparts, that is, those in the upper middle class and the landed aristocracy. It was said of the military officers that, like their civilian counterparts, "few were out and out anti-Semites. [Although regrettably, some were.] They generally regarded Jews with disdain rather than hatred."[32] Like everyone, they were children of their time, and the era of the late nineteenth and early twentieth centuries was an age of racial prejudice, much of it anti-Semitic.

Racism never had been an exclusively German phenomenon. For centuries dating from the Middle Ages, every nation in the Western world practiced anti-Semitism in varying degrees of intensity. Famously, France was rocked by an anti-Semitic scandal in 1894 when Alfred Dreyfus, a Jewish captain in the French Army and the first man of his faith to be admitted to the general staff, was falsely convicted of treason and sent to prison on Devil's Island. The trial itself had been a mockery of justice, and many people in public life challenged the verdict. Several years later, Dreyfus was released from prison, and eventually he was completely exonerated.[33] Although broader issues surrounded the "Dreyfus affair," the question of his religion was definitely a significant part of the episode. Could a Jew be a true patriot and an officer in the military establishment of his country and still practice his faith? Could a German Jew be both German and Jewish? This was the substance of the "Jewish question," and it permeated virtually all of Europe. Anti-Semitism was particularly rife in France and Russia. To illustrate its intensity, the historian Richard Evans relates the following story:

> A historian once speculated on what would happen if a time-traveller from 1945 arrived back in Europe just before the First World War, and told an intelligent and well-informed contemporary that within thirty years a European nation would make a systematic attempt to kill all the Jews of Europe and exterminate nearly six million in the process. If the time-traveller invited the contemporary to guess which nation it would be, the chances were that he would have pointed to France.

Another likely candidate might well have been Tsarist Russia in the late nineteenth and early twentieth centuries. This period was stained by a series of vicious pogroms that led to many Jewish deaths. German Jews, in contrast, had become assimilated into the mainstream of German society quite successfully.[34]

* * * *

In addition to the growth of racial violence after 1935, a second issue was beginning to produce a deepening sense of disquiet and unease within the ranks of the officer corps of the Wehrmacht. Having consolidated his power within Germany and having confirmed the Third Reich as its governing system, Adolf Hitler began to make plans and take action in the pursuit of his ultimate goal, which was the creation of a "racially pure" Germanic empire in Eastern Europe. Accordingly, his pronouncements were becoming increasingly bellicose and strident, and his foreign policy was becoming more reckless and adventurous. Already, Hitler was pushing Germany relentlessly toward a war for which it was ill prepared. This problem was worrisome for those civilians and military officers who would soon become active in a conspiracy to overthrow Hitler and his hooligans.

They soon faced an ethical and moral issue, however. As much as they detested Hitler and the Nazis, they nonetheless supported many of the Führer's short-term foreign policy goals, especially those that would rectify the alleged injustices perpetrated by the Allied powers at the end of the Great War. Specifically, there was the issue of the German Army, which had been reduced to a token military force of one hundred thousand men and officers. Additionally, the Rhineland area of Germany was to be permanently demilitarized. All military installations in the territory of the German nation west of the Rhine River, plus a strip of territory fifty kilometers to the east of the river, were prohibited. These and other demands placed upon the German nation outraged its people. Virtually everyone in Germany – even the future conspirators against Hitler – welcomed the attempt to rectify these conditions. The problem lay not with the goals but with the method Hitler planned to use in order to achieve them, which was war, or at least the threat of war. Almost no one outside the circle of Hitler's immediate associates supported either military action or its threat. This issue of goals and methods became an especially burdensome problem for the resistance movement in the days ahead.

The Conservatives

Despite all Nazi attempts to complete the work of creating their Volksgemeinschaft, dissent and resistance remained. Three groups were becoming an active presence in what soon would become an anti-Nazi resistance movement. The first group can be described as the "conservatives." Used in the historic European sense, the term refers to those of the aristocracy and upper middle class whose political and social views led them to support tradition and traditional institutions. Clearly defined social and economic classes had been a significant part of the foundations for the prewar world in which they had lived. Their dislike of democracy was almost innate, because they believed that it led to instability and ultimately to social and political chaos. These individuals came from families "of affluence, education, influence, and privilege."[35] For many of this class, the modern age of "mass man" had created a very disquieting world – unstable, corrupt, and immoral. These people were the vestigial remains of the ancient system of feudalism that had been the bedrock of European society since the demise of the Roman Empire. Their political values reflected the feudal tradition, which was royalist, authoritarian, and antidemocratic. Two of the best representatives of this group were Carl Goerdeler and Ulrich von Hassell.[36]

The feudal tradition remained particularly strong in Germany for reasons that can be found in the nation's late nineteenth- and early twentieth-century experience. As late as 1850, Germany was still a largely agrarian society. Yet within scarcely fifty years, the nation had become a modern industrial giant and a major world power, although the feudal foundations remained in place even as the German Empire was proclaimed in 1871. The magnitude and speed of these revolutionary changes inevitably produced "extremely acute economic, social and political problems."[37] Germany had become almost a hybrid nation, in which a feudal-minded aristocracy – now supported by an upper-middle-class industrial elite – continued to dominate society, but where an emergent working class was embracing socialism in its variant forms. The legacy of this conflict and its stresses would be felt well into the twentieth century and would have a dramatic impact on the resistance movement.

Of all the various anti-Nazi resistance groups, the conservative resistance was the most important, because these were the people from whom the governing elites and army leadership traditionally came. They were the ones who, aside from the Nazis themselves, had the greatest access to the actual centers of power. This was particularly true of the military leadership, especially the army. Of the three branches (army, navy, and air force) of the Wehrmacht (armed forces), the army was most free from the taint of Nazism, and it was here that actual planning for a military coup took place.

Reichsmarschall Hermann Göring, a thoroughgoing Nazi and member of Hitler's inner circle since the early 1920s, commanded the air force (Luftwaffe). In addition, the modern Luftwaffe was largely Hitler's creation, and he took a special interest in its modernization and expansion, because it would have an important role to play in the new type of warfare

– blitzkrieg (lightning war) – envisioned for the evolving German military establishment. He ensured that heavy subsidies went to the Luftwaffe for this purpose, and for that reason alone he enjoyed the loyalty of most Luftwaffe officers. Thus, any anti-Hitler plot was very unlikely to emanate from this branch of the Wehrmacht. Although the navy had a longer tradition, it too was a most unlikely source of anti-Hitler activity. Its commander, Grand Admiral Erich Raeder, though not a dedicated Nazi, was a longtime admirer of Hitler and doubtlessly would have effectively squelched any anti-Nazi plot.

The army, however, was another matter. It was the one institution in Germany that had a reasonable chance of eliminating Adolf Hitler in that it had the greatest access to the man himself. Thus, any serious attempt to overthrow Hitler would require the army's support and participation. The army leadership met regularly with Hitler and his personal staff, especially as war planning and war itself became central features of the Third Reich. It also had access to weapons and explosives essential to any coup attempt, something the civilian resistance did not have. Most importantly, however, was the fact that a small but growing group of anti-Hitler officers was taking shape by the late thirties. The Führer's disturbing jingoism and the Nazi Party's increasingly violent behavior caused the army growing concern. As the oldest and largest German military establishment, it was closest to the noblest of the German military traditions, with a direct connection to the Prussian Army itself. Many of the dissenting officers, who represented those traditions, were at last awakening to the Nazi peril.

The conservatives also were doubtlessly the most paradoxical and contradictory of the many resistance groups. Their fundamental opposition to democracy and democratic principles, plus their intense distaste for the emerging mass society of the twentieth century, inevitably produced an actual hatred for the Weimar Republic and all that it represented. They believed that the creation of the republic was "an act of political betrayal" and that it "had undermined the sense of common purpose in Germany."[38] For these people, the republic was simply "un-German" and unrepresentative of German traditions and values. In addition, many conservatives were convinced that Nazism was "a product of popular forces and energies unleashed by democracy."[39]

A body of evidence suggests that this assertion has a basis in fact. At this critical point in its history – that is, post-1918 – Germany desperately needed continuity in government and social institutions in order to adjust to the prevailing postwar conditions; military defeat and domestic chaos had swept continuity aside. The trauma of an uncertain peace had replaced the trauma of a lost war. Without the ability of familiar institutions to stabilize Germany during this time of transition, many people understandably turned to the false promises of a charlatan posing as a political messiah. Better than a democratic republic would have been a constitutional monarchy for Germany. A modification of the existing constitution – plus the abdication of the kaiser in favor of the crown prince – might well have provided the foundation for a more representative government and given Germany the continuity essential for a more orderly transition from war to peace.[40]

We can never know whether this approach would have been successful. We do know, however, that contributing to the instability of the republic was its democratic system of governance, which was more akin to the Anglo-Saxon model and was not part of the historic German tradition. That is why some of the conservative members of the anti-Nazi resistance movement, such as Carl Goerdeler, wished to restore the monarchy. He believed that this was the best form of government for a postwar Germany. His candidate for a restored throne was Fritz von Hohenzollern, the grandson of Germany's last emperor, by then living in England. Others agreed with Goerdeler: men such as Colonel General Kurt von Hammerstein-Equord – a determined anti-Nazi officer who had served as commander in chief of the army during the Weimar Republic – and Colonel General Ludwig Beck, chief of the army general staff from 1935 to 1938.

The diplomat Ulrich von Hassell and Dietrich Bonhoeffer's brother Klaus also hoped to restore the monarchy.[41] Though not necessarily complete authoritarians in their political convictions, they entertained "serious doubts" about the long-term viability of parliamentary government. These men sincerely believed that a more tradition-oriented society, such as a monarchy, was better for the German nation than a system based upon mass democracy. A modified imperial government was at the heart of their vision for a post–World War II Germany. They had serious doubts about the suitability of popular sovereignty in a restored, post-Nazi Germany.[42]

* * * *

Among the greatest of the historic German traditions were those associated with the name of Prussia and its military establishment. Prussia's ruler, Friedrich Wilhelm von Hohenzollern, who is better known to history as the Great Elector, founded the Prussian Army in 1640. Ultimately, it became the most important institution within the Prussian state. In some ways it *was* the Prussian state. Prussia, it has been said, was not a state, but rather an army with a territory that it used for its billeting area. This comment was not far off the mark. The history of Prussia is the history of its army. Without it, Prussia never would have become a dominant state in Germany or in Europe. In fact, the Prussian army actually guaranteed the survival of the Prussian state itself. Yet, though militaristic, Prussia was not necessarily warlike. It most certainly was no more warlike than its European contemporaries. In fact, "Prussia spent fewer years at war during Frederick's [*i.e.,* Frederick the Great] reign than any major European power," and though a "highly militarized *state* ... [Prussia was] not necessarily a highly militarized society" (italics in original). The Prussian Army and state came to embody the finest military virtues to be found anywhere in history.[43]

With German unification achieved in 1871 under Prussian leadership, Prussian values became German values. This ethos permeated all of Germany in the years following 1871, and was marked by the privileged position that the officer corps enjoyed throughout German society. This in no small measure was due to the Prussian Army's role in securing German unification, which, after all, had been achieved through war.

The militaristic state that Germany became in the late nineteenth century was certainly not unique in the Europe of that era. The dominant European ethos of that day was extreme chauvinism, reinforced by the prevailing doctrine of Social Darwinism (see appendix C). The enthusiasts of Social Darwinism applied this concept to the prevailing nation-state system of the late nineteenth century, declaring that "societies had natural, hereditary enemies and that conflict among them was inevitable." French military authorities, for example, characterized Germany as a "deadly and determined enemy to France." The feeling was reciprocated. By 1900, the possibility of war confronted all the European powers, and preparation for war was seen as the prime responsibility of statesmen.

The ubiquity of war as part of the human experience served to reinforce the conviction that modern industrial society must accept this fact with a state of military preparedness that far surpassed the efforts of earlier generations. Large standing armies became essential to the security of the nation, or so it was believed. All the major states – except Great Britain – maintained mass reserve armies, each of whose personnel were numbered at the unprecedented figure of at least one million or more.[44]

This increasingly virulent and militaristic nationalism brought significant changes to the major powers. For example, the "Germany of the poets and thinkers became the Prussia-Germany of efficient and aggressive power." Unfortunately, Imperial Germany's foreign policy from 1890 to 1914 exhibited a predilection for bombastic theatrics, further reinforcing the belief that arrogant and bellicose behavior was an innate part of the Prussian-German character. Emperor Kaiser Wilhelm II personified this stereotype. Although a large body of opinion inside Germany greeted this bellicosity with repugnance, the drums of war drowned this out with increasing ferocity as the day of reckoning approached in the summer of 1914.[45]

The experience of the Great War further confirmed these perceptions of Germany, however distorted and simplistic they may have been. Thanks in no small measure to Allied propaganda, Prussia-Germany was vilified as a warmonger solely responsible for precipitating a cataclysm of unprecedented proportions. One writer, commenting on the effects of anti-German propaganda on American opinion during the war, concludes, "The American public, after a year and a half of propaganda and patriotic oratory, had become so passionately anti-German as to be in a state resembling mass hysteria." By war's end, this propaganda had destroyed much of what had been German in American culture, and the darkest of terms were used to depict Germany as a warlike and unregenerate nation.[46] Reality produces a different picture, however.

Historic Prussia held values that can be succinctly summarized as follows: order, duty, obedience, and social responsibility. A spirit of true chivalry permeated the Prussian-German military establishment that represented Germany at its best. The men of the Prussian officer corps enjoyed special rights and privileges in Prussian society, but with these rights and privileges came duties and responsibilities to serve the state well. Prussia had most certainly been a classic authoritarian state (Obrigkeitsstaat). Those on the bottom rungs of the socioeconomic ladder had absolutely no political power, responsibilities, or privileges. Nonetheless, Prussia's rulers, motivated by a strong religious ethos, had a deep sense of social responsibility for their subjects, a fact that could not have been lost on the socialist leaders of the Weimar Republic. Additionally, these rulers were committed to effective, honest, and competent government. Prussian commercial policy was based upon the belief "that commerce must be for the benefit of the state and through the state for the benefit of all rather than for the exclusive enrichment of the individual." This policy prefigured the program of the twentieth-century socialist movement in Germany, especially in Prussia. Additionally, Prussia's authoritarianism "was tempered by the rule of law, some liberal administrative practice and an established tradition of religious toleration."[47]

An Emergent Resistance

Frederick II (the Great), who ruled his state from 1740 to 1786, epitomized this tradition. A true child of the Enlightenment and a freethinker, he was a despot – that is, an authoritarian ruler – but an enlightened and benevolent despot. He considered himself to be the first servant of the state. And he was. He had a genuine concern for the welfare of his subjects and tried to rule in a manner that he believed served their best interests. He introduced the singularly modern concept of equality before the law for all his subjects, from the highest aristocrat to the lowliest peasant. Absolute religious freedom became a distinguishing feature of Prussian society, and Prussia became a haven for religious dissenters throughout Europe. Jews fleeing persecution found a new home in Prussia. (Ironically, many of their descendants would become the first victims of Nazi persecution.) Freedom of speech and the press allowed open criticism of government policy, and books proscribed elsewhere in Germany and Europe were widely available in Berlin. Torture, still practiced as a part of the legal system in much of eighteenth-century Europe, was absolutely prohibited in Prussia. Prussia's leaders had a clear sense of social responsibility to everyone who was a part of the community that comprised the Prussian state. Though far from perfect, their community was a true Volksgemeinschaft.

The tradition of Prussian paternalism as practiced by Frederick II had its nineteenth-century echo in the policies of the great Prussian statesman Otto von Bismarck, who, like his illustrious predecessor, was committed to state paternalism. Although the conservatives effectively controlled Imperial Germany, a genuine interest in the welfare of the entire nation and a veneration of the cultural inheritance of the German national community was an integral part of state policy. By the end of Bismarck's tenure as chancellor in 1890, he had created what has been described as "Europe's most progressive system of social insurance." This program was continued by his successors, and Kaiser Wilhelm II pledged his support as well. Pre–World War I Germany has been described as "the classic welfare state." Thus, as Germany entered the twentieth century, a solid foundation had been laid for the creation of a modern social service state that transcended the narrow-minded militarism that for many has defined the modern German nation. The best expression of this tradition is found in the Prussian civil service, whose finest qualities have been summarized as "intelligence, character and accomplishment." It developed a reputation for honesty, integrity, devotion to duty, and efficiency that became the envy of the rest of Europe. The Prussian bureaucracy was almost totally incorruptible. An ethos of selfless service to the state became its hallmark.[48]

An additional element reinforcing this value system was the Prussian state church, which was itself influenced by Calvinist theology. The Prussian version allegedly demanded "severity, dignity, abstinence from the pleasures of life, attention to one's duty, loyalty, honesty, indeed self-denial, and a somber scorn for the world." A kernel of truth can be found in this rather large overstatement. An examination of the behavior of the kings of Prussia reveals a rejection of the trappings of royalty found among contemporary ruling families of Europe. There was a complete lack of ostentatious display. The Prussian kings historically preferred military uniforms to royal regalia, for example. Their watchwords were "austerity," "frugality," and "simplicity." This attitude remained a significant part of the Prussian ethos throughout its history. "In a world of abundant comfort, a high value was put on renunciation, on knowing how to do without. There was a fear of indulgent luxury, of ostentation, of excessive ease, all of which bore the danger of decline and decadence."[49]

These were the values that the conservatives who became part of the anti-Nazi resistance prized so highly. This helps to explain the animus they held for the Weimar Republic, which introduced Germany to the age of materialism and consumerism that became the hallmark of the twentieth century. Many who rejected this emergent world came from the most distinguished families in Prussian history.

For example, the forebears of Henning von Tresckow, who was one of the prime movers of the army conspiracy to assassinate Hitler, had a three-hundred-year tradition of military service to Prussia. Twenty-one generals in the Prussian Army bore the name von Tresckow. Henning's father, a cavalry general in the Prussian Army, had been present at the 1871 ceremony in the Palace of Versailles when King Wilhelm I of Prussia was crowned emperor of the new German Empire.

Erwin von Witzleben, born in Breslau (now Wrocław, Poland), which was the capital city of Silesia, a province of Prussia, also descended from a military family of very long standing. Had the July 20, 1944, bomb plot been successful, he would have assumed command of the Wehrmacht. Ewald von Kleist-Schmenzin was a civilian who embodied the best of the Prussian conservative tradition. A committed monarchist, Christian, and determined opponent of Hitler, he was one of the few conservatives who recognized the danger of Nazism well before Hitler assumed power. Another member of the resistance, Ulrich von Hassell, was the scion of a family that also was part of the traditional Prussian landed aristocracy. His name was prominent on several lists of prospective cabinet officers – in his case, foreign minister – to serve in a provisional government that would replace the Nazis subsequent to a successful coup d'état.[50]

One man who was not part of the Prussian tradition but who exemplified its ethos was Admiral Wilhelm Canaris, who served as chief of the Abwehr. He typified the many military officers who had nourished the ultimately false hopes of a revived and rejuvenated Imperial Germany. Born in a small town near Dortmund in the Ruhr Valley of western Germany to a wealthy industrialist, Canaris joined the navy while still in his teens, and served as a U-boat commander during the last year of the Great War. Initially, he enthusiastically supported the Nazis, not awakening to the reality of Nazi rule until the late 1930s. It was said of Canaris that he was a "'gifted officer conscious of his duty, an old nationalist, [who] was called to an important position [and] did the best he could in fulfilling his task.' All he had wanted was to serve his country." This was, in fact, true of all of the conspirators who had supported the Nazis early in their careers.

> All of them believed that in serving Hitler they were serving Germany, that in defending the Third Reich they were defending their nation and their people. They could not see, because they did not really want to see, the dark underside of National Socialism, its cruelty and oppressiveness, its rapacity and heartlessness, its dehumanizing worship of brute force. They knew only that the Nazi regime was making possible the political and military revival of their country, and for them that was enough.[51]

This quote provides the key to the reason for the failure of the generals to move against Hitler early on. They did not comprehend the essentially evil nature of the Nazi ideology until it was too late. Tragically, these men confused ends with means. They most certainly understood that the means the Nazis employed were occasionally violent, "crude, and reckless," but they also believed that the ends sought were "essentially legitimate and justifiable." Therefore, for many, their reluctance to act was not the result of a lack of courage. Rather, they had to break away from a mind-set that had prevented them from seeing Nazism for what it was until quite late in the game. They had to reorient their thinking and "move from nonviolent to violent, legal to illegal means in opposing the head of state."[52] Some could not make the transition.

This ill-fated story is a classic example of people wanting to believe something so badly that they ignore the underlying reality. In sum, the generals had put on blinders. They represented the very best of the Prussian historical tradition, and this helps to explain their antipathy toward the Weimar Republic. They believed that the republic had destroyed these noble Prussian virtues. Some, believing that the Nazis, once in power, would restore those values, supported Hitler at first. Others, with great prescience, were determined opponents from the beginning.

* * * *

Conservatives were not alone in believing that the republic had destroyed Prussian virtues. There was a general rejection of the Weimar Republic that cut across social and economic classes. The facts were there for all to see. The Weimar Republic had capitulated to the enemy in 1918; it had signed the Treaty of Versailles. In the eyes of many Germans, it was decadent and corrupt; hedonism was rampant; it was incompetent; it violated traditional values; and it not only condoned but also actually encouraged licentiousness and sexual immorality. Hence, there was "a broad perception that the country was experiencing a breakdown of cultural and moral values." The republic was held responsible for these conditions, and therefore it was reviled. Republican Germany was seen as a "moral-political swamp."[53] It had become materialistic and secular; mere commercial values had replaced spiritual and moral values. Even the political institutions of the republic, especially parliamentary democracy, were declared to be alien to the German ethos.

The word "mass" was everywhere. There was mass production and mass consumption, bringing to an end what was left of the small, craft-oriented community of an earlier age. There was mass entertainment for a mass audience, such as the cinema and spectator sports. And there was mass politics, which found expression in mass political parties. Thus, the Weimar Republic was the very antithesis of all those Prussian virtues that the conservatives held in such high esteem; it was alien to the "German spirit." Additionally and perhaps most importantly, there was an understandable frustration and despair over a feckless government seemingly incapable of accomplishing anything. It was demonstrating a total inability to cope with the enormous problems facing Germany by 1930. The experiment in liberal democracy was seen as a catastrophic failure. It had led to social chaos, economic collapse, and political disaster. An objective look at the fourteen-year period from 1918 to 1933 makes these conclusions of the conservatives hard to refute.

Such a look also makes it easier to understand why so many conservatives, some of whom later became anti-Nazi conspirators, welcomed the Nazis to power. They believed that the Nazis would bring stability to Germany and would restore to the fatherland those "traditional Prussian values" that the republic had trampled underfoot. "Many of them [had] cheered the fall of the Weimar Republic, which appeared to them to embody all the weakness of mass rule, party politics, military ineffectualness and crass materialism. The Third Reich, by contrast, seemed to hold out the promise of a civic and spiritual revival. Clearly the duty of every patriotic citizen was to support its efforts."[54] Thus, the Nazis would bring about the "national revival" that so many Germans sought so desperately.

Nazi Distortions

The conservatives were caught in a contradiction, however. Most of them believed that Nazism was the product of Weimar democracy, yet they also believed that the Nazi Party, with its mass appeal and plebian nature, actually represented their best hope of restoring the society that war and revolution had swept away. By portraying themselves as the guarantors and protectors of those German traditions that the conservatives valued so highly, the Nazis shrewdly promoted this conviction. They claimed to be the standard-bearers of order, obedience and submission to authority, devotion to duty, and commitment to the community. In sum, they claimed to represent the bedrock of traditional German values.

What was not seen at the time was the way in which the Nazi system would corrupt and debase all of these values. Thus, a significant number of conservative leaders, many of whom ultimately became active in the resistance, naïvely believed that the Nazis provided the best hope for a restoration of the Germany they had known in their youth – or at least the Germany they *thought* they had known. They had an ambivalent attitude toward the Nazis. On the one hand, they saw Nazis as guttersnipes and barbarians. On the other hand, Nazis seemed to represent the vanguard of leadership in a revived and restored fatherland. Hitler would lead Germany back to its true imperial greatness. This ambivalence ultimately brought much grief to the conservatives.

* * * *

Though anxious to support strong and dynamic leadership, the conservatives had a decided distaste and dislike for the obvious crudeness and vulgarity that was evident in the Nazi movement. The conservatives saw the Nazis as part of the lumpenproletariat (the dregs of German society). For example, historian Terry Parssinen comments that General Ludwig Beck, who became an active participant in the resistance, characterized the Nazis as "vulgar and distasteful."[55] In the eyes of people such as Beck, Nazism was "an upstart political movement whose leaders were corrupt, hypocritical, murderous, unpleasant and vulgar."[56]

This perception was in part a reflection of the class consciousness that was inherent in Prussian-German, as well as European, society. Beck and others like him believed that the Nazis were people who had to be controlled. Though they welcomed the introduction of "strong government" in 1933, they disliked – and eventually feared – much of what the Nazis brought with them. Most particularly, they feared Hitler's arbitrary rule and ultimate tyranny, as well as his growing predilection for "irresponsible risk-taking," particularly in foreign affairs.[57] These conflicted attitudes help to explain the inconsistencies that eventually developed within the resistance.

* * * *

By 1939, many conservative members of the resistance had become completely disillusioned with Nazism, and they began to look beyond the war itself to a subsequent peace without Hitler. They also saw clearly that the Nazis had debased, corrupted, and ultimately spurned the traditional values that they had promised to restore. In many ways, those in the conservative resistance were tied to the past. Schooled in the traditions of the empire, they sought a return to an authoritarian government resembling the empire, especially its monarchy. They wanted a restoration of the "old, traditional virtues of German political life: selflessness, responsibility, duty, sacrifice, and obedience."[58] Most of them also were committed to a restoration of the geographical boundaries of the old empire, and this ultimately created a significant obstacle in their dealings with the Allied countries before and during World War II.

The conservatives wanted to recover a lost world. This goal became increasingly impossible to achieve with the passage of time, and it merely reinforced Allied prejudices against the resistance. The Allied leaders tended to believe that all Germans were Nazis, or at least Nazi sympathizers.

* * * *

The Nazis exploited the conservative value system with great skill. They combined traditional norms of behavior and thought with their perversions, and in so doing, they co-opted the army leadership. Thus, Nazi success was based on deception. The Nazi ideology was cleverly presented as a part of the historic German ethical, religious, and philosophical tradition. The examples are many. There was an "unqualified obedience to authority" that accompanied the commitment to duty "and its execution with devotion and unrelenting thoroughness."[59] An illustration of this "devotion to duty" can be found in the career of Adolf Eichmann.

A member of the SD, Eichmann, an Austrian, was given responsibility for carrying out the final solution to the Jewish question. He escaped to Argentina at the end of the war but was apprehended by the Israeli secret service, taken to Israel, tried, found guilty, and hanged in 1962 for crimes against humanity. During an interrogation while in captivity, he was asked why he had participated in the Holocaust. Reportedly, he said, "Es war den Auftrag den ich hatte [*sic*]. Ich hatte den Auftrag zu erfüllen" (It was an assignment that I had. I had an assignment to fulfill). In other words, *Ignore the moral implications of my actions; I was just doing a job to the best of my ability.* He in fact claimed to have acted in a morally responsible way in that he'd fulfilled his duty.[60]

The almost sacred notion of one's "calling" is a major part of the German tradition. The German translation of the English word "job," that is, an occupation or paid position of regular employment, is "Beruf," which comes from the verb *rufen*: "to call." It has distinctly religious connotations, as described by Max Weber in his seminal study *The Protestant Ethic and the Spirit of Capitalism*.[61] It implies that the individual should find satisfaction in the job well done, however menial it might be. Again, we see how the Nazis perverted this ideal to include the perpetration of the most heinous crimes; their history shows how easily excessive devotion to ideals can corrupt individuals. The notion of selfless service and the subjugation of one's own interests to the interests of the community, the Volksgemeinschaft, was profaned to serve the cause of vicious racism.

The Nazis debased and desecrated everything they touched. Political morality degenerated into a perverted and rancid bureaucratic ethic of "service."[62] Noble Prussian values and virtues were totally corrupted, resulting in complete moral confusion. This process has been aptly depicted as a poisoning of the moral wines, as described in the following passage: "Thus the vast majority of a people, as they looked back in 1945, stood aghast at the route they had marched and were totally bewildered. For they knew they could not have done the immoral; had they not acted in accord with the traditionally cherished values?"[63]

The answer to that question, of course, is no. In reality, they had not followed those "cherished values." The values they had followed appeared to be traditional, but in fact were not. The people had allowed themselves to be deceived. Without fully realizing it, the German nation had made a Faustian bargain with the Nazis. Although the Nazis claimed to be a bridge from the glorious imperial past to a glorious utopian future, they, like contemporary fascists in other countries, totally rejected the Western intellectual tradition and all of its shared wisdom and values. Theirs was a barbaric world in which brute force ruled. It was a world where, in the words of the English political philosopher Thomas Hobbes, life was "poor, nasty brutish and short."[64]

The German nation, in rejecting the Weimar Republic and not understanding the nature of this Faustian bargain, thought that it was returning to an idealized past in the form of the pre–World War I empire. In fact, it was heading down an ever-darkening road, whose end in 1945 brought the nation to total destruction. At that point, an accounting had to be rendered. As the endgame approached, those few in the army who now realized what was going on resolved to eliminate the man who was leading their nation to the approaching catastrophe, with the hope of mitigating its worst consequences.

Some, however, had refused from the outset to be a party to the bargain. They saw with great clarity what was taking place in their homeland. Early on, they saw the perversions that were an integral part of the Third Reich. They saw how virtues of an earlier time were being subverted to serve the interests of a patently evil regime. With uncommon prescience, they foresaw the endgame and what it would be like, and they became the nucleus for an active resistance movement. Civilians such as Dietrich Bonhoeffer and Ewald von Kleist-Schmenzin, together with military officers such as Hans Oster, Helmuth Groscurth, and Kurt von Hammerstein-Equord, were among the first true resisters.

The moral courage of these men who were willing to engage the all-powerful Nazi government provides a lesson for all time. The perversion and corruption of moral and ethical values are perennial problems for every culture and every society no matter what type it may be, whether democratic or authoritarian. Too often, the corrections come far too late to prevent or even to limit the grim consequences of the failure to take timely action.

The Churches

Like other conservative institutions, the Roman Catholic Church and the Protestant Evangelical (state) Church welcomed the end of the Weimar

Republic. Both churches held an intense dislike for the "secularism" and middle-class "materialism" of the republic. These phenomena, though little understood at the time, actually were representative of the age of high mass consumption that was dawning in the Western world, and had little to do with the republic itself. Nonetheless, the republic became an effective scapegoat for the critics of the emergent twentieth-century world. Reinforcing this prejudice against the republic was the conviction that it espoused a moral relativism and hedonism that tolerated "the forces of Socialism, Communism, and atheism."[65]

Thus, many clergymen welcomed the Nazis to power, because they, like many of their conservative compatriots, naïvely believed that the Nazis represented a return to traditional cherished social and political values. Some clergy even indulged in effusive and fulsome comments in support of the Nazis. Such comments often were grotesque, approaching obscenity and even sacrilege. The people who indulged in this sort of thing were among those opportunists found in any society who are willing to compromise their integrity and even their souls for temporary advantage.[66] Clergy who supported the Nazi-organized and short-lived "Reich Church" were the worst offenders.

As with the soldiers and the conservatives, so it was with many of these church leaders. They allowed Nazi rhetoric to deceive them with what today would be called "buzzwords" and "talking points." The Nazis promised to recover a "lost world," to restore "family values" and "traditional values." They also would demand "responsible behavior" among "good" Germans. Therefore, churchgoing Germans, like many others, clung to the myth that the Nazis intended to restore those dearly held traditional values.

Hitler made the most of this naïveté with a grandiose display of Nazi theatrics in an elaborate ceremony to commemorate the opening of the newly elected Reichstag on March 23, 1933, at the garrison church in the Berlin suburb of Potsdam. The day and venue had historical significance, for exactly sixty-two years earlier, Otto von Bismarck had convened the inaugural Reichstag of the German Empire in this same garrison church. Moreover, Potsdam had been the residence of the Prussian kings and German emperors, and the church was considered the "symbolic locus" of the Prussian monarchy.[67] President Paul von Hindenburg attended, along with many other dignitaries, civilian and military. Standing next to the vacant Hohenzollern throne and resplendent in his Prussian field marshal's uniform, Hindenburg received the homage of the newly appointed chancellor, Adolf Hitler, who was wearing a simple frock coat and top hat.

The symbolism of it all was obvious. The civilian Hitler was submitting to the Prussian tradition in Germany, implying that he intended to follow in that tradition as he assumed the powers of governance. The prominence of the garrison church in these theatrics also suggested that the Evangelical Church would regain its preeminent position in German life and society. The throne and altar were to be restored, if not literally, then most certainly figuratively. No effort was spared to place Hitler and his Nazis in the tradition of Germany's greatest rulers, much of it in the kitsch style that was characteristic of Hitler's artistic tastes. For example, a postcard promoting what came to be known as the Hitler cult appeared about this same time, showing him as the direct successor of Paul von Hindenburg, who was preceded by Otto von Bismarck and thence to Frederick the Great. The caption reads, "Was der König eroberte, der Fürst formte, der Feldmarschall verteidigte, rettete und einigte der Soldat" (What the king conquered, the prince shaped, the field marshal defended, the soldier saved and united).[68]

* * * *

Once the Nazis came into power, most of the Christian clergy, regardless of denomination and including those who were highly suspicious of the Third Reich, walked a tightrope, trying not to offend the Nazi Party while also trying to preserve their own autonomy. Obviously, this tightrope act did not work. The demands of a complete totalitarian system ultimately overwhelmed the churches. They were forced to choose: Would it be capitulation or resistance? Most, though not all, chose resistance. These people exemplified a true Volksgemeinschaft that contrasted sharply with the Nazis' spurious notion of "community."

Despite their initial enthusiasm for the regime, the organized churches were the first of the German institutions to openly confront the Third Reich. They were able to do so because the Nazi leaders realized that attacking organized religion too harshly risked a backlash against the regime. Hence, the Nazis tried to co-opt the churches.

> [They] did not think that they could risk complete destruction of the churches. They were confronted here with barriers which they could not understand – the fortitude and integrity of religious conviction, conscience and a sense of responsibility for one's fellow men which were not to be extinguished by regulations and prohibitions.[69]

Because of such barriers, a state like the Third Reich must engage in intense and effective propaganda.

The situation also demonstrates a basic fact of politics: governments must maintain a delicate balance between force and consent. The state that is able to maximize consent and minimize force is ultimately stronger and more stable than the one that must resort to force and blatant propaganda in order to ensure consent. The Nazis' ultimate goal was total control of the mind and body. This would give them total domination and ultimately total power, but the church was an effective barrier to their pretensions. In fact, the churches "were the only major organizations to offer comparatively early and open resistance; they remained so in later years."[70] As a consequence, the Christian clergy were able to speak in a relatively open manner and could "articulate political dissent in the guise of pastoral stricture."[71]

There was a problem, however. Many clergymen sought advantage for their respective institutions within a political and social system that was fundamentally evil. "They were fighting ... not for religious faith or moral principle but for denominational autonomy and confessional authority. Their struggle ... was in essence not against but within the system."[72] Like many people in other walks of life, they practiced a moral relativism that ultimately produced a catastrophe.

* * * *

Each specific institutional church dealt with the Third Reich in its own way, based upon that church's historical relationship with German society and government. The Nazi leadership faced an especially difficult problem in its attempts to bring the Roman Catholic Church under its control, and was forced to concede that the Catholic Church was part of a "worldwide ecclesiastical community subject to a non-German Pope."[73] Consequently, the struggle between church and state in this instance proved to be especially acerbic.

Hitler, as well as several other top Nazis, had been raised in the Catholic Church, and they recognized its power over its communicants, as well as its intricate organizational structure that was capable of reaching all parishes, large and small, with its message. These close ties represented a challenge to the Nazi Party, especially because this church had preached an anti-Nazi message that has been described as vehement.[74] With approximately one-third of the German nation holding membership in the Roman Catholic Church, the Nazis faced a formidable obstacle to their Gleichschaltung policy. The Nazis realized that the international character of the Catholic Church demanded swift yet careful action to bring the church under their total control.

For their part, most members of the Catholic clergy concluded that overt opposition was an exercise in futility. Hence, they initially pursued a nonconfrontational strategy toward the Nazis, hoping to maintain at least a degree of control over their own affairs. They tried to establish what ultimately became an uneasy balance between religious and political or secular authority. Initially, the ensuing struggle between the two organizations, "though fierce, remained largely submerged. Each party, for reasons of its own, helped maintain the fiction that their relations were cordial and harmonious."[75] And a fiction it was, because Germany was a totalitarian state; its goals remained unchanged. All phases of national life were to be brought under the control of the Nazi Party. Furthermore, this uneasy balance did not last long.

In an attempt to regularize relations between the two authorities, the Papacy concluded a concordat with Berlin in July 1933. The concordat guaranteed the integrity of the Catholic Church, together with its assets and institutions, in exchange for its agreement to refrain from political activities. Within a very short time, however, this concordat proved to be "not worth the paper it was written on." Catholic lay property was seized, and the activities of most church-related organizations, including various Catholic publications, were severely restricted, if not banned outright.[76]

The struggle persisted, and Nazi relations with the church continued to deteriorate into the mid- and late thirties. For example, a firestorm broke out over the published works of the so-called Nazi "philosopher" Alfred Rosenberg, especially his book *The Myth of the Twentieth Century*. In this book, he claimed that Catholicism was the "creation of Jewish clericalism." The Catholic clergy of Germany reacted with outrage. Even the German Christians in the Nazi-controlled Reich Church criticized Rosenberg's work severely. The Papacy placed Rosenberg's publications on the Index of Prohibited Books. The German cleric Clemens von Galen, bishop of Münster, attacked Rosenberg's book vociferously with the words, "There are heathens again in Germany." He then went on to condemn Rosenberg's racism. Rosenberg responded with his own attack on Galen at a party rally in Münster.[77]

The Catholic laity thereupon entered the fray by making a statement of their own. The city traditionally held an annual celebration in July commemorating the successful resistance of the local Catholic church to Bismarck's "Kulturkampf" (struggle for culture or civilization) against Catholicism, which had taken place over a half century earlier. Coincidentally, this particular celebration also commemorated the defeat of the Anabaptists, who had instigated a reign of terror against those who dissented from their religious beliefs and practices some four hundred years earlier. In this specific year, 1935, the faithful, some nineteen thousand, which was double the usual number, turned out for the annual procession through the city streets. Galen, speaking to his supporters, "issued a ringing declaration that he would never give in to the enemies of the Church."[78]

The quarrel was intensifying, and the Nazis reacted to the controversy with growing alarm. They resorted to taking several steps designed to bring matters under control, such as censoring Catholic publications and limiting public meetings of various Catholic organizations, all without success. Goebbels and his Ministry of Propaganda also got into the act, "releasing a flood of accusations [all lies] against Catholic organizations for financial corruption."[79] He, too, failed. The Catholic community continued to remain faithful to its church, and the protests against Nazi behavior increased. The Gestapo reported in May 1935 that "numerous clerics are now taking a very critical position from the pulpit towards Rosenberg's *Myth* and his new work *To the Obscurantists of Our Day*. They curse the spirit of the new age, the Godless and the heathen, by which they mean National Socialism."[80]

An example of the irreparable damage done to the Nazis as a result of the Rosenberg affair can be found in Oldenburg, a small rural area in northwestern Germany. The reaction of the residents included resignations from the Nazi Party, the self-dissolution of a branch of the Brownshirts, and a sharp decline in support for the Nazis. Despite "massive manipulation and intimidation," the Reichstag elections of 1938 recorded only a 92 percent favorable vote, as compared with a 99 percent favorable vote two years earlier. Although the outcome of this election was a foregone conclusion, the "massive manipulation and intimidation" failed to achieve the desired result of complete unanimity. It will be remembered that this was a time when the Nazi Party carefully controlled these so-called "elections" and only Nazi candidates could stand for office. In many parts of the country, "a largely spontaneous war of words" broke out between local parish priests and party officials over issues involving control of Catholic youth groups and schools. These conflicts reportedly were "the only cause of open political dissent within Germany by the mid-1930s."[81]

A group of German senior Catholic clerics, seeking support for their resistance efforts, met with Pope Pius XI in early 1937 to discuss the feud.

This meeting led to the famous papal encyclical *Mit brennender Sorge* (With Burning Concern), which condemned the Third Reich in the severest terms. To emphasize its importance, the encyclical was written in the German language. The Nazi leadership was enraged and alarmed – enraged because of the encyclical's incendiary language in condemning Nazi rule, and alarmed because the Catholic Church had demonstrated its ability "to organize a nationwide protest without arousing the slightest suspicion in advance even from the Gestapo."[82]

All of this gives a hint of the potential opposition that existed among German Catholics even during the high tide of Nazi power in the midthirties. Inevitably, repression, intimidation, and harassment followed, and the church, fearing further reprisals, reduced its outspoken condemnation of the regime.[83]

* * * *

Unlike the "international" Catholic Church, the (Protestant) Evangelical Church was considered to be a "German" institution. It was created in the early nineteenth century with the merger of the Lutheran and Calvinist confessions. This merger brought with it a three-hundred-year association with the Prussian state and monarchy. Martin Luther himself had taught that Christians should willingly submit to temporal authority, and this conviction remained a significant part of the Lutheran tradition. Lutheran bishop Otto Dibelius was quoted as saying that the Lutherans were "more like a department of ecclesiastical affairs than a church."[84] The political position of the Evangelical Church has been described as "extremely conservative," and by the twentieth century, "it was clear that, for many, nationalism and Protestantism had become two sides of the same ideological coin."[85]

The Evangelical Church and the Nazis shared a mutual animus toward the Weimar Republic. Together, they denounced both popular democracy and the "spirit of liberalism" associated with the republic, and demanded a rejection of the Treaty of Versailles. The church leaders believed that Nazi rule would bring with it a revival of traditional values. Consequently, their "common hostility to the Weimar Republic" appeared to make the Evangelical Church a natural ally of the Nazis. Hitler's nostrums merely reinforced the belief that a Nazi-led religious revival would soon be forthcoming. For reasons such as this, many church leaders strongly supported National Socialism. They welcomed the Nazis to power.[86]

An Emergent Resistance

For the most part, this enthusiastic support did not last long. As Hitler subjected the Evangelical Church to increasing pressure not only to conform but also to endorse Nazi ideology and incorporate it into church doctrine, resistance began to build almost immediately. The two most important leaders of the Evangelical resistance were Dietrich Bonhoeffer and Martin Niemöller. Bonhoeffer, in particular, understood from the beginning the true nature of Nazism, and he persistently spoke out against it with uncommon foresight. He "recognized where a Nazi regime was likely to lead."[87] However, at this point in time, his was but one voice. He alone among his fellow resisters resolved the issue of resistance to – versus acceptance of – Nazism "without [a] prolonged inner struggle." He was practically alone in recognizing the consummate evil that lay at the core of the Nazi system. Moreover, "his opposition to it was based on deep-rooted spiritual conviction rather than compelling national interest."[88]

As early as 1933, Bonhoeffer realized that a conflict between the church and the Nazi state was inevitable, and he called for the former organization to take a principled stand against Nazism; this was at a time when many – perhaps most – of his fellow clergy were trying to reach an accommodation with Nazism.[89] He was the "only well known member of the ecclesiastical community who from the outset criticized the regime's racial program, openly, repeatedly, and consistently."[90] Even as early as 1933, he was drawing "more radical conclusions [in the issue of church–state relations than] most of his teachers and friends."[91] His biographer, Ferdinand Schlingensiepen, claims that Bonhoeffer's foresight lay in the fact that he "was the first Lutheran theologian to think this particular matter through."[92]

Bonhoeffer believed there were three possible positions that the church could take vis-à-vis church–state relations:

> *First*, questioning the state as to the legitimate state character of its actions, that is, making the state responsible for what it does. *Second* is service to the victims of the state's actions. The church has an unconditional obligation towards the victims of any societal order, even if they do not belong to the Christian community. "Let us work for the good of all." … The *third* possibility is not just to bind up the wounds of the victims beneath the wheel, but to seize the wheel itself. Such an action would be direct political action on the part of the church. This is only possible and called for if the church sees the state to be failing in its function of creating law and order.[93]

Thus, Bonhoeffer was counseling direct action against the Nazis as quickly as possible. A year earlier, just before the Reichstag elections of July 1932 that brought the Nazis to the peak of their popularity, he spoke prophetically of a future under Nazi rule. "Hitler's nationalistic party abuses democratic opportunities and seeks the establishment of a dictatorship." He went on to give what has been described as "an uncanny prophesy":

> "The victory of the Hitler party would have unforeseeable consequences not only for the development of the German people but also for the development of the whole world." All Christians must therefore unite in a struggle against the forces "that mislead countries into a false nationalism, that promote militarism, and that threaten the world with an unrest out of which a war could arise."[94]

Regarding his second point, he allegedly was the only member of the future resistance movement to take an early and forthright stand against anti-Semitism. Although he evidently shared some of the traditional theological and cultural biases of his social class toward the Jewish community, he totally rejected the notion of racial anti-Semitism. Rather, his views of the so-called "Jewish question" were shaped by his religion and theology. A Jew converting to Christianity, for example, was to be accepted as a communicant into the Christian Church without exception, "without differentiation or discrimination." For Bonhoeffer, the "Jewish question" was solely a matter of religion, not race.[95] But regardless of conversion or not, his stand on the issue was clear; he rejected anti-Semitic activity of any sort, and this was the main source of his early and absolute rejection of Nazism.[96]

His third point was a call for an organized and active church-centered resistance movement. "He was standing before his church and demanding that it develop a political conscience and take determined action."[97] Regrettably, no one in a position of power and authority – especially within the military establishment, but also within the church – was willing to take that "determined action" against Hitler at this early phase of Nazi rule. Too many of these people were willing to temporize, to wait and see. Perhaps the Nazis would implode. Perhaps the "extremists" and "hooligans" within the party would go too far and be reined in by the "responsible" Nazi leaders. Such people failed to realize that the word "responsibility" was not part of the Nazi vocabulary and that extremism was innate to Nazism.

Whether action such as that proposed by Bonhoeffer would have produced effective results remains an open question, but we will never know the answer because that action was never taken. Bonhoeffer encountered what would be the besetting problem for the resistance movement: lack of a high-profile dynamic leader able to challenge Hitler, someone who could organize mass support against the Nazis. These two essential ingredients – leadership and organized mass support – remained absent from the resistance movement from beginning to end. This was the curse of the resistance movement.

Unlike most of his fellow clergymen, Bonhoeffer was not committed to a restoration of the conservative system that lay at the heart of Imperial Germany, nor was he especially attached to the traditional values held by his conservative colleagues. Although he shared the same sense of injustice that his fellow countrymen felt toward the Treaty of Versailles, he evidently was the "only prominent member of the resistance to defend the democratic system [that is, the Weimar Republic] in its hour of crisis" and to lament its demise.[98] As is the case for everyone, the influence of family, friends, and the experiences of Bonhoeffer's youth shaped his Weltanschauung (worldview). By the standards of his day, he had traveled extensively, to Italy, Spain, Cuba, Mexico, England, and the United States. While pursuing his studies at Union Theological Seminary in New York City, he participated in a youth program at the famed Abyssinian Baptist Church in Harlem, where he gained a much-broader perception of Christianity and the Christian Church and its relationship to a world that was far removed from the upper-middle-class society of his personal experience. He spoke of this time as seeing the world "from below, from the perspective of the outcasts, the suspects, the maltreated, the powerless, the oppressed and reviled, in short from the perspective of the suffering."[99] Schlingensiepen refers to this time as "one of the learning experiences that made him a man for the Resistance."[100] For reasons such as these, Bonhoeffer's entire perspective on Nazism and a proper response to it remained at variance with all but a very few of those like him who grasped the monstrous nature of Nazism from the start: men such as Ewald von Kleist-Schmenzin and Kurt von Hammerstein-Equord.

Dietrich Bonhoeffer's associate in the soon-to-be-created Confessing Church, Martin Niemöller, initially was much unlike his friend in social and political outlook. Born in a northern province of Rhineland Prussia in 1892 to a very conservative family in the tradition of the Evangelical Church, Niemöller – whose father was a Lutheran pastor – has been described as a classic "personal example of the fusion of patriotism, militarism and religiosity in the mainstream of German Protestantism."[101] Niemöller initially chose a career in the Imperial Navy. He enlisted as an officer cadet and served on various submarines in the Great War, where he participated in several naval battles. At war's end, he was a submarine commander. Germany's collapse left him devastated. Writing in his memoirs *From U-Boat to Pulpit*, he said of his return to his homeland, "[I was] a stranger in my own country."[102]

Subsequent to his discharge from the navy, he became active in several antirepublican right-wing causes and organizations before turning to religious studies. He had decided that Germany's deplorable postwar condition could only be cured through religious renewal. "His recipe for national renewal was as much spiritual as political."[103] He began a program of religious studies and was ordained a minister in the Evangelical Church in 1924.[104] His political journey through the Weimar Republic was typical of those who shared his authoritarian and antidemocratic convictions. He and his coreligionists especially despised Marxism and all of its derivations, from communism to social democracy, because of its secularism. Its ideology was essentially atheistic.[105]

Typical also was Niemöller's susceptibility to the blandishments of Hitler, as the Führer continually reassured the conservatives of his intention to restore the German churches to their position of power and influence that the Weimar Republic had destroyed. With Hitler in power, religion would experience a new day; the ceremony at the garrison church on March 23, 1933, offered reassurance that this indeed would be the case. Niemöller remained optimistic even as Nazism's malevolent shadow began to fall across the churches of the land. His sermons reflected this optimism. Speaking of a "vast reconstruction" of the Evangelical Church, he asserted that "the forces that press forward are filled … with honest purpose and with an enthusiasm that is contagious and irresistible."[106] This, he believed, would produce "a new and fruitful relationship between temporal and spiritual authority." He even went so far as to predict a "national moral revival" under Nazi rule, and claimed that "National Socialism and Protestantism were not incompatible but complementary forces in the spiritual life of Germany."[107] Germany would experience a spiritual rebirth under Nazi rule. This was not an untypical view of many clergymen within the Evangelical Church.

Even long after he had broken with the Nazis, Niemöller continued to support many of the foreign policy goals of the Third Reich because he believed those goals to be legitimate. He eagerly endorsed any and all measures taken to neutralize the provisions of the despised Treaty of Versailles, and welcomed Germany's withdrawal from the League of Nations. He also, along with many of his fellow clergy members, heartily approved of the remilitarization of Germany.[108] Like many resistance activists, he fully supported Germany's war effort and war aims once World War II began, and he offered to return to active naval service even though he was incarcerated in the Sachsenhausen concentration camp at the time for his opposition to Nazi attacks against the churches. Love of country motivated him. He realized that a Nazi victory would come at the cost of his country's soul, but he also recognized that defeat could well bring an end to Germany as a nation. Thus for him and other conservatives, defense of the fatherland had primacy. Speaking after the war, he said, "I could see no other way for myself, either as a Christian or a German." The Nazis, obviously wishing not to create a potential anti-Nazi war hero, rejected his offer.[109] This episode says much about Niemöller's extreme nationalism, to which he gave voice in 1945: "If there is a war, a German doesn't ask is it just or unjust, but he feels bound to join the ranks."[110] Thus, his behavior during the Nazi era can be succinctly described as "ambivalent and often contradictory."[111]

As with many conservatives, nationalism and religion remained at the heart of Niemöller's value system. Religious revival and national revival were two sides of the same coin. Hitler naturally manipulated this conflation to his great advantage. A second comment that Niemöller made at the end of the war also says much about his belief system. He said that he had not really taken issue with the Third Reich over matters of politics, but that his opposition was based solely on the fact that the Nazis sought to control not merely "man's body [but also] his soul."[112]

Unsurprisingly, Niemöller shared the anti-Semitism of many conservatives, although his was not a racial anti-Semitism. The distinction was faith, not race. Like Bonhoeffer, he believed that any Jew who converted to Christianity had to be fully accepted as a communicant in the Christian Church on the basis of full equality.[113] As with many Christians of his age – and of all ages – he believed that the Jews were responsible for Christ's crucifixion, but that "their punishment should be left to divine judgment, not human retribution." Speaking directly to this issue, Bonhoeffer said, "It can never … be the mission of any nation to take revenge on the Jews for the murder committed at Golgotha." That, he declared, was for God to decide.[114]

Largely because of the Jewish–Christian issue, Niemöller was one of the first clergymen to take an active role in resistance to the Nazi assertion of power over Germany's churches. In 1933, he created the Pastors' Emergency League as a protest against the Aryan Paragraph, a Nazi law that required the Evangelical Church to dismiss pastors with a Jewish heritage.[115] Out of this organization came the Confessing Church, cofounded by Niemöller, Bonhoeffer, and the Swiss theologian Karl Barth. The Confessing Church challenged the Nazi attempt to turn the Evangelical Church into an instrument of the Nazi state.

Martin Niemöller remains one of the more enigmatic and controversial figures in the history of the anti-Nazi resistance. A very outspoken man, he voiced both warm support for and bitter opposition against the Third Reich, and he paid a heavy price for his opposition. The Nazis treated him very harshly. He was twice incarcerated in concentration camps and suffered severe physical punishment.

Later in his life, Niemöller rejected many of the assumptions that had formed the basis for his Weltanschauung. For example, he renounced the intense nationalism that had been one of his core beliefs, and he became an outspoken pacifist and antiwar activist. He also was a driving force behind a statement issued by the Council of the Evangelical Church in Germany in October 1945, entitled "The Stuttgart Declaration of Guilt." Though controversial, especially in Germany, it represented an attempt to come to terms with the moral issues surrounding the behavior of the Evangelical Church during the Nazi era. Niemöller, much more than other signatories to the document, chose to publicize it widely in his sermons.

Niemöller also lectured forcefully on issues of war, peace, and disarmament. Speaking of his own political transformation, he said, "I began my political responsibility as an ultra-conservative. I wanted the Kaiser to come back; and now I am a revolutionary."[116] He is remembered as the author of a poem that has been widely published over the years:

When the Nazis came for the communists,
I remained silent;
I was not a communist.

When they locked up the social democrats,
I remained silent;
I was not a social democrat.

When they came for the trade unionists,
I did not speak out;
I was not a trade unionist.

When they came for the Jews,
I remained silent;
I wasn't a Jew.

When they came for me,
there was no one left to speak out.[117]

As World War II progressed, Niemöller, as well as those who thought as he did, tried to make a distinction between the German nation and the Nazi regime. Some went so far as to declare that what they perceived as Nazism's original goal – specifically, the elimination of the Weimar Republic and its replacement with a new regime that represented a return to the ideals and values of Imperial Germany – had been valid and that the original Nazi ideals had been good and sound. The problem as they saw it was that the Nazi regime itself had been corrupted by self-serving and corrupt individuals. Hence, these people tried to find a way to preserve the Nazi successes in foreign policy – specifically, its territorial acquisitions – and yet bring an end to Nazi rule. Carl Goerdeler held this hope. It was a vain hope, however. Only Germany's total military defeat could resolve the issue of party versus nation.[118]

This issue dogged the resistance to the very end. The belief that a "pure" Nazism had ever existed was utter fantasy. Those who held to this conviction failed to perceive the absolute evil that lay behind the facade of what appeared to be the good. Once more, Hitler's deceptions proved to be very appealing, very powerful, and very diabolic. The most significant difference between Dietrich Bonhoeffer and Martin Niemöller was their perception of Nazism and its connection to the nation. Bonhoeffer recognized the evil character of Nazism well before Adolf Hitler took control of the German government, and his opposition to it was absolute. He realized quite early that once the Nazis had taken control of the German nation, no distinction between regime and nation was possible. Germany, he believed, had become infected with an almost fatal virus that, once war broke out, could only be cured by total military defeat. Together, these two men represented the diversity of views that prevailed in the resistance movement. Everyone within the resistance agreed that Hitler had to be brought down, but their aspirations for a future non-Nazi Germany diverged widely. This problem contributed significantly to the inability of the movement to achieve unity, find a charismatic leader, and mobilize the masses for a coup.

Luther's doctrine of the two kingdoms further complicated matters for clergymen trained in the Lutheran tradition of obedience to civil authority but who abhorred Nazism and all it represented. The situation became especially painful as wartime conditions descended upon the fatherland. "It was not easy … to break their oath to a ruler even if his name was Hitler, especially during a war when such an act might bring about Germany's defeat."[119] Not all clergymen shared Dietrich Bonhoeffer's moral clarity. This issue – loyalty to the ruler and to the nation vs. loyalty to moral principle – proved to be the single most important question for the church, as well as for all members of the resistance movement, especially the military officers.

* * * *

The Evangelical Church soon encountered a serious challenge from the Third Reich. Not content to merely secure the cooperation of the Catholic and Evangelical Churches, Hitler sought to control the Evangelical Church from within by establishing a new Reich Church, complete with a "religious doctrine" compatible with Nazi ideology. Known as the "German Christian Movement," it was totally controlled by Hitler and his party. Hitler appointed Ludwig Müller, a former army chaplain who was sympathetic to the Nazi movement, to the newly created position of Reich bishop. Under Müller, these "German Christians" attempted to merge Christian doctrine with Nazi ideology and with German mythology. Specifically, they sought to purge the Christian religion of its Jewish roots. For example, Jesus of Nazareth was turned into an "Aryan hero," and Old Testament studies were eliminated from the curriculum of Christian schools.

This Reich Church became a grotesque perversion of the Christian religion. Some examples of the bizarre Nazi practices are as follows:

> Some churches, such as Brunswick Cathedral, became Nazi shrines, and Nazi forms of baptism and weddings were introduced. The annual harvest festival ceremony at Bückeburg, the climax of the year for farmers, was a pagan affair; and a German farmers' calendar for 1935 showed the Christian festivals replaced by dates from the Nazi Pantheon – Christmas Eve was given over to the celebration of the birth of Baldur, guardian of light, and Good Friday was remembered for the 4,500 Saxons slaughtered by Charlemagne.[120]

A reaction to the Reich Church was not long in coming. In September 1933, a few courageous clergymen, led by Martin Niemöller, created the Pastors' Emergency League, the purpose of which was specifically to resist the Nazi-imposed anti-Semitic strictures placed upon the Evangelical Church and, more generally, to resist Nazi efforts to create an alternative religion. The league's specific objective was "to protect Biblical Christianity against the new idolatry of race and nationalism" and to resist "any adulteration of the evangelical faith by Germanistic or other non-Christian ideas."[121] Niemöller has been described as the "moving spirit" behind the organization. He and Bonhoeffer worked closely together in this effort.[122]

Within a year, some 7,036 clergymen, over one-third of the Protestant clergy of Germany, had joined the league, which became the nucleus of the subsequent Confessing Church.[123] A large meeting took place in the city of Ulm in April 1934 to protest the anti-Semitic activities of the German Christians. A synod of Lutherans and Calvinists followed in May. This second meeting produced a document known as the Barmen Declaration. The Swiss theologian Karl Barth authored the six-point statement defining the Articles of Faith, which can be summarized as follows: "Jesus Christ is the ultimate authority and revealer of God's mystery; and ... the Christian owes his duty first and foremost to God, and his obedience to God's laws."[124] The new Confessing Church "united all the dissident Evangelical elements in Germany in a brotherhood dedicated to combating Nazi extremism."[125]

Repression of the Confessing Church took many forms: Confessing pastors were banned from preaching or had their pay withheld, and they were not allowed to teach in the schools. Theological students were forced to join Nazi organizations. A Protestant publishing house was confiscated, and a Protestant church in Munich was destroyed. Martin Niemöller was arrested, and though acquitted of the charges against him, he was immediately rearrested and sent to Sachsenhausen concentration camp. He was but one of many pastors who were imprisoned for their resistance activities. By 1938, some seven hundred had been imprisoned for such things as disobeying gag orders on sermons and refusing to submit to various regulations and decrees, such as those restricting fund-raising for the Confessing Church. These attacks were especially severe in the Berlin–Brandenburg region. One hundred and two pastors were arrested in the Potsdam district in 1935 for reading aloud the declaration of the Confessing Church synod.

There is an interesting footnote to these latter arrests. Upon their release, these pastors "were welcomed home by triumphant demonstrations of members of the Steel Helmet (Stahlhelm), breaking free momentarily from their incorporation into the brownshirts."[126] The Stahlhelm was a reactionary right-wing organization of Great War veterans who had opposed the Weimar Republic and had venerated the empire. After the Nazi accession to power, they were incorporated into the SA. In addition to this episode, a subsequent Gestapo report on the actions taken against the Confessing Church at this time gives an indication of the church's strength: "All the measures taken so far against the Confessing Church ... have proved to be inadequate, and only made the pastors more insubordinate still."[127] Moreover, the Nazis noted with growing alarm that the Confessing Church was gaining "respect and influence" and "that in court it was almost always found to be in the right."[128]

Thus, as early as June 1933, "a 'first focus of resistance' had formed" within the Confessing Church, and Bonhoeffer and Niemöller emerged as two of its most important leaders.[129] The very thing the Nazis had feared had come to pass, and this is precisely why they tried so hard to suppress the movement and to create a substitute religion.

In their determination to counter the Nazi assault on the Confessing Church, Bonhoeffer and Niemöller resorted to a subterfuge in order to pursue their cause. By 1935, the Reich Church was already providing seminary training for its future clergy, but the attempts of the Confessing Church to follow suit with its own seminary training were thwarted. Such efforts were "considered 'illegal' before they even started their work."[130] Nonetheless, the Confessing Church proceeded with its plan and created five seminaries in 1935, one of which was located at Finkenwalde in north Germany, with Bonhoeffer as the director. Remarkably, all were able to function until 1937, when the Gestapo closed them down. The fact that they survived undisturbed for two years has led some to ask a question that has never been answered definitively. Bonhoeffer's biographer, Ferdinand Schlingensiepen, comments, "Were the authorities purposely looking the other way?" He also avers that "members of the Gestapo had protected Confessing Church pastors and their work." The question is unanswerable. Meanwhile, some sixty-seven "illegal" seminarians continued their now clandestine studies with Bonhoeffer until 1939.[131]

Regrettably, the Confessing Church confined itself to doctrinal issues and failed to take a principled stand against Nazi political activity, especially the persecution of Germans of the Jewish faith. For example, it neglected to condemn the infamous Kristallnacht episode in any way, choosing instead to just ignore it.[132] Consequently, a schism soon developed between those who wished to achieve an accommodation with the Third Reich, and Bonhoeffer and his Finkenwalde associates, who were determined to resist the Nazis in any way they could. The issue was no longer heresy. It had become a straightforward question of obedience to the state. Should the Confessing Church submit to the Third Reich and acquiesce to its demands for total submission or not? This issue produced a bitter split within the Confessing Church, with the Finkenwalde seminarians becoming an avant-garde in the controversy. "The Confessing Church seemed to be falling apart."[133] Yet despite this conflict, Bonhoeffer himself remained committed to the Confessing Church, although the approach of war in the late thirties brought a significant change to his life and work as he eventually became a double agent in the Abwehr. As for the Confessing Church, it suffered more and more Nazi proscriptions, and ultimately was reduced to irrelevance. By 1938, it "was no longer an institution."[134]

The German Christian Movement went nowhere as well. A total failure, it secured only minimal support from the laity, and only members of the clergy who were opportunists and without moral integrity endorsed it. Hitler soon abandoned the project, although the organization technically lasted until the end of World War II. Müller proved to be completely inept and was replaced by a lawyer named Hans Kerrl, who also failed to meld German Protestantism with Nazi ideology.[135] Müller committed suicide in 1945.[136] In the end, all of Hitler's efforts to bring the Christian churches under his total control failed.

The Socialists

The socialist movement provides an interesting contrast to the beliefs and actions of the conservatives. Unlike the latter, the socialist leaders recognized the innate evil of the Nazi movement almost immediately, which leads to an obvious question: Why did the socialists have a much-clearer understanding of the Nazi phenomenon than the conservatives? Answers to such questions are always speculative, but history demands that an attempt be made. Perhaps a clue can be found in the attitudes toward the Weimar Republic held by the conservatives and the socialists and in the philosophical orientation that separated the two groups.

As has been stressed, conservatives passionately hoped for a return to the values and traditions of Imperial Germany. Yet those same people who initially embraced the Nazis did not comprehend the depraved nature of the Nazi ideology. Socialist ideals, on the other hand, were rooted in the emergent twentieth-century world. Social Democrats espoused the values of

Western liberal democracy that found expression in the Weimar Republic. Whereas the conservatives looked backward to a glorious mythical past, Social Democrats looked ahead to a glorious mythical future. The clash of values found here – namely tradition vs. change – represent one of the most pervasive sources of conflict in all of history. The historian Richard Bessel has commented, "All human endeavor can probably be seen as a search for stability which is doomed to disappointment in a constantly changing world."[137] The consequence of this unfortunate dispute helped to deepen the divisions within the resistance movement, further weakening attempts to create a broad united front against the Nazis.

One of the more intriguing what-if questions in the history of the German anti-Nazi resistance movement is as follows: What if the Social Democratic Party had been able to make common cause with the conservatives – including the military establishment – in staging a coup d'état against the Third Reich? It is an intriguing question, because such an alliance could have provided the requisite leadership and mass support for a successful coup. Yet for two reasons, this notion is completely fanciful. First of all, the conservatives held an almost visceral contempt for socialism that dated from the mid-nineteenth century. Secondly, the Nazis had effectively destroyed social democracy as a potential center of resistance almost at the outset of Nazi rule. Nevertheless, a proper understanding of the resistance and its ultimate failure to depose Hitler and destroy the Third Reich requires an appreciation of the place the SPD held in German society and politics. This in turn requires a side trip into late nineteenth- and early twentieth-century German history.

* * * *

The rapid industrialization that took place in nineteenth-century Europe brought with it extreme political, economic, and social dislocation. The dream of universal prosperity accompanied the grim reality of abject poverty. Socialism had its origins in these conditions. Social reformers quickly realized that direct political action was essential to the realization of their goal of a more just and equitable society. They began to promote a system of economic organization in which the means of production, distribution, and exchange were publically – that is, government – owned.[138] Thus, they became socialists.

Before they could put these changes into effect, however, they had to capture control of the government. There were two ways to bring this about, either through the political process – namely, elections – or violent revolution. The struggle of these two contending ideas encapsulated the history of socialism for the next century and a half. This struggle was nowhere more sharply defined than in Germany.

By the beginning of the twentieth century, the Socialist Workers' Party (SAP), founded in 1875 and renamed the Social Democratic Party (SPD) in 1890,[139] had established itself as the champion of the industrial proletariat, and it quickly became one of Germany's major political parties. By 1912, it held 110 seats, making it the largest single party in the 397-seat Reichstag.[140] Nevertheless, internal divisions within the socialist movement contributed to its failure to forge a governing majority. These divisions were the result of a deep philosophical and ideological chasm that cast a very long shadow into the twentieth century and impacted the anti-Nazi resistance movement in a profound way. The pivotal figure in this phase of socialist thought was Karl Marx.

Marx produced a rigid ideological system that predicted the future course of industrial society, arguing that capitalism ultimately would collapse under the weight of its own contradictions and that a short-lived dictatorship of the proletariat would replace it. Once the last vestiges of capitalism were removed and everyone was subsumed into the proletariat, however, the need for government would cease and the state would gradually wither away. The end result would be a workers' paradise. In order to achieve this paradise, however, violent revolution was both necessary and inevitable, because it was the only way to break the power of the middle-class capitalist oligarchy – or so Marx believed. This was the inflexible ideology that a group known as the "orthodox" or "revolutionary" socialists proclaimed, and it produced what has been aptly described as "dogmatic immobility."[141]

This rigid interpretation of historical events provided the orthodox Marxists the ideological foundation for their support of the Russian Revolution. The revolutionary socialists within the German Social Democratic Party laid the groundwork for the creation of the German Communist Party in 1919.

That being said, many within the German social democratic movement embraced an older philosophical tradition that was much more pragmatic and much less ideological than that of the revolutionary group. Those who represented this older tradition remained prominent within German social democracy, and shortly after Marx's death in 1883 they issued a challenge to many of the orthodox Marxist assumptions. This second group, now known as "revisionist" or "evolutionary" Marxists, completely rejected the idea of the imminent collapse of capitalism and an inevitable revolution. Instead, working as an organized political party, they championed that older tradition of democracy and social justice. They proposed to work within the existing political system to bring about evolutionary rather than revolutionary change. Thus, they would promote social democracy by means of the ballot box rather than the bullet and barricade. The two words "socialism" and "democracy," which had been integral parts of the German socialist movement from its beginnings in the 1840s, reasserted themselves in the late nineteenth century.[142] Of course, the conservatives totally rejected both terms as inappropriate for Germany.

The man considered as the founder of revisionist socialism as well as its dominant figure was Eduard Bernstein. Born in Berlin in 1850 to a railroad engineer, he became a bank clerk for a short while and was soon attracted to socialism. He joined the Socialist Party at the age of twenty-two and remained active in the socialist movement until the end of his days. He was elected to the Reichstag in 1902, was reelected a number of times, and served in that body until 1928. Less than six weeks after his death in December 1932, the democratic republic for which he had labored so devotedly fell before the onslaught of Adolf Hitler and the Nazi Party. Throughout his life, he remained committed to the belief that the task of the socialist movement was "to organize the working classes politically and develop them as a democracy and to fight for all reforms in the state which are adapted to raise the working classes and transform the state in the direction of democracy."[143] In this statement, he was reiterating a party program of 1869 calling "for the establishment of a free democratic state [and pledging itself] to struggle for the abolition of all class domination and the attainment of full economic and political emancipation of the working classes."[144] The future Germany envisioned by Bernstein and his supporters hardly conformed to the socialist ogre that the enemies of the Weimar Republic imagined as they worked assiduously to bring about its demise.

* * * *

By 1900, the split between the evolutionists and revolutionists was complete. The evolutionists, now known as the Majority Socialists, became the dominant faction within the SPD. They also became a bulwark of the Weimar Republic. Those who remained faithful to the original orthodox and doctrinaire ideology were the nucleus of what ultimately became the Communist Party. These two groups – the revisionists and the revolutionists – became implacable enemies. However, few Germans who were not part of the socialist movement recognized these divisions or their significance. The conservative political leaders of the empire and the Weimar Republic lumped all socialists together as potential, if not actual, enemies of the German nation. The middle and upper classes did not grasp the nuances within socialism and viewed all socialists as "Bolsheviks" who were hell-bent on revolution and destruction of all that was considered sacred. They saw the Weimar Republic as a viper's nest of socialism.[145]

These accusations were completely unfounded. In fact, the Majority Socialists achieved a degree of success in restoring order to Germany that bordered on the miraculous. Against incredible odds, the leader of the Majority Socialists, Friedrich Ebert, successfully guided the ship of state through the shoals of left-and right-wing extremism, brought the Great War officially to an end, albeit with a peace treaty with highly unsatisfactory provisions for Germany but over which he had no control, and helped to set Germany on a course toward a system of parliamentary democracy with a new constitution.

Ebert, a saddler by trade, became chairman of the SPD in 1913, served as provisional chancellor of the national government from November 1918 to February 1919, and was president of the Weimar Republic from 1919 until his death in 1925 of natural causes.[146] Tragically, Ebert's achievements did not last. Thanks in no small measure to Nazi efforts, the German nation never embraced the Weimar Republic wholeheartedly, and the Majority Socialists never received proper recognition for their achievements. They "received no credit for saving the fatherland, for preventing foreign occupation and for bringing the troops home. They were merely denounced and held in contempt as traitors."[147] Thanks also to the Great Depression and inept political leadership by politicians not part of the SPD, the demise of the Weimar Republic became inevitable.

Thus, as we know, the Nazis prevailed in 1933 against all opposition, but not without a spirited resistance put up by the SPD leadership and not without a display of incredible personal courage on their part. Almost immediately after Hitler's appointment as chancellor, the Nazis moved to consolidate their power. An important first step was the passage by the Reichstag of the Enabling Act (Ermächtigungsgesetz), a law giving all legislative and budgetary powers to the cabinet, thereby creating a dictatorship. The Enabling Act gave Hitler the ostensibly legal authority to rule by decree, and effectively reduced the Reichstag to a mere rubber stamp for his policies. The SPD was the only political party to vote against this law.

The vote was scheduled for March 23, 1933. The session convened in what has been described as an "atmosphere heavy with violence and intimidation."[148] "SA mobs [the infamous Brownshirts] were audible outside, greeting deputies with calls of 'Centre pig' [that is, the Catholic Center Party] or 'Marxist sow,' while SA and SS men lined the walls, looming over the shoulders of Social Democrat deputies, of whom 94 ... were present."[149] SPD member Wilhelm Hoegner recalls the scene vividly: "When we Social Democrats had taken our places on the far left, the SA and SS men placed themselves by the exits and along the walls behind us in a half-circle. Their attitude did not bode well for us."[150]

In the debate that followed, another Social Democrat, Otto Wels, gave "an exemplary and brave speech,"[151] in which he "defended democratic ideals, including a 'real national community' based on 'equal rights.'"[152] Wels went on: "Freedom and life can be taken from us, but not honour." The historian Richard Evans has written the following description of the episode:

> Wels was not exaggerating: several prominent Social Democrats had already been killed by the Nazis, and he himself was carrying a cyanide capsule in his waist pocket as he spoke, ready to swallow should he be arrested and tortured by the brownshirts after delivering his speech. His voice choking with emotion, he ended with an appeal to the future: "In this historic hour, we German Social Democrats solemnly profess our allegiance to the basic principles of humanity and justice, freedom and socialism. No Enabling Law gives you the right to annihilate ideas that are eternal and indestructible."[153]

When the vote finally took place, only the SPD delegates – all of them – voted no.[154] Unsurprisingly, the Nazis singled out the SPD for "special attention" in the years that followed. They were condemned as "Communist sympathizers"; additionally, they had the audacity to openly resist Hitler's expressed intent to completely extirpate any semblance of responsible government from Germany. The SPD had been consistent in its support for the Weimar Republic, and it was consistent in its opposition to the Nazis.

Although some SPD leaders had believed as early as 1930 that the republic was doomed and that some accommodation would have to (and could) be reached with the Nazis, the reality of Nazi rule soon disabused them of this misconception.[155] They, together with the Communists, were among the first groups to be suppressed by the government of the Third Reich. The German Communist Party was proscribed on March 7, 1933. On May 22, 1933, the SA and SS raided "every Social Democratic–oriented trade union office in the land, took over all the trade union newspapers and periodicals, and occupied all the branches of the trade union bank."[156] Leading union officials were taken into "protective custody" and placed in concentration camps. "The once powerful German trade union movement had disappeared without a trace virtually overnight."[157] The SPD was proscribed on June 22, 1933, and most of its leaders escaped to Prague.[158]

By August 1933, "almost all the ... leading Social Democrats who had remained in Germany were in prison, in a concentration camp, silenced or dead."[159] The Nazis replaced the unions with the Nazi Labor Front (Deutsche Arbeitsfront, or DAF), an organization whose single purpose was to keep labor powerless and in line. Thus by 1939, "there was no working-class underground movement in Germany worth mentioning."[160] Only uncoordinated and unorganized underground "cells" remained. There was no united front of socialists whatsoever. For all practical purposes, the working class had neither an organizational structure nor leadership.[161]

As Germany entered the high noon of Nazi popularity in the mid-thirties, many of its citizens, now enjoying the benefits of a revived economy, jettisoned their ties to the now defunct Social Democratic Party and cast their lot with the Nazis.[162]

But not all of them did. Many workers themselves maintained a continued opposition. They even had a loosely organized resistance movement and engaged in "stubborn refusals to co-operate on an everyday basis."[163] Such activities included sabotage in the workplace and distribution of anti-Nazi leaflets, as well as behavior that can best be described as nonconformist: refusal to attend party rallies or failing to give the obligatory "Heil Hitler" and Nazi straight-arm salute when circumstances demanded it.

Such nonconformist activity, though insignificant in a normally functioning society, represented a serious breach of proper behavior in Nazi Germany and could earn a stiff reprimand for the miscreant, or even worse. This is a classic example of a totalitarian state at work. Such behavior by definition constituted a violation of the norms of the Nazi-defined Volksgemeinschaft.

According to files in the Wiedergutmachungsamt [Reparations Office] for the city of Dortmund, a total of 1,925 names of people

> persecuted for political resistance are known. Of these, 511 were Socialists and 1,250 Communists ... In Oberhausen the names of 382 victims of political persecution are known. Twenty percent of these were miners and 16 percent metal workers; a bare 10 percent of the victims were not workers ... The fact remains that workers took part in resistance in disproportionately high numbers.[164]

According to Gestapo records found after World War II, 11,687 arrests were made in 1936 "for spreading illegal socialist propaganda." In that same year, 17,108 trials were held, and 1,643,000 illegal pamphlets were confiscated. What makes all of this especially significant is that these socialist activities were taking place at the high tide of Nazi popularity in Germany.[165]

All of this strongly suggests that a nucleus for mass action existed within the socialist ranks. Had the socialist leadership not been decimated after the March 5 Reichstag elections and had the conservatives not held the socialists in such mistrust, an organized anti-Nazi mass movement with strong leadership just might have evolved. The fact that some of the leaders of the two factions established contacts even before the war began in order to discuss the issues surrounding a coup d'état suggests that the potential for joint action existed.

Sadly, however, old animosities and prejudices ultimately frustrated attempts to achieve a coordinated and united front against the Hitler state. For example, SPD leader Wilhelm Leuschner, together with other Social Democrats, met with General Beck – then retired – in the fall of 1939 to discuss a general strike that would be coordinated with a generals' coup that the Wehrmacht chief of staff, General Franz Halder, was planning. Upon learning of the conversation, Halder acidly replied, "If that were so, then the workers should initiate the coup from below." General Walther von Brauchitsch, chief of the Army Command, responded in a similar manner. He "maintained that if the workers were really so anti-Hitler, then they should overthrow him by means of a general strike." When Leuschner learned of Brauchitsch's comment, he "was furious and said that these gentlemen, the officers, would then, of course, fire on the workers – they always fired on the Left but never on the Right."[166] Regrettably, Leuschner's statement was correct.

The memory of those early Weimar years produced a barrier between the conservatives and Social Democrats that ultimately was fatal to the cause of a united front against Nazism, and to the cause of the resistance as well. Neither side could overcome the burden of history. We shall never know just how effective such a united front might have been. What we do know, however, is that ideological blindness and ignorance were effective in keeping the resistance movement tragically divided from beginning to end, even as many were trying to build the framework of a post-Nazi Germany. Many conservatives, both military and civilian, were prisoners of their own social milieu, unable to break free from their ideological straitjackets and form a solid core of resistance together with their supposed adversaries. They lived in a world that was far removed from that of the Social Democrats. They should have read their own national history a bit more objectively. This experience suggests that those in positions of political leadership should always be aware of the ways in which blind prejudice can distort their decision-making processes.

* * * *

And yet, attempts were made to build a united opposition. Of those few social democratic leaders who remained in Germany after 1933, several eventually became active in the resistance movement. For the most part, they were not so much conspirators as planners for a postwar, non-Nazi Germany. They tried to find a common ground with their conservative counterparts who were planning for a new Germany once the war was over. Julius Leber, Wilhelm Leuschner, and Jakob Kaiser are representative of this group.

Julius Leber, a veteran of the Great War, served in the Reichstag as a member of the SPD from 1924 to 1933. After being arrested by the Nazis and sent to a concentration camp for several years, he returned to private life. Later, during World War II, he established contacts with Carl Goerdeler, as well as with the Kreisau Circle resistance group, in planning for a post-Nazi government. He also was Claus von Stauffenberg's choice for chancellor in this proposed government. Thanks to Stauffenberg, Leber became an intimate associate of the most significant and active leaders of the conspiracy. This gave a decided leftward tilt to the resistance and raised the possibility of creating a genuine mass movement. Both men shared a pragmatism and political realism that transcended ideology. Arrested after the aborted bomb plot of July 20, 1944, Leber was executed in early 1945.[167]

Like Leber, Wilhelm Leuschner was a veteran of the Great War. He also was a longtime member of the SPD – he joined the party in 1910 – and a trade union leader. Arrested by the Nazis in May and again in June 1933, he was released in 1934. Shortly thereafter, he became active in anti-Nazi resistance activities. As early as 1936, he was running a small manufacturing business that came to be known as "the hub of the 'illegal Reich leadership of German unions.'" He also made contact with the Kreisau Circle and with Carl Goerdeler. Leuschner was considered a likely candidate for the vice chancellor's position in a post-Nazi government. Arrested in August 1944, he was executed in September after a sham trial.[168]

The political career of Jakob Kaiser began during the Weimar Republic. A member of a Catholic trade union, he joined the Catholic Center Party and served as a leader of the Christian labor movement. He was an ardent anti-Nazi as well. He, too, made contacts with both Goerdeler and Stauffenberg, and for this reason he was forced to go into hiding after the failure of Operation Valkyrie. Kaiser survived the war and became active in rebuilding the Catholic Center Party, which was reorganized shortly after World War II and renamed the Christian Democratic Union. Today it is one of Germany's major political parties. Kaiser died in 1961.[169]

An early example of clandestine activity pursued by the outlawed Social Democrats was a group known as the "Markwitz Circle." (The source of this name is obscure.) These people distributed prohibited literature and helped individuals who were threatened with arrest to escape from Germany. Regrettably, an informer betrayed them to the Gestapo in 1935.[170]

Yet another example of underground social democratic activity can be found in a meeting that took place in the winter of 1938–1939 in the home of a prominent former SPD member, Ernst von Harnack. Among those in attendance were Leuschner, Leber, and Dietrich Bonhoeffer's brother Klaus, who was a lawyer and a trustee of the Lufthansa and who was also heavily engaged in resistance activity. These people "discussed the possibilities of resistance activity with a view to overthrowing the regime and concluded that progress might be restarted by formation of a 'Unity Front' combining all opposition tendencies, both civilian and military, without regard to party political [*sic*] background."[171] This "Unity Front" never became a reality, but the meeting led to an exchange of views that helped to create a sense of common purpose, which in turn inspired the resistance movement to continue working for an end to Nazi rule.

These men helped to lay the groundwork for subsequent anti-Nazi activity that took place during the war years. A common conviction united all of these various anti-Nazi factions, from Left to Right, civilian and military. They knew that a system of consummate evil had seized control of their nation, and they committed themselves to its eradication.

Hence, though gravely wounded and reduced to political impotence, the social democratic resistance movement nonetheless survived. Its leaders, especially Leuschner, Kaiser, and Leber, made contact and established ties with others in the civilian and military resistance movement. As a consequence of these connections, Leuschner and Kaiser were able later in the war to set up "an invisible network" of opposition cells with various workers' groups – such as railway workers – "throughout Germany to provide broader support" for Operation Valkyrie. The idea was to use these "cells" to "whip up the public support and cooperation that would be essential to its [*i.e.,* Operation Valkyrie] success."[172] Leuschner made it clear, however, that the military coup had to take place first, indicating that the workers' general strike would follow immediately thereafter. This would prevent a replay of events that took place at the end of the Great War, when a premature strike launched by the socialists helped to bring down what was left of the imperial government. That strike further discredited the SPD in the eyes of many Germans, especially the conservatives.[173] The comments of Generals Halder and Brauchitsch about a general strike doubtlessly were on his mind as well.

Two Resistance Groups

In addition to the formal institutions in the resistance movement, such as church, army, and political party, there were groups and individuals who did not necessarily participate directly in active resistance to Nazi rule but who, rather, engaged in various forms of dissent, some of which have been discussed already. Most of this dissent was not formally organized. It will be remembered, however, that the Nazis considered any form of dissident behavior or nonconformist activity to be a threat to their rule and an impediment to the creation of their Volksgemeinschaft. Such activity was officially declared to be treasonous.

These dissenters were an eclectic group of men and women from widely different socioeconomic backgrounds, with widely divergent philosophies and sociopolitical beliefs. They could be found at every point across the political spectrum, from the extreme right to the extreme left. They included Social Democrats and authoritarian monarchists, and spanned a wide spectrum of age groups, from youth to the elderly.

In retrospect, however, only two groups – aside from the army, which is discussed in chapter 4 – "were able to forge closer ties over the years and develop a strategy that posed a genuine threat to the regime."[174] The first was the Beck–Goerdeler group, so named for the two men who provided its leadership, Carl Goerdeler and Ludwig Beck. The second group is remembered as the Kreisau Circle. Helmuth James von Moltke was its leader, and it met several times at Kreisau (now Kryżowa, Poland), his estate in Silesia; hence the name of the group.

* * * *

By 1938, Carl Goerdeler had come to realize that the Nazi influence in Germany was pernicious in the extreme, and he decided that he had to do something about it. He, together with many of his countrymen, also was becoming increasingly apprehensive of Hitler's expansionist foreign policy and obvious warlike intentions, specifically, his imperialistic designs on Eastern Europe. Subsequent to his resignation as mayor of Leipzig in April 1937, Goerdeler accepted an offer from his friend, the industrialist Robert Bosch, to become head of the Bosch Corporation's overseas sales division. This appointment gave him a legitimate opportunity, or "cover," to establish many overseas contacts promoting the increasingly significant resistance movement inside Germany. Thanks also to his long career in public service, he had extensive contacts with individuals in the civil administration of German society on the regional and local level as well as in the national government. Goerdeler was in regular contact with "business owners, trade union leaders, clergymen, and financiers, and he kept in constant touch with opposition leaders in the military. Goerdeler was himself a rallying point and organizer for a number of diverse political, civilian, and military opposition groups."[175]

Goerdeler, who ultimately became one of the most influential leaders of the civilian resistance, has been described as a key player in every anti-Hitler conspiracy from 1938 to 1944.[176] The late historian Harold Deutsch described him as the "principal motor" of the opposition.[177] His strength of character became an important element in the resistance movement. Possessed of a "keen, analytical mind," he also tended to be "inflexible and narrow in his point of view."[178] This latter characteristic was reflected in his rejection of the Weimar Republic and its system of social democracy, as well as in his commitment to the aristocratic values of an Imperial Germany that was quickly receding into the shadows of history, never to return. He and others within this group of resisters envisioned "the creation of a true national community dominated by the traditional aristocracy," an idea that for obvious reasons was completely unacceptable to the Social Democrats.[179] Unfortunately, the conflict between the Social Democrats and the conservatives continued to burden the resistance.

Despite his "inflexible and narrow" perspective, however, Goerdeler was constantly negotiating with men of diverse and even opposing views, and he understood fully that the essence of politics is compromise. Hence, "he could see no other way to create a broad basis for a coup except negotiations, and so he continued them almost down to the last day."[180] There was no other way to achieve his goal of a unified resistance movement. As he worked to build a broad anti-Nazi coalition within Germany, he developed a "close working relationship" with Wilhelm Leuschner and especially Jakob Kaiser. Kaiser subsequently became one of Goerdeler's "most influential advisers."[181] Thanks doubtlessly to people such as Kaiser and Leuschner, Goerdeler eventually moderated his views on which was the best form of government for a post–World War II Germany.

Later, during the war, at least one ultraconservative member of the Beck–Goerdeler group, former jurist and Prussian Minister of Finance Johannes Popitz, "accused Goerdeler of having lost his way, by which he meant his alliance and agreements with the socialists."[182] Harold Deutsch has stated that Goerdeler had a "profound distaste for everything that smacked of authoritarianism [and that] he had been a passionate advocate of home rule and of wide participation by the citizen in self-government."[183] These contradictions that Carl Goerdeler embraced within his own mind reflected the contradictions that lay at the heart of the resistance movement itself. It was a microcosm of the conflict between the Social Democrats and the conservatives and their respective views of the kind of postwar society they wanted for Germany. Should it be a new and improved Weimar Republic, or should it be a restored though modified Imperial Germany? This question bedeviled the resistance movement from beginning to end.

The year 1937 not only marked Goerdeler's departure from public life but also was the year he first met General Ludwig Beck, the man with whom he would soon form close ties in their mutual struggle to remove the Führer from power. Beck became the military counterpart to Goerdeler and his work in the civilian branch of the resistance movement. This military–civilian team worked together to recruit members of a resistance movement to rid Germany of its Nazi plague.

Ludwig Beck was born in 1880 in the town of Biebrich, a suburb of Wiesbaden, "into a quiet, respectable, upper-middle-class family." His father, an iron mine owner, was "a highly skilled metallurgical engineer, with a strong academic bent." The son inherited that bent, and it became one of his "most outstanding characteristics."[184] Young Ludwig also was musically inclined; he played the violin. The place of his birth – the Rhineland, rather than old Prussia – together with his upper-middle-class origins, meant that he was never a part of the historic Prussian military aristocracy; he was, in fact, the mirror opposite of the stereotypical Prussian officer. For example, he was "a fervent admirer of French culture," and "he exhibited nothing of the stiffness, the fixed ways, and the limited horizons often associated with old-style military professionals."[185] His political philosophy has been described as liberal, which presumably means that he was committed to the values of constitutionalism and civil liberties and rights.[186]

As with Bonhoeffer and Niemöller, so it was with Beck and many of his colleagues in the army. The differences in social and cultural background produced differences in social and cultural outlook. It was said of Beck that he "seemed largely free of the social prejudices displayed by many aristocratic members of the officer corps."[187] Moreover, he was a man of impeccable character and integrity. Perhaps for these reasons, Hitler especially feared Beck. In early 1938, he expressed these fears during a conversation with his minister of justice about plans he was formulating to gain total control of the army: "The only one whom I fear is Beck. That man would be capable of undertaking something."[188] However, one thing that Beck and others of the as yet unformed resistance did share with the traditionalists in the officer corps was a desire for Germany's military revival. As a result, they welcomed Hitler's emphasis on a rearmed Germany. The cost of that revival was not yet evident in 1937 and 1938.

Beck attended Wiesbaden University before joining the army in 1898. Subsequently, he entered a course of study at the Berlin War Academy, where he excelled in studies on military strategy and organization. This led to his selection for general staff training, which he completed in 1911. He also had a talent for writing, and in 1930 he published an army field manual that has been described as "one of the most renowned of German military publications." In addition to its clarity, his writing style displayed an unusual degree of literary refinement.[189] He served as a staff officer during the Great War and rose to the rank of major. He remained in the army – renamed the Reichswehr in 1919 – after the war. By 1931, he had risen to the rank of major general. On October 1, 1933, he was named head of the Truppenamt (Troop Office), a kind of shadow general staff – the latter had been officially dissolved by the Treaty of Versailles – and given another promotion, this time to lieutenant general. The Truppenamt was redesignated general staff in 1935, and Beck retained his position as head of the organization.

An Emergent Resistance

As with many of his fellow military officers, Beck had a brief infatuation with Nazism. As early as 1934, however, he, together with others in civilian and military life, was beginning to have serious concerns about Hitler's long-range plans. These concerns increased significantly over the next four years.

* * * *

By 1938, the path of German history was soon to change direction in dramatic fashion. Already, Adolf Hitler was preparing to pursue his policy of imperialist expansion through military action – that is, war. Those of the officer corps who had a realistic appraisal of Germany's military potential knew that the fatherland was not prepared for such an adventurous policy. Beck and his allies were absolutely opposed to what they considered to be Hitler's foolhardiness. Thus began a stirring of nascent resistance activity within the military establishment that soon would become a full-blown anti-Nazi conspiracy. Moreover, a civilian resistance group complementing the activities of Ludwig Beck and Carl Goerdeler also began to form. This was the Kreisau Circle.

The men who became part of the Kreisau Circle were younger than the leaders of the Beck–Goerdeler group, and not surprisingly they held values and ideals that differed somewhat from those of their elders. Rather than a group of conspirators, these men were more of a discussion group looking for an exchange of ideas on what sort of Germany would arise from the detritus of the Third Reich, which they confidently expected ultimately to fail.[190] The founder and leader of the Kreisau Circle, as mentioned previously, was Helmuth James von Moltke, who descended from one of the most distinguished families in German-Prussian history. Several meetings of this group were held at the Moltke estate, Kreisau, which prompted the Gestapo to name the group the "Kreisau Circle" after they had broken it up.[191] Most of the time, however, they met at the Berlin home of Peter Yorck von Wartenburg, who was the scion of another illustrious Prussian military family.

As Yorck was the "heart" of the Kreisau Circle, Moltke was its "engine."[192] The Kreisau Circle was quite loosely organized and had a diversity of participants – "members" is not really an appropriate term – that, in addition to Moltke and Wartenburg, included three members of the SPD who had remained in Germany after 1933, namely, Julius Leber, Wilhelm Leuschner, and Jakob Kaiser, plus theologians such as the Jesuit priest Alfred Delp and the Protestant clergyman Eugen Gerstenmaier.

Dietrich Bonhoeffer also had close connections with the group. Kreisau "brought together a fascinating collection of gifted men from the most diverse backgrounds: noblemen, officers, lawyers, socialists, trade unionists, churchmen."[193] Though they represented a broad spectrum of social, political, and economic views – with aristocrats and socialists outnumbering representatives of the middle class by a significant margin – they were united by a common philosophy that is best described as Christian and socialist.[194] The "strong religious leanings" of this group, together with its ability to attract "devoted but undogmatic socialists," have been described as its "most striking characteristic."[195]

Helmuth James von Moltke was the great-grandnephew of General Helmuth von Moltke the Elder, who had served as commander of the Prussian Army in the Franco-Prussian War and as chief of the Prussian, later German, General Staff. Additionally, he was the grandnephew of Helmuth von Moltke the Younger, who was chief of staff of the Prussian Army at the outbreak of war in 1914. His mother, Dorothy (née Rose-Innes), was an English South African, whose father, Sir James Rose-Innes, was a leading jurist in the Union of South Africa. Both parents were active members of the Christian Science Church, and Moltke himself, though not a practitioner of Christian Science, had a very accurate moral compass that was based upon Christian values that he obviously had received from his parents. Quite early on, he recognized the totality of Nazi depravity. The passage of time only deepened his disgust for and outrage over the regime.

Writing to his wife in the summer of 1941, he commented on the mass murders taking place in the east, observing that the German people would have to bear the burden of "a blood-guilt that can never be expunged in our lifetime and can never be forgotten."[196] A year later he wrote the following words in a letter that was smuggled to his British friend Lionel Curtis:

> Today, not a numerous, but an active part of the German people are beginning to realize, not that they have been led astray, not that bad times await them, not that the war may end in defeat, but that what is happening is sin and that they are personally responsible for each terrible deed that has been committed – naturally, not in the earthly sense, but as Christians.[197]

He has been compared to Dietrich Bonhoeffer in his sensitivity to the "inherent inhumaneness of racial persecution."[198] Also, like Bonhoeffer, he recognized the depravity that lay just beneath the surface of the Nazi system at a time when others were trying to explain it all away as an aberration that time would eventually heal.

In 1935, Moltke began a law practice in Berlin. His specialty was international law, and he used his expertise to help victims of Nazi persecution to emigrate safely. He rejected the opportunity to become a judge because he would have had to join the Nazi Party. He was a regular visitor to Great Britain, where he continued his legal studies at Oxford and London. Doubtlessly because of his mother's influence, he spoke English fluently. With the outbreak of war on September 1, 1939, he was conscripted into the Abwehr. His work was primarily the task of gathering information on political and military matters from various sources, such as foreign newspapers and military attachés.[199]

It has been said of Helmuth James von Moltke that he "remained essentially a man of ideas rather than deeds, a theorist more than a pragmatist," and that he never was a "hard-core activist in the resistance." The same could be said of the Kreisau Circle. These people were "reluctant in principle to use force as an instrument of political change." Kreisau initially was "opposed to any attempt to overthrow the dictator."[200] They were idealists rather than activists.[201] Moltke has been characterized as the Hamlet of the resistance movement, "agonizing over the cruel dilemmas and exigencies of a time out of joint."[202] He was especially pessimistic about the prospect of successfully assassinating Hitler. Opposed at first, he later came to support the idea, all the while doubting that the attempt would succeed; he also questioned whether it would make much difference even if it should be successful.[203] His abhorrence of violence lay at the heart of his initial rejection of assassination. He desperately wanted to move beyond the use of "all force and brutality even in countermeasures" against a regime that was one of the most brutal in history, at least in terms of the numbers of its victims.[204] Yet, he did change his mind on the question of assassination and reluctantly came to the conclusion that Hitler had to be eliminated. Together with other members of the Kreisau group, he actually cooperated with the military conspiracy in planning for a post-Nazi Germany. Though naïve on many matters, Moltke was anything but an ideologue.[205]

Because the Kreisau Circle had a very diverse membership, accurate generalizations about its beliefs and attitudes are difficult to make without resorting to oversimplification.[206] Nonetheless, an attempt must be made. More of a discussion or social group than a true resistance organization, it had been in existence since at least 1937.[207] It essentially was a study group anticipating a post-Nazi, post-Hitler Germany. They were asking the question, What kind of Germany do we want to create to replace the system of terror under which we are living?

Their ultimate goal was twofold. First of all, they wanted a Germany purged of all Nazi elements and transcending what they considered to be the dead weight of the past. They anticipated nothing less than a thoroughgoing social revolution for Germany. Therefore – unlike the Beck–Goerdeler group – they had no interest in restoring the Germany of Bismarck and Wilhelm II. Rather, they wanted a clean break with the past and a fresh start, which though never defined precisely, presumably would have had a strong commitment to social justice, with an amalgam of the socialist and Christian values that they espoused.[208]

Secondly, they anticipated a new Europe arising out of the ashes of the old. This Europe would be some sort of a federation transcending national sovereignties and ideologies and resembling the United States of America. Therefore, they rejected any kind of expansionist foreign policy such as envisioned by the Beck–Goerdeler group. Recognizing that Germany would have to pay a high price for the Nazi depredations, they had few illusions about a restoration of German imperial greatness. For example, they knew that Germany's territorial boundaries would be significantly reduced in a post–World War II world.[209] On the other hand, some within the Beck–Goerdeler group clung to the fanciful idea as late as May 1944 that Germany would be able to retain its 1914 borders, including autonomy for Alsace Lorraine. They also hoped to retain Austria and the Sudetenland area of Czechoslovakia, regions that the Nazis had seized in 1938.[210]

Because of their commitment to a federal system for Europe, the Kreisau Circle participants have largely been dismissed as a group of utopian dreamers. Furthermore, they believed that "all social and political systems were reaching a dead end and that capitalism and communism, no less than Nazism, were symptomatic of the crisis deep and all-encompassing in modern mass society."[211] They had a profound suspicion of capitalism and its attendant mass society. In fact, together with the Beck–Goerdeler group, they considered mass society to be "the great scourge of the time." Its egalitarianism "appalled" them.[212] Both groups wished to replace the undifferentiated and atomized totalitarian world of "mass man" with a restored sense of a genuine "organic community," or "rootedness and belonging based upon Christian values and local identities" transcending the fraudulent Nazi Volksgemeinschaft.[213] Some within the Kreisau Circle embraced what has been described as utopian socialism, in which the state not only protects the individual family but also provides its daily requirements, including "food, clothing, housing, a garden and health." Additionally, these people declared that "work must be so organized that it promotes a ready acceptance of responsibility."[214] This latter provision was similar to some of Goerdeler's ideas.

Doubtlessly recalling the unlamented Weimar Republic, many within the Kreisau group were at one with the Beck–Goerdeler group in their condemnation of the modern world that emerged out of the post-1918 experience. They both rejected the Western style parliamentary democracy that was part of the Weimar experiment.[215] Both wished to restore the rule of law and to reclaim basic individual freedoms that the Nazis had destroyed.[216] These goals were not necessarily incompatible with the restoration of an authoritarian government envisioned by some within the Beck–Goerdeler group. Basic freedoms had been guaranteed under the old empire, even though its government was authoritarian.

Until well after the outbreak of war, the strong religious convictions held by many within the Kreisau Circle prompted them to reject the use of force, or indeed any violent move of any sort – especially assassination – to achieve their goals. They were at one with Moltke on this question.[217] Although they agreed with the Beck–Goerdeler group that the period immediately following a successful coup would doubtlessly require a semiauthoritarian government, the Kreisau group was looking beyond the contemporary world to a post-Nazi Germany that would experience a "far-reaching social revolution," something the Beck–Goerdeler group did not envision.[218] However, the historian Peter Hoffmann has correctly dismissed "their ideas on the integration of classes and interests and elimination of social discord [as] romantic and idealistic – hardly compatible with a search for compromise and coalition politics."[219]

As the progress of the war increasingly pointed to Germany's ultimate defeat, Moltke, well aware of the inevitable outcome, pressed with an increasing sense of urgency to bring the ghastly conflict to a swift conclusion by means of a coup d'état. Accordingly, he began working with the military establishment in late 1943 to create conditions for a coup. Hence, from this point on, he was not "merely thinking"[220] about postwar Germany but actively working for an end to a conflict that was obviously all but lost. He fervently hoped to reduce further loss of life. This cooperation was enhanced with the appearance of Claus Schenk von Stauffenberg, whose leadership qualities and single-minded determination to destroy Hitler had thrust him into the leadership of the military conspiracy.[221] The Kreisau

Circle assisted in the planning for the coup and a provisional government and its personnel once Hitler was overthrown.

The Beck–Goerdeler group was more conservative in its outlook than the Kreisau Circle. Many in the former group, such as Hassell, envisioned a quasi-corporatist state for postwar Germany. Like the Kreisau group, however, they anticipated a moral rebirth in postwar Germany based upon Christian values. Both groups "regarded Christian values as the all-important foundation for the re-emergence of a morally upright Germany."[222]

Julius Leber and his fellow Social Democrats had serious reservations about the role of religion, however. Though definitely in favor of religious toleration and the elimination of proscriptions against the Jews, "they were strictly against mixing government activities with religion in any form."[223] In other words, they firmly believed in the separation of church and state, something the traditionalists and conservatives rejected, since such separation had never been a part of German history. Instead, the ecclesiastical leadership within the Evangelical Church proclaimed beliefs that had long been part of their tradition: "submission to legitimate authority, obedience to established traditions, avowal of national loyalty, and acknowledgement of religious faith."[224] Many conservatives within the resistance held fast to these convictions. As the socialists recalled the bitter conflicts between them and conservatives during the years of the Weimar Republic, they doubtlessly believed that this strong emphasis on the role of established religion in a post-Nazi Germany might well lead to a replay of those earlier days.

The ceaseless battle between social democracy and the forces of German conservatism continued unabated in the resistance movement, and especially within the Kreisau Circle. The ghost of Weimar continued to haunt the resistance movement. In the end, no agreement was ever reached among the resisters as to what kind of government a post-Hitler Germany should have. The resistance "tore itself apart in controversies" over several issues, such as socialism.[225] Although the two groups attempted to find unity in their plans for a post-Nazi Germany, they could not find common ground. "Moltke considered Goerdeler a reactionary, while more politically experienced men like Hassell thought many of the 'youngsters' unrealistic."[226]

From beginning to end, the civilian resistance suffered a debilitating lack of unity. It remained "a motley collection of individuals who differed greatly in their social origins, habits of thought, political attitudes and methods of action."²²⁷ These differences created insurmountable barriers. Vital questions remained unanswered: What exactly must be done to actually bring about the changes they all so fervently desired? Is assassination acceptable or not? Once it is decided *what* should be done, the next question was, *how* should it be done? What form should it take? What should replace the Nazi state? Should there be a social democracy, a monarchy, or something in between? These two civilian resistance groups – namely, the Kreisau Circle and the coalition that had formed under the leadership of Ludwig Beck and Carl Goerdeler – never provided adequate answers to these questions.

Individuals and Small Groups

As has been noted, an anti-Nazi resistance had been in existence from the beginning of Hitler's rule. Threats against Hitler's life had surfaced as early as the summer of 1933. Hitler himself, obviously aware of the danger, calculated that seven assassination attempts had been made in the first six years of the Third Reich's existence.²²⁸ The danger only increased as the "high noon" of Nazi popularity began to fade in the late thirties. By then, "a complex and widespread conspiracy was gathering. Whether their names have been quoted or not, all these people 'did' something to sabotage the government and assist in bringing about the fall of the regime."²²⁹

Yet they were completely unorganized. Many were individuals acting entirely alone. Georg Elser, the 1938 Munich Bürgerbräukeller bomber, is a prototypical example of these people. Others joined in very small groups of a few dozen or even less. They were motivated by the growing fear of an impending war and by an increased awareness of Nazism's true nature. Once that fear became reality, the incentive to remove Hitler increased dramatically, especially as the fortunes of war turned against Germany after 1942. It was said of them that they "did everything possible to undermine the Nazi tyranny."²³⁰ In many instances, opposition was expressed as simple dissent. Many individuals merely refused to conform to Nazi standards of behavior, such as giving the obligatory Nazi salute. In other instances, it was active opposition and conspiracy.

Particularly noteworthy in all of this was the realization of these people that even mere talk that was critical of the regime was dangerous activity. Such talk was an offense punishable by death under an infamous "treachery law." Those who "did no more than 'merely' express their abhorrence of the regime and talk about ways and means of dealing with it" were literally risking their lives.²³¹ Once World War II began, the situation became increasingly dangerous, especially as the conflict progressed to its dénouement. Yet these dissenters and conspirators were not deterred. In effect, they became prisoners of their own consciences. As evidence of the vile nature of Nazism mounted, people from every segment of German society responded as best they could with the means at their disposal. In some cases, it was simply taking an individual stand on moral principle, risking and in some cases sacrificing their lives in the process. Tragically, these groups and individuals had no leadership capable of mobilizing them for collective action. The army was the only institution that could have made a difference, but its leadership remained hopelessly divided.

* * * *

The name Franz Jägerstätter is, practically speaking, unknown to history. Yet it is a name that deserves to be honored. This man was a true martyr to his Christian faith and to his public rejection of Nazism and all it represented. He was very similar to Georg Elser in several ways. Both came from a humble background, both were among the faceless masses that are part of any modern society, and both had a white-hot hatred for the Nazis. In one respect, however, they differed. Whereas Elser took a path of active resistance, Jägerstätter was simply a dissenter and nonconformist. Nevertheless, he ultimately suffered the same fate as Elser.

Born in 1907 in the Upper Austrian village of Saint Radegund, Jägerstätter was the illegitimate child of very young parents – Rosalia Huber and Franz Bachmeier – who were too poor to marry. Both were servants. Later in life, Jägerstätter wrote of his poverty as a source of discrimination that he experienced as a youth. Presumably because of Rosalia's penurious condition, the care of his early life was given to his maternal grandmother, although Bachmeier evidently did provide support for Rosalia.[232] Subsequent to Bachmeier's death in the Great War as a soldier in the Austro-Hungarian Army, Rosalia married Heinrich Jägerstätter, a relatively prosperous farmer, who gave young Franz his surname.[233] This change also gave the young boy access to a small theological library. His former schoolmates remembered him as an avid reader.[234] His contemporaries also remembered him as "fun-loving and popular."[235] His interests ranged from bowling to dancing to playing the zither to studying shorthand. He purchased the first motorcycle in his village. He also is alleged to have led a rather unruly life in his youth, although the degree of its intensity has been disputed.[236]

After completing his schooling, Jägerstätter worked as a farm laborer and in a nearby iron mine for a time, but ultimately he returned to Saint Radegund to work on his adoptive father's farm. In the interim, he underwent a profound religious conversion that some – but not everyone – described as "sudden and complete."[237] Regardless of the speed of his transformation, all agreed that it was significant. He became a "new man"[238] and contemplated entering the priesthood, but his parish priest dissuaded him, arguing that Franz should take over management of the family farm and also care for his aging mother and adoptive father.

Jägerstätter's religious conversion and his anti-Nazi convictions are directly related. Gordon Zahn, his biographer, spent a considerable period of time in Saint Radegund interviewing villagers who knew him, and he has written the following account of those interviews:

> The villagers' memories of the changed man emphasize two major points: his intense and open religiosity and his thoroughgoing opposition to the Nazi regime. These two characteristics of his later thought and behavior are so closely interwoven that it is sometimes difficult to treat them separately.[239]

Jägerstätter's contemporaries considered his marriage to Franziska Schwaninger in 1936 to be a significant influence in his transformation from a rather rowdy and unruly youth to a very devout and dedicated Christian, because she was a woman of faith and deep spiritual conviction. Many years later, she said, "We helped one another go forward in faith."[240]

In the meantime, the world around the couple was changing rapidly. The Nazis had come to power in Germany in 1933, and by the summer of 1938, they also were in control of Austria. Moreover, thanks to Hitler's insane ambitions, Europe was headed toward war. Soon, Franz Jägerstätter's life would change dramatically – and fatally. March 1938 brought the Anschluss (connection) to Austria, when the Austrian government capitulated to Nazi demands for annexation under threat of military force. Although this event produced what has been described as "unbelievable euphoria" throughout Austria, "popular enthusiasm was by no means universal."[241]

Jägerstätter was one of those who greeted these changes with consternation and dismay. His opposition to the Nazis was evident from the outset and has been described as "thoroughgoing."[242] For some time, he had observed the Nazis' murderous activity just across the Saltzach River in Bavaria, and he had gotten a close-up view of them in 1934, when the Austrian Nazis – a branch of the German Nazi Party – made an abortive move to seize power in their own country. The so-called "legitimization" of the 1938 Anschluss by means of a carefully controlled and staged plebiscite in which the Austrian public gave its virtually unanimous approval dismayed Jägerstätter and is said to have been "one of the darkest days in [his] life."[243] His active opposition to the Nazis began with a pointed decision to vote *nein* in that plebiscite. His negative vote was the first step on a road of opposition to Nazi rule that led to his death five years later.[244] Like Georg Elser, he outwardly and flagrantly displayed his loathing for Hitler and the Nazis. For example, he regularly responded to the mandatory "Heil Hitler" salutation with "Pfui Hitler" (Pooh on Hitler).[245]

The buildup of the Nazi war machine, which had been going on for several years, became even more intense after 1938, and Austria, now a part of Germany, found itself being swept into the vortex of Nazi militarism. Inevitably, Austrian males were being called to military service in the Wehrmacht. Jägerstätter received his orders to register for conscription in April 1939.[246] His actual conscription came in June 1940, although he was released within a very short time because both his wife and mother became seriously ill and he was needed at home to take care of their needs. He was conscripted two more times over the next year and a half, but in each case, he was released from military service because the local authorities in Saint Radegund secured an exemption for him based upon his work in a "reserved civilian occupation."[247] Jägerstätter made no attempt to secure an exemption on his own behalf, however.[248] An exchange of correspondence with his wife indicates that he did not wish to become beholden to the local party officials in Saint Radegund. Instead, "he initially even chose military service rather than having to go to the village officials, whom he regarded as representatives of the Party, to ask for their support in gaining exemption."[249] He now was a civilian released from military obligations.

Over the next two years, Jägerstätter's convictions about military service to the Third Reich became more fixed. His limited experience as a military recruit had convinced him that "he could no longer be part of [the army]."[250] Franziska Jägerstätter, speaking of her husband years later, said that after his return from military service in April 1941, he vowed "never to serve in the army again."[251] He spoke freely to others in Saint Radegund about this decision, and he resisted all efforts to dissuade him. This was a time when he became more committed than ever to his faith. Shortly after his discharge, he was appointed sacristan (i.e., he was in charge of the church sacristy, where the sacred vessels, vestments, and so on are kept). Also, while still in the army, he became a novice in an organization of laity and clergy within the Roman Catholic Church known as the Third Order of Saint Francis. He became more firmly convinced than ever that Nazism represented unspeakable evil and that an unbridgeable chasm existed between Christianity and Nazism. Simply stated, he saw the issue as a struggle between good and evil.

He was recalled to active duty in February 1943. The year is significant because the Battle of Stalingrad had recently taken place and German military forces were now in a full retreat, a situation that would end two years later in unconditional surrender. The casualties were mounting, and the armed forces needed every able-bodied man – and some not so able-bodied – that they could put their hands on. This time, however, Jägerstätter refused to serve. On March 1, 1943, he wrote to his wife, "Today I am going to take the difficult step."[252] He then went to the induction center at the nearby town of Enns, whereupon he declared his intention to refuse the conscription order, "because [according to the Reich court-martial papers] he rejects National Socialism (Nazism) and therefore does not wish to perform military Service."[253] Subsequently he was arrested and sent to a military prison at Linz.[254] On May 4, he was transferred to Tegel Prison in Berlin.[255] Throughout this period, people from all walks of life tried to persuade him to change his mind, but he refused.

The court-martial trial was held on July 6, 1943.[256] As could be expected, it was a parody of true justice. The comment of General Wilhelm Keitel, chief of the OKW, tells us something about the integrity of the court-martial system within the Wehrmacht with the following words: "It goes without saying that it is a prerequisite that each judge, of whatever rank, should be firmly rooted in the National Socialist (Nazi) worldview, and should orient his work according to its principles."[257] Like all else within the Nazi state, the military establishment's judicial process was fraudulent. The judges were committed "to safeguard the rule of the Nazi state."[258] Jägerstätter was charged with "harming the war effort." The specific language of the penal law reads as follows:

> The death penalty shall be levied against ... anyone who publically advocates or incites the refusal to perform the required service in the German army or one allied with it or otherwise openly seeks to weaken or undermine the desire of the German people or any allied with it to maintain its military effectiveness.[259]

One last thread of hope remained, Jägerstätter's expressed willingness to serve as a military paramedic. After his execution, his widow, Franziska, spoke to her husband's court-appointed lawyer and asked him about the question of medical service. The writer Erna Putz, who interviewed Franziska, describes the lawyer's response as "cynical," because it suggests that Jägerstätter's doom had been sealed even before judicial proceedings were initiated. "We could certainly have done that, but we didn't," was his reply.[260] In sum, the lawyer simply neglected to investigate the possibility of allowing Jägerstätter to became a medical aide in lieu of performing regular military service. That neglect led directly to Jägerstätter's death. The anticipated guilty verdict was declared shortly after the trial, and the sentence was immediately carried out. He was beheaded on August 9, 1943.

Throughout this entire ordeal from 1941 to 1943, Franz kept up a voluminous correspondence and held discussions with family, friends, clergy, and former comrades in arms about his religious convictions and his ultimate rejection of military service. As this surviving correspondence suggests, it all came down to a simple question of individual responsibility, a position that bears a striking resemblance to the one taken by Dietrich Bonhoeffer. Jägerstätter's biographer, Gordon Zahn, has summarized his belief as follows:

> Jägerstätter justified his stand by insisting that this was the kind of a moral judgment that ultimately has to be made by the individual conscience, especially since the point at issue concerned precisely the distinction between the "things that are Caesar's" and the "things that are God's."[261]

Although others, such as Jägerstätter's attorney, tried to persuade him that he had a responsibility to his wife and children, as well as to other members of his family, he responded, in Zahn's words, that "the dictates of conscience must always be given precedence even over such personal considerations."[262]

Franz Jägerstätter died not because of any treasonous activity. He died because of the demands of his conscience. He said, "I cannot reconcile my conscience with fighting for the Führer."[263] He proclaimed his absolute opposition to the Third Reich simply because he saw it as "an intrinsically immoral government which could have no claim on the loyalty of a Christian subject."[264] His moral compass showed remarkable accuracy, clarity, and consistency when he stated, "I do not believe that Christ ever said that one must obey such rulers when they command something that is actually wicked."[265] This comment summarizes almost perfectly the stand taken by others – especially military officers – who ultimately would engage in a conspiracy to kill Hitler and overthrow the Third Reich.

In this instance, we have a simple, untutored Austrian peasant, lacking erudition and sophistication, acting alone, but demonstrating a wisdom and perception far beyond many who were much more highly educated and accomplished than he. Jägerstätter recognized "both the evil of the day and the responsibilities it placed upon him as a believing Christian – and [he accepted] those responsibilities though they led to the grave."[266] Perhaps the very simplicity of his faith and the isolation of living in a small community virtually untouched by the distractions of a complex outside world made the difference. Perhaps it was these conditions that gave him a moral sensitivity that many of his contemporaries lacked. It is known that Jägerstätter never had contacts with anti-Nazi groups. He was a solitary witness to his faith.[267]

* * * *

Georg Elser declared his opposition to the Nazis with a single act of resistance taken by one lone individual. Franz Jägerstätter's opposition was an expression of simple dissent. He refused military service. Kurt Gerstein represented a third path of opposition. He became part of the Nazi system in an attempt to undermine it from within. He was, in the words of the writer Saul Friedländer, a "counterfeit Nazi."[268] Gerstein was born in Münster in the state of Westphalia in 1905 into what has been described as a "conventional German middle class family"[269] of Prussian origin. His father, who had been an officer in the Prussian Army and later became a "pious and emotionally unbending judge,"[270] was intensely nationalistic to the point of being a racist. Gerstein had deep religious convictions and was active in the Evangelical Youth Movement, but paradoxically he joined the Nazi Party and the SA in 1933 in an attempt to reconcile his religious beliefs with the ultranationalistic politics of his family. He also developed close ties with the Confessing Church of Bonhoeffer and Niemöller.[271]

These contradictions could not be resolved, however. Gerstein became increasingly disillusioned with the Nazis, and as early as 1935, he openly expressed his disapproval of Nazi behavior in a variety of ways. This earned for him not only expulsion from the party but also arrest and subsequent incarceration in a concentration camp on two separate occasions. Thereafter he studied medicine and mining engineering. By the early war years, he decided that the best way to work against the apparatus of death was from within. In his words, he wanted to "see things from the inside."[272] In March 1941 he joined the SS and became a "spy for God,"[273] explaining in a letter to his wife, "I joined the SS ... acting as an agent of the Confessing Church."[274]

In January 1942, Gerstein became head of the Technical Hygiene Section in SS headquarters. In this position, he was responsible for obtaining the poison gas used for the extermination of concentration camp victims. Although he was able to sabotage consignments of the poison gas, his primary objective was to tell the outside world what actually was going on inside the death camps. He contacted foreign government representatives, such as a Swedish diplomat and a Swiss press attaché, plus several clergymen, in what proved to be a vain attempt to expose the gruesome work of these camps. He hoped that these revelations would cause a worldwide furor and also induce the German people to rise en masse against the Nazis. Many German citizens at the time were defying the Nazi authorities and listening to the BBC's radio programs. Nonetheless, Nazi control over the German nation made the dissemination of the facts of Nazi horrors virtually impossible, and Gerstein's efforts to rouse his nation against its rulers were futile. Moreover, the very magnitude and scope of the crimes was so great that initial news of them was greeted with skepticism and disbelief both within and outside Germany, and international news sources did not carry the story with sufficient determination to affect the course of events.[275]

The end of the war found Kurt Gerstein in Reutlingen, Germany, where he surrendered to the Allies. Initially treated sympathetically, he later was transferred to a French military prison, where it is believed that he was treated as a war criminal.[276] Tragically, he had deliberately implicated himself as an accomplice and participant in the Holocaust because of his work in the SS. Evidently the strain of the war and the double role he had played in it, coupled with his arrest as a war criminal, overwhelmed and broke him. He committed suicide in July 1945. His story is an object lesson in "the pitfalls of opposing a totalitarian regime from the inside."[277]

* * * *

A brief glance at just four of many very small, dedicated, and diverse dissenting groups within the Third Reich provides a hint of the widespread character of the resistance movement. The people who were part of these groups were not involved in any plot to overthrow Nazi rule, nor were they at all committed to do so, although one of the groups did carry out minor acts of sabotage on occasion. Their mere existence gave lie to Nazi pretensions of a racially and ideologically pure Volksgemeinschaft. Therefore, they had to be mercilessly suppressed. And for that, many of them paid with their lives.

First, there was a group of young German teenagers known as the Edelweiss Pirates (Edelweiß Piraten), who wanted to enjoy a social life free from the suffocating control of the Hitler Youth. These young dissenters engaged in a variety of nonconformist and illegal activities, including dancing to "degenerate" American jazz and swing music. Especially during the war years, they increasingly participated in actual resistance activities, such as giving protection to army deserters, participating in minor acts of industrial sabotage, surreptitiously distributing anti-Nazi leaflets dropped by Allied bombers, writing anti-Nazi graffiti in streets and subways, and even participating in pitched battles with the Hitler Youth. The government reacted with a vicious crackdown. Several Edelweiss Pirates leaders in Cologne were hanged in late 1944.[278]

There also was the White Rose (Weiße Rose), whose leaders were Sophie Scholl and her brother Hans, students at the University of Munich, who printed a series of clandestine pamphlets condemning Nazi rule and calling for resistance to it. Together with several like-minded students, all of whom were inspired by their Christian faith and commitment to humanistic ideals, they distributed these pamphlets throughout Germany and Austria. Arrested in 1943, they were brought to trial before the infamous People's Court, with the equally infamous Roland Freisler as the presiding judge, of whom more will be said subsequently. The inevitable guilty verdict brought with it the sentence of death by beheading. Almost immediately thereafter, a Nazi-inspired rally was held at the university condemning the White Rose and its activities, accompanied by the obligatory "Sieg heil"s and pledges of loyalty to the regime. Nonetheless, graffiti appeared on the walls of the university several days later that read, "Despite Everything, Their Spirit Lives On. Scholl Lives!"[279]

A third resistance group was the "Solf Circle," so named for Hanna Solf, who was the widow of Wilhelm Solf, a highly regarded former German diplomat. It was said of this group that it was in no way subversive but that it "consisted of ... like-minded people who simply wished to oppose and counter the oppression, persecution, humiliation, and degradation of human beings by the regime."[280] All of them were arrested in 1944, largely because several had attended a social gathering the previous September in which highly critical comments had been made of the Nazis. Informers in that gathering reported the comments to the Gestapo. Arrests also included people whose only offense was membership in the group. Several were executed merely because they "had stood up for humanity." One such person was Albrecht Graf von Bernstorff, a retired senior counselor in the foreign office. He has been described as "one of the most courageous opponents of Hitler; he concentrated mainly on helping émigrés and Jews to escape and saving their belongings." He, too, died at the hands of the Nazis.[281]

A fourth group, the Rote Kapelle (Red Orchestra), had a Marxist orientation, but it was independent of Moscow. Rather than a single organization, it has been described as "a series of overlapping and functionally rather different clandestine groups."[282] Total membership of the Rote Kapelle numbered about 150 men and women.[283] What's more, "it was subject neither to Communist discipline nor to Stalinist ideology."[284] Their activities included helping political refugees to escape from Germany, distributing anti-Nazi literature, and passing information about Nazi war crimes to both the Soviet and American Embassies. Its leaders were Arvid Harnack, a civil servant in the Nazi Economics Ministry, and Harro Schulze-Boysen, an attaché to the Air Ministry. Harnack's American wife, Mildred Harnack-Fish, also was active in the Rote Kapelle. Arrested in September 1942, they, along with over 50 other members of the group, were executed after rapid sham trials. This brought an end to the group's activities. Rote Kapelle was but one of several left-wing resistance organizations, most of which were much smaller in membership numbers.[285]

All of these individual and small-group actions that were taken against the Third Reich during its twelve-year rule were magnificent statements of moral purpose, but they lacked the two ingredients essential to a successful overthrow of Nazi rule: leadership and mass support. Absent pure chance, a successful decapitation of the Nazi state by such groups was highly unlikely. Adolf Hitler was a wily and elusive target. Only a well-developed plan and inspired leadership could ensure success in any conspiracy capable of freeing Germany from the iron grip of National Socialism. Success required the active participation of the German Army in any plot to remove Hitler from power. The army had to take control of the anti-Nazi resistance movement. It is to this topic that we now turn.

CHAPTER 4

An Organized Resistance

Of all the groups that became part of the anti-Nazi resistance, the one with the greatest potential for forming a conspiracy capable of actually overthrowing the Nazi regime was the German Army. Aside from the Nazi Party itself, only the army had direct access to Hitler.

Like others, however, many within the army leadership had an ambivalent attitude toward Hitler and the Nazi Party. Their initial support for Hitler and his so-called "movement" was very strong. Most of the older generals displayed the prejudices of their social class in their disdain for the plebian nature of the Nazis, and they naïvely believed that they could control the Nazis and use them for their own purposes. This proved to be one of the greatest miscalculations in all of modern history.

The Blood Purge
Within a year of Adolf Hitler's accession to power, several higher-ranking officers who initially had supported the Nazis were beginning to have second thoughts about this man; so much hope had been placed on him for restoring the German nation to its former great-power status and purifying it of the perceived corruption and moral decay that had accompanied the recently departed and unlamented Weimar Republic. However, a first warning of darker times ahead went unheeded, and the consequences were grim. That warning came on June 30, 1934, when Hitler instigated the infamous Night of the Long Knives, or blood purge, which was a preemptive assault launched against his enemies, perceived and actual, both within and outside the Nazi Party. Among those shot were his longtime Nazi Party associate Ernst Röhm, who at the time was head of the Nazi "army," that is, the SA (Sturm Abteilung, or storm troopers), as well as General Kurt von Schleicher, who had helped to engineer Hitler's appointment as chancellor, and Gustav von Kahr, who had been minister-president of Bavaria at the time of the Beer Hall Putsch episode. Each man had incurred Hitler's wrath in one way or another.

From Hitler's perspective, Röhm represented the most dangerous threat. He was the leader of a left-wing Nazi faction that was promoting a "second revolution." The first had been the so-called "Machtergreifung," or "seizure of power" that had taken place on January 30, 1933. Röhm and his followers wanted a thoroughgoing social revolution that would displace the ruling classes and replace the professional army – the Reichswehr and its officer corps – with the SA, which would become a national "people's army." These "wilder spirits"[1] were especially incensed because they believed that they had been denied the spoils of victory. Hitler had betrayed them, and the "establishment" was still in power.[2]

However, Hitler still needed the support of the conservatives, especially the army, and he could not afford to alienate them at this point. Furthermore, these people – the army leadership in particular – were demanding that he take action against Röhm's increasing indiscipline. Defense Minister General Werner von Blomberg, Commander in Chief Werner von Fritsch (army), and General Ludwig Beck, chief of the army Truppenamt (Troop Office), were deeply concerned about the implicit threat coming from Röhm and his SA. Fritsch, in particular, was a prototypical Prussian officer, and he especially held "an arrogant contempt for the vulgarity of the Nazis."[3]

In addition to the entreaties of the army leadership to "do something" about Röhm and his SA, Hitler recognized the threat that Röhm represented to his absolute control of the party. For these two reasons, therefore, Hitler's former friend and partner was at the top of his hit list.[4] Schleicher was near the top of the death list as well, because he had frustrated Hitler's bid for the chancellor's office in the summer of 1932, when the Nazis were at the peak of their power in the Reichstag. Although Schleicher had helped to engineer Hitler's appointment in January 1933, Hitler had never forgotten the earlier affront, and he was determined to wreak his vengeance. General Kurt von Bredow, Schleicher's aide, was marked for death as well. The reason for Kahr's death is obvious. He had broken up Hitler's coup attempt at the Bürgerbräukeller in 1923.

Thus, old scores were settled and personal rivals were liquidated.[5] In the predawn hours of June 30, Hitler dispatched units of the SS and Gestapo throughout the length and breadth of Germany to administer Nazi-style "justice" to the miscreants who had dared to challenge, or even question, his authority. The rampage lasted for some forty-eight hours,[6] and it effectively destroyed the SA as a political threat to the Third Reich and as a military threat to the Reichswehr, although it remained in existence and continued to precipitate violence on occasion.[7] The actual number of persons murdered as a result of the blood purge may never be determined with absolute accuracy. Estimates vary widely, from less than one hundred to over a thousand.[8] Hitler himself, "explaining" the episode in a "tense and often contradictory speech"[9] to the Reichstag the following July, admitted to seventy-four deaths. At least eighty-five are known to have died.[10] Regardless of the actual number, the important point is that this was the first mass murder perpetrated by the Third Reich. The dead had been executed "without trial, without a chance to defend themselves, victims of a brutal Party and gang intrigue."[11]

While this orgy of mayhem and murder was going on, the army sat on its hands. Not only did it do nothing to prevent the SS and Gestapo from carrying out their gruesome work, but also it actually was complicit in this affair in that it had supplied trucks and weaponry to the killers. In an act of almost stupefying moral obtuseness, the army leadership, especially Defense Minister von Blomberg, who already was "favourably disposed to the Nazis" as well as being a "naïve, weak and somewhat unrealistic" man,[12] together with others, including some of the men who a few years hence would become the solid core of the army conspiracy against Hitler, expressed their satisfaction that the SA had been dealt a mortal blow.

The late historian Gordon A. Craig has written, "It is difficult to avoid the conclusion that the leaders of the army closed their eyes to the slaughter and their minds to everything but the thought of the advantages which the elimination of the S.A. would bring to them."[13] General Erwin von Witzleben, who would become one of the dominant figures in the as yet unformed resistance movement within the army, reportedly responded with the word "splendid" when he learned that the SA had been destroyed as a military organization. Even the young lieutenant Claus von Stauffenberg, who would place the bomb at Hitler's headquarters on July 20, 1944, likened the episode to the "lancing of a boil."[14]

Aside from the obvious satisfaction of seeing a rival's demise, perhaps the only rational explanation for the behavior of these men is that they allowed themselves to be blinded by their own prejudices. They were fixated on the memory of Germany's recent imperial greatness, when the army enjoyed a privileged position in German society, and they believed that a "purified" Nazi party led by a Führer now freed from the debilitating and noxious influence of Röhm and his SA minions would be able to pursue Hitler's goal of building a restored and revitalized fatherland. This fixation distorted their moral perspective to such a degree that they did not even respond to the murder of two of their own, Schleicher and Bredow. The behavior of the army leadership in this entire affair has been correctly described as "moral capitulation."[15] Such are the dangers of nostalgia.

Even so, many of the officers were dismayed not only by the extent and ferocity of the episode but also, more importantly, by its implications for the future. General Ludwig Beck was one of those officers. Henning von Tresckow and Hans Oster were two others. Thus, the "tightly closed ranks of the army began to crack."[16] The blood purge was a warning to the army of what lay ahead, but many failed to heed it. The Reichswehr leadership congratulated itself that their army was now free from the menace of an SA state. However, a much more threatening and sinister organization was now poised to challenge the army. An SS state would become a reality all too soon.[17]

An Oath of Allegiance

Without realizing it, the officer corps of the Reichswehr were already playing Faust to Hitler's Mephistopheles as early as the summer of 1934. The first indication was the blood purge episode. The second came just thirty-four days later at the death of Germany's president Paul von Hindenburg.

Hindenburg was a war hero of almost mythic proportions. He – and his chief of staff, Erich Ludendorff – had brought to Germany its first military victory of the Great War at the Battle of Tannenberg against the Russians, an event that had catapulted him to national prominence. The German people, desperate for a hero in 1914, idolized him. He became a revered figure, a modern Siegfried. He acquired an aura of invincibility that never left him, even after the ignominious defeat in 1918.[18] These facts are a clear indication of the reason for Hitler's attempt to identify himself with the honored field marshal at the time of the garrison church ceremony in 1933. Hindenburg retired from the army in June 1919. However, he returned to the public arena in 1925, when he was elected president of the Weimar Republic, replacing SPD leader Friedrich Ebert, who had died. He was reelected in 1932. At this point, the republic was near death. With considerable misgivings, he submitted to the importuning of General Kurt von Schleicher and Franz von Papen and appointed Hitler as chancellor on January 30, 1933. By the following year, however, the aged field marshal's health was deteriorating rapidly.

Hitler bided his time, and when Hindenburg died on August 2, 1934, at the age of eighty-four, he moved within one hour to combine the offices of president and chancellor, creating the position of leader and chancellor of the realm (Führer und Reichskanzler), an action that significantly increased his power and prestige. It also was an act of blatant illegality and unconstitutionality. A day earlier, the government, that is the cabinet, not the Reichstag, had unanimously passed a "law" combining the two offices into one, to be put into effect immediately after the death of the president. A carefully controlled referendum, that is, a sham plebiscite, affirmed this "law" on August 19.[19] Preceding all of this was an earlier law passed the previous January – the Act for the Reconstruction of the Reich – allowing the government to "lay down fresh constitutional legislation."[20] However, this January law violated Article 2 of the Enabling Act of March 1933, which had specifically prohibited "the government from making any changes to the office of the Reich president."[21]

The implications for the military establishment were profound. As with other parliamentary systems, the Weimar Constitution had stipulated that the president was the chief executive and that the chancellor (prime minister) was head of government. Unlike the chief of state in many parliamentary governments, however, the president of the Weimar Republic had substantial powers, which included control of the army. Article 47 of the Weimar Constitution stated this power in unequivocal terms: "The Reich President has the supreme command over the armed forces, in their entirety."[22] That system, still in place in 1934, came to an abrupt end with Hindenburg's death. As Führer und Reichskanzler, Hitler now was in a position to assume complete control over the nation's military establishment. "So by unconstitutional methods Hitler obtained constitutional authority over the Reichswehr."[23] A coup d'état against the army had taken place.

There was more. On the afternoon and evening of that same day, August 2, a new oath of allegiance was introduced to the Reichswehr. It was very simple and clear: "I swear by God this holy oath, that I will render to Adolf Hitler, Führer of the German Reich and People, Supreme Commander of the Armed Forces, unconditional obedience, and that I am ready, as a brave soldier, to risk my life at any time for this oath."[24] It thus declared complete loyalty to the person of Adolf Hitler rather than to the office he held, and was required of every single member of the German Army.

According to Hitler's biographer, Ian Kershaw, the coauthors of the oath were General Walter von Reichenau, a man known for his pro-Nazi sympathies, and General Werner von Blomberg, minister of defense. Evidently their goal was to "cement a special relationship" between Hitler and the army that would separate him from the party.²⁵ The oath also may have represented an attempt to induce Hitler to make a similar commitment to preserve and protect the army. Such a statement was soon forthcoming. Hitler fulsomely expressed his gratitude for the document and declared that since "the officers and soldiers of the Wehrmacht have pledged themselves to the new State in my person, so will I at all times regard it as my highest duty to intercede in behalf of the stability and inviolability of the Wehrmacht."²⁶ The phrase "in my person" has been described as the ultimate expression of the totalitarian system that was descending upon Germany. The oath itself became the single most important obstacle to effective resistance activity on the part of the army.²⁷

The reason for the existence of this obstacle can only be found in the history of the Prussian Army. Prussia, as a constituent state of the German federation, had occupied a dominant position in Imperial Germany, and its army and traditions provided the foundation for the modern German Army. For example, many – indeed most – of the senior officers had been trained in Prussian military schools, and the Prussian General Staff became the German General Staff after Germany's unification in 1871. In fact, an "imperial army" did not exist in the German Empire. Instead, there were the armies of several states, of which the Prussian Army was dominant. Practically speaking, the national army was the Prussian Army writ large. During wartime, command of the other armies came under the command of the Prussian Army and General Staff.²⁸ For these reasons, a proper understanding of the place of this oath of allegiance in the German military tradition and its importance to the Reichswehr requires a proper understanding of that oath in the Prussian military tradition. This, in turn, requires one more excursion into Prussian-German history.

* * * *

Deeply embedded in the Prussian ethos was a personal oath of allegiance to the head of state that dated back to the seventeenth century. It represented a kind of social contract between the king and the Junker aristocracy, which was the social class from which members of the officer corps were recruited. This contract provided the foundation for the officer corps and indicated a system of mutual rights and obligations in which the king granted the Junkers complete freedom in the control they exercised over the peasants who lived on their estates in exchange for an oath of fealty pledging their service to the king. Unlike contemporary armies of seventeenth- and early eighteenth-century Europe, the social prestige that accrued to the members of the Prussian officer corps was considerable and was based upon the fact that they were soldiers of the king rather than members of a social class. This further cemented the relationship of the king to his army.[29] Prussian officers viewed their oath as a "personal link with their Head of State," which they saw as "the essence of their military honour." Additionally, they took "great pride [in the fact] that they had publicly indicated their willingness to lay down their lives in his service. To him they pledged unconditional obedience, simply because conditional obedience was the antithesis of the discipline that formed the basis of military life." Even though these men were not the king's property, "they were bound to obey him, and he could launch them on any operation that he saw fit."[30] The creation of the Prussian officer corps has been described as a marriage between the soldier-king and the Junker aristocracy.[31] To at least one member of an earlier generation of Prussian officers, this oath also represented a bond between a Prussian officer and his monarch that was an echo from the ancient German tribal past, a time when covenants of mutual duty and fealty were sworn between the chieftain and his warriors. This was the relationship that Hitler corrupted.[32]

The traumatic changes that came to Germany with the conclusion of the Great War brought a significant alteration to the entire military establishment. Gone was Imperial Germany, together with its traditional military organization. In its place was the new Weimar Republic. A liberal democracy had replaced an authoritarian monarchy, creating confusion and ambivalence for the officer corps. This new political structure brought with it a system of governance and a set of values that were entirely unfamiliar to the German nation and its army. This was nowhere more evident than in the new oath required of the officer corps in the reorganized military establishment that was now known as the Reichswehr. It was an oath not to defend the head of state but to defend the Weimar Constitution.

A written constitution had been created for Imperial Germany as well, although the army did not swear an oath to defend it.[33] Thus, an oath to defend an abstract document such as the Constitution of the Weimar Republic had no precedent in the history of the Prussian Army, and an oath to protect what for them was a meaningless document – a mere scrap of paper, as it were – made no sense whatsoever.[34] Moreover, this new oath only increased the overweening disdain they already held for the republic.

These soldiers, regardless of rank, were committed to the ethos of that earlier time, when an oath of allegiance was, from their perspective, a sacred trust. The tragedy underlying this entire matter is that they – or most of them – did not anticipate the extent to which their leader would betray that trust. These men failed to grasp the fact that Adolf Hitler would desecrate and corrupt that sacred oath all too soon. Too many officers failed to comprehend the difference between an oath of allegiance given to a Frederick the Great or any other Prussian king and that same oath given to an Adolf Hitler. Tragically, the hatred that most members of the German military establishment held for the unlamented Weimar Republic blinded them to this fact. All but a very few failed to grasp the significance of what they were doing. By swearing the oath, they were unwittingly descending into a moral quagmire because they did not understand that Hitler had absolutely no intention of honoring his commitment to maintain the "stability and inviolability of the Wehrmacht." He, in fact, cared not for the protection and preservation of the army. His sole interest lay in using the military establishment as an instrument enabling him to create a totalitarian state, which then would provide him with the means of pursuing a monstrous foreign policy of limitless expansion and genocide.

The officers did not understand that in giving their word of honor and making a pledge or promise to follow Adolf Hitler unconditionally, they were giving their fealty to a man who would lead their nation inexorably over a moral abyss to absolute catastrophe. When the ultimate realization did come, it was too late. For the less principled, the oath provided a rationale for inaction and a convenient excuse not to take part in any resistance activity. Regardless of their motives, they exercised incredibly poor judgment when they handed this gift to Adolf Hitler, because his pledge of support for the Wehrmacht was worthless, a dead letter from the start. "After all, an oath is but an empty form of words if the substance, the idea that lies behind it, is dead."[35]

This entire episode is yet one more illustration of the way that Hitler perverted and corrupted the noble and honored traditions of the nation he ruled and then used them to serve his demented purposes. This became one of the major hallmarks of Hitler's behavior as Germany's Führer. In this particular case, the victim had contrived to hand the executioner the weapon of his own destruction. The army leadership was guilty of "moral capitulation."[36] What appeared to be a return to the historic Prussian values was in fact a step toward the complete emasculation of the German Army.

Most of those who were part of the army leadership willingly accepted the new oath without question. Others, however, had serious misgivings. They had a premonition of darker days ahead. A "depressed mood" is recorded in the personal memoirs of some of these men. Baron

Rudolph-Christoph von Gersdorff, who would play an important role in the conspiracy against Hitler in the war years, believed that the members of the officer corps had been "coerced" into accepting the oath. Its net effect was to raise doubts about Hitler, especially among the younger members of the officer corps. Heretofore, most of these men had been "unstinting in their trust and confidence" in the Führer and in his message.[37] Their apprehensions would only increase with the passage of time.

General Ludwig Beck in particular expressed his darkest forebodings of what the consequences might be. He described August 2 as "the blackest day of my life," and seriously considered resigning his commission.[38] One of the earliest critics of the Nazis, he played an active role in the resistance from the beginning. Beck represented the older generation of officers, whose doubts about Hitler and his "movement" became ever greater with the passage of time.

Many younger officers shared these doubts. Though they were the sons of the Prussian aristocracy, the ethos of the Prussian officer corps and the restoration of the old order were much less important to them than to their fathers. Hence, they were less inhibited by the oath than were their elders. Typical of these men was Adam von Trott zu Solz, a lawyer who became an ardent opponent of the Nazis and who was executed in August 1944 after the failed bomb plot on Hitler's life. He declared that these younger men should "avoid any hint of being reactionary, of gentlemen's clubs, or of militarism."[39] Another man who personified this younger group was the aforementioned Hans Oster, whose hatred of the Nazis was absolute. He had an uncommon clarity in his understanding of the Nazis and realized that Hitler had no intention of restoring a vanished world. He also saw that National Socialism was an "entirely new phenomenon" and that "it was an ideology of such sinister immorality that traditional values and loyalties no longer applied."[40] Therefore, the so-called "Hitler oath" was completely meaningless for him.

* * * *

The burden of this oath of allegiance became extremely heavy for practically all the members of the officer corps, regardless of their political convictions and their attitudes toward the Nazis. The word of a Prussian officer was considered inviolate and was part of a sacred code of honor. None of these men took the oath lightly. Even several of the most dedicated army conspirators wrestled with their consciences as they deliberately violated that oath. We have the example of Henning von Tresckow, who described

Hitler as the "destroyer of his own country" and the "source of all evil," but who nonetheless struggled to reconcile the fact of the oath with his contradictory behavior as a conspirator. Not long before his death by suicide on July 21, 1944, he declared, "We aren't really criminals," which, according to his biographer, gives a clear indication of his self-doubts.[41] It has been said that the anti-Hitler conspiracy "was probably the first time in Prussian history that generals had plotted against the civilian power, and it was particularly significant because the whole notion of conspiracy was incompatible with the traditionally sacred officer's oath."[42]

This tragic situation demonstrated both Hitler's uncanny, almost demonic, charismatic powers of persuasion and the incredible naïveté of some members of the officer corps. They failed to grasp the underlying reality of an oath, namely that it is a proverbial two-way street. "If such solemn undertakings are to be given they presuppose a degree of moral and political obligation on the part of the individual to whom they are given."[43] Nazi Germany was a land without justice. All norms of ethical behavior had disappeared. The government was undermining the very foundations of the society that it was committed to uphold, preserve, and protect. Its commitments, national and international, were completely worthless. Consequently, the oath of allegiance extracted from the army had absolutely no validity. It was, in fact, illegal, because it violated not only the Weimar Constitution that technically was still in place but also a law passed by the Nazis themselves on December 1, 1933. This law, known as the Oath Act, committed those who took it to serve the people and nation; but there was no reference to the person of Adolf Hitler. The oath of August 1934 was a vow of loyalty not to constitution or nation, but only to the Führer.[44]

Tragically, those generals who were determined to uphold this latest oath displayed a kind of tunnel vision. It was as if they had put blinders on and could not or would not see their responsibilities either to their fatherland or to the outside world. Too many of them, such as General Franz Halder, exhibited behavior characterized by "weakness, devotion to military duty and formalism,"[45] which allowed Nazi rule to flourish and ultimately bring total devastation to their homeland. The position of Field Marshal Günther von Kluge is a special case in point. He has been described as "a gifted commander but a weak man."[46] It was said of him that he "typified the inability of many senior German officers to break the bonds of tradition, obedience and patriotic loyalty." Whenever the time came for him to commit to the resistance, he would demur and "always reverted to the oath of loyalty he had sworn."[47] The only way to free such men as these from this excessive devotion to their oath was to eliminate the man to whom the oath was given. Hitler had to be assassinated.

The resistance leaders grasped the issue clearly. To them it was a conflict between honor and obedience, between conscience and duty. They neither could nor would hide behind the rationalization "I was only following orders." The others, those who followed obedience and duty, were being corrupted even as they were obedient and performed their duty; but either they didn't realize it or they refused to acknowledge it.

The events of World War II became the catalyst for a resolution of this clash of values between oath and conscience. As the war ground on, its ultimate conclusion was obvious even to the most obtuse. One can only imagine the sense of desperation that many officers felt as they contemplated the impending destruction of their homeland. The fact that the conspirators were willing to embark upon this journey of resistance to kill their chief of state and supreme military commander demonstrates clearly their commitment to moral values that transcended their oath of allegiance.

Tragically the leaders of the Allied coalition failed to realize this. With no appreciation for the ever-widening chasm that had opened between Hitler and some of his generals, they were unable to exploit an opportunity that conceivably could have changed the course of World War II, thereby saving countless lives and preventing needless destruction.

Rearmament and the Rhineland

The apprehensions that the blood purge and the oath of allegiance had unleashed in the summer of 1934 faded a bit in early 1935. Much to the delight of the military establishment, Hitler, on March 8, announced the creation of a new air force (Luftwaffe), followed one week later by an announcement that Germany was repudiating all of the military restrictions imposed upon the nation by the Treaty of Versailles, especially its size limitation of a 100,000-man army. The Reichswehr, renamed the Wehrmacht, was to be enlarged to 550,000 officers and soldiers comprising thirty-six divisions. Conscription was introduced in May.[48]

The senior members of the officer corps were obviously delighted by this turn of events, which they had helped to initiate. Still laboring under the delusion that they were in control of military matters, they forged ahead with plans designed to implement Hitler's declaration, even though the foreign office expressed concern about the foreign and diplomatic consequences of Hitler's announcement, and Hjalmar Schacht, president of Germany's central bank, the Reichsbank, raised questions about the economic and financial consequences of this rearmament program for the nation. In truth, military expansion had begun over a year earlier and was well under way by the time of the announcement.[49] Unsurprisingly the rearmament program had a beneficial impact on the economy over the short run. Unemployment, aided by conscription, dropped. Germany, it seemed, was emerging from the worst economic catastrophe in its entire history.[50]

Understandably Hitler's popularity soared. These events presaged the arrival of the "high noon of the Nazi regime."[51] For most Germans, the future appeared to be bright with promise. While these conditions prevailed, any attempts to create an opposition movement, whether civilian or military, were doomed to futility. Those who still doubted remained quiescent.

* * * *

However, the year 1936 brought with it a whiff of change that swept across Germany. Its source lay not in the domestic scene but in foreign affairs. It marked the beginning of military adventurism. Although most of the Treaty of Versailles had been torn to shreds by this time, one contentious issue remained, namely, the Rhineland. The region was still demilitarized as per the terms of the treaty. This was an affront to the German nation and its people. Hitler, sensing an opportunity to achieve a redress of grievances on his own terms, decided to make his move to rectify the situation. From his perspective, the early months of 1936 seemed to be a propitious time to act. Neither Great Britain nor especially France appeared either willing or able to respond to Nazi Germany's increasingly defiant behavior. Economic issues were forcing both countries to concentrate on internal matters. Moreover, aside from an official protest from the British government,[52] neither country had responded to Hitler's earlier repudiation of the military status quo when he announced his intention of rearming Germany. Finally, the failure of these two countries to offer an effective challenge to Italy for its invasion of Ethiopia earlier in the year convinced Hitler that he could rearm the Rhineland with impunity.

The danger for Germany was the threat of war. The step that Hitler planned to take was, under the terms of the treaty, one that "would have justified, and indeed required, immediate military action by the other signatories."[53] Such an action doubtlessly would have precipitated a conflict that was well beyond the capability of the German military establishment to pursue successfully, and the generals – all of them – knew it. Though they supported the idea of a rearmed Rhineland for military reasons, they were apprehensive about this entire operation. They "had their doubts."[54] The army chief of staff, General Ludwig Beck, and Army Commander in Chief Werner von Fritsch both were opposed to "adventures in foreign policy."[55] Even General Werner von Blomberg, who was not one to cross Hitler, expressed his doubts about the viability of the operation, although he was "nervously supportive" and ultimately "went along with Hitler."[56]

Thus, the military establishment was conflicted. Although they and others within the government applauded the goal, they opposed the proposed method. The Foreign Ministry, for example, was hoping to resolve the issue through negotiations, not military force.[57] Even Hitler himself had his doubts about the advisability of the operation. It was said of him that virtually up until the last minute "he continued to waver."[58] But he was a gambler and was committed to the military option in order to resolve this issue. And a gamble it was. It has been estimated that "one French division would have sufficed to terminate Hitler's adventure."[59] But the French Army failed to move.

Thus, in the very early morning hours of March 7, 1936, thirty thousand Wehrmacht troops, augmented by police units to make the forces appear to be larger than they really were, marched into the demilitarized zone of the Rhineland. Three thousand men crossed the major bridges spanning the Rhine River and penetrated deep into the region, while the remainder deployed along the east side of the river.[60] The only international response consisted of "empty protests."[61]

Hitler won the gamble. Reason and logic counseled against a military operation, but he had defied both and achieved his goal. A comment that he made several days after the event provides a clear indication of his growing megalomania: "Neither threats nor warnings will prevent me from going my way. I follow the path assigned to me by Providence with the instinctive sureness of a sleepwalker." In this instance, his *schlafwandlerische Sicherheit* (sleepwalker's assurance) did not fail him.[62]

This was but the first of many such episodes that would occur over the course of the next several years, proving – to Hitler's satisfaction at least – that instinct was more reliable than reason as a guide to decisions related to the issues of war and peace. The entire Rhineland affair became a watershed moment for the Führer. His generals' advice to exercise restraint had been wrong. "Perhaps nothing did more to destroy Hitler's respect for the generals than their behaviour on this occasion." He became convinced that they were "incurable pessimists, who need not be taken seriously."[63] Ever the egomaniac, he now was convinced more than ever of his own infallibility and invincibility.[64] Adolf Hitler was now locked in the deadly embrace of hubris. Inevitably, his nemesis was waiting in the wings.

The Rhineland affair had significant international implications. It totally repudiated the Treaty of Versailles. The international security system that the European nations, with Weimar Germany's cooperation, had carefully constructed over the previous ten years and more by means of a series of treaties also lay in shambles. The affair altered the balance of power in Western Europe. German armies were now in a position to outflank France in the event of a military confrontation. France was weakened both militarily and politically. The descriptive word for European international relations was no longer "security." It had become "insecurity." For the more-perceptive Europeans, including those in Germany, that whiff of change noted earlier brought with it a premonition of an increasingly somber future.

And what about the anti-Nazi opposition in all of this? What was the reaction of these people? How did they respond? What did they do? In the words of Ian Kershaw, "Opposition groups were demoralized." The overall reaction among the general public throughout Germany was elation and euphoria.[65] The German people (at least most of them; that feeling was far from universal) believed that a terrible injustice had been rectified at minimal cost. Thanks to the Führer, the "Diktat of Versailles" (dictated Treaty of Versailles) had been undone and the German nation had recovered its dignity, honor, and self-respect. Germany now controlled its own destiny. "High noon" had arrived. Hitler's popularity continued on its upward trajectory, which would prevail for another four years. How could an opposition group secure any kind of popular support in such an atmosphere?

For all practical purposes, Hitler's conquest of Germany was complete. The nation was totally under his control – or so he believed – and he now was in a position to implement his plans for the creation of a Greater Germany that would dominate European and world affairs. Only one German institution remained a potential threat to him: the army. Some members of the officer corps were his enthusiastic supporters. They included Defense Minister (War Minister after 1935) General Werner von Blomberg, General Walter von Reichenau, a field commander who later broke with Hitler and the Nazis, and General Alfred Jodl, who served in various administrative offices in the Wehrmacht. It was said of Jodl that he, "along with many other officers, had been enthralled by Hitler's non-violent success – the introduction of general conscription in 1935 and the occupation of the demilitarized zone of the Rhineland in 1936."[66]

Nevertheless, the Rhineland episode did not meet with universal support, even among the civilian population. Many were apprehensive given the bellicose implications of Hitler's audacious actions. Memories of the Great War still haunted them. One contemporary observer – a Social Democratic agent – summarized these fears with the following comment: "The people are very worked up. They're afraid of war, since everyone is clear that Germany will lose this war and then will go to its downfall."[67]

Individuals in positions of command and authority within the government and the military establishment also had serious reservations. There was a palpable sense of unease among these men. What were the diplomatic implications of all of this? they asked. How much longer would France and Great Britain stand aside and allow Germany to continue down the path that Hitler had charted? What about the impact of rearmament on the German economy? The rapid pace and magnitude of the rearmament program threatened to drain the national economy of its resources to such a degree that total economic collapse was a distinct possibility.[68] For the first time, hints of a resistance movement began to appear.

Two men, displaying considerable courage, spoke openly to the Supreme Command of the Army (Oberkommando des Heeres, or OKH) against the military and economic implications of the Rhineland affair. Theirs was a "campaign of enlightenment" designed to give the army a realistic appraisal of actual conditions, both domestic and international. The first spokesman for this nascent opposition group was Hjalmar Schacht, who at this time was minister of economics. He "spoke out with amazing frankness to audiences of officers" about the implications of the Nazi-created war economy, or Raubbau (bandit economy) as its opponents described it.[69] The second spokesman, General Georg Thomas, was director of the War Economy Department of the War Ministry. Speaking with equal clarity and courage, he "took issue with notions of quick and easy victory though 'lightning war' … [and] stressed German vulnerability in any extended conflict."[70] Significantly, the efforts of these two men were centered on the OKH, since, of the three military services, the army was the least infected with the Nazi virus. The Luftwaffe (air force) was a highly politicized "Nazi institution," and the Kriegsmarine (navy), though less pro-Nazi than the Luftwaffe, was nonetheless politicized and unreliable.[71]

Partly as a result of Thomas's and Schacht's efforts, a few military officers were beginning to have doubts about Hitler and his ultimate goals. A very few had entertained doubts from the beginning of Nazi rule. These were the men who would become the nucleus of an army conspiracy to decapitate the Nazi state. One such man was Hans Oster. He had caught that original whiff of change and sensed the increasingly reckless nature of Hitler's foreign policy. More importantly, he perceived its essential immorality, something that most of his fellow officers did not yet recognize. To the extent that apprehensions about Hitler's leadership did surface within the officer corps at this time, the fears of most of these men were focused more on the risks associated with Hitler's adventurous foreign policy than on moral considerations. Oster's moral concerns were shared by only a few of the future resisters. But regardless of their motivation, all of them felt a sense of futility. "As long as Hitler had been able to get away with bullying the western powers, most Germans had shrugged off whatever doubts they may have had about the Führer."[72] Hence, Hitler's successes, both foreign and domestic, effectively quelled any potential opposition, either military or civilian.

Civilians like Carl Goerdeler shared the future resisters' sense of futility. He knew that so long as Hitler continued to produce spectacular successes like the ones that neutered the Treaty of Versailles, the man was unassailable. These civilians recognized that they lacked leadership, organization, and the means to bring Hitler down. And they lacked organized popular support. Under these circumstances, active civilian opposition was futile. Consequently, they began to look to the army for help. "As they became more convinced that the overthrow of the government from below was out of the question and a coup d'état from above was the only feasible answer, these efforts began to center on the Army."[73] Subsequent events would demonstrate, however, that even the army had serious weaknesses that fatally compromised the resistance movement.

Ultimately:

> ... the German military tradition in the last analysis did not constitute a real foundation for political resistance. Opposition remained confined to the personal initiative of intellectually and morally independent officers. Its basis was not the tradition of the Army but the conscience of individuals whose eyes were opened by the reality in unquestioning military obedience, and, finally, who were ready to step out of the narrow framework of military thinking and make contact with the civilian resistance.[74]

This brief statement summarizes the dilemma of the entire German anti-Nazi resistance movement almost perfectly. The army as an institution was just not equipped to deal with the unique issues of Nazi rule, and without institutional support, the prospect of men acting individually or in pitifully small groups achieving success in deposing Hitler was minimal. The fact that they almost achieved success on several instances under these constraints is a testimony to their courage and commitment.

The following two years only confirmed the worst fears of those who saw the inexorable march toward war. Hitler spoke with increasing clarity of his warlike intentions at a secret conference held on November 5, 1937, at the Reich Chancellery in Berlin with his service chiefs and foreign minister, Konstantin von Neurath. Although Hitler offered no specific plan of military action, his comments clearly indicated what his intentions were – war. "'Germany's problem,' he declared, 'could be solved only by the use of force.'"[75] The problem, he said, was Germany's need for Lebensraum (living space), specifically in Eastern Europe. Only here could Germany find the resources essential to realize Hitler's goal of complete autarchy, or economic self-sufficiency. Only here could the German "racial stock" thrive and grow. Implied in this megalomaniacal worldview was the reduction, or preferably the complete elimination, of the inhabitants of this region.

Although some of Hitler's military officers accepted this Weltanschauung without question, others were appalled by its implications. Something obviously had to be done if the march to the abyss were to be stopped. The demands being placed on the military establishment – especially an ever-shortening timetable for military action – were causing considerable strains. Those officrs who feared the prospect of war began to see Adolf Hitler for what he was: a completely irrational and amoral gambler who was acting with an increasing recklessness that threatened the safety and security of the fatherland.[76]

Because several of the senior officers at the November 5 meeting either expressed their doubts about his plans or failed to respond with sufficient enthusiasm, Hitler decided that he must get rid of them. He viewed them as stumbling blocks to the realization of his grandiose scheme.[77] More compliant officers would have to replace them. Many old conservatives still occupied prominent positions within the military establishment, and these were the men who were seen as the stumbling blocks. They had to go.

Two men in particular were targeted for removal. They had committed the unpardonable offense of openly expressing doubts about Hitler's plans: Army Commander in Chief Werner von Fritsch and Minister of

War Werner von Blomberg. Fritsch was forced to resign after a completely fabricated charge of homosexuality was brought against him. Blomberg's removal was much easier. He managed to present his own head on a platter to Hitler because of his mésalliance with a woman, one Eva Gruhn (also known as Marguerite or Erna), who – according to an anonymous telephone call to General von Fritsch – had registered with the police as a prostitute. She also allegedly had posed for pornographic photographs.[78] Blomberg resigned in disgrace.

With these two men removed from the scene, Hitler was able to reconfigure the armed forces to suit his purposes. On February 4, 1938, he issued a decree that completely reorganized the German military establishment. The decree contained the following sentence: "Henceforth, I will personally exercise immediate command of the whole armed forces."[79] Sixteen generals were dismissed, forty-four senior officers were reassigned, and an entirely new command structure was created. No one was appointed to fill the now vacant position of war minister, thereby effectively eliminating the War Ministry as a factor in military planning. Furthermore, a new organization, das Oberkommando der Wehrmacht (OKW, or Supreme Command of the Armed Forces) was created to coordinate the activities of the newly established subordinate ministries of the three armed services.

These changes signified that Adolf Hitler was now the supreme commander of all of the German armed forces. The OKW, in effect, became his personal staff, which in turn meant that all military plans required the Führer's approval. General Wilhelm Keitel, an open admirer of Hitler and a man whom many considered to be a spineless toady – some referred to him as the rubber lion (Gummilöwe) or the nodding donkey (Nickesel) – was named chief of the OKW.[80] Hitler "had outmaneuvered, defeated, humiliated and dragooned the German army."[81]

These events brought the German Army to an end as an independent force. It now was under Hitler's total control, and Gleichschaltung, or "coordination," was complete. Army, party, and nation were one. Hitler no longer needed the conservatives. He had used them in order to reach the pinnacle of power, and now he could discard them. Tragically, the army leadership had allowed its moral integrity to be destroyed for the sake of an illusory belief that it had regained all it had lost after the Great War. In fact, "it was now completely at Hitler's mercy."[82] In a speech delivered to the Reichstag on February 20, 1938, Hitler declared quite accurately that the armed forces were now "dedicated to this National Socialist state in

1938: A Pivotal Year

Viewed in its historical context, 1938 was perhaps the most important year in the history of the resistance. For the first time, a bona fide organized resistance movement, centered in the army, began to materialize; it was a movement to remove Hitler from office, either by arrest and imprisonment or by assassination. This was a turning point. Mere talk was replaced by action. "For the first time since Hitler's rise to power, some of those who had been his supporters and allies began to think seriously about opposing him not only with arguments and pleas but with force. A concrete, organized resistance against the Third Reich was finally coming into existence."[84]

The reason for this change is quite clear. Hitler's foreign policy was becoming much more strident and aggressive, and the subject of war was appearing with increasing frequency in his conversations and his planning sessions. For example, he had written a memorandum in 1936 declaring that the Wehrmacht should be ready for war within four years. Although he revealed its contents only to Luftwaffe Chief Hermann Göring and Minister of War Werner von Blomberg, his subsequent actions gave a clear indication of his intent.[85] One example will suffice. War production increased dramatically during the late thirties, and by the end of the decade, Germany had a formidable military establishment, with 103 fully equipped army divisions, an air force that was second to none in size, and a sizable navy, which included 57 submarines. The nation's state of readiness has been described as a "potent factor in the crises of 1938 and 1939."[86] The dates refer to the Anschluss and Czech crises of 1938 and the Polish campaign that marked the beginning of World War II, respectively.

Their numbers were few, but the men of the resistance had great determination. They also had a very clear-eyed understanding of the reality that lay behind the humbug of the Third Reich. They saw what had just happened to their army, they saw what was happening to their beloved fatherland, and they foresaw what would happen if Hitler were to remain in power. The enormities of the Nazi system were revealing themselves for all who would or could see, and a sense of moral outrage over Nazi behavior was beginning to penetrate the inner circle of what would soon become a full-fledged resistance movement. It was time to remove Hitler, by violence if necessary.

The infamous Kristallnacht episode ultimately convinced many of the doubters of Nazism's inherent evil. The resisters recognized that the only way to forestall an almost certain catastrophe was a coup d'état against the Nazi state. Only then could a war that most assuredly would bring not only calamitous defeat to the German nation but also its possible destruction be avoided. Therefore, 1938 became a critical year for those who opposed the Nazis, as they began to seriously consider the elimination of Adolf Hitler. "Opposing war was the most effective way of enlisting support against the regime. Getting rid of Hitler more and more appeared to be the sole way to prevent (and later put an end to) war."[87] Hitler was at the epicenter of National Socialism, and he had to be eliminated before any other anti-Nazi action could be contemplated.

* * * *

The infamous Fritsch episode of January 1938 that led to the man's abrupt dismissal outraged members of the officer corps. In addition, the more perceptive officers grasped the significance of the changes that Hitler initiated in the wake of Fritsch's dismissal quite clearly, and the government's increasingly bellicose atmosphere only deepened their apprehensions. The day after Hitler's confrontation with Fritsch, three military officers – Army Chief of Staff Ludwig Beck, Abwehr commander General Wilhelm Canaris, and his subordinate Lieutenant Colonel Hans Oster – met to discuss the possibility of taking advantage of the baseless charges brought against Frisch to organize a strike against Hitler. Thus began an organized anti-Nazi resistance movement within the military establishment.

Oster was emerging as the de facto leader of the effort. In addition to the obvious reasons for making this attempt, Oster had a personal reason. He had served under Fritsch in the Reichswehr before the Nazis came to power, and the two men had become good friends. He wanted to rescue his former commander's reputation as a "model German army officer." Upon learning of the sordid affair, he reputedly said, "I have made the Fritsch case my own."[88] Canaris's original support for the Nazis had diminished considerably by 1938. His position as head of the Abwehr brought him into personal contact and conflict with Heinrich Himmler, commander of the SS and the Gestapo, where he began to see the dark side of Nazi rule. Hitler's foreign policy adventurism also deepened his concerns, but it was the Fritsch affair that finally and irrevocably turned him against the Nazis.[89] By this time, Ludwig Beck also had lost whatever early enthusiasm he may have held for the Nazis. First, there was the oath of allegiance, and now there was the Fritsch crisis. His growing fears of an impending war convinced him that the time for action had come.

Beck's "actions," however, were pitifully inadequate. He tried to convince Hitler by way of rational argument that Germany's military forces were insufficient for the demands being placed upon them and that, absent substantive policy changes, Germany was headed toward destruction. Naturally the Führer rejected Beck's arguments out of hand. Here, in Hitler's eyes, was one more example of the general's faintheartedness. Described as a "cautious, shy and withdrawn man,"[90] Ludwig Beck was a conservative not merely in his social and political views but also in terms of his personality and behavior. He was a circumspect man, although it was said of him that "he was prepared to take risks, after due consideration."[91] He was not yet ready for risk-taking, however, and found the idea of mutiny or revolution to be absolutely repellent. He also was incredibly naïve in his estimation of Nazi duplicity. Although he held a healthy suspicion of such men as Göring and Himmler, "he found it … difficult to believe that men could be capable of so dirty a trick as that constituted by the intrigue against Fritsch."[92] Just the day prior to Fritsch's resignation, Beck reacted to a suggestion that the army should raid the headquarters of the Nazi-controlled Secret State Police (Gestapo) in Berlin with the comment that this would be tantamount to "mutiny, revolution," and added that "such words do not exist in the dictionary of a German officer."[93] Ludwig Beck did not become an active participant in the army's anti-Nazi conspiracy until the following summer.[94]

Nonetheless, a true resistance movement began to take shape. Contact was established between military officers, mostly within the Abwehr, and civilian resistance leaders such as Carl Goerdeler and Hjalmar Schacht. Others joined the emerging conspiracy, including General Erwin von Witzleben, commander of the Berlin military district, and Hans Berndt Gisevius, a friend of Oster and former employee of the Ministry of Justice.[95] Unable to secure effective support from the top military leadership – Beck as chief of the general staff was opposed to a coup, and Fritsch had been dismissed as army commander in chief pending his court-martial – these resistance leaders could not depend upon the army to be a factor in any effort to prevent Hitler from carrying out his plan to destroy whatever remained of an independent army.

Even so, Oster, Gisevius, Goerdeler, and Schacht decided to contact various military commanders throughout Germany to enlist their support for direct action against the Nazis.[96] The reactions they received can be described as mixed. Some were very sympathetic, others much less so. The idea of a mass resignation of the generals was contemplated, but success required unanimity, and this was highly unlikely, especially since the officer corps had been undergoing a process of expansion and dilution since 1933. Many within the officer corps now were pro-Nazi in their sympathies. This included younger men within the Junker aristocracy who considered themselves to be members of the racial elite thanks to "centuries of breeding." Moreover, the rapid expansion of the military establishment after 1935 gave these younger men an opportunity to pursue a military career in the officer corps, which had been the special preserve of their forbearers for centuries. At the very least, Hitler's personal magnetism attracted many of the younger officers.[97]

A second alternative was an actual coup d'état. Its success, however, would require actual troops, and the conspirators had none at their disposal. The newly appointed army commander in chief, Walther von Brauchitsch, was not one to lead such an operation, and those generals located in the various military districts across Germany faced almost insurmountable odds in launching such a strike. For example, General Wilhelm List, commander of the military district around Leipzig, pointed out to Carl Goerdeler that three days would be required to move a division to Berlin and that it doubtlessly would be vulnerable to Luftwaffe attacks. Thus, "Leadership for a coup must come from the center and the highest level of the army. If a coup was to succeed, it would have to have the full support of the army high command and be led by a troop commander in the Berlin district."[98]

To make matters worse, General Erwin von Witzleben, who commanded the Berlin military district, was hospitalized during these critical hours and did not return to duty until the middle of February, well after the Fritsch crisis had been resolved in Hitler's favor.[99] Adolf Hitler achieved his goals. Fritsch and Blomberg were gone, the OKW was in place, and the Führer now had absolute control over the entire military establishment. The plans for a coup came to nothing, and the mad dash to the abyss continued unabated.

Treason

The events of the year 1938 highlighted an issue of significant moral relevance for the emergent resistance movement, especially for the military officers who were actively plotting Hitler's overthrow. The issue was treason. It was inextricably connected with the questions of assassination and the infamous oath of allegiance – or unconditional obedience – that was extracted from Germany's soldiers beginning in 1934. It then was highlighted by the reorganization of the military establishment that took place in early 1938. As a consequence of these changes, the German Army no longer served the interests of the nation. It had become the servant of the Nazi Party and of its Führer.

Consequently, the army now faced the issue of treason under altered circumstances. Under these new conditions, the meaning of the term had changed significantly. With the new arrangement, any kind of political activity in opposition to the Nazi Party or to Hitler himself could be defined as treasonous activity. This had special relevance for those army officers such as Hans Oster, Henning von Tresckow, and Claus von Stauffenberg, all of whom recognized that the path that Hitler had charted would lead to calamity unless something could be done to change course. That "something" obviously was the removal of Hitler from power; but how could this be accomplished?

The army leadership was hopelessly divided on the question. First of all, there were the generals who exhibited unquestioning loyalty to the Third Reich. They were devoted to Hitler and would not countenance any kind of resistance. He was the Führer and had to be obeyed regardless of the consequences. Secondly, there were the generals who heartily despised Hitler and all he represented. They knew, however, that any action taken against him was tantamount to rebellion, and this they would not sanction. Most of the officers in this category were imbued with the ethos of the Prussian military tradition, which absolutely forbade any behavior that bore even the slightest resemblance to rebellious action. A third category was a group of generals who were mere opportunists. They wanted to be on the winning side, whether Nazi or anti-Nazi. It mattered not to them which group it was. Their moral compass was broken beyond repair. The fourth group consisted of the Tresckows, Osters, and Stauffenbergs, as well as the clergyman Bonhoeffer, who, along with many others, despised the Nazis with all of their moral fiber and who were willing to risk all to free Germany from the Nazi leviathan. Finally, there were several generals who shared with the fourth group a disgust of the Nazis but who lacked the moral courage to take a stand against a manifestly evil political system. Within this small group were several generals in key positions, whose support just might have made the difference between success and failure in several coup attempts against Hitler. This, of course, is pure speculation. We shall never know what the outcome would have been had they cast their lot with the resistance.

An important question remained unanswered: How far could an army officer go in resisting his government? And was there any moral justification for taking an action that could be considered treason? This issue lay at the very heart of the entire resistance movement, and it became one of the thorniest questions that the army leadership – from the generals to the junior officers – had to answer as the power of the Führer and his Nazi Party increasingly overwhelmed the nation. This was an especially critical question for the army because it was the only institution capable of removing Hitler from power. No resistance movement could hope for success without the cooperation and participation of the army. And yet the generals never resolved their differences. This schism was the primary reason for the ultimate failure of the army conspiracy against Hitler. But those within the army resistance became ever more determined to remove the dictator as the passage of time brought greater clarity of the dangers of continued Nazi rule.

By the late thirties, those in the army resistance recognized that the very integrity and survival of the German nation was at stake. Thus, these men faced a terrible dilemma. What should they do in such circumstances? What was their responsibility? What was their patriotic duty? Where did their loyalties lie? Was it possible to be both a traitor and a patriot? Specifically, was resistance to Nazism treason, or was it patriotism? In fact, the Nazis had successfully conflated loyalty to National Socialism, especially to Hitler, with loyalty to the nation. The Nazis asserted that "whoever is a really good soldier will also be a good National Socialist." Historian Theodore Hamerow, reflecting on this statement, declared that the Nazis had erased the distinction between the German state and the Nazi Party.[100]

Faced with the choice of continued Nazi rule or treason, these officers of the resistance movement made their decision. Morality and true patriotism demanded the removal of Hitler from power. They were trying to save lives. Hans Oster attempted to take direct action against Hitler, first in 1938 and then in 1940. It was said of him, "His purpose was not to damage the Reich or his country. It was precisely the opposite."[101] He wanted to save lives and prevent war.

The name of Dietrich Bonhoeffer is placed alongside those of the soldiers who were part of the resistance because of the consistency, moral clarity, and determination he displayed in his opposition to Nazi rule. He never faltered and never hesitated to denounce the evil that was an integral part of the Nazi system. He never in any way made allowances for their bestial behavior. He also spoke and wrote with great clarity about the issue of treason.

Well before Hitler came into power, Bonhoeffer recognized Nazism for what it was and what it represented. The Nazis' virulent anti-Semitism especially outraged him. Moreover, he publicly denounced Hitler and his hooligans from the very beginning of Nazi rule. Reputedly he was the first public figure in Germany to do so. He and "a pitifully few ... perceived from the earliest days that the practitioners of cherished and not ignoble values were unwittingly standing in the service of an unsurpassed criminality."[102] As war approached in 1939, he wrote to his friend, the American theologian Reinhold Niebuhr, the following words: "Christians in Germany will face the terrible alternative of either willing the defeat of their nation in order that Christian civilization may survive, or willing the victory of their nation and thereby destroying our civilization."[103]

Bonhoeffer's statement summarizes precisely the moral dilemma facing everyone who was a part of the anti-Nazi resistance. Which would be worse, the victory of Nazism or the defeat of Germany? Although Bonhoeffer's Lutheran heritage had taught him to obey the civil authorities virtually without reservation, the world in which he now lived had turned all the conventional definitions of morality upside down. He recognized that the Nazis had totally corrupted the terms "treason" and "patriotism." Therefore, he resolved to "[be a doer] of evil in order to prevent evildoers from doing worse."[104] In fact, this "doer of evil" was willing to countenance the murder of Adolf Hitler.

Bonhoeffer was in New York City just before the outbreak of hostilities in 1939. After a short period of soul-searching, he decided to return to Germany. His American friends tried unsuccessfully to dissuade him. Before leaving the United States, Bonhoeffer wrote the following words to Niebuhr: "I shall have no right to participate in the reconstruction of Christian life in Germany after the war if I do not share the trials of this time with my people."[105] Realizing that this step was tantamount to signing his own death warrant, Bonhoeffer nonetheless refused to be deterred. The conviction behind this decision can be found in a statement of his that represents the quintessence of his beliefs: "When Christ calls a man, he bids him 'come and die.'"[106]

* * * *

The issue of treason was rendered even more complex by German law. The general definition of "treason" is "a crime of betrayal, especially of one's country." It implies an attempt to kill the leader(s) or overthrow the government. The historian Peter Hoffmann has defined the term as "an intent or deliberate act designed to damage one's own country."[107] In fact, the term technically can be used to describe action taken against virtually any institution or even individuals. Its best synonym is the word "betrayal." Historically, the word "treason" has been used to describe "betrayal of trust or faith; treachery."[108]

With slight variations over time, the German law code has traditionally recognized two types of treason. The first is Hochverrat, or high treason. As defined in post–World War II German law, it is "a violent attempt against the existence or the constitutional order of the Federal Republic of Germany."[109] The earlier, pre–World War II definition was "betrayal of the head of state." The second type of treason, Landesverrat, is now considered to be the crime of espionage, but in earlier usage, it carried a much more sinister connotation. It was considered to be betrayal of country, and it has been described as a "much more odious crime," for which there was "absolutely no tolerance within the army."[110]

Some army officers were willing to countenance a coup d'état before World War II and during the short-lived period of military inaction after the conclusion of the Polish campaign in the autumn of 1939 when it appeared that a further widening of the conflict could be avoided. However, these men totally rejected the prospect of overthrowing Hitler once hostilities began in earnest in 1940. Staging a coup from this point on was for them Landesverrat. Even Stauffenberg initially was included in this group. He and his compatriots were soldiers, and for them, the defense of the nation had first priority. According to his brother Berthold, Claus said, "First we must win the war. Things of this sort (that is, rebellion) should not be done during a war … But then, when we come home, we will get rid of the brown pestilence."[111] Just how they could accomplish this within an atmosphere of Nazi triumphalism was never explained.

The legal system of the Third Reich, such as it was, conflated the two types of treason. Hitler was declared to be the actual personification of the state, the nation, and its people. This concept represented the complete consummation of totalitarianism. Hitler was the Führer, the leader. He was above the law, a virtual demigod, far superior in intellect and ability to mere mortals. Hence, any action against him was ipso facto Landesverrat. Hitler certainly was not the only political or military leader to strive for this position. History is replete with examples of those who have aspired to such an exalted status. Few have achieved it with such finality as Hitler, however.

By 1938, the distinction between the two types of treason had become a matter of critical importance to those in the army who also were members of the resistance. They recognized a growing gap between loyalty to the nation and loyalty to the Führer. "The soldier's oath had long since lapsed since Hitler had not observed his own obligations but was in the process of sacrificing Germany to his own crazy purposes."[112] Thus, these men were willing to commit Hochverrat for the sake of preserving the integrity of the fatherland.

By any objective analysis, their proposed actions did not even fall under the category of Hochverrat, because the Nazi accession to power was a grim parody of legality and justice. Threats, intimidation, manipulation, distortion of fact, and plain lies were an integral part of the Nazis' modus operandi. The Nazis had made illegality "legal." These soldiers of the resistance, like all the others who participated in the resistance movement, essentially were working against an illegitimate government. The highest standards of patriotism and loyalty motivated them. They wanted to save Germany and all of Europe from a catastrophe of unprecedented proportions. Their goals have been accurately described as "the antithesis of treason ... When so monstrous, devilish and erratic a criminal as Hitler, appears both willing and able to subjugate a whole continent, national boundaries in the strict and formal sense lose their significance; the interests of all peoples then become similar."[113]

Anschluss and Sudetenland

In the midst of the turmoil precipitated by Hitler's preemptive strike against Germany's military establishment in early 1938, the international scene was darkening significantly. As Hitler was plotting his move against the army, he also was planning the seizure of Austria and incorporating it into Germany as part of his greater Third Reich. This was the first step in his plan of conquest, to be followed by the seizure of the Sudetenland region of Czechoslovakia.

The campaign against Austria began early in 1938 with a venomous propaganda attack as part of a political offensive against the government of Chancellor Kurt von Schuschnigg. Its purpose was to bully the Austrian government into submission to Germany's demands for an Anschluss, or connection/union, between the two countries on Nazi terms. For reasons deeply embedded in German history, a considerable degree of popular support for an Anschluss could be found on both sides of the border. Even many of those who soon would become the most active members of the resistance shared these sentiments.

An understanding of the reasons for such feelings is essential to an explanation of the contradictions inherent in the position of the people who held them. How were these men able to reconcile their abhorrence of Hitler's imperial pretensions with their desire for Anschluss with Austria, and later with their support for the acquisition of the Sudetenland of Czechoslovakia? Were they or were they not imperialists, desirous of territorial expansion of the fatherland? Did they or did they not support Hitler's megalomania? An answer to these questions can be found only by examining the long history of Germany's relations with Austria and Czechoslovakia. This in turn requires yet another journey through German and Central European history.

* * * *

For centuries, Austria had been at the center of German political life. This was long before there was a united "Germany." Instead, there were the Germanies, literally hundreds of completely independent German states that were joined in a very loose confederation known as the Holy Roman Empire. From the fifteenth century on, the Austrian Habsburg family occupied the imperial throne. With the demise of the empire in 1806, the Habsburg rulers assumed the title Emperor of Austria. From 1815 to 1866, the Germanies were reorganized into the German Confederation under Austrian leadership. However, Prussia's rapid rise to political and economic power in the nineteenth century led to the Austro-Prussian War in 1866. Prussia's victory in that conflict resulted in the expulsion of Austria from Germany. Austria subsequently was reorganized the following year as a "dual monarchy," with Hungary as an equal partner with the Austro-German lands in what had become a multinational and multilingual state, now known as Austria-Hungary. The Habsburgs remained on the throne. An ally of Germany in the Great War, Austria-Hungary suffered defeat in 1918 and the Habsburg Empire came to an end. The rulers were forced into exile, and Austria, shorn of its non-German territories, was reduced in size to the original ducal Habsburg lands.

Understandably, Austria wished for a union – or reunion, to be more precise – with Germany after the defeat in 1918, but the Allies would have none of it. In their view, the vanquished enemy should receive absolutely no compensation whatsoever.[114] Thus the erstwhile great power was now a virtual client state, that is, of second or even third rank in terms of power and importance in international affairs. It also suffered what today would be called an identity crisis. Were they "Austrians" or were they "Germans"? They were, of course, both. The centuries-long association with the Holy Roman Empire had conditioned the Austrian Germans to view themselves as an integral part of Germany, as indeed they were. Though a numerical minority, they also had considered themselves to be the dominant part of the Austro-Hungarian Empire. But now that empire was gone, and the Austrians were prohibited from joining Germany. It was almost as if they were orphans living in a strange land. At this point, their sense of Austrian nationalism apart from Germany was at best only rudimentary.[115]

Just what was this new "Republic of Austria," and where did it belong? Should Austria become a sovereign state in its own right, or should it be joined with Germany? The social, political, and economic divisions that opened up as a result of this trauma plagued the new Austria for the next twenty years. The Anschluss of 1938 seemed to provide a way out of the dilemma resulting from the losses sustained in 1919. Indeed, viewed within the broad sweep of German history, its logic appeared to be almost irrefutable. The problem for the resistance lay not so much with the fact of the Anschluss, but rather with the reasons behind it. The Anschluss was merely a prelude to Hitler's ultimate goal, the creation of his Greater Reich, and the Republic of Austria became the first territorial acquisition on the road to war.

Thus, in the midst of the crisis of army leadership associated with the Fritsch affair, Hitler took that anticipated first step. On March 12, 1938, German troops crossed the frontier with Austria. The Anschluss was officially proclaimed on the thirteenth, and Hitler took formal possession of the country of his birth on the fourteenth. He had achieved a bloodless victory that was greeted with a wild enthusiasm approaching hysteria on both sides of the border. The episode came to be known as the Blumenkrieg (flower war).[116]

Those in the nascent resistance greeted the Anschluss with mixed feelings. As German nationalists, they were understandably delighted to see the union – or reunion – of the two German states. Both Ludwig Beck and Carl Goerdeler were representative of this group. They believed that the Anschluss was legitimate and historically justified, although Goerdeler in particular deplored the way in which the union was achieved, specifically "the bluster and bullying, the strutting and posturing."[117] He would have preferred the Anschluss to be part of a broader political settlement between Germany and the Western powers – that is, France and Great Britain – by means of a policy of "moderation, restraint, [and] judiciousness, and a willingness to compromise."[118] The conviction that history justified the Anschluss remained with these men almost to the end.

Even after the outbreak of World War II, Beck remained convinced "that the incorporation of Austria was warranted as well as irreversible."[119] Claus von Stauffenberg held this belief as well. He expressed this view scarcely a month before his assassination attempt on July 20, 1944.[120] Hence, the desire of all Germans to see the rectification of what they considered to be a great injustice transcended both ideology and party affiliation. Even the Social Democrats Julius Leber and Wilhelm Leuschner supported the Anschluss. "Of all Hitler's diplomatic achievements, the Anschluss aroused the most enthusiasm and the least concern among [the members of the resistance]."[121] Hitler's dazzling triumphs seemed to mesmerize everyone.

Nonetheless, memories of recent past actions in the Rhineland were recalled. The methods that Hitler used to achieve his goal in that 1936 episode had been greeted with grave misgiving among the incipient resisters. Now, two years later, the Anschluss affair was conducted in the same way, arousing those same fears. A disquieting pattern was becoming increasingly evident.[122]

* * * *

The ease with which the Anschluss was achieved only whetted Hitler's appetite for more territorial acquisitions. Hence, the successes of March 1938 led directly to the Czech crisis of April to September 1938, when Hitler launched his campaign to seize the Sudetenland, the westernmost portion of Czechoslovakia. A German-speaking population inhabited this region that for centuries had been an integral part of the old Holy Roman Empire and, following that, of the now defunct Habsburg Empire. Like the Anschluss, the Sudeten crisis had its roots deep in the complexities of Central European history. The two episodes also are interconnected and provide a classic example of how the past continually shapes our contemporary world.

Bohemia and Moravia, which today comprise the Czech Republic, had been an integral part of the Holy Roman Empire since the tenth century. By the seventeenth century, the region, now ruled by the Habsburg family, had become the Kingdom of Bohemia and was a major pillar of the Habsburg Empire.[123] Bohemia bore a heavy geographical and historical burden. German-speaking lands virtually surrounded it. The inevitable migration of peoples in the Middle Ages ultimately brought the Germans into contact with the Slavs living to the east and south of the German lands, the region known as the Sudetenland. This migration had the support of the Bohemian kings and began as early as the tenth century, lasting for several hundred years.[124]

Tragically, the two peoples never assimilated. Although assimilation showed initial promise, conflicts between the two groups arose by the late thirteenth century and only grew more numerous and intense with the passage of time. Thus, "in spite of more than three centuries of attempted Germanization by Vienna, the German-Czech conflict was not resolved."[125] The rise of nationalism in the nineteenth and twentieth centuries, together with the peace settlements after the Great War, exacerbated the problem. Although the Bohemians, Moravians, and Slovaks secured their own independent nation-state – Czechoslovakia – many within the German minority in Bohemia and Moravia, especially in the Sudetenland, remained unreconciled to their new circumstances. Heretofore, they had been part of the dominant national group within the Habsburg Empire, even though they were a numerical minority. Now, however, they were a cultural, social, and linguistic minority as well. The Germans "never felt they entirely belonged"[126] in what was seen as an artificial Slav state. Once again, the principle of national self-determination had been denied to the Germans. "To Germany, the position of Bohemia and Moravia ... was not that of a Czech majority and a German minority, but of a small Czech island in an immense Teutonic ocean."[127]

Despite their minority status, however, the Germans fully enjoyed all the rights of citizenship and participated actively in Czechoslovakia's parliamentary democracy. They also had the right to use their native tongue in normal discourse and for official business. Additionally, they had their own schools and universities, as well as their own newspapers. Furthermore, relations between the Czechs and Germans in this hybrid nation were relatively stable and conflict-free in the decade that followed the Great War. And yet, the Germans were still a minority population in a Slav state. This situation was perfectly suited for exploitation by nationalist demagoguery, especially if something should happen to disrupt the normal course of events. That "something" was the Great Depression.

The economic collapse was especially burdensome for the Germans living within the borders of Czechoslovakia, because much of the industry in the German areas was devoted to light industry that produced consumer goods, such as textiles and glass. These industries were particularly vulnerable to the economic downturn. Consequently, an estimated two-thirds of the unemployed in Czechoslovakia were ethnic (popularly known as Sudeten) Germans. However, the government's social welfare system was stretched to the breaking point, which meant that it was unable to respond adequately to the economic and financial needs of the German community, which in turn suggested to them that since the Czech government was failing to respond to their needs, it had no interest in their fate.[128] This was a perfect setting for Nazi-inspired exploitation, and they made the most of the opportunity.

Once again, Hitler was able to use his demagogic talents to fan the flames of mass discontent. Those Germans living on the eastern slopes of the Erzgebirge (the Ore Mountains) along the German-Czech border were merely the latest objects of manipulation for his evil purposes. The grievances of this minority obviously could become "a pretext for intervention sufficiently plausible to divide and weaken external sympathies [for Czechoslovakia]."[129]

Just as our brief survey of Austria's role in German history indicates a rationale for Germany to argue that eventual Anschluss was only just and right, so this snapshot of Bohemian history gives some perspective on the attitudes of those Germans who believed that ultimate union of the Sudeten Germans with the fatherland also was inevitable, logical, and just. The tragedy lurking behind these positions was that for Hitler, the union of these two entities with Germany was but a prelude to even greater conquests in the east. He had no interest in rectifying an unjust peace settlement that denied Germans the right of self-determination. Rather, he wished to build a springboard for the next step in his grand strategy, which was the invasion of Poland and the Soviet Union. Victory in this war would lead to a completely reordered international political system, giving Germany its necessary Lebensraum. This new system would conform to the Nazi concept of a German-dominated and racially restructured Europe.[130] This most certainly was not the vision held by those within the resistance movement who supported union with Austria and acquisition of the Sudetenland, but the distinction was not all that clear in 1938.

What *was* clear, however, was the realization that plans for an attack against Czechoslovakia in the autumn of 1938 at the latest were well under way by late spring. No sooner had the Anschluss become a fait accompli than rumors began to circulate within Germany and throughout the capitals of Europe that a German assault against Czechoslovakia would be forthcoming shortly.[131] On March 18, 1938, only days after the Nazi seizure of Austria, Hitler gave a speech to the Reichstag, in which he spoke of "brutal violation of countless millions of German racial comrades" throughout Europe. Later, on May 28, he spoke to the military high command and key personnel in the foreign office, declaring that he was "utterly determined that Czechoslovakia should disappear from the map," and two days later, he revealed his military plans "for implementing his 'unalterable decision to smash Czechoslovakia by military action in the foreseeable future.'"[132]

* * * *

As these events were playing out on the international scene, the resisters began to plan a course of action to remove Hitler from power. The resistance movement – especially the generals – was becoming more and more apprehensive of the military gamble that was unfolding in the summer of 1938. Hitler was betting that neither France nor Great Britain would respond to his challenge with military force. His generals were very dubious, especially those men who were part of the emerging resistance movement. Most of them approved of the goal to incorporate the Sudetenland into Germany proper as a matter of simple justice. As it had been with the Anschluss, so it was with the Sudetenland. They also remembered the statements of US President Woodrow Wilson, who had championed the cause of "national self-determination" at the Paris Peace Conference in 1919. The idea was very simple and direct. It declared that any people claiming a common national identity had the right to unite as one independent sovereign state. In both instances, Germany had been denied this right.

Most of the conspirators wanted to rectify what to them was a miscarriage of justice. Like Goerdeler, however, they believed that the goal should be achieved peacefully through negotiation and compromise with the other European states. There should be a general policy of reconciliation. The approach they advocated contrasted sharply with Hitler's diplomacy of the bludgeon. War, they believed, should be considered only as a last resort to solving the problem of German minorities, and certainly not before Germany had achieved military parity with the European powers. The year 1938 was not the time for military action, because German rearmament still was very incomplete. The army leaders believed that Hitler's plan for Czechoslovakia would lead to a military confrontation with France and Great Britain, and the result for Germany would be a terrible military defeat. Consequently, the conspirators believed that the only way to foil Hitler's plans was to remove him from office, and assassination was the only way to do it.

CHAPTER 5

The Army — Four Rounds of Resistance[1]

Four distinct rounds of resistance activity can be identified in the subsequent history of the Third Reich. Round I took place during the period of July to September 1938, with the major resistance activity centered within the Supreme Command of the Army, together with the general staff and their civilian supporters. The Abwehr, in the person of Hans Oster, provided the leadership for this effort. Round II had two parts. Part 1 began with the opening phase of World War II in September 1939. It collapsed in November largely because of cowardice on the part of several generals, leaving the resistance movement and its leaders at least temporarily discomfited. Nevertheless, Part 2 resumed a short time later and came to an end in May 1940 with the German military strike against Western Europe. Henning von Tresckow, an officer serving in the high command of Army Group Center (one of three army groups on the Eastern Front), provided the leadership for Round III, August 1942 to October 1943. The last phase, Round IV, took place between March 1944 and July 20, 1944. The replacement army command staff directed this last phase, which culminated in Operation Valkyrie and the bombing of Hitler's headquarters in East Prussia by Claus Schenk von Stauffenberg.

* * * *

Any study of the anti-Nazi conspiracy has to deal with the fundamental question, why did it fail? Why was Hitler not killed? Ultimately, the answer lies with the German Army, specifically its leadership. Absent the decisive and determined action of its generals, success was unlikely. All of the moral outrage over the criminal behavior of the Nazis and all of the fierce and grim determination of the conspirators to eliminate the one man who stood at the apex of this criminal regime ultimately proved to be insufficient to achieve the goal. A general with adequate command authority over troops and with the dedication to carry out the mission was absolutely vital to success. In the end, there was no one on whom the conspirators could depend to play that role.

As passionately as men like Hans Oster, Henning von Tresckow, Claus von Stauffenberg, and those who stood by their side wished to liquidate the Nazi scourge, they could not carry out their mission without troops on the ground to support them. Too many generals in positions of high responsibility were willing to sacrifice principle for expediency. Too many tried to "straddle the fence" and play both ends against the middle. They wanted to be on the winning side, wherever it might be. Too many either were truly paralyzed by the oath of allegiance and were unable to join with the conspirators or, more likely, used the oath as a convenient pretext for doing nothing. Too many lacked the moral courage and conviction of the conspirators. Still others – perhaps most of them – never completely understood the true nature of Nazism until it was too late to prevent disaster. These men shared this myopia with many civilian conservatives.

In addition to the problem of ignorance and moral equivocation, a sense of fatalism and even hopelessness prevailed among some of the generals. They believed that "an indomitable fate was at work and would follow its predestined course regardless of what they might say or do."[2] For example, General Werner von Fritsch, commander in chief of the army from 1935 to 1938, declared early on that "Hitler was 'Germany's destiny for better or worse, and this destiny will run its course. If he tumbles into the abyss, he will take us all with him. Nothing can be done.'"[3] Others concurred, saying that "it was impossible to resist Hitler."[4] An almost Calvinist sense of predestination prevailed among many members of the officer corps, and they resigned themselves to what was, in their minds, inevitable.

Round I: The Oster Conspiracy, July to September 1938

As Round I began to evolve, three sectors of opposition either within or close to the government coalesced into a single resistance movement that was about to become a conspiracy to overthrow Nazi rule. First, there was the civilian sector, which included many who had been affiliated with the political parties of the Weimar Republic, as well as others who had at least tangential connections with its public life. In sum, this sector "embraced all civilian elements outside the foreign office."[5]

At its center was the group led by Carl Goerdeler. Also included were members of the government bureaucracy, jurists, and union leaders, along with teachers and university professors. They were men such as Ewald von Kleist-Schmenzin of the Prussian landed aristocracy, a monarchist and a committed Christian who loathed all that Hitler and the Nazis represented, and Fritz-Dietlof von der Schulenburg, a lawyer who joined the Nazi

Party in 1932 but was expelled in 1940 because he became "politically unreliable." These men were representative of a fairly extensive collection of individuals who had significant contacts both within Germany and beyond its borders. This civilian sector eventually made common cause with the general staff, most particularly with its chief, Ludwig Beck. Thus emerged the Beck–Goerdeler group, discussed earlier. Despite the severe constraints placed upon it by a powerful and well-organized police state, it had a broad base of support.[6]

The foreign office represented the second sector of opposition within the various circles of government. These men were professionals in the best sense of the word. They were sophisticated, highly educated, well trained, cultured, cultivated, pragmatic, and nonideological, with a realistic understanding of world affairs. They represented the best of the historic Prussian ethos. Equally important, they were completely free of Nazi taint; they held it in complete disgust and contempt. This intense dislike undoubtedly reflected their own aristocratic pedigree and their strong sense of class consciousness, which deeply resented the "guttersnipes" who now were wielding almost unlimited power in a manner that represented a mortal threat to the fatherland.

Yet despite their antipathy toward the Nazis, few were drawn into the active resistance. The foreign office never became a "hotbed of resistance to the regime and its policies." Instead, most of the foreign ministry personnel took the route of "inner rejection" that many of their compatriots followed. With a few notable exceptions, they did not participate in any conspiratorial activities. Theirs was a classic case of "internal exile." They went along with the prevailing Nazi ethos without enthusiasm or commitment. Doubtlessly most of them would have actively supported the resistance had Hitler been removed. Ernst von Weizsäcker, the state secretary in the foreign office, personified the conflicted attitudes that prevailed within the foreign office. He "traveled a slippery path between conformity and accommodation on the one hand and resistance on the other, with all the attendant illusions and entanglements one might expect."[7]

Two exceptions to people holding this general attitude were the brothers Erich and Theo Kordt, important men in the foreign office who also became very active in the resistance. They had many diplomatic contacts with foreign governments as well as with the German military establishment. They also played a significant role in the first round of resistance activities centered on the international crisis that Hitler's actions against Czechoslovakia precipitated in the summer of 1938.

The Army – Four Rounds of Resistance

The third resistance sector was the army – specifically, the Supreme Command of the Army (Oberkommando des Heeres, or OKH), together with the general staff plus the Abwehr section of the OKW. The army was the most important of the three sectors because no movement to remove Hitler and his henchmen from power could hope for success without its cooperation and participation. Only it had the requisite means, namely, access to Hitler and weapons, to actually carry out an assassination plot. Army Group Center, which would provide the leadership for Round III of the resistance, did not become active until the midsummer of 1942, more than a year after the military campaign against the Soviet Union that began in June 1941.

Within the OKH, the two key figures were Ludwig Beck, chief of the Truppenamt (Troop Office) from 1933 to 1938,[8] and Franz Halder, chief of the general staff from 1938 to 1942. Both men despised the Nazis and all they represented. Both men wrestled with the moral issues implicit in serving the Nazi state. And tragically, both men ultimately failed to stem the tide of Nazi expansionism and aggression. Beck, in particular, had struggled with these moral issues ever since Hitler's accession to power. Like many fellow officers of his generation, he had initially welcomed the Nazis, because he believed that they would restore to Germany the military power that had been lost in 1918. Nevertheless, the dark side of Nazi rule became more manifest with the passage of time, and Beck's disillusionment increased accordingly.

Two events occurring in 1934 especially disturbed him. The first was the new oath of allegiance. The second was the infamous blood purge episode of 1934.[9] The Rhineland adventure of 1936 only increased Beck's apprehensions as he, together with Generals von Fritsch and von Blomberg, tried without success to induce Hitler to "alter the nature of the operation."[10] Although they wished to see military installations restored in the Rhineland, these three men had serious misgivings about Hitler's determination to move in open defiance of the provisions of the Treaty of Versailles. His success in this adventure only increased their anxieties.

* * * *

The ultimate turning point for Beck and for those in the military sector who supported him came with the realization that Hitler was planning a military assault against Czechoslovakia in 1938 over the Sudetenland issue. Beck's journey thus far had included "years of agonized self-examination,"[11] but now he crossed his personal Rubicon. Having made his decision, he forged ahead, regardless of the consequences. Hitler, he concluded, had to be removed from power. In contemplating the unfolding events during the summer of that crisis year, he penned the following words:

> History will burden those military leaders with blood guilt who fail to act according to their professional knowledge and their conscience ... There is a lack of stature and a failure to recognize one's mission when a soldier in highest position in such times conceives of his duties and problems solely within the restricted framework of his military assignments and in unawareness that his highest responsibilities are toward the entire nation. Abnormal times require deeds that are also out of the ordinary.[12]

This is one of the most eloquent statements of a soldier's ultimate responsibility ever written, and undoubtedly reflects Beck's deeply held religious convictions. He has been described as "a believing Christian."[13] Whatever the source of his convictions was, the statement describes unequivocally the existence of a morality that transcends conventional definitions of treason. Ironically, Beck was unable to take an active part in the attempted coup against Hitler at the time of the Czech crisis because, on August 18, 1938, he resigned in protest over Hitler's policies.[14] Despite his departure from the general staff, he remained a part of the resistance until the very end, and paid with his life for his actions.

In addition to the OKH and general staff of the army, the Abwehr also became a significant center of the resistance movement, partly because of its contacts with foreign governments, but largely because of the efforts of three men: Admiral Wilhelm Canaris, head of the Abwehr, Hans Oster, and Helmuth Groscurth. By the summer of 1938, the three sectors – civilian, foreign office, and army – had melded their activities into a single movement. Beck from the army, Goerdeler from the civilian sector, and Ernst von Weizsäcker, the career diplomat who at that time was secretary of state in the foreign office, provided the initial leadership for each respective sector in the growing conspiracy.

A network of potential resisters had been building for the past several years, especially between the civilians and the military establishment. By this time, Carl Goerdeler was seen as the pivotal figure of the civilian segment of the resistance movement. His extensive experience in public life had enabled him to establish many contacts with other notable individuals within German society, both in government service and in private life – contacts such as the industrialist Robert Bosch. He also was well known outside Germany. His foreign travels took him to some twenty-two foreign countries – especially France, Great Britain, and the United States – between June 1937 and the end of 1938, with the ultimately unsuccessful goal of securing foreign support for the resistance movement.[15] Moreover, his clashes with the Nazis, especially over the Mendelssohn statue affair in Leipzig, were well known.

Goerdeler and Beck – who by now had made the irrevocable decision to support the resistance wholeheartedly – had become two foci for resistance activities, the former for the civilians and the latter for the army. Goerdeler remained the "principal motor" and "the driving force of the civilian opposition."[16] This was especially true for the conservatives who had cast their lot with the resistance,[17] which, thanks to the increasingly ominous turn of events over the preceding four years, had grown considerably in numbers. Remarkably, the activities remained secret. This is testimony to the degree of cohesion that prevailed, especially within the army leadership. Even though some generals did not approve of the resistance activities, they did not betray the conspirators. Moreover, the resisters only spoke candidly to those whom they knew well and who shared their revulsion for the Nazis.

All was now in place for Round I of the resistance movement to begin. The quality of its leadership and organization, together with its broad base of support among the generals committed to the cause, offered the best hope for success of any of the anti-Nazi conspiracies. It has been said that the general officer corps was closer to mutiny at this time than it ever would be again.[18] The plot ultimately failed, not because the resistance acted improperly, but because foreign governments did not act at all.

The Sudetenland question had much greater significance than either the Rhineland or Austrian affairs, because international treaty obligations were part of this issue. Both France and the Soviet Union had committed themselves to the preservation of Czechoslovakia's territorial integrity. Additionally, Great Britain, with informal ties to France, could be dragged into the controversy as well, even though the British government had indicated its reluctance to go to war in the defense of Czechoslovakia. British Prime Minister Neville Chamberlain himself had disingenuously declared that he did not wish to engage in hostilities that were the result of "a quarrel in a faraway country between people of whom we know nothing."[19] Nonetheless, the Wehrmacht generals understood fully that Hitler's determination to press the issue regardless of the consequences could precipitate a general conflict.

These events especially perturbed General Beck.[20] He was convinced that a war with France, probably Great Britain, and perhaps even the Soviet Union over the Sudetenland would be suicidal for Germany. On May 5, he revealed his doubts to Hitler, who summarily rejected his fears with ridicule. Subsequent efforts either to induce Hitler to change his mind or to persuade the generals to take drastic action proved fruitless. Discouraged by his inability to reverse the course of events, Beck resigned from his position as chief of the general staff on August 18, 1938.[21]

The increasingly bellicose atmosphere spurred the conspirators to greater activity. Rational argument had failed. Hitler refused to be deterred. Therefore, determined action on the part of the conspirators appeared to be the only way to stop his mad dash to war. By the summer of 1938, several conservative groups, civilian and military, younger and older, had coalesced in a concerted effort to eliminate Hitler and remove his accomplices from power. Government officials like Abwehr commander Canaris, State Secretary von Weizsäcker, and Erwin von Witzleben, who was the military commander of the Berlin district, and civilians such as Schacht, Goerdeler, von Kleist-Schmenzin, and von der Schulenburg, together with a group of younger men such as the Kordt brothers, Hans Bernd von Haeften, and Adam von Trott zu Solz, all of whom had served in the Foreign Ministry at one time or another, became part of this conspiratorial group. Also included were former members of the senior civil service, such as Hans Berndt Gisevius, previously an assistant secretary in the Interior Ministry, and Count Peter Yorck von Wartenburg, one of the very active members of the Kreisau Circle who had served in the office of the Reich Price Commissioner.[22] The two most important military officers within this conspiracy, especially after Beck's departure, were Groscurth and Oster.

These conspirators began to "meet in small groups ... informally to grumble, criticize and warn, and to make plans – some legal, some half-legal, and some illegal – to prevent a war for which the nation was not ready."[23] The growing apprehensions of these men were leading them to "outright sedition."[24] They began to make plans for a coup d'état. This effort included putting out feelers to other like-minded individuals, working on the details for troop deployments, drawing up lists of potential leaders and officials for a new provisional government, and developing a plan of action that would coordinate their respective activities, especially between the army and the proposed civil administration. High on their list was the question of Hitler's fate. Should he be arrested or assassinated? No definitive answer was reached at this point. Foreign contacts were made as well, but nothing of any substance came of them. Although there were "polite expressions of interest ... [there were no] concrete pledges of support."[25]

With Beck's departure from the general staff, the most important figure to emerge from this diffuse group was Hans Oster. Beck has been described as the commander in chief of the military wing of the resistance, and Oster its chief of staff.[26] Oster assumed command of the conspiracy almost immediately upon Beck's resignation.[27] From this time forward, until his dismissal from the Abwehr in 1943, Hans Oster was the dominant figure in the active resistance movement within the government. Many of his comrades in the struggle against the Nazis considered him to be "the greatest figure in the opposition."[28]

A pastor's son, Oster was a career soldier who was thoroughly immersed in the Prussian tradition of selfless service to the state. He described himself as totally apolitical as a young man: "There were no politics for us. We wore the king's uniform and that was enough for us."[29] His social values were "conservative and royalist."[30] He served his country well during the Great War and was completely undone by the military collapse of 1918. Although he totally rejected the concept of republicanism, he nevertheless elected to remain in the Reichswehr, the army of the Weimar Republic, with the hope that he and his comrades could "help our nation to survive this difficult period."[31]

Like many of his generation and political persuasion, Oster gave cautious support to the Nazis and to their avowed goals of restoring Germany to what they considered to be its rightful place within the international community. The prospect of a revived and effective military establishment was especially appealing. Nonetheless, there was much about Nazism that Oster found repellent, especially the Nazi goal of politicizing the entire nation, including all social relationships.[32] After the Nazis assumed power, their behavior – such as arbitrary arrest and punishment of their opponents, plus the establishment of the concentration camp system – only reinforced his revulsion. The final turning point for him came on June 30, 1934, with the Night of the Long Knives, Hitler's murderous preemptive strike against his enemies. This episode convinced Oster that Hitler and the Nazis were a menace to Germany "and must be overthrown."[33] Worst of all from Oster's perspective, the army itself had been complicit in the affair, thus demonstrating its moral obtuseness and its inability to comprehend the depth of Nazi depravity.

Another significant source of Oster's hatred for the Nazis was their virulent anti-Semitism. Doubtlessly his deeply held Christian convictions significantly contributed to his attitude. His moral compass indicated that the Nazis represented ultimate evil, and it pointed to the course of action he must follow. "It was his sense of right and decency which ... dictated Oster's rejection of Nazism. He loathed it with a hard white heat that admitted no reservations, qualifications or extenuating circumstances."[34] Hence, he was prepared to take any measures necessary to exorcise these demons now possessing the soul and spirit of the German nation. It was said of Oster that he was willing to fight fire with fire – that is, "to use the tools of criminals [in order] to contend with them." Such tools included "deception, treason and murder."[35] In sum, Oster was willing to go to any length and use any methods, moral or immoral, just or unjust, in order to eradicate the Nazi scourge.

Oster's incredible courage, commitment, and acute moral sensibility distinguished him from most of his fellow officers in the resistance during these early years. They were less concerned with the moral issues raised by Nazism than with Hitler's "reckless foreign policy."[36] These men obviously did not yet comprehend the full implications of Nazism. They did not realize that "National Socialism represented an entirely new phenomenon: an ideology of such sinister immorality that traditional values and loyalties no longer applied."[37] The full scope of Nazi savagery did not become apparent to them until the Polish and especially the Russian campaigns of World War II.

One man who grasped the depth of Nazi moral depravity quite early was Erich Schultze, a very close friend of Oster. They spoke freely between themselves about the growing menace, and they came to recognize the necessity of removing Hitler from power. Schultze, in an interview with the late historian Harold Deutsch in 1972, spoke the following words: "Oster and I had complete trust in each other during the Third Reich and were able to talk openly. From early on there was no doubt in our minds about the necessity of Hitler's removal; only how was left unanswered."[38] Schultze said that they reached this conclusion as "conscientious and concerned Christians who were very worried about the increasing danger facing the entire world," rather than as "soldiers and officers."[39] Additionally, their growing concern over the fate of Germany's (and ultimately Europe's) Jews became their primary incentive for taking action against the Nazis. Said Schultze, "We suddenly felt we were responsible before God for their [the Jews'] rescue."[40]

Oster first met Wilhelm Canaris in 1931. In 1934, Oster joined the Abwehr as a civilian because he had lost his military commission as a result of an indiscretion with the wife of a superior officer. The relationship of the two men was rather complex and is difficult to define. Evidently they never became close friends, and they did not work in close harmony. Whereas Canaris initially supported the Nazis, Oster from the outset found them to be repellent. However, the two men eventually did become of one mind in their opposition to Hitler and the Nazis. Canaris was given command of the Abwehr in 1935, whereupon he immediately restored Oster's commission and gave him, if not quite carte blanche, at least wide discretion to begin building an anti-Nazi network within the Abwehr. The network that Oster created is known today as the "Oster conspiracy." Canaris ultimately promoted Oster to the position of second-in-command of the Abwehr, which made him, in effect, Canaris's chief operating officer.[41] Canaris did not play an active role in the conspiracy but acted more as a "protector" for the conspirators.[42]

Oster has been described as "a gregarious and charismatic man [who] made friends easily and inspired the trust of others."[43] These talents were put to good use as he began assembling his group of conspirators. He meticulously began recruiting officers to work with him in turning the Abwehr into a center of anti-Nazi activity.[44] One of the group, Franz Marie Liedig, said that "Oster's office was a port of call for all those members or associates who were self-acknowledged opponents of National Socialism."[45] Oster's efforts over the next three years produced an organization comprised of dedicated and talented individuals, with a well-thought-out plan that, according to some historians, had "reasonably good prospects of success," although others have expressed their doubts.[46]

During the summer of 1938, Oster wrote a plan, known to history as the Oster Study (Studie Oster), that has been described as a "concise analysis of takeover problems, and a delineation of measures to be taken" in order to carry out a successful coup d'état against the Third Reich.[47] Oster had conferred with Beck during the initial stages of the plan's development.

The concept behind the plan was straightforward. Oster proposed to use the growing fear throughout Germany of a war with Great Britain and France over the Sudetenland as a pretext to dispatch Hitler. He created a small paramilitary assault party that would raid Hitler's quarters at the Reich Chancellery and kill the Führer. Simultaneously, various military units within the Berlin military district, under the overall command of General von Witzleben, would surround the city of Berlin and occupy "the ministerial buildings, the more vital government agencies, post and telegraphic offices, radio stations, central communications offices, air ports [*sic*], police stations [that is, SS and Gestapo headquarters], and party offices."[48] The plan also included a list of Nazi officials to be apprehended, plus a second list of individuals to serve in a provisional government pending elections for a permanent government. Ludwig Beck was the proposed permanent government's designated head. Additionally, the raiders were to apprehend top party officials, namely, Joseph Paul Goebbels, Hermann Göring, Heinrich Himmler, Martin Bormann, and Rudolf Hess. Assisting Witzleben in the military part of the plan was General Walter Graf von Brockdorff-Ahlefeldt, who commanded the Twenty-Third Infantry Division garrisoned in the Berlin military district.[49] The Berlin police, commanded by Wolf Heinrich Graf von Helldorf, were to participate in the coup as well.

The coup attempt was to commence immediately upon receipt of orders from the army commander in chief, Walther von Brauchitsch.[50] As with many such operations, however, the devil was in the details, one of the most important of which was Great Britain. Would the British – and the French – government initiate hostilities in defense of Czechoslovakia or not? Therein lay the key to the success or failure of Oster's plan. If the two democracies would respond militarily, the coup would go ahead. The Oster plan was predicated on the prospect of war between Germany and its two antagonists, France and Great Britain.

A second, potentially fatal problem lay with the chain of command. Only Brauchitsch could give the order for the conspirators to take action. The chief of staff – in this case, the newly appointed Franz Halder – commanded no troops, and he could issue orders only in the name of the commander in chief.[51] Regrettably, Brauchitsch was the weakest link in that chain of command. On paper, his credentials were impeccable. His distinguished upper-middle-class family had a "long tradition of unquestioning service to the Prussian state."[52] He was educated at the War Academy, served on the general staff in Berlin, and was decorated for exceptional performance as a staff officer in the Great War.[53] Unfortunately he was a deeply flawed man. He has been described as "hapless" and "weak-kneed," a man with "little intestinal fortitude."[54]

In truth, his moral compass was severely, even fatally, damaged. His relations with Hitler were indicative of his weakness of character. Although he disdained Nazism itself, he admired the Führer personally, even though he entertained serious doubts about Hitler's "political and military judgment."[55] He could not stand up to the man. Hitler intimidated him. In speaking of their relationship, Brauchitsch confessed to Halder, "When

I confront this man, I feel as if someone were choking me and I cannot find another word."[56] He could never free himself from Hitler's grasp. Doubtlessly a personal matter between the two men contributed to this state of affairs. Hitler had given Brauchitsch a gift of 250,000 reichsmarks to relieve him from financial distress caused by an acrimonious divorce.[57] Thereafter, Brauchitsch could never free himself from his sense of obligation to the Führer. Hitler had bought him. All of these elements would have serious consequences for the success of the Oster plan, as well as other plots against Hitler.

As the Oster conspiracy grew throughout the spring and summer of 1938, the Nazi government was moving to implement its plans to invade Czechoslovakia. Storm signals were raised on May 19–20, 1938, with the discovery of German troop movements near the Czech border. The Czech government responded with a partial mobilization of its nearly 180,000-man military reserve. When news of these events reached the European capitals, the response was a flurry of diplomatic activity. A sharp retort from London and Paris to Berlin suggested that Britain and France would respond militarily to any German attack on Czechoslovakia. However, nothing of substance took place. British reconnaissance reports on May 22 indicated that German military activity within the area in question did not appear to be of a threatening nature.[58] Consequently, the crisis dissipated, but not without subsequent ramifications of great importance to the resistance.

The world was given the mistaken impression that Hitler had backed down because Britain and France had threatened to take military action against Germany in the event of a German invasion of Czechoslovakia. In reality, he had no intention of invading Czechoslovakia at that particular time. His timetable called for a military strike later in the year. Nonetheless, the suggestion that the Nazis had rescinded their invasion plans because of Western threats of a military response infuriated him. Hitler had suffered a loss of face within the international community. Consequently, he revised his timetable and ordered the Wehrmacht to prepare for an attack against Czechoslovakia by October 1 at the latest. This plan – with the code name Fall Grün (Case Green) – was given at the time of the aforementioned May 28 meeting when Hitler revealed his determination to eradicate Czechoslovakia. If the execution of this order resulted in war with Great Britain and France, so be it. Such was Hitler's attitude.

Oster's main task at this point was to convince the generals of the need to take decisive action against the Nazi leadership, that is, against Hitler himself. As early as mid-July, he and Beck, the latter of whom was still chief of staff, discussed the possibility of the generals refusing to follow orders to attack Czechoslovakia – essentially a mutiny – to be followed by their mass resignation as a protest against Hitler's orders.[59] The success of such a venture, however, required at the very least virtual unanimity, and this was highly unlikely. Nonetheless, a few generals already supported Oster. Certainly, Beck could be counted on. Two others in this category were Generals Georg Thomas and Erwin von Witzleben. Thomas, the War Economy director, had declared his position as early as 1936 at the time of the Rhineland episode, and he remained active in the resistance to the end. Shortly after the invasion of the Soviet Union in 1941 and while working with the Beck–Goerdeler group, he visited several commanders on the Eastern Front, trying to enlist their support for a coup, but he was unsuccessful. Unlike many of his contemporaries in military service, Witzleben's ultimate goal had been not merely to prevent war but to eliminate Hitler and to remove the Nazis from power. His opposition to the war provided a convenient pretext to achieve the larger goal. In this, he was at one with Oster.[60]

Franz Halder, Beck's successor as chief of staff, though certainly sympathetic to the Oster conspiracy, was among those men who were less reliable. He detested Hitler and the Nazis. "In principle he was usually ready to proceed against them."[61] It was said of Halder that he "considered [Hitler's] rule highly illegitimate because it stood outside all tradition; truth, morality, patriotism, even human beings themselves were only instruments for the accrual of more power. Hitler in Halder's view was 'the very incarnation of evil.'"[62] Yet, like so many of his compatriots in the army, he invariably would hesitate at the critical moment. Did his oath of allegiance inhibit him? We shall never know.

Hans Berndt Gisevius, an active member of the resistance who survived to tell his story, said of Halder: "What [he] lacked was not intelligence nor awareness of his position nor patriotism. He lacked will."[63] It was said of the conspirators in general, "those who had the will lacked the opportunity, whereas those who had the opportunity lacked the will."[64] This reality became the curse of the resistance. It was one of the most formidable obstacles the conspirators faced.

As the Czech crisis deepened throughout the spring and summer of 1938, those in the Oster conspiracy who had foreign contacts worked assiduously to build international support for their proposed actions. For all practical purposes, this support was the key to success. Most of Germany, and the rest of Europe as well, greeted the prospect of an international conflict over the Sudetenland with much fear. They were opposed to military action of any sort. Thus, the potential for securing a strong popular base for resistance activities was there, but it could only be achieved with international, that is, British, support. "Nothing less than the specter of a full-fledged European war could hope to secure that wide popular support needed for an anti-Nazi coup."[65] Hitler was approaching the apogee of his popularity. The only way to effectively and successfully challenge that popularity was through the threat of war, and that threat had to come from Great Britain, and also from France.[66]

Moral and ethical issues aside, the rationale for a coup at this time had to be presented as an attempt to prevent war. The greatest international challenge to Hitler's ambitions for an expansionist foreign policy, especially the Sudetenland issue, lay with Great Britain. The British government was clearly the leader in the tacit alliance of the two Western democracies. Its actions would determine the response to the Nazi challenge. Therefore, on several occasions during these months of crisis, members of the resistance traveled to London, either at the behest of others or on their own initiative, in an effort to convince the Western powers to stand firm against Hitler and his bellicose threats. Oster, in particular, wanted to convey to the British government the urgency of the situation and of the need for a firm British stand against Hitler. He wanted assurances that the inevitable consequence of a German attack against Czechoslovakia would be a general European conflict, and he especially wanted the German public to have a clear understanding of the dangers.[67] This above all was the essential ingredient in securing the mass support essential to the success of the Oster conspiracy. Goerdeler's earlier travels had helped to lay the groundwork for this latest attempt.

Oster and Beck chose the Prussian conservative Ewald von Kleist-Schmenzin to serve as their emissary on a mission to London for this purpose. He had contacts in England and already had warned them about Hitler's imperial pretensions on previous occasions. In the preparatory conversation among the three men, Beck spoke to Kleist the following words: "Bring me certain proof that England will fight if Czechoslovakia is attacked and I will make an end of this regime." In response to Kleist's question of what constituted proof, Beck responded, "An open pledge to assist Czechoslovakia in the event of war."[68] Thus began the Kleist mission.

Secrecy was of the utmost importance given that Kleist's anti-Nazi sentiments were well known to the authorities in Berlin. Thus, subterfuge and deception were essential to the success of the mission. The first step in this process was the flight to London, which took place on August 17, 1938. Kleist's cousin, who was a general and who obviously supported the resistance, secured a military car that was able to take him directly to the tarmac of Templehof Airport, thus avoiding the normal customs and currency control checks. With his cousin the general "running interference," Kleist was able to board the airplane without incident. Upon his arrival in London, he registered under an assumed name at the Park Lane Hotel, located in the fashionable Mayfair district. The hotel was chosen partly because of its large size, which, it was thought, would help Kleist to retain his anonymity.[69]

Kleist's primary contact in Great Britain was Ian Colvin, a "well-connected British journalist," who held membership in Berlin's prestigious Casino Club. This membership "opened many doors for him."[70] Colvin counted Ewald von Kleist-Schmenzen as one of his closest friends in Germany. Through the influence of Colvin, Kleist met with several members of the British government, including an antiappeasement member of Parliament, Lord Lloyd, and told him that everything was in place for the coup, but that success in toppling Hitler demanded a firm stand by the British government against the dictator's adventurism. Only a valid threat of military action by British – and presumably French – forces could precipitate a coup d'état.[71]

Kleist then met with Sir Robert Vansittart, the chief diplomatic adviser to the British Foreign Office, and tried to impress upon him the absolute necessity of a clear and unequivocal statement from the British government that Great Britain would defend the territorial integrity of Czechoslovakia by using all requisite means, including military force. Unfortunately, Vansittart had a very simplistic and unrealistic view of conditions inside Germany. He believed that there were two categories of German politicians, the "moderates" and the "extremists," and that "Hitler was a relatively passive leader who floated between the two factions that were grappling for control of the Third Reich."[72] This perception was not far removed from the one held by Prime Minister Chamberlain.[73] Kleist tried to disabuse Vansittart of this gross misperception without success. He urged that someone of authority in the British government should make a clear and unequivocal statement of Great Britain's unconditional support for Czechoslovakia.[74]

Vansittart sent a report to Lord Halifax, the foreign secretary, who forwarded it to Chamberlain.[75] In Chamberlain's response to the report, he compared Kleist and the conspirators to the friends of King James II of English history, who had been deposed in the Glorious Revolution but whose friends tried unsuccessfully to restore him to the throne. He said that "Kleist was clearly anxious to stir up his friends in Germany to attempt to overthrow Hitler, that he therefore was prejudiced and that a good deal of what he said must be discounted."[76] He considered Kleist "to be a traitor, pure and simple. For Chamberlain, Kleist's message held no significance."[77] Kleist's mission to Chamberlain was an abject failure. It "achieved nothing."[78] It is said of the British that throughout this whole period, they "remained impassive, stoic, and distrustful, offering little more than empty words."[79] Subsequent attempts to influence British policy proved just as fruitless.

Kleist did, however, meet with Winston Churchill at the latter's country home, Chartwell, where the atmosphere was more cordial. Churchill was sympathetic to Kleist and his cause, and he subsequently sent a letter to Vansittart fully supporting Kleist. He clearly perceived the danger that Hitler presented to peace and stability in Europe, and he had written extensively about the Nazi threat. However, he had been out of office since 1929 and was currently serving as a backbencher in Parliament. Consequently, he lacked both power and influence to determine foreign policy. Nonetheless, he assured Kleist that he would do all within his power to promote the cause that he represented. Regrettably, that power was pitifully minimal at this time.[80]

Almost three weeks later, yet one more attempt was made to contact the British government and impress upon its ministers the gravity of the situation in Germany. Erich Kordt, a deputy to Nazi Foreign Minister Joachim von Ribbentrop, passed a message to his brother Theo, who at the time was counselor at the German Embassy in London, asking Theo to convey the message to the British that he was "the delegate of an influential group in German military and political circles which wished to prevent the war with Czechoslovakia planned by Hitler and, subject to certain conditions, had the power to do so."[81] The success of this venture required British action.

> It must be made totally clear that war with Czechoslovakia would mean war with Britain. If, in spite of this, Hitler continued with his policy, then the German Army leaders would intervene by force of arms; German patriots saw no other method of stopping the crime of war. The prerequisite for such a step was a foreign

policy defeat for Hitler, which the declaration would imply; this would in practice signify the end of Nazi Germany.[82]

Thus, the conspiracy was prepared to move against Hitler immediately – to precipitate a coup d'état – upon receipt of news confirming that the British government was taking military action against Germany. Kordt's statement could not have been clearer. Everything depended upon the British government. Since Erich Kordt wished to remain in Germany during this time of growing crisis – the invasion of Czechoslovakia was scheduled for the end of September – he found a courier in the person of his cousin Susanne Simonis, a foreign correspondent for a German newspaper, *Die Allgemeine Zeitung* (General Gazette), who ostensibly was doing research for an article. To ensure secrecy, she memorized the contents of the message that she was to give to Theo. The date was September 5, 1938.[83] Upon receipt of the message, Theo contacted Sir Horace Wilson, described as "one of Chamberlain's most important advisers on foreign policy"[84] and a man with whom Kordt had previous dealings.

The message so impressed Wilson that he made arrangements for a meeting between Kordt and Lord Halifax, the foreign secretary, so that Kordt could repeat its contents to Halifax. In order to maintain as much secrecy as possible, the meeting took place on September 7 at 10 Downing Street rather than at the foreign office. Kordt entered the premises unnoticed through a side door that opened into the garden.[85] He left the meeting, again through the side door, with the reasonable assurance that "an unequivocal British declaration would shortly be made."[86] But nothing came of this meeting. Chamberlain remained unmoved. The Chamberlain government had no desire to antagonize Hitler. Later, after the Munich Conference had concluded, Halifax admitted to Theo Kordt: "We were not in a position to be as frank with you as you were with us. When you passed your message to us, we were already considering Chamberlain's mission to Germany."[87] Once again, the conspirators were thwarted by the failure of the British government to act.

Even a strongly worded message to Hitler that Halifax himself had drafted on September 9 was never delivered to its intended recipient, because British ambassador Sir Neville Henderson had strongly objected to its tone and contents. He was able to convince his superiors to scrap it. Henderson was deeply committed to the appeasement policy and has been described as being "intent on ingratiating himself with the Nazis."[88] The conspirators were up against a proverbial stone wall in trying to induce the

British government to take a strong stand against Hitler's determination to seize the Sudetenland.

The behavior of the British government during these crisis weeks had already been foreshadowed at the time of the May 1938 crisis, and this behavior provided an explicit example of the direction the government would take in the weeks and months ahead. Believing that the policy was too risky, the Chamberlain government altered course. He and Foreign Secretary Lord Halifax decided that the price of continued confrontation with Germany over Czechoslovakia was too high. If necessary, Czechoslovakia would be sacrificed to preserve the peace.[89] The mistaken belief that the Czech government had "concocted the rumors" and had misrepresented the episode of May 20–22 to serve its own interests reinforced their decision. The British government had a convenient excuse to abandon the Czech nation in its hour of need.[90] This decision would result in disaster for the Oster conspiracy, and ultimately for Europe and the world.

Naturally, the resistance did not and could not know that the Chamberlain government had changed course since the May crisis. Encouraged by the apparently firm stance that Chamberlain and his cabinet had taken in May, Oster and his fellow conspirators went ahead with their plans. Understandably, Oster believed that Hitler had overreached himself with his arrogant dismissal of both the British and the French as potential adversaries in this crisis. Obviously he could not know that Hitler's assessment of the two nations was the correct one.

The reasons for the British change of policy are many and varied and are much too complex to recount here. Suffice it to say that the Chamberlain government totally misread the nature of the Oster conspiracy and the entire German resistance movement. An important element in the unfolding Greek tragedy was Neville Chamberlain himself, who has been described as "a man of limited insight and imagination, repeatedly prone to wishful thinking." This was coupled with a stubborn refusal "to recognize reality." Nevertheless, he was supremely confident that he was fully equipped to deal with the nuances, subtleties, and intricacies of foreign policy, even though he was totally unversed in foreign affairs. His self-confidence bordered on arrogance.

Several entries in his personal diary during the thirties reveal:

> … his emerging self-image as the indispensable man, superior to any of his fellow-ministers. His abundantly justified self-confidence

was increasingly edged with condescension, sometimes verging on contempt, for his colleagues, and a growing disposition to take over their responsibilities and himself make decisions that were properly theirs.[91]

Despite his ignorance in these matters, he had "decided opinions" and pursued them forcefully. He believed that a new approach to world politics was essential for the preservation of world peace. A "new realism" was required that would "discover the real grievances of the dictators, ... correct them, and ... attain general appeasement." He failed to consider that his goals could only be achieved at the expense of other nations.[92] He also failed to consider the man with whom he was dealing.

The Chamberlain government also was very suspicious of the anti-Nazi conspirators. For one thing, there seemed to be something strange about German citizens urging the British government to take action against the German government.[93] Many within Chamberlain's cabinet, including Chamberlain himself, saw these men as little better than "a gang of traitors."[94] This perception doubtlessly reflected an anti-German mood in Great Britain that was a remnant of the anti-German propaganda of the Great War, even though many believed that Germany had just grievances against the Treaty of Versailles. The stereotypical image of the militaristic Prussians was still very strong, and Germany was seen as an unregenerate warlike nation, "innately evil, or at any rate inclined in that direction, as a result of that nation's historical and cultural heritage."[95]

Hence, many in Great Britain failed to see much of a difference between the Nazis and the resistance. They could not – or would not – see the moral and ethical differences between Hitler and the men who were trying to overthrow him.[96] Thus, Chamberlain's prejudices and ignorance of the facts laid the foundation for the collapse of the Oster conspiracy. Others in Chamberlain's government shared his attitude. "[They] did not understand that German conservatives and nationalists might be moral and religious men who were appalled at the lawlessness, brutality and inhumanity of the Nazis."[97]

The August weeks of 1938 passed quickly, and international tension continued to build. The drums of war, beating ever more loudly, announced Hitler's determination to launch a military strike against Czechoslovakia in order, in his words, to alleviate the suffering of these "poor, tortured creatures" [that is, the Sudeten Germans] and free them from "oppressive" Czech rule.[98] Oster's hopes that the generals would refuse to obey Hitler's orders to attack Czechoslovakia were fading. In an attempt to secure the help of the OKH, Oster sent the diplomat Erich Kordt on a mission to the army's commander in chief, Walther von Brauchitsch, to secure his cooperation for the proposed generals' strike. Kordt had been working with Oster in tandem, although not in direct cooperation, in an effort to disrupt Hitler's mad dash to the abyss. Brauchitsch listened to Kordt attentively but gave no assurances of his support for the plan.[99] With no hope of achieving unanimity, the prospect of a generals' mutiny was quashed. The only route now open to the conspirators was a coup d'état and probably assassination.[100] Nevertheless, one final, unexpected turn on the thorny path to the Sudetenland was yet to be taken. That turn was the melodrama of the infamous Munich Conference that would play out at the end of September.

It was now the end of August. The date for the invasion of Czechoslovakia was set for October 1.[101] Options available to the conspirators were diminishing rapidly. Additional attempts to secure the cooperation of the British government proved unavailing, and rational argument obviously would not dissuade Hitler from continuing his path to war. Oster concluded that the only logical way to preserve peace was to remove him from power, and assassination appeared to be the only alternative.[102] Ironically, while the conspirators in Berlin were planning to eliminate Hitler, the Chamberlain government in London remained determined to appease him.[103]

Yet there were glimmers of hope. Despite his tendency to equivocate, Halder, who had just replaced Beck as chief of staff on September 1, completely supported the goals of Oster and his men. Thus, despite the failure to secure the help of General von Brauchitsch, Oster was able to maintain contact with the general staff. Additionally, General von Witzleben, commander of the Berlin military district, remained an important figure in the Oster group, and several field commanders in the nearby military districts who actually commanded troops could be counted on to support a coup or at least "remain neutral."[104] Unfortunately Halder's support now began to waver. Halder lacked Oster's audacity and ruthlessness, two qualities absolutely essential for success in this effort. Though wholeheartedly behind the goal of Oster's plan, he balked at some of its details. Specifically, he was opposed to preemptive action and wanted to be certain that Hitler had "ignored all warnings and issued final instructions to launch a war."[105] Then and only then would he move.

Although the debate over various details of the coup continued, plans for its execution were now in place. Halder was prepared to take action immediately after Hitler's order to initiate Case Green, the invasion of Czechoslovakia, and this could occur at any time. Understandably, the tension among the conspirators was extremely great. One of the gravest concerns was over Halder himself. Would he give the necessary order, and would it be at the right moment?

The answer to that question will never be known, because a thunderbolt from London completely blindsided the conspirators and threw their plans into total disarray. On the evening of September 13, Neville Chamberlain announced to the world that he wished to meet with Herr Hitler to discuss the Sudetenland crisis. Hitler himself reportedly said after receipt of Chamberlain's proposal for a meeting, "Ich bin vom Himmel gefallen" (I am flabbergasted).[106] The news devastated the conspirators. Even worse, the Chamberlain government appeared ready to capitulate. If so, the prospects for a successful coup were nil.[107] Hitler once again would be proclaimed a genius, achieving his goals without war. The conspirators would be bereft of popular support.

Two days later, Hitler and Chamberlain met at the Berghof, Hitler's mountain retreat in Berchtesgaden, Bavaria. The discussions went as could have been predicted. Hitler demanded that Czechoslovakia cede to Germany all of the regions within its borders that had a majority of German inhabitants.[108] Chamberlain accepted the conditions and returned to London to confer with representatives of the French government. Together they essentially imposed them on the Czech government. Chamberlain returned to Germany, where on September 22–23 he met a second time with Hitler. The venue was the resort town of Bad Godesberg along the Rhine River. The purpose of the meeting was to confirm the agreement reached at Berchtesgaden. Much to Chamberlain's shock and dismay, Hitler increased his demands to an unacceptable level.[109] Hitler apparently was going to get his war after all.

As this diplomatic imbroglio unfolded, the conspirators continued to work feverishly on their plans for a coup. By mid-September, everything appeared to be in place. The leaders had conducted a series of meetings to work out the details of the plot even as the Berchtesgaden and Bad Godesberg conferences were taking place. One last meeting of the "inner circle" was held in Oster's apartment on September 20 to make final preparations for the assault.[110] Included in that meeting were Oster, Captain Friedrich Wilhelm Heinz (of whom more will be said momentarily), Witzleben, Goerdeler, Franz Marie Liedig, who was a close friend and associate of Oster in the Abwehr, and presumably Groscurth, Gisevius, and Hans von

Dohnányi, a lawyer and jurist attached to the Abwehr.[111] The plan called for Witzleben, who assumed overall military command of the operation, to lead a group of reliable officers from his headquarters and, accompanied by a raiding party, go to Hitler's personal residence on the Wilhelmstraße. Once there, Witzleben intended to arrest the Führer and demand his immediate resignation.[112] Additionally, units of the III Army Corps, under the overall command of Witzleben, were given orders to simultaneously "occupy Berlin and crush the anticipated resistance from the SS."[113]

Units from Hitler's personal bodyguard, the Leibstandarte SS Adolf Hitler, protected his residence as well as the Reich Chancellery. This bodyguard numbered some thirty-nine men in all, of whom approximately one-third were on duty at any given time. One security guard each was stationed at the entrance to the main Chancellery at #78 Wilhelmstraße and at Hitler's personal quarters, #77. In addition, several armed guards were stationed at various positions inside the residence area, in the front yard, and on the garage ramp, and the garden area was patrolled at night by an armed guard with a dog. This security force was described as "significant but not impenetrable."[114]

The conspirators were confident that a commando-like raiding party that they had assembled to provide protection to Witzleben and his companions could overpower Hitler's bodyguard in what doubtlessly would be a deadly clash between two armed groups. The leader of this raiding party was Captain Friedrich Wilhelm Heinz, a veteran of the Great War, whose political sympathies were right-wing and antirepublican. He had joined the Stahlhelm (Steel Helmet), the nationalist organization of veterans, and had served in the Ehrhardt Freikorps (a free corps brigade led by Captain Hermann Ehrhardt), one of the many private armies created in 1919 to fight the Communists and promote extremist nationalism. By the late thirties, Heinz, like many of his former comrades in arms, had become completely disillusioned with the Nazis, and he welcomed the opportunity to join the conspiracy to overthrow them and, in the process, dispatch Hitler. There was a remarkable similarity between Heinz and Hitler.

> Both were misogynist and anti-Semitic proponents of violence. Like Hitler, Heinz glorified war, and both had found the companionship in the trenches that had been missing from other parts of their lives. Heinz, like Hitler, had been nurtured in the nest of right-wing terrorist organizations that had befouled postwar Germany. Heinz had also been fired from his job as a

journalist for the Nazi Party for being too irascible and violent. Oster had found the right man for the job.[115]

Heinz had the ruthlessness, courage, and determination requisite to the success of the operation. The group that now assembled for the strike consisted of some twenty to sixty men (the numbers vary depending upon the source cited) from widely diverse backgrounds; they were "rough, brash young officers, students, and workers trained in the use of firearms."[116] It has been argued that the diversity of these men was deliberate, "calculated to show that the action was not just a military putsch to seize power for the Army, but a broad-gauged action by widely representative elements of anti-Nazi Germany."[117]

The calendar now read September 27. Several days earlier, Hitler had issued an ultimatum to the British government: the demands he had made at Bad Godesberg had to be accepted by 2:00 p.m., September 28, or else he would initiate action against Czechoslovakia.[118] Hitler followed this ultimatum with an order on the twenty-seventh, secretly sending some seven divisions to the Czech border in preparation for an assault anticipated on September 30 or October 1 at the latest. He hoped to surprise the Czechs. On the twenty-seventh, Hitler also marched his troops through the streets of Berlin in an attempt to whip up enthusiasm for war, but this met with the Berliners' sullen rejection.[119]

In the meantime, Heinz had moved his assault force, or commandos, to various private residences near the Chancellery and Hitler's residence on the Wilhelmstraße. Everything was in place. The plans had been carefully and meticulously made. "Preparations were more thorough and prospects of success greater than at any subsequent period."[120] Troops were at the ready. Even Brauchitsch appeared to be on board, although it is not clear even to this day just how committed to the coup he really was. Graf von Helldorf, police president of Berlin, had given his support to the plot somewhat earlier, thus guaranteeing the cooperation of the Berlin police.[121] Although assurances were given to several conspirators, such as Halder and Witzleben, that Hitler would be arrested and not killed, Oster and Heinz agreed between themselves that assassination was the only guarantee of success. Therefore, an "incident" would be manufactured that would result in Hitler's death.[122]

In the early morning hours of the twenty-eighth, Heinz assembled his commandos at army headquarters and distributed weapons, including small arms and ammunition plus hand grenades. The attack against

Czechoslovakia was anticipated at any moment, and a declaration of war from France and Britain was expected to follow shortly thereafter. These two events would provide the signal for the conspirators to take action, and since Halder would be the first to know about Hitler's order to launch Case Green, he was the logical contact person to give the signal to the leaders of the conspiracy, who could then give the order for the coup to commence. His call would be the trip wire,[123] but the signal was never given. Instead, an appeal came from an unlikely source for a four-power conference to include Germany, Great Britain, France, and Italy – but not Czechoslovakia – to resolve the crisis without a military confrontation. That source was the Italian dictator Benito Mussolini. For reasons that will never be completely clear, Hitler agreed to the appeal.[124]

The conference, held in Munich, the capital of Bavaria, on September 29, 1938, acceded to all of Hitler's demands. Czechoslovakia lost about 10,000 square miles of territory, which included fully one-third of its population, or approximately 3.5 million inhabitants, of whom some 700,000 were Czechs and 2.8 million were German. This area also included the nation's most heavily industrialized and most heavily fortified region.[125] The truncated remainder of Czechoslovakia would survive as an independent state for barely six months.

For three years, Adolf Hitler's virtually unparalleled string of political successes had dominated the headlines; the Rhineland, the Anschluss, and now Munich had demonstrated his audacity. His diplomatic method was threat, bluff, bluster, and intimidation – and it was successful. He had achieved his goals without war. Supporters as well as enemies called him a genius, doubtlessly the greatest statesman of his age, or perhaps any age. The Munich Conference is still considered to have been the pinnacle of his diplomatic success. Ironically, he had wanted neither a conference nor diplomacy. He had wanted war.

This turn of events had a calamitous impact on the resistance, which now was devastated and paralyzed. There would be no war after all. This, Hitler's "greatest international triumph,"[126] had rendered him virtually impregnable to any kind of domestic opposition. His popularity continued to soar to unprecedented heights. Who would dare to challenge him now? With peace seemingly assured for the foreseeable future and Hitler basking in the glory of his diplomatic "brilliance," his position was unassailable. The conspirators now had absolutely no way to secure popular support for a coup, "even on such an issue as preventing a major war."[127] That threat had been removed. What army officer now would be willing to participate in a coup d'état? The Oster conspiracy was reduced to a "mood of bitter helplessness."[128]

Munich, said Halder, had "decimated' the opposition."[129] They had come so close. Even as Hitler was in the final planning stages for his assault against Czechoslovakia, Hans Oster had finalized his own plans for an assault against the Third Reich. These men literally were within hours of launching a raid on Hitler's headquarters at the Reich Chancellery when news of the impending Munich Conference reached them. It was now over. There would be no coup d'état. The Oster conspiracy collapsed, and Round I of the resistance movement came to an end.[130]

These torturous events had taken the members of the Oster conspiracy on an emotional roller-coaster ride through the month of September 1938. First, the announcement of the Berchtesgaden meeting dashed their hopes. Then, they experienced a brief moment of euphoria when they learned the results of the Bad Godesberg meeting. But the announcement of the Munich Conference once again plunged them into deep despair.[131] It was a sad end to a journey that had shown much promise.

To this day, lingering questions hover over this whole tragic affair. Why did the conspirators not go ahead with the assassination plot? Why did they not follow through with their plan to eliminate the tyrant? The clarity of hindsight vision affirms that the opposition to Hitler's rule at this point in time was not based upon moral considerations – those would come later – but rather upon the issue of war or peace; and since peace had been preserved, there was no longer a need for a coup. This issue led directly to the fatal flaw in the plans for Round I of the resistance movement. The resisters in the summer of 1938 "had made their actions dependent on events they could neither accurately foresee nor control."[132] Success for the Oster conspiracy depended upon two external factors. First, Hitler had to order and initiate the invasion of Czechoslovakia; and second, Britain and France had to declare war. Oster and his group obviously had no control over these two actions. Under these constraints, the prospect of securing the degree of mass support essential to a successful coup d'état was extremely remote. The issue has been described as a "self-imposed dependence on external circumstances."[133]

And yet the question remains: What else could the conspirators have done? What other course of action could they have taken? Given the limitations imposed upon these men as a consequence of the conditions under which they struggled, any alternative approach was highly unlikely to meet with success. Over time, only a handful of officers, such as Hans

Oster, Helmuth Groscurth, Henning von Tresckow, and Claus Schenk von Stauffenberg, had the sheer audacity, singleness of purpose, and ruthlessness essential to the success of such a venture. And their numbers were too few.

* * * *

The Munich episode was a watershed moment for the resistance. Never again would the conditions for a coup d'état be as favorable as they were in September 1938. The debacle left the conspirators shattered and demoralized.[134] Writing well after the event, two of the most dedicated and active members of the resistance stated in very simple terms the effect of the Munich Conference on the conspiracy. The diplomat Erich Kordt declared, "The Munich Conference prevented the coup d'état in Berlin."[135] The lawyer Hans Berndt Gisevius was even more blunt and succinct: "Chamberlain saved Hitler."[136]

General Erwin von Witzleben eloquently expressed his dismay at the failure of the plot in a statement couched in terms of "heavy sarcasm" and reflecting the "bitterness" all the conspirators felt:

> You see gentlemen, for this poor foolish nation he is once again our big dearly beloved Führer, unique, sent from God, and we, we are a little pile of reactionary and disgruntled officers or politicians who dared to put pebbles in the way of the greatest statesman of all times at the moment of his greatest triumph … If we tried to do something now, history, and not just German history, would have nothing else to report about us than that we refused to serve the greatest German when he was the greatest, and the whole world recognized his greatness.[137]

This statement provides us with a mere glimpse into the sense of despair these men experienced as they contemplated the future course of events for their fatherland. It anticipates the grim, almost insurmountable barriers they faced in pursuing their conspiracy during wartime. Despite these obstacles, however, they persevered.

The organized resistance now entered a period of decline and disintegration that accompanied mutual recriminations and a growing sense of mistrust among its members.[138] The bonds uniting the individuals from the three sectors of German society forming the backbone of the resistance – civilian, foreign office, and army – began to crumble. Many of the leaders remained steadfast in the determination to topple Hitler from power – men such as Beck, Oster, Schulenburg, Gisevius, Goerdeler, and Witzleben. Others, however, became disheartened by the turn of events. Hitler's popularity was never higher than it was at this point. Nazi triumphalism reigned supreme in the Third Reich. Hitler and the Nazis were more firmly ensconced in Germany than ever, and the possibility of a coup d'état was gone.

Franz Halder, for one, believed that a coup attempt after Munich was futile. He and others within the resistance movement – especially the military officers – believed that only a crushing diplomatic or military defeat would undermine Hitler's support among the general population and the overall army leadership. Those generals on the fringes of the resistance found an excuse to remove themselves from any resistance activity. An assassination at this point would accomplish little, if anything, of a positive nature. Many believed a more likely result would be civil war.[139]

Hitler held all the reins of power. The resistance had none. Moreover, his reorganization of the military establishment became a factor in the overall picture. As noted, the OKW was little more than his personal staff and had to do his bidding. For example, Wilhelm Keitel, the head of the OKW, was little more than the Führer's lapdog. For his part, Hitler deliberately sowed discord between the OKW and the OKH (Supreme Command of the Army), which was the bastion of the old Prussian officer corps. "In the light of Hitler's foreign policy successes ... the ranks now began to waver." Some senior army officers became distressed over the fact that the OKH was showing a demonstrable lack of faith and confidence in the Führer. General Alfred Jodl, another one of Hitler's OKW flunkies, wrote of the OKH as the "enemy side."[140]

Hitler took advantage of the situation to dismiss other generals who were showing a decided skepticism toward his plans. These were men who had escaped the purge that had taken place earlier in the year.[141] Thus, the military branch of the resistance movement was effectively paralyzed. "After Munich ... the military could no longer be persuaded into a coup d'état."[142] Even the occupation of Prague and the destruction of the remains of an independent Czechoslovakia the following March failed to galvanize what was left of the resistance movement to further anti-Nazi action. Despite the discord that now existed within the ranks of the military establishment, the esprit de corps remained. Remarkably, none of those officers who opposed the resistance betrayed the conspirators.[143]

From now on, any renewal of a reorganized resistance movement – absent a disastrous military defeat – had to be built upon moral and ethical foundations. Mere opposition to war was insufficient. Only with the revelations of Nazism's evil nature and criminality could the resistance hope to recover its soul and renew its efforts. The war in the east ultimately would provide those revelations and inspire a renewed effort to rebuild the resistance movement.

* * * *

Despite the mood of despair that permeated the resistance, a remnant of the leadership remained resolute in the pursuit of their goal. Somehow, Hitler had to be eliminated. A pitifully small number of men, including Ludwig Beck, Hans Oster, Hans Berndt Gisevius, Erwin von Witzleben, and Carl Goerdeler, remained committed to bringing Hitler down. For the present, however, they could do nothing. They no longer had an effective organization, and they lacked the power and resources to carry on.[144] Thus, the goal remained unchanged: Hitler and the Nazis must be removed from power. The unanswered question also remained unchanged: How is the goal to be achieved? The search for an answer to this question would underlie the activities of the resistance for the next five years.

Round II, Part 1: The Abwehr, September to November 5, 1939

As the resistance leadership withdrew to recover and rebuild its shattered organization, events were moving swiftly toward a military confrontation in Poland. Hitler's success in bringing thousands of ethnic Germans "home" to a Germany with expanded frontiers not only failed to satisfy his territorial ambitions; it also encouraged him to engage in further expansionist activity in pursuit of his ultimate goal of a German empire in the east. On March 14, 1939, Slovakia, under threat of a German invasion, declared its independence from Bohemia and Moravia and became a satellite state of the Third Reich. On the fifteenth, German troops occupied Prague. The following day, the sixteenth, the German government announced the creation of "the Protectorate of Bohemia and Moravia." Thus the "abscess of an independent Czechoslovakia" was "lanced,"[145] and Neville Chamberlain's appeasement policy was in tatters. Czechoslovakia disappeared from the map of Europe, and Hitler achieved his "last great victory of ... statecraft by intimidation."[146] The Sudetenland had been a mere way station on the road to the creation of the "Greater Reich."

The march toward war in the east continued unabated through the spring and summer of 1939, with hostilities scheduled to begin on September 1. The pretext for the invasion was the border question, specifically the Polish Corridor that separated East Prussia from Germany proper. Hitler admitted, however, that the attack had a much-broader purpose. "What is involved for us is the consolidation of Lebensraum in the East and the safe-guarding of our food supply."[147] The construction of the Greater Reich was about to commence.

In a last, desperate effort to dissuade Hitler from ordering an attack, the British and French governments on March 31 announced that they would guarantee Polish territorial integrity. The communiqué from the Chamberlain government read in part as follows: "[In the event] of any action which clearly threatened Polish independence, and which the Polish government accordingly considered it vital to resist with their national forces, His Majesty's Government would feel themselves bound at once to lend the Polish government all the support in their power."[148]

Hitler's last step on the road to war was the infamous Nazi-Soviet Nonaggression Pact, signed on August 23. This treaty, a classic diplomatic bombshell, meant that German forces could now invade Poland with impunity. The Red Army (that is, the Soviet Army) would hold its fire. In fact, a secret protocol appended to the treaty provided for the dismemberment of the Polish state, with German forces coming in from the west and forces of the Soviet Union coming in from the east. Poland's doom was sealed.

* * * *

The long-anticipated and long-feared invasion of Poland commenced on September 1, 1939, with a frightening display of blitzkrieg, or lightning war. It represented a new type of warfare, mechanized and highly mobile, glimpses of which had been seen in the closing phases of the Great War. The Luftwaffe (air force) and panzer (armored) units struck first in coordinated attacks and were followed by infantry assaults. The focus was on offensive operations. The defensive side of the military equation was ignored. Stationary trench warfare of the type found in the Great War was relegated to the history books. Blitzkrieg tactics allowed Germany to seize and hold the initiative throughout the conflict, which, it was believed, would be short, though sharp and violent.

The Polish campaign represented a brilliant display of modern mobile warfare. By September 21, German forces had completely overrun western Poland. The capital city of Warsaw held out until September 27, when its surrender brought the conflict to an end. In the meantime, Soviet troops, in accordance with the terms of the Nazi–Soviet pact, invaded Poland from the east. By the end of September 1939, Poland, like Czechoslovakia, was no more.[149] Once again, Hitler had achieved his goal at minimal cost. War, his preferred method of resolving international disputes, had brought him great success.

This time, however, his instincts failed him and he made a serious miscalculation. Unexpectedly, both Great Britain and France honored their commitment to Poland and responded with declarations of war against the Third Reich on September 3. Hitler had anticipated a series of short wars, but now the limited war against Poland threatened to become a much wider and much more open-ended struggle. Whether it would become that long-feared general conflict depended largely upon decisions made in Berlin. If Germany were to limit its objectives and assume a defensive posture, then a diplomatic resolution of the war, though remote, just might be possible. This obviously was not to be, however. Adolf Hitler was playing a dangerous game: all or nothing, Weltmacht oder Vernichtung (World Power or Destruction). It was not the nature of Nazism to accept moderation or restraint. Thus, the seeds of Germany's destruction already were being sown in Eastern Europe.

The apprehensions of this ultimate result were very strong in Germany in the late summer of 1939.[150] Official reports described the mood of the general populace at the end of August as "depressed," and the actual outbreak of hostilities produced a "general 'despondency' amongst the population."[151] The correspondent William Shirer, who had reported the sullen mood of the Berliners at the time of the Czech crisis a year earlier, described the reaction on September 3, 1939, to the announcement of the British war declaration with the following words:

> I was standing in the Wilhelmstrasse before the Chancellery about noon when the loudspeakers suddenly announced that Great Britain had declared herself at war with Germany. Some 250 people – no more – were standing there in the sun. They listened attentively to the announcement. When it was finished, there was not a murmur. They just stood there. Stunned. It was difficult for them to comprehend that Hitler had led them into a world war.[152]

Shirer went on to describe his perception of the general mood among the Berliners: "On the faces of the people astonishment, depression ... In 1914, I believe, the excitement in Berlin on the first day of the World

War was tremendous. To-day no excitement, no hurrahs, no cheering, no throwing of flowers, no war fever, no war hysteria."[153] "Apprehension and anxiety were the commonest emotions as Germany entered a state of war."[154]

State Secretary for Foreign Affairs Ernst von Weizsäcker was not an especially active member of the resistance, but he was nonetheless sympathetic toward and cooperative with its operations and goals. On September 3, he wrote:

> And now the struggle has begun. God grant that not everything that is good and valuable will be utterly destroyed in it. The shorter time it lasts the better. But one must remember that the enemy will never conclude peace with Adolf Hitler and Herr von Ribbentrop [the Nazi foreign minister]. What does this mean? As if anyone could fail to see what it means.[155]

His somber assessment was all too prophetic.

An obvious question immediately arises: Why did the conspirators not take advantage of the situation to stage a commando-like strike against Hitler, similar to the one planned for the previous year at the time of the Munich Conference? The answer is as simple as it is tragic. The resistance movement was in complete disarray as a consequence of the fiasco that had occurred a year earlier. The leadership had disintegrated. For example, in November 1938, General von Witzleben, one of the most important members of the military opposition, was transferred from Berlin to assume command of a military unit located at Frankfurt am Main in western Germany, thus removing one of the most dedicated and active anti-Nazi military officers from the center of resistance activities. He was taken out of the loop. In addition, the collapse of the Oster conspiracy had demoralized General Halder, who thereafter had become a participant of doubtful reliability. Though he despised Hitler and the Nazis, his confidence in the prospect of a successful coup had waned considerably. He had lost heart. It has been said of the entire officer corps in general and of Halder in particular that they probably never again would be "as mutiny-prone as [they had been] in September 1938."[156] Moreover, the army resistance had been further weakened by the personnel changes that Hitler had made in 1938, when he replaced men of doubtful loyalty with those whom he could fully trust. Under these circumstances, a successful coup d'état was highly unlikely. The leadership problem continued to torment the resistance movement.

Furthermore, even with the prospect of a much-wider war looming as a consequence of the Polish campaign, Hitler's prestige within the nation at large remained at such a high level that the ability of the resistance to rally support for a move against him remained in great doubt. Speaking of Hitler's diplomatic victory at Munich a year earlier, historian Harold Deutsch has written, "His prestige was now so great as to place in question the ability of an Opposition to rally the nation against him, even on such an issue as preventing a major war."[157] The events of September 1939 proved the accuracy of this statement.

Now that war had come, the declared duty of every German, civilian and soldier alike, was to protect the fatherland and to prosecute the war to a victorious conclusion. Thus, any thought of resuming resistance activities at this point was absolutely out of the question. "All will to resist seemed to disappear for an extended period after the war began, in part because of the deep irrational feelings of loyalty that the outbreak of war always arouses, regardless of right and wrong."[158] This was true of the military leadership and of the German nation as a whole. Nationalist ideology and military victory, enhanced by the barrage of Nazi propaganda, effectively suppressed any expressions of dissent. The brilliant success of the blitzkrieg against Poland produced a heightened sense of professional pride within the officer corps, even for such anti-Nazi stalwarts as Helmuth Groscurth, Hans Oster, and Henning von Tresckow, as well as others who were part of the resistance. The story is told of General Georg von Sodenstern, "who ten days before the outbreak of war had conferred with Witzleben over far-reaching plans to topple Hitler. But in September, when war had been declared, he turned 'to the military duties incumbent upon him and away from any thought of a violent uprising.'"[159] A spirit of intense nationalism had taken command of the German nation.

* * * *

The conquest of Poland produced the first hints of just what a Nazi-dominated Eastern Europe would look like, and the picture was gruesome. Here, systematic mass murder was visited upon people whose sole crime was membership in a group officially designated as fit only for liquidation and extermination. These "lesser peoples" (Untermenschen) had to be eliminated so that the "superior peoples" (Übermenschen) could survive. This was at the heart of the Nazi ideology, and those who implemented this program were little men playing God. This horrid chapter in German and world history is a sobering object lesson on ideologies of whatever kind and on the dangers they present to all people for all time, both to the victims and the perpetrators.

Almost immediately after the cessation of hostilities at the end of September, an administrative structure was put into place for the purpose of achieving the goal of implementing Nazi ideology as it pertained to Poland. General Halder summarized this goal when he told Major Helmuth Groscurth that "it was the intention of the Führer and Göring to destroy and exterminate the Polish people."[160] The heart of this administrative structure was the Schutzstaffel, or SS (Security Staff). By the war years, the SS effectively controlled Germany; the Nazi Party had established a complex SS administrative superstructure that superseded and supplanted the traditional governmental apparatus. The Reich Security Head Office, or RSHA (Reichssicherheitshauptamt), operating parallel to but essentially outside the state, provided a "single, centralized directorate" that circumvented the "'normal' pillars of justice and administration through secret and special authorizations."[161] In effect, the party was now the state, and the SS was the instrument of party rule. Under this system, "police power became political power."[162]

One of the most important parts of the SS organization was a series of administrative units noted earlier, namely, the Einsatzgruppen (operations groups, or task forces). Their responsibility was "the safeguarding of political life,"[163] which was a euphemism for a program of rampant terror and annihilation for anyone perceived to be an enemy of the Third Reich.

As hostilities commenced, a two-part process of subjugation emerged. First, the Wehrmacht initiated military operations against the Polish Army. Second, as Polish territory was overrun, the Einsatzgruppen took over jurisdiction of the conquered areas. Though ostensibly under the army's military justice system, the Einsatzgruppen, in fact, were under Himmler's command.[164] Their "task" can be described very simply: they were mobile killing squads whose sole purpose was to eliminate the Untermenschen who occupied the conquered territories. Ethnic Germans, then, were to become "colonists" in the now vacant land. This was, in effect, "a grandiose program of demographic engineering based on racial principles that would involve moving hundreds of thousands, indeed ultimately millions, of people like so many pieces on a checkerboard."[165]

The ideological justification for this "program" was very simple. The need for Lebensraum required the application of a crude Social Darwinist policy to the conquered territories in the east.[166] The German "colonists" themselves would be resettled from their historic communities located in various parts of Eastern Europe, such as the Baltic Sea states. The Jewish population from Germany, as well as from the conquered territories, was to be "resettled" in areas of Poland known as the Judenreservat (Jewish reservation), pending a determination of their ultimate fate.[167] The war thus was an essential part of the Nazi program. It "finally freed the Nazi regime of all tactical restraints and opened the way" for the realization of its insane goals.[168] The Polish experience was but a foretaste of what would take place in the Soviet Union a few years hence.

Deplorably, the Einsatzgruppen were allowed to carry out their homicidal activities without any serious challenge from the army leadership. As in the past, the generals once again failed to take action on an issue of profound moral significance. Realistically, there was little they could do, because the army had no control over the SS and its operational groups. Nevertheless, the army was now complicit in the nefarious SS activities. Although its highest-ranking generals completely understood the criminal nature of the SS and of its plans for Poland, they failed to take a principled stand against the mass murders that were already taking place in September 1939. After all, the army's conquest of Poland had made all of this possible.[169] "Once again, as had happened so frequently since 1933 ... the Army became the accomplice of a policy which a majority of its officers, frequently against their better judgment, followed to the end, in blind obedience to the Leader."[170] This long-standing pattern of behavior would ultimately lead to the army's total moral ruin.

Additionally, most of those within the military leadership shared an understandable, if lamentable, professional pride in military victory, even though it was achieved against an admittedly inferior army. They also could rationalize their victory with the claim that it rectified an injustice perpetrated against Germany at Versailles. The "Polish Corridor," which had been created to give the revived Polish state access to the Baltic Sea, of necessity took territory away from Germany, separating historic East Prussia from Germany proper. The German nation viewed this act of the peacemakers in 1919 as an abomination and a crime to be rectified at all costs, whereas Hitler considered this issue to be a mere pretext for the pursuit of his greater goal, which – as noted – was the complete subjugation and ultimate depopulation of the Polish nation. This distinction was not evident at the time. Regardless, the generals chose to ignore the moral implications of their victory. The relentless corruption of the Prussian ethos continued its lamentable course. In essence, the superior officers of those soldiers actually carrying out the horrid work of killing the innocent told their men, "Don't worry about what you are doing. Just follow orders and do your work with professional pride." It was the same message that had been conveyed to Adolf Eichmann.

A second moral offense was committed when the senior army leaders failed to share with fellow officers, who were ignorant of what was going on in the occupied territories, their knowledge of the barbarities being committed by the Einsatzgruppen in the name of the German people. These senior leaders could not reconcile the distinction between loyalty to their government and devotion to the "moral norms of their profession and culture." In essence, they participated in a "conspiracy of silence."[171] Understandably, these men wished to protect the junior officers from this moral dilemma, and therefore they withheld information about the actual conditions on the ground in Poland. Regrettably, this only made matters worse, because it allowed these killing squads to continue and even expand their despicable work.

Many within the officer corps, "not yet morally numbed"[172] by the obscene behavior of the Einsatzgruppen, might well have provided a solid foundation for a united resistance against the latter. That would have required clear knowledge that the Einsatzgruppen were acting not contrary to orders, but at the actual behest of the government in Berlin, namely, Hitler. Only a very few army officers at the very top of the command structure – men such as chief of the OKW, General Keitel; chief of the general staff, General Halder; commander in chief, General von Brauchitsch; and quartermaster general of the OKW, Eduard Wagner – were fully aware of the source of this hideous program.[173] However, instead of raising their voices and speaking out, they immersed themselves in the strictly military aspects of the Polish campaign and turned the proverbial blind eye to what was actually going on. They took refuge in "strict military duty."[174] Their moral myopia came at great cost to them and to the institution of which they were a part.

Many senior military officers chose this path, most notably Walther von Brauchitsch and Franz Halder. As noted earlier, both men had contacts with and were sympathetic to the resistance and its objectives. They had known about the Oster conspiracy of 1938 and, at the very least, did not oppose it. Halder even gave it a significant degree of support. Nevertheless, their behavior in the Polish war betrayed a kind of moral obtuseness that prevented them from taking direct action in opposing the patent criminality of the regime they were serving. To their credit, they tried, when possible, to mitigate some of the most heinous actions of the Einsatzgruppen. They "remained at their posts with the praiseworthy intention of 'preventing something worse'"[175] and, in so doing, doubtlessly mitigated some of the evils they encountered. And yet, for the most part, they hid behind the facade of military duty, choosing to ignore the moral implications of their inaction. Their behavior has been aptly judged as follows: "Participation in crime, even in the hope of perhaps sabotaging it, is always questionable."[176] Yet they were typical of many fellow officers within the Wehrmacht command structure who were afflicted by a moral paralysis that prevented them from taking the kind of action demanded of them. Their devotion to "duty" blinded them to the horrid realities of the world in which they were living. They were incapable of becoming traitorous patriots, incapable of pursuing a higher moral path. As with most, they chose to look away – most, but not everyone.

* * * *

Although the outbreak of hostilities in September 1939 temporarily suppressed any thought of resistance activities against the Third Reich, there was still a dedicated remnant of those who had been at the center of the 1938 conspiracy and whose loathing for Nazism and all it represented continued unabated. Although the failures of that critical year deeply discouraged them, they were determined to carry on. Their numbers, however, were pathetically small, and the obstacles they faced were more formidable than ever. The brilliant success of the blitzkrieg in Poland silenced the critics of the war, as Hitler had scored yet another victory that further enhanced his reputation as a political and military genius.[177]

Consequently, the resistance was "at its wits' end" for a short time. "No one knew what to do now."[178] No longer could they take action in order to prevent war, because, unlike in 1938, Germany was now at war. A coup attempt at this point would be viewed as treasonous, both in a legal and moral sense. Defense of the nation against the declared enemy now took precedence over all other considerations. The issues of Nazi immorality could be dealt with later, or so the members of the resistance thought. "For now, all loyal Germans, whatever their political convictions, should rally to the defense of the fatherland."[179]

Paradoxically, however, two issues directly connected with the Polish campaign became rallying points for the resistance movement and contributed to the renewal of conspiratorial activities within the government, especially the army. First, there were the moral issues arising as a consequence of the monstrous activities of the Einsatzgruppen. It was becoming more apparent that the question of Nazi immorality could not be postponed indefinitely. Second, more and more people were questioning the logic of continued warfare now that the issue of the Polish Corridor had been resolved in Germany's favor. The resistance leaders knew, however, that Hitler's victory in Poland would only spur him on to more military campaigns. Consequently, peace would require his overthrow. The resistance, it seemed, was beginning to regain its footing.

* * * *

As knowledge of the murderous behavior of the Einsatzgruppen became more widespread, a growing sense of moral outrage began to permeate the ranks of the Wehrmacht officer corps.

> Some of [the conspirators] began to speak not only about protecting the welfare and security of Germany but about defending vital moral principles and universal spiritual values. Their condemnation of National Socialism gradually shifted from criticism of its recklessness or willfulness to denunciation of its essential immorality.[180]

The growing revulsion of the army over the activities of these state-sponsored "murder squads" (the term was coined by Henning von Tresckow, soon to become a prominent resistance figure) led to renewed hopes for a coup d'état.[181] Denunciations such as Tresckow's began to be heard with increasing frequency from army officers. The written reports of Colonel General Johannes Blaskowitz, commander of the occupation forces in Poland, have been described as among the "most forthright and courageous denunciations" of SS savagery found anywhere.[182] In scathing terms, he condemned the "criminal atrocities, maltreatment, and plundering carried out by the SS, police, and administration." He declared that the "animal and pathological instincts" of the SS had resulted in "the slaughter of tens of thousands of Jews and Poles."[183] He also said, "Every [German] soldier feels sickened and repelled by the crimes committed in Poland by agents of the Reich and government representatives."[184] Thus, "opposition to the Nazis within the army was no longer based solely on Hitler's fool-hardy foreign policy and the military risks he ran but also on fundamental moral questions."[185] The general mood of the resistance had changed perceptibly within a few months. Whereas the patriotism of early September had required support for the military actions then taking place, the patriotism of December called for opposition to the evil nature of Nazism as well. Interest in a coup d'état was renewed.[186]

In fact, this renewed interest could be noted well before the outbreak of hostilities in September 1939. The most indomitable members of the resistance had resumed their work as early as the autumn of 1938, attempting to rebuild an effective opposition movement. Three men in particular – Witzleben, Oster, and Goerdeler – had remained in contact with each other after the collapse of the Oster conspiracy.[187] They fully understood that civilian and military coordination and cooperation were essential to the success of any future coup d'état. They also realized the need to have on hand those who could "assume administrative responsibilities" once Hitler was removed from the scene.[188] The gathering storm in the summer of 1939 enabled them to regain their "focus and purpose that led to a second major effort to assemble [their] resources for an attack on the Hitler regime."[189] Thus began Round II, Part 1, of the army resistance.

Hans Oster remained at the forefront of the resistance. Without him, the movement undoubtedly never would have been rebuilt. The historian Harold Deutsch states, "It is, in fact, solely due to Oster that it is at all possible to speak of an organized resistance. Through him the principal sectors were linked and achieved whatever capacity they had for coordinated action."[190] Oster's work made the Abwehr the operational center of the resistance for the next nine months.

Admiral Canaris, "who was now impatient to proceed,"[191] gave Oster fresh encouragement. Helmuth Groscurth, now a lieutenant colonel, continued to work closely with Oster to rebuild an effective resistance movement. Groscurth was chosen to serve as chief of the army intelligence liaison group on the general staff. This post brought him into direct and regular contact with Commander in Chief von Brauchitsch and Chief of Staff Halder in the OKH. It was said of Oster that he "wanted someone permanently at Halder's elbow to jog it when needed."[192]

Oster also brought other like-minded people into the Abwehr, one of the most significant of whom was Hans von Dohnányi. Dohnányi's entry into the inner circle of conspirators brought a man who has been described as "a jurist of wide experience and extraordinary talent."[193] Depicted as "Liberal [and] Christian ... without party commitments,"[194] he had been an implacable opponent of the Nazis from the beginning and had been collecting evidence since 1933 in a special secret file in preparation for a (presumed) criminal trial of Hitler.[195] His "final moment of truth" came with the aforementioned Fritsch episode, when Army Commander in

Chief Werner von Fritsch was court-martialed on a trumped-up charge of homosexuality.[196] At that point, Dohnányi joined the resistance and eventually became head of the Office of Political Affairs in the Abwehr. He was intimately involved in the 1938 coup attempt, as well as a subsequent attempt in 1939, plus an assassination plot in 1943.

Dohnányi also was able to recruit new participants. Doubtlessly the single most important member of this group was his brother-in-law Dietrich Bonhoeffer.[197] It was a fortuitous choice. Bonhoeffer had been an active participant in international ecumenical affairs for a number of years, and this gave him "cover," allowing him to move with relative impunity within the international religious community and also to serve as a clandestine courier for the Abwehr in its ultimately vain attempts to secure international support for its anti-Nazi activities.

* * * *

The conclusion of the Polish campaign brought a pause to significant military activity. Ground operations for all practical purposes came to a halt, although there was some action on the high seas and in the air. This period is known to history as the "phony war," or the "Sitzkrieg" (sitting war). In the west, the French and British remained quiescent throughout the entire period from September 1939 to April 1940. The reasons are not difficult to discern. Rampant defeatism had paralyzed the French government and high command, and Great Britain, with its relatively small army, was hardly in a position to launch major ground operations against Germany without French participation. In the east, both Germany and the Soviet Union moved quickly to claim the spoils of victory as Polish territory was parceled out to its conquerors.

The relative calm of this period suggested that perhaps negotiations could be renewed, peace could be restored, and further bloodshed could be avoided. This theoretical possibility produced a flurry of diplomatic activity that foundered on the shoals of political reality, however. Three insoluble problems ultimately destroyed any hope for a negotiated peace settlement. First of all, the prospect of foreign governments legitimizing the Nazi conquest of Poland was highly unlikely. Second, Hitler's unlimited goals for Eastern Europe remained unchanged. Finally and most importantly, Hitler was determined to attack his western neighbors as soon as possible, and he would not brook any opposition on this point.

By this time, the reality of Hitler's warlike intentions was beginning to permeate the entire officer corps. Almost everyone, whether they were part of the resistance or not, began to realize that the man represented a growing menace not only to the Wehrmacht but also to the entire German nation. This knowledge prompted the conspirators once more to take action. From September to November 1939, they made still another attempt to stop Hitler in his tracks before he could do more damage. Once again, however, several key generals demonstrated their timidity, and this plot, like all the others, fell apart.

The source of this latest resistance effort lay with a meeting that Hitler held with the highest leaders in the chain of command on September 27, 1939, the same day the Polish campaign came to an end. At this meeting, he declared his intention to launch an immediate military offensive in Western Europe, and he ordered the men to plan for operations to commence as early as November 12. In truth, the army was ill-prepared for such a campaign in the autumn of 1939, and the generals all knew it.[198] Their reaction to this order was almost universally negative. In a word, they were aghast. General von Brauchitsch expressed his opposition openly.[199] Officers who generally supported Hitler's initiatives were dismayed as well. Even General Keitel, the infamous "rubber lion" who was totally under Hitler's control, had his doubts.[200]

Another unexpected opponent was Colonel General Walter von Reichenau, the general staff officer who had been closely identified with the Nazis from the outset. Although many of his associates considered him to be "Hitler's man,"[201] Reichenau displayed an increasing tendency to challenge Hitler. His behavior strongly suggests that ultimately he was his own man. In this particular instance, Abwehr chief Admiral Canaris, much to his own surprise, easily persuaded Reichenau to draft a personal memorandum to Hitler expressing his opposition to the planned attack in the west.[202] Naturally, the Führer's mind could not be changed, and Reichenau's subsequent contacts with Hitler convinced him that the use of logic and reason were useless in conversations with the man.[203] Others, such as General Walter Warlimont, who at the time was deputy chief of the Wehrmacht Operations Staff, also reflected the "broadly negative reaction" to Hitler's plans.[204] Together, Reichenau and Warlimont were representative of those officers who had no connection to the resistance but who nevertheless were becoming increasingly apprehensive over "the insanity of Hitler's intentions."[205] The members of the resistance who were part of the military establishment believed that the western offensive "would bring about 'the end of Germany.'"[206]

As a consequence of this growing anxiety, conditions once more favored a renewal of resistance activities. The process of rebuilding the network that had been initiated almost a year earlier continued, as "various old and new contacts were established."[207] In addition, moral concerns increasingly accompanied political and military questions as reports of the abominations being perpetrated in Poland began to filter back to Berlin. General Ludwig Beck, now retired but still closely connected to the resistance, issued a memorandum to the conspirators in which he reiterated his conviction of the previous year, that the soldier's highest responsibility was to his nation, not to his government.[208]

Admiral Canaris renewed his efforts as well. In September 1939, he visited the headquarters of several commanders in the various western military districts of Germany not only to ascertain their views of the prospects of success of the projected western offensive but also, if possible, to enlist their support for a coup d'état.[209] About the same time, Helmuth Groscurth also embarked on a trip of his own to the western military districts "in a mission of subversion along the Rhine."[210] Although several of the commanders expressed sympathy for the resistance, the key to any successful army coup lay with Brauchitsch and Halder, and both men lacked the requisite audacity to lead such an effort. This was especially true of Brauchitsch, whose fainthearted behavior would lead to the collapse of a second coup attempt in November.

While the generals in the OKH dithered, one general in the west decided to take matters into his own hands. He was Kurt von Hammerstein-Equord, a former commander of the Reichswehr. The historian Harold Deutsch has described him as an "independent-minded" Hanoverian with "wide interests" who cultivated relationships within a broad political spectrum, including those on the moderate left, men such as the Social Democrat Wilhelm Leuschner, so much so that some of his associates referred to him as the "Red General."[211] Retired in 1934, he was recalled to active duty on September 7, 1939, and was given command of "Army Section A," described as "an ad hoc force formed for the defence of the West Wall"[212] and headquartered in Cologne.

Unlike many of the fellow officers of his generation, Hammerstein had been an "uncompromising opponent" of National Socialism from the beginning, and Hitler considered him to be one of his "most dangerous enemies."[213] Hammerstein later regretted that he had not eliminated the "brown scum" when Hitler assumed power in 1933.[214] Heinrich Brüning, who was the Weimar Republic's last true constitutional chancellor and was now living in exile in the United States, described Hammerstein as a man "'without nerves' who, if it came to a coup, 'would light up a Brazil cigar, seat himself in his easy chair, and give the order to fire.'"[215] Upon hearing these words, Hammerstein allegedly "smiled grimly" and responded, "Just give me some troops, and I won't fail."[216] That, of course, was the point. He had no troops. Those troops under his command were not suitable for the kind of military operations that a coup d'état would require. More importantly, he held his command for a few weeks only. By the end of the month, he was transferred to a deputy command and subsequently retired.[217]

Almost immediately after assuming his duties in Cologne, Hammerstein devised a scheme to eliminate Hitler that was the epitome of simplicity. He proposed to invite Hitler to his headquarters for the purpose of inspecting the troops, and then arrest him. What would have happened next remains a matter of conjecture. Some writers state that the next step would have been "appropriate judicial proceedings," whereas others declare that Hammerstein's intent was "to render [Hitler] harmless once and for all – and even without judicial proceedings."[218] This statement obviously was a euphemism for assassination. Whatever Hammerstein's ultimate intent was, the opportunity to carry out the plan never arose.

Despite invitations given "with embarrassing frequency" – which may have aroused Hitler's suspicions – they were never accepted.[219] Hitler "refused to play [the] fly to Hammerstein's spider."[220] Doubtlessly, Hitler's finely tuned sense of danger continued to serve him well. Once more shunted into retirement, Hammerstein succumbed to cancer in April 1943. Thus died one of the most determined opponents of Nazism to be found within the ranks of the German military establishment. The words of the British historian John W. Wheeler-Bennett provide an eloquent epitaph to the man and his life: "Not only had he courage and daring, and clear vision in military affairs, but he was also a very wise man and one of indisputable integrity and patriotism ... He died honoured and regretted by all who knew him."[221] Kurt von Hammerstein-Equord had a remarkably accurate moral compass. He was a true traitorous patriot.

As General von Hammerstein-Equord was doing his best to neutralize Hitler, events in Berlin were moving to a climax of sorts, as the autumn of 1939 became yet another testing time for the conservative resistance, especially the conspirators within the OKH and Abwehr. There was general recognition that, absent the actions of a lone assassin such as Georg Elser, who had almost succeeded in November 1939, the military establishment – specifically the army leadership – was the only organization with sufficient power to bring down the entire edifice of the Third Reich.[222] The issue was clear. If the western offensive were to be stopped, Hitler had to be eliminated.[223]

These October weeks have been described as probably "the most complicated and difficult to unravel period in the history of Round II."[224] At the risk of oversimplification, the picture can be described as follows:

> On one side [of Brauchitsch and Halder] stood Hitler, clinging relentlessly to his projected offensive. Confronting him, if the term does not imply too much, were the hand-wringing chiefs of OKH, shaken and at times well nigh unmanned by the pressures to which they were subject. On the other side of the two generals were the ranks of Opposition-oriented elements importuning them both to thwart the Führer's plans and to end the war by raising a *coup d'état* against him.[225]

To his credit, Halder recognized that the only way to stop Hitler was to remove him from power, and he supported the members of his staff who were actively plotting a coup – men such as Lieutenant Colonel Groscurth and Lieutenant Colonel von Tresckow, as well as several others. Although Halder did not play an active part himself, he nonetheless continued with his own planning for that eventuality.[226] He realized, however, that success required the active support of Commander in Chief von Brauchitsch, because a chief of staff did not have command authority over troops. Yet, as noted, the reliability of Brauchitsch remained in doubt. Had Halder been blessed with a boldness and audacity to match that of Oster or Groscurth, he still might have been able to lead a coup. However, he lacked those qualities. It has been argued that "he deserves credit rather than blame for recognizing that fact."[227]

Still, he continued to wrestle with the question of assassination from the autumn of 1939 to the summer of 1942. It was said that "within his heart he was against assassination but he knew perfectly well that [Hitler could not be deposed] any other way."[228] Only then could the "Nazi pestilence" be eliminated. Hence, he contemplated playing the role of assassin himself. He subsequently revealed to Groscurth that he carried a loaded pistol in his pocket on several occasions with the purpose of shooting Hitler. Groscurth recorded in his diary the following words: "With tears in his eyes, [Halder] said that he had been going to see Emil [Hitler] with a pistol in his pocket for weeks in order to possibly shoot him down."[229] In the end, however, Halder just could not do it. He later commented to an aide that "to assassinate Hitler, one had to be born an assassin, and he had not been born to be one. Such was his dilemma – and his tragic inconsistency."[230] In an interview after the war, he "said that he could not bring himself as 'a human being and a Christian to shoot down an unarmed man.'"[231]

Halder, like many generals in the officer corps, was unable to commit to the violence requisite to Hitler's removal from power. Together, Generals Hammerstein-Equord and Halder represented two variant positions held by those within the army leadership who opposed the Nazis. There were too few of those who wished to take direct action and too many of those who were unable to commit to direct action. The men of this latter group busied themselves with the technical aspects of military operations and either suppressed or ignored the frightening moral issues that surrounded those technical aspects. Halder was never able to resolve the conflict that tortured him. Later, in the spring of 1940, with the war in the west about to resume with a fury, he not only failed to take action against Hitler but also refused to do so. "[He said that] Britain and France had declared war on Germany and the war must now be fought out. The Wehrmacht could not act on its own to overthrow the government. [It could only act] in [the] face of imminent defeat."[232] The historian Peter Hoffman comments on this statement with the following words: "This was in fact naïve and worse – it was irresponsible."[233]

It was said of both Brauchitsch and Halder that "they could not make up their minds either to fulfill their military duty in the true sense of the word or to do their ethical and moral duty."[234] The choice was clear: either conscience and honor or duty and obedience. The continued vacillation of these two men and all those within the officer corps who behaved as they did remains a stain on their reputation that can never be removed. It also remains a primary reason for the ultimate failure of the resistance.

* * * *

As events moved toward a confrontation (of sorts) between Hitler and his generals, the foreign office was taking action of its own, especially on the international level, functioning as the focal point of a resistance network for "gathering and disseminating intelligence, for facilitating rapid communication between the different groups, and especially ... for bringing pressure to bear at critical points on individuals who showed a disposition to flag in what was expected of them."[235] A "shadow" foreign office was created as part of a renewed effort to reestablish contacts with foreign governments[236] and achieve peace "through negotiation and compromise."[237] With the Polish campaign successfully concluded and the stalemate of the Sitzkrieg in place, this appeared to be an opportune time to bring about a cessation of hostilities. At the center of this foreign office operation was Ernst von Weizsäcker.

Ernst Freiherr (Baron) von Weizsäcker, whose official title was State Secretary (that is, Deputy Foreign Minister) at the foreign office, played a role in the Foreign Ministry similar to that of Wilhelm Canaris in the Abwehr. He was not an active participant in the conspiracy against Hitler, but he gave support to those within the Foreign Ministry who were active, such as the Kordt brothers.[238] Though his animus toward Hitler and the Nazis deepened with the passage of time, he remained in office "in order to prevent and restrain as much as he could."[239] He played the role of the spoiler and did not resign from office until 1943.[240]

With Weizsäcker's tacit support, Erich Kordt became the point man for a reorganized resistance group within the foreign office. It had a twofold mission: first, to establish "outposts from which peace negotiations could be inaugurated" immediately after a successful coup, and second, to tighten "existing and [fabricate] new connecting lines to other resistance sectors."[241] The conspirators inside the foreign office also planned to use their shadow directorate to assume the responsibilities of office the instant the Nazis were deposed.[242] Out of this scheme ultimately came a communications network extending far beyond Germany's borders that kept the resisters apprised of all matters relating to resistance activities. This included liaison between the members of the resistance who were in the foreign office or in the army.

Two general officers, Colonel Generals von Witzleben and von Hammerstein-Equord, were participants in these activities.[243] These two men had impeccable credentials as ardent anti-Nazis. Another officer intimately connected with these liaison efforts was Major (later Lieutenant Colonel) Helmuth Groscurth.[244] The primary purpose behind their activities at this point in time was to avoid widening the conflict with Great Britain and France and, if possible, bring it to an end. As early as October 1939, efforts were under way to bring about a cessation of hostilities, possibly through intermediaries in Sweden or the Vatican. An entry in the diary of a liaison officer who represented Weizsäcker in these negotiations reads, "In all peace negotiations one is confronted by the categoric [sic] demand for the removal of Hitler and the reestablishment of Czecho [sic] in some form."[245] The message to the conspirators was absolutely clear: If negotiations for a cessation of hostilities were to proceed, Hitler must be deposed. That should be their immediate goal.

However, the question of Czechoslovakia was more intractable. What were its implications? What kind of a Czechoslovakia was to be "reestablished"? Where would its westernmost border lie? Would that border restore the Sudetenland to Czechoslovakia or not? Questions of this sort ultimately produced an impasse between the conspirators and the enemy powers – that is, Great Britain and later the United States and the Soviet Union – that was never resolved. At issue were the lands that Hitler had acquired since the spring of 1938, specifically Austria, the Sudetenland, and now the Polish Corridor. As noted, virtually every German citizen, regardless of social class or political persuasion, including the conspirators themselves, believed that Germany's claims to these lands were historically and ethnically justified. Given the methods by which those lands were acquired, however, the prospects of bringing hostilities to an end in the autumn of 1939 without forsaking the acquired lands were nil. This issue remained the main stumbling block to an accommodation between the conspirators and the Allied powers throughout World War II.

The attempt of the foreign office to reconnect the disparate resistance sectors brought a renewal of contacts with what was left of the German social democratic movement. Ludwig Beck and Carl Goerdeler made contact with Wilhelm Leuschner, one of the very few leaders of the Social Democratic Party still inside Germany. Leuschner was a longtime acquaintance of General von Hammerstein-Equord. Connections with Hans Oster and Wilhelm Canaris in the Abwehr were established as well. Together these men tried to form a coalition to bring about the downfall of the Nazi government. They forged a plan toward the end of the year 1939 that would combine a military coup with a general strike. At this point, the social democratic movement was beginning to recover as a potential political force inside Germany.[246] Leuschner and his social democratic associate Jakob Kaiser assured Beck that the workers were "extremely opposed to the war and in favor of a coup; a general strike was being prepared in support of it."[247]

A significant part of the foreign office operations was the posting of reliable personnel in strategic diplomatic locations worldwide. Among the more important postings was that of Theo Kordt to Berne, Switzerland, where, as previously noted, he established contacts with the British government.[248] Another diplomatic assignment of some significance was given to Adam von Trott zu Solz, a young lawyer who, after a flirtation with Nazism in the early years of the Third Reich,[249] became a determined member of the resistance. His studies had taken him to Great Britain

– he had been a Rhodes scholar at Oxford – and to the United States. Consequently, he was well acquainted with and had numerous friends in both countries. The "shadow" foreign office put this knowledge to good use.

In late October 1939, Trott traveled to the United States, ostensibly to attend an international peace conference. His actual mission, however, was to establish contacts between the Allies and the resistance and to bring about peace with a Germany free of Hitler. He hoped to deliver a simple message to the US government from the resistance, as follows: a significant anti-Nazi resistance movement existed in Germany, and it was working fervently to depose Hitler. Specifically, he wished to develop an "association between the Allies and the forces of Opposition in Germany."[250] He departed for the United States in September 1939 on the last ship sailing from Genoa. After an arduous journey, which included slipping through a British blockade at Gibraltar, he arrived in New York, whereupon he immediately made contacts with the German exile community, including former chancellor Heinrich Brüning. A series of discussions ensued, which led to "an extensive memorandum on ways of achieving a fair peace with a non-Hitler Germany." Trott and Paul Scheffer, a German expatriate writer who was former editor of the newspaper *Berliner Tageblatt* and now living in the United States, coauthored the document.[251]

As explained in the memorandum, the resistance had two major concerns at this point. First of all, they feared that the Allies, the United States included, had a growing perception that all Germans were Nazis, and that the end result of this perception would be an Allied doctrine of collective guilt. This, in turn, would produce a draconian peace settlement in the event of a Nazi defeat, resulting in a replay of the Treaty of Versailles of 1919. Publication of these Allied war aims would then drive the German people to despair of achieving a just peace and induce them to give wholehearted support to the Nazis.[252] Sadly, this last scenario is what actually unfolded to a significant degree when the Allies proclaimed their demand for the unconditional surrender of the Axis powers at the Allied conference at Casablanca in January 1943. Nazi propaganda had a proverbial field day when news of the demand for unconditional surrender became known. Trott's second concern was the fear that London and Paris might actually negotiate a peace of appeasement with Hitler, a not irrational concern at this point in the war. The Polish campaign had ended, and no significant hostile activity was taking place at this time.

The memo ultimately reached Cordell Hull, the US secretary of state. Additionally, the influential American columnist Walter Lippmann wrote an article, published on October 10, that "caused considerable stir, even in official quarters." Lippmann:

> ... argued for a public statement of war aims. "If the Germans," he contended, "can be made to see that a military victory is impossible but that a decent peace is possible, Europe may yet be spared the incalculable horrors of a war to the bitter end." So the time had come for the Allies, "to state their war aims with a view of making clear to the German nation that the siege can be lifted whenever they have a government with which it is possible to negotiate."[253]

We can never know exactly how much influence Trott had in shaping the substance of this article. He did have an interview with Lippmann prior to its publication, and we do know that it reflected his message with almost exact precision. Trott impressed those whom he met, both in private life and in government, very favorably.

Nonetheless, his mission ended in failure. Some strategically placed individuals, such as Supreme Court Associate Justice Felix Frankfurter, who had a nodding acquaintance with Trott from their days at Oxford, did not consider Trott to be completely trustworthy. Also, some of his acquaintances from his time at Oxford considered him to be an "appeaser," that is, someone whose ultimate goal was a compromise with Hitler, a view that was entirely wrong but willingly believed. Evidently some comments that he had made in that earlier time were taken out of context and now used against him. In addition, a strong anti-German prejudice was once again descending on the United States, just as it had during the years 1914 to 1918 and after. Once again, the German people – according to American propaganda – were marching in lockstep with their Prussian military masters, who were hell-bent on war. The FBI considered Adam von Trott zu Solz to be nothing more than a spy. He was shadowed by FBI agents, who opened a file on him entitled "Subject: Espionage Activities, Adam von Trott in the US (Case no. 862.20211)." It was a tragic end to a mission that held much promise at the outset. Ironically, Trott was a direct descendent on his mother's side of the first American chief justice, John Jay.[254]

About this same time, the resistance, through an intermediary, tried to establish contacts with the British government through the good offices of the Vatican. The resistance leaders, especially Hans Oster, hoped to negotiate a peace treaty between Great Britain and a post-Nazi German government with the help of the Holy See. Most unfortunately, however, these efforts were thwarted in part by an episode that took place in northern Germany on November 9, 1939. It appeared to be connected to the Elser bomb plot, which occurred at the exact same time.

In September 1939, two agents of the British Intelligence Service, Captain R. H. Stevens and Major S. Payne Best, made contact with a German émigré at the Hague who claimed to have ties to Wehrmacht officers who were part of an anti-Nazi conspiracy. Ultimately, the two groups met and held several meetings at Backhus near Venlo, in the Netherlands, which at the time was neutral. An additional meeting was scheduled for November 9. However, the British agents had no way of knowing that the men with whom they were meeting were not anti-Nazi Wehrmacht officers, but rather agents of the Sicherheitsdienst and the Gestapo. At their meeting on November 9, the Nazi agents seized the British officers at the border, took them into custody, and returned with them to Germany for questioning.[255]

The fact that the bombing of the Bürgerbräukeller and the Venlo incident occurred almost coincidentally raised suspicions that the two events were directly connected. In the end, the consequences of this assumed connection were far-reaching and brought considerable harm to the resistance movement. Many within the Nazi establishment, Hitler included, believed that the British were somehow involved in the Elser plot. The timing alone, November 9, seemed to suggest more than mere coincidence. For their part, the British believed that the Nazis had hoodwinked and outmaneuvered them by means of a bogus resistance movement. Consequently, they became more suspicious than ever of German anti-Nazi resistance activities, regardless of their source, and the resistance movement was seriously discredited in the eyes of the outside world.[256] Although the resistance and the British government continued to maintain contact, mostly through the Vatican, rapport between the two groups was seriously, perhaps fatally, damaged.[257]

In the end, the resistance suffered a serious setback. Elser's effort, though commendable from the perspective of the conspirators, did them more harm than good, and the Nazis scored a propaganda victory. Britain was excoriated as the perpetrator of the dastardly deed, and Hitler's popularity soared. Fulsome expressions of thanksgiving for his unscathed survival appeared in churches. "Ordinary Germans" sent "countless letters and telegrams" to the Führer expressing gratitude for his survival. One adoring German composed a poem to commemorate Hitler's escape:

He lives! The enemy's plans were thwarted!
He lives! Our thanks to the Almighty,
That the death of our Führer does not leave
A sorrowful Germany – a people to grieve.[258]

* * * *

As the Sitzkrieg had prompted the conspirators to seek a way to end the war, so the British government itself appeared to be reaching out for a compromise to end hostilities, which, so far at least, had not spiraled out of control. Scarcely twenty-four hours after Great Britain's declaration of war against Germany on September 3, Prime Minister Neville Chamberlain broadcast a speech to the German nation in the German language stating that the British nation had no quarrel with the German people, but only with their "unscrupulous" leader and his tyrannical regime. Several weeks later, Chamberlain reiterated his position in the House of Commons when he said, "It is no part of our policy to exclude from her rightful place in Europe a Germany which will live in amity and confidence with other nations." He went on to express his support for a peace settlement that would consider "the just claims and needs of all countries."[259] Statements such as these were heartening to the resistance. The main stumbling block remained the person of Adolf Hitler. Hence, his removal by whatever means possible became the main focus of their efforts.

Hitler's reply to Chamberlain's peace effort naturally made matters worse. He responded to Chamberlain's statements with his own "peace offensive," as he assumed the role of the "reluctant warrior, the reasonable, moderate statesman,"[260] a pose that he maintained throughout the autumn of 1939. On several occasions he expressed his desire for a settlement with Great Britain and France. There was no need to continue the struggle, he declared. All he was asking for was international recognition of the changes that had taken place in Poland. It was all a fraud, of course. Britain and France neither could nor would accede to the "changes" that had occurred in Eastern Europe. To do so would forfeit what little credibility was left to them after Munich and the events that followed, a fact of which Hitler was well aware.[261]

More importantly, Hitler's plans for a military strike against Western Europe were still in place. The November 12 deadline for a military assault was rapidly approaching, and his generals – all of them – knew of this fact. Thus, the challenge to the resistance was simple, if formidable. If Hitler could be removed from power, the western offensive could be stopped, and the admittedly remote chance of a genuine peace settlement just might become a reality. Perhaps even the issue of Germany's conquests might be resolved peaceably. This was the conspirators' hope. However, they recognized that only a successful coup could bring this about. "The removal of Hitler from power was as important as stopping the western offensive. The one would follow from the other."[262] The events of late October suggested that such an action might actually take place.

By then, the top leadership within the OKH, especially General Halder, had become convinced that a coup d'état – without violence if possible, but with violence if necessary – was the only way to prevent a complete military debacle in the west.[263] By whatever means, Hitler had to be removed from power. Halder directed his deputy chief of staff, General Karl-Heinrich von Stülpnagel, to initiate preparations for a coup. For the next week or more, Stülpnagel was the "central figure" in the OKH conspiracy. On October 31, Halder and Stülpnagel together ordered preparations to be made for a coup attempt.[264]

Meanwhile, conspirators within the Abwehr were actively plotting a coup as well. This group, evidently unknown to either Halder or Stülpnagel, was formed by a group of younger officers, and is known to history as "Action Group Zossen," because of its location at army headquarters (OKH) in Zossen, a small town some twenty miles south of Berlin. When notified of Halder's decision, a pleasantly surprised Groscurth resurrected the Oster Study (Studie Oster). The final plan of Action Group Zossen essentially was an updated version of Oster's 1938 plan, and consisted of four parts: "eradicating Hitler, eliminating the SS and Gestapo, cordoning off the main centers of power, and even forming a provisional government."[265]

A significant difference between the original version and the revised plan was the clearly stated intention to kill Hitler. As previously mentioned, the earlier plan at the time of the Munich Conference had called for a raid on Hitler's living quarters but had left the question of assassination unanswered. Nevertheless, Oster and Heinz had agreed between themselves that an "incident" would be manufactured to dispatch the man. The revised study also included plans for Beck to give a radio address to the nation, indicating that he was assuming command of the Wehrmacht, that he was declaring a state of emergency and martial law, that he would hold national elections as soon as possible, and – most importantly – that he would open peace negotiations immediately.[266]

As the conspirators resumed their planning for a coup, the OKH was moving ahead under Hitler's orders with its own plans for a strike against the west, to commence on November 12. Before actual military operations could begin, however, a week or more of preparation was necessary, meaning that the "fatal hour" for Hitler to issue the preparation order was set for 1:00 p.m. on November 5. In one last attempt to dissuade Hitler from giving the fatal order for the "mad attack," Brauchitsch arranged for an interview with him. The meeting took place on the fifth at noon in the Congress Hall of the old Chancellery, scarcely one hour before the preparation order was to be given.[267] Brauchitsch had said that he wanted to give "a 'calm' presentation of points which 'might be decisive' for some of the Führer's 'political aims and decisions,' as well as for the 'further conduct of the war.'"[268] The meeting proved to be anything but "calm."

As it began, Brauchitsch gave Hitler a memorandum that was a summary of the points he wished to make. He then commenced with his verbal presentation with technical arguments against the impending offensive, which Hitler completely dismissed. As he went on, Brauchitsch unfortunately committed several tactical errors, such as hinting at Hitler's interference with military operations in Poland and referring to episodes of indiscipline and lack of aggressiveness among the troops. This latter accusation was an indirect criticism of the Nazi youth training. He then compounded his error when he contrasted these weaknesses with the spirit that had characterized the imperial army in the Great War. At that point, Hitler erupted into one of his classic paroxysms of rage. He unleashed a torrent of vituperation and vitriol against the army and its generals. A cascade of insults, including charges of cowardice, descended upon Brauchitsch. Hitler's fury at the reference to the Great War very possibly was prompted by the "constant and gnawing sense of inferiority he felt when facing aristocratic holdovers from imperial days."[269] The contrast between these men and Hitler's own petit bourgeois origins was a constant reality that affected his overall conduct.

His behavior also may have been part of a calculated maneuver designed to intimidate his opponents, in this case, General von Brauchitsch. At one point in the tirade, he called his deputy, OKW Chief General Wilhelm Keitel, into the room. The "nodding donkey"[270] naturally did nothing to support Brauchitsch. Hitler also made a passing reference to "the spirit of Zossen," declaring that "some fine day he would ruthlessly stamp [it] out."[271] How much, if anything, Hitler actually knew about the conspirators at Zossen is impossible to ascertain. He certainly knew of the opposition to his plans for a western offensive, although it is highly doubtful that he had any knowledge of the actual conspiracy. Subsequent events tend to support this belief. Nevertheless, this passing remark had far-reaching consequences.

Brauchitsch emerged from the twenty-minute meeting totally discomfited. The confrontation completely unnerved him. Witnesses described him as "chalk-white and with a twisted countenance."[272] After leaving the Chancellery, he returned to Zossen with Halder, who had accompanied him to the interview but had remained in the antechamber during the interview. Brauchitsch was described as being "exhausted and in a state of collapse, [whereas] Halder [was] apparently composed."[273] However, in the course of their conversation about the just-concluded disastrous episode, Brauchitsch, who was completely unaware of the Abwehr activities at Zossen, made reference to Hitler's comment about the "spirit of Zossen."[274]

It was now Halder's turn to become panic-stricken. Upon their return to Zossen, he immediately ordered the destruction of all incriminating evidence relating to the proposed coup, fearing an imminent Gestapo raid. Unfortunately, much of value was lost, although both Groscurth and Dohnányi were able to salvage some important papers. As the hours passed, no "black shirts" appeared at Zossen, indicating that Hitler was indeed unaware of the coup plans.[275]

Immediately after his arrival at Zossen, Halder spoke to Groscurth, telling him that "the offensive in the west must now go forward … There was nothing to be done about it. The coup could not take place." Groscurth recorded in his diary Halder's own words: "Thus the forces that had been counting on us are no longer under obligation. You understand what I mean."[276] In sum, Halder had completely reversed his position, and he refused to reconsider that position even though the anticipated Gestapo raid never took place. What had prompted this complete reversal? The following statement by historian Peter Hoffmann offers several reasons: "The only explanations for the change in Halder's attitude are panic, inability to make up his mind, insincerity or the belated realization that he could not count on Brauchitsch, who had command authority over the troops."[277] Most scholars believe that Halder suffered from a "crisis of nerves rather than one of conscience."[278]

Meanwhile, the actual mobilization order had not yet been delivered to army headquarters. The one o'clock deadline for the order had passed without notice in the confusion that resulted in the aftermath of the explosive meeting. The belated order was given in writing to the OKH later in the afternoon that same day, November 5, and continued in force until it was postponed two days later.[279] The behavior of both Brauchitsch and Halder during the critical hours of November 5 probably can be best described as tragically incompetent. Initially, Brauchitsch calmed down to a point that allowed him to look at the situation with a degree of objectivity. Nonetheless, he declared that, for his part, the coup attempt was at an end. Although he believed that the western offensive would be a disaster for Germany, he stated clearly that he would have nothing more to do with a coup. He told Halder, "I shall do nothing [to aid the conspirators,] but I also shall do nothing if someone else does something."[280] Evidently he still believed in the necessity of stopping the western offensive, but he refused to do anything to stop it himself.[281]

As early as the evening of November 5, the plan began to fall apart. Arguments pro and con over the question of what to do next continued to vex the conspirators over the next several days. Should they continue to plan for a coup or not? Through this entire time, however, one incontrovertible fact could not be avoided. Two leaders at the top of the military command structure had forsaken them. They were Wehrmacht Commander in Chief Walther von Brauchitsch and Army Chief of Staff Franz Halder. They had abandoned ship. At this point, the only viable option was assassination. A willing assassin had stepped forward in the person of the diplomat Erich Kordt, who offered to become a suicide bomber in order to eliminate Hitler and thereby free the generals from their inhibitions, especially their oath of allegiance. However, tightened security measures initiated as a consequence of Georg Elser's assassination attempt prevented Kordt from securing the necessary explosives, and the whole idea was squelched.

About this same time, Hans Oster and fellow conspirator Hans Berndt Gisevius tried to build support for a coup attempt in the form of a mutiny, whereby the military commanders in the west would refuse to obey orders to launch the military strike against Germany's western neighbors. To this end, they visited various military commanders in the west to enlist their cooperation for their plan. Contact was made with General Erwin von Witzleben, who now was commander of the First Army, headquartered at Bad Kreuznach in western Germany. Though he still supported the resistance wholeheartedly, he was very pessimistic about the prospect of a generals' mutiny. Additional communication between and among various individuals confirmed this assessment.[282]

By the middle of November, this second coup attempt within a year was dead. The whole sorry affair was a further demonstration of the fact that no coup could succeed without the support of the army, "but the Army would not march without orders. Only Brauchitsch could give the orders."[283] And he refused. Once again, the army leadership, this time in the persons of Franz Halder and Walther von Brauchitsch, demonstrated its fecklessness in dealing with Adolf Hitler. These men completely misunderstood the basic irrationality of the Führer's character. He neither could nor would ever be convinced of anything by reasoned argument.

Additionally, Halder and Brauchitsch in particular lacked the determination, consistency, and strength of character to remove him from power. They had allowed those admirable Prussian traits of order, duty, obedience, and social responsibility – the ethos by which they thought they were living – to be perverted in the service of an evil man and an evil system. They had allowed a twisted sense of duty to compromise them ethically and morally. They also behaved in a manner that could harshly, though justly, be described as cowardly. The tragic and fatal flaws that characterized these men allowed unimaginable horrors to be visited upon their nation and the world. It is said of Brauchitsch that he "lacked the strength of character and moral commitment even to be considered for the role of tragic hero."[284] As for Halder, he "had followed a course of service without loyalty, and duty without honour."[285]

Had neither the stakes been so high nor the consequences so horrid and so calamitous, one could argue that this whole affair might have served as the inspiration for an opéra bouffe by Jacques Offenbach. Thus, the highly regarded German journalist Joachim Fest has written, "For the second time in a year, a coup plot had sputtered and failed. The conspiracy of November 1939 was more tragedy than farce, yet there is indeed something farcical about a coup that was foiled simply by the angry outburst of a tyrant."[286]

This tragic episode reflected the contradictions and inconsistencies that plagued the resistance from beginning to end. Their planning for this coup attempt has been described as "contradictory and uncoordinated," as well as "inadequate and probably even stunningly inept."[287] As severe and accurate as these criticisms are, however, we must recall the circumstances under which these men labored. The incredible obstacles they faced, the emotional stress, and the frightening conditions they endured must be taken into account. The Third Reich was a totalitarian police state completely under the control of the Nazi Party, and the secret police apparatus was omnipresent. Furthermore, Brauchitsch and Halder bore two additional severe – even fatal – handicaps. Not only did they have virtually no popular support, but also they had no strong leader capable of drawing all of the disparate elements of the resistance together and inspiring them to take the necessary action. Instead, the members of the resistance were "brooding individuals, estranged by contradictory goals and approaches and united only by their disgust for the regime."[288] The assassination question is a prime example. Many of the generals never reconciled their detestation of the Nazis with their unwillingness to accept tyrannicide as the necessary means to the goal of freeing Germany from the Nazi plague. Theirs was a "lack of political will to commit an act that ran against the grain of all their traditions and patterns of thought."[289]

Round II, Part 2: The Abwehr, November 6, 1939, to May 1940

As the autumn days of 1939 faded into approaching winter, Hitler still had not given the definitive order to invade Western Europe. Instead, he issued a series of postponements between November and December, until finally, on January 16, 1940, he announced that the long-awaited offensive would not take place until the following spring.[290] Ultimately, he postponed the date for the western offensive some twenty-nine times between the autumn of 1939 and the spring of 1940. These postponements would have unfortunate consequences for the resistance in the months ahead. For the present, however, they gave the most persistent conspirators the opportunity to try yet again to bring an end to the Third Reich. Thus began Round II, Part 2.

One man who remained undeterred was Ludwig Beck, the retired chief of the general staff. As early as November 20, he sent an extensive memorandum to General von Brauchitsch analyzing Germany's current political and military position. He concluded that despite the unbroken string of diplomatic and military victories, the fatherland faced a grim future absent an immediate end to hostilities. At a time such as this, he declared, the senior military commanders must consider "the limits of their responsibility," which "are set solely by their own conscience, by their sense of responsibility towards the Army and the people and by the judgement which history may be expected to pronounce."[291] He sent a second memorandum just after the first of the year that quite accurately predicted the consequences of continuing the war, which he said Germany could never win.

These memoranda fell on deaf ears. Both Brauchitsch and Halder once again displayed their weakness of character that prevented them from fulfilling their duty either in a military or in an ethical and moral sense. They could not cope with the associated risks and uncertainties of a coup.[292] Although subsequent attempts were made to bring Halder around, these proved to be fruitless.[293]

Traitors or Patriots?

Beck was not alone. Hans Oster also was at work. His resolve to rid his beloved fatherland of the Nazi plague remained undiminished, and he was willing to use any means in order to achieve his goal. In many ways, he was the greatest and most daring of the traitorous patriots. In the autumn of 1939, he took the "ultimate and most extreme action"[294] against his own government that he could possibly take. He committed literal treason in the hope that the anticipated war in the west could be brought to a swift conclusion with the collapse of the German military offensive.

The historian Terry Parssinen paints a vivid and poignant picture of the episode:

> On the night of November 7, 1939 – two months after Germany's successful campaign against Poland … Franz Maria Liedig drove Hans Oster to the Berlin apartment of Colonel Gijsbertus Sas, the Dutch military attaché in Berlin and Oster's good friend since 1936. During the drive Oster was very quiet. Liedig waited in the car while Oster entered the apartment to talk to Sas. When Oster returned, his garbled sentences were barely comprehensible. But Liedig soon understood that his friend was deeply troubled, and that he had "crossed the Rubicon." Oster said quietly, "There is no way back for me." Liedig asked him what he meant, and Oster replied, "It is much easier to take a pistol and kill somebody; it is much easier to run into a burst of machine-gun fire than it is to do what I have done."[295]

What Oster had done was to give Sas "the entire German plan for the invasion of Western Europe, then scheduled for November 12."[296] As we know, the assault was postponed and was the first of the twenty-nine postponements that would delay the actual invasion until the early morning hours of May 10, 1940. Nonetheless, Oster, like others in the resistance, had indeed crossed his own personal Rubicon and could never go back. Under the standard German definition, he had committed "high treason" (Hochverrat), that is, treason against the government and head of state, even though the legality of that government was questionable considering the means it had used to acquire and consolidate its power. Did Oster betray his country as well? Did he commit Landesverrat? A definitive answer to that question may never be found to everyone's satisfaction.

His arrest in 1944 and subsequent trial by a kangaroo court and execution a year later at war's end brought his conspiratorial activities to light. The Nazis obviously exploited these revelations to their great propagandistic advantage, so much so that long after the collapse of the Third Reich, the name of Hans Oster was held in derision by most of the German nation. Oster himself fully recognized and accepted the burden that accompanied his deed. He completely understood that in taking this step, he was putting the lives of German soldiers at risk. According to his own calculations, German casualties might number as many as forty thousand. He included himself in that number. As he struggled with his conscience, however, "he concluded that such casualties must be accepted in the face of the certainty that, failing an initial defeat, the war, with its millions of victims and untold misery and destruction, would most certainly be a long one."[297] His prophecy tragically proved to be all too accurate. For this reason, therefore, "formal legal scruples could no longer carry weight in a fight against a demon of destruction like Hitler, to whom the word 'humanity' meant nothing; the object must be to prevent as much damage, misery and death as was possible." Ludwig Beck agreed with him completely.[298]

Oster reasoned that a timely warning to the Dutch and Belgians would give them an opportunity to prepare an adequate defense against a blitzkrieg and Hitler would be denied his coveted quick victory. Oster's goal was simple. He wanted to spare his country – and Europe – the consequences of a "vast, bloody war of conquest" that Germany would almost certainly lose.[299] His moral perspective was both broad and deep, giving him the ability to transcend the narrow legal and political constraints that impeded others. He saw the danger that Nazism represented to Germany and to the world. The following words, spoken of Ludwig Beck, applied to Oster as well. Both men were serving a "higher morality" that "rejected blind obedience to orders endangering Germany's survival as a great power."[300] Sadly, Oster's reputation – and also his family's reputation – suffered greatly as a consequence of his treason. Long after World War II had come to an end, the name Oster was still held in derision in Germany.

Even the Allied powers viewed Oster's actions with disgust. They had condemned the German nation, especially its military leaders, for their lack of "moral courage" because of their failure to overthrow Hitler and the Nazis, yet they saw Oster as a "morally despicable traitor."[301] All of this doubtlessly would not have deterred Oster one iota even had he known about it. In a conversation with his friend Gijsbertus Sas, he spoke to the issue: "One may say that I am a traitor to my country but actually I am not that. I regard myself as a better German than all those who run after

Hitler. It is my plan and my duty to free Germany and thereby the world of this plague."[302] His determination to destroy the Third Reich remained undiminished regardless of the personal cost to him and his family. "He represented that highest patriotism, which is knowing when to be ashamed of one's country."[303] Hans Oster was a man of incredible courage and integrity. Had others in the resistance shared his moral courage, their efforts may well have met with success.

Meanwhile, Hitler's continued indecision over a western offensive restored a degree of hope within the resistance. A short-lived period of promise between mid-December 1939 and mid-January 1940 replaced the "disastrous and demoralizing" months of October and November.[304] Bold action might yet halt the seemingly inevitable march toward war in the approaching spring. Efforts to awaken the military commanders to the grisly work of the several Einsatzgruppen in Poland continued, although some officers greeted these revelations with incredulity. Additionally, an episode involving the SS occurred shortly after the first of the year 1940, raising the spirits of the conspirators. Late in 1939, SS Chief Heinrich Himmler issued a circular note implying that his elite guard was available for stud service to German women for the purpose of increasing Germany's population, especially to those women whose husbands were in military service away from the homeland. A commentary printed in *Das Schwarze Korps* (the Black Corps), the official publication of the SS, soon followed. It equated young women who refused to perform "the duty of contributing to population increase with deserters from the colors."[305] A protest voiced by Lieutenant General Theodor Groppe was one of many indignant reactions. He read the *Schwarze Korps* article to his men at a divisional staff meeting on January 4, 1940, and commented on it with the following words: "Gentlemen, we have been told at the New Year that this year will bring a decision between us and England. From what I have just read to you, it seems to me that a decision must be reached between God and Satan."[306] In retaliation for these remarks, Groppe was relieved of his command.

* * * *

The position of the resistance became even more precarious as February 1940 approached. Time was running out. With the coming of spring, there was a general apprehension that the Sitzkrieg would soon come to an end and Western Europe would be engulfed in a military conflict for the second time in the twentieth century. The only question was exactly when and where the anticipated invasion would occur. In fact, the first major military action of 1940 took place not in Western Europe at all, but in Scandinavia.

Hitler decided in early 1940 that a strike against Denmark, and especially Norway, had to take precedence over an invasion of Western Europe. The German war machine needed Swedish iron ore, and Hitler feared that the British navy might seize control of the sea-lanes to Narvik, the northern port of Norway, through which most of the iron ore passed on its way to Germany.[307] Although Oster, working with Sas, did his best to warn the Norwegian government, their efforts met with failure. Hitler's repeated postponements had produced considerable skepticism within the foreign offices of his intended victims. Neither Oster nor Sas was taken seriously anymore.

The resistance greeted the impending Scandinavian adventure with what has been aptly described as a mixture of "shame, dread and hope"[308] – shame over Germany's willful expansion of the war, dread over the potential consequences of this step, and hope that it might produce one last opportunity to stop Hitler. Just possibly, so the reasoning went, those generals who were not active members of the resistance but who nonetheless were very unhappy about the prospect of a wider war could be persuaded to take action at long last. This final chance before the attack in the west had a "make or break element for both the conspirators and the regime."[309]

The planning and execution of this operation, known by its code name Weserübung (Weser Exercise, for the Weser River), was essentially the exclusive brainchild of Hitler himself. Although Grand Admiral Erich Raeder, the commander of the Kriegsmarine (navy), supported the operation, the generals of the OKH vehemently opposed it almost to a man. Even the man called "Hitler's General," Walter von Reichenau, was now almost completely disenchanted with Hitler and the Nazis, and was dead set against an expansion of the war. He already had adamantly voiced his opposition to the launching of Fall Gelb (Case Yellow), the strike into Western Europe. Additionally, the wretched behavior of the SS in Poland increasingly outraged him.[310] He had resorted to the same sort of treasonous behavior as Oster when, in the autumn of 1940, he warned the Belgian, Dutch, and Danish governments through his own intermediaries of the planned German attack.[311]

In addition to the admittedly faint hope of a generals' revolt, the resistance was counting on a military disaster in Norway. It was not an unreasonable hope, because the operation became Hitler's own pet project, and he assumed responsibility for the overall command of it. Operational planning, normally the responsibility of the OKH, especially its general staff, was in this instance given to the OKW, which was ill-equipped for the task. The OKH had declared the entire operation to be "a lunatic venture,"[312] infuriating Hitler, who turned the project over to the OKW, which, as noted before, was completely subservient to him.

The resistance leaders within the general staff and Abwehr thus believed, not without reason, that in the event of a failed military action, Hitler would be discredited in the eyes of his generals and the nation to such an extent that an overthrow of the regime just might be possible.[313] In addition, military action in Norway, with its mountainous terrain and some fifteen hundred miles of coastline filled with deep, narrow fjords, presented a formidable challenge to the German military forces. Besides, the British Navy could be expected to contest the Kriegsmarine for control of the North Sea and the waters off the Norwegian coast; and of the two navies, the British fleet was by far the superior force.[314]

Weser Exercise was launched on April 9, 1940, with a combined air, sea, and land offensive against Norway and a land assault against Denmark. The latter surrendered within a few hours. Norway held out until the end of the month, and sporadic fighting continued until June. An Anglo-French expeditionary force landed in Norway in the middle of April but suffered a humiliating defeat and was forced to withdraw within two weeks.[315] The German victory was complete, and Hitler's position was unassailable. He had achieved another spectacular victory, and the resistance had suffered another disastrous setback. As with the previous attempts, this last chance to prevent an invasion of Western Europe had ended in frustration and failure.

On the other hand, the victory had not been achieved without cost. In its encounters with the British Navy, the Kriegsmarine sustained significant losses, from which, according to the late Harold Deutsch, it never fully recovered.[316] Among those losses were a newly commissioned battle cruiser, ten destroyers, and fifteen transport ships, plus damage to two battleships.[317] More significantly, Hitler's performance as the generalissimo of Weser Exercise proved to be less than stellar. He displayed characteristic signs of emotional instability, as well as a "startling lack of nerve."[318]

On at least one occasion, he suffered what has been described as a panic attack. Also, his orders often were contradictory and inconsistent. Officers who observed him at close physical proximity began to realize that his capabilities as a military commander were severely limited. Consequently "ripples of anxiety" began to spread throughout the high command.[319] Nevertheless, the spectacular success of Weserübung and the subsequent victories in Western Europe that were just weeks away pushed these concerns into the background. But the victories of the first year and a half eventually gave way to stalemate and defeat, and the cold, hard reality of a shallow amateur leading his country to catastrophe eventually replaced the legend of the infallible Führer.[320]

* * * *

With the success of Weserübung assured, the long-anticipated Nazi invasion of Western Europe began in the predawn hours of May 10, 1940, with a combined air and ground assault against France, Belgium, and the Netherlands. Using the blitzkrieg tactics that had brought stunning success in Poland the previous September, units of the Luftwaffe began the attack with a strike against airfields in Belgium, the Netherlands, and northern France, in order to neutralize the Allied air forces and thereby secure command of the air.[321] A ground offensive was launched simultaneously against Belgium and the Netherlands, catching both countries completely by surprise. The twenty-nine postponements of the invasion had taken their toll, and Oster's latest warning had been ignored. He had completely lost his credibility. Overwhelmed by superior planning and organization, the countries were hard-pressed to offer any effective resistance. Even units of both the French and British armies dispatched to Belgium and the Netherlands were unable to halt the German juggernaut.

The Dutch government surrendered within four days, and Belgium capitulated on May 27.[322] Striking through the very hilly and heavily forested region of the Ardennes along the Franco-Belgian border, the Wehrmacht broke through into northern France near the city of Sedan (site of a crucial battle during the Franco-Prussian War in 1870), crossed the Meuse River on May 13, and reached the English Channel by May 20, essentially sealing the fate of the Allied armies. The Allied troops north of the German line were trapped. Their last hope of escape came with the famous Dunkirk operation, in which a ragtag armada consisting of ships of the Royal Navy and private boats rescued some 338,000 British and French troops from the beaches and transported them to safety in England. To the south, German troops advanced swiftly toward Paris and captured the City of Lights on June 14. On June 22, the French government accepted German terms for an armistice, and three days later all fighting ceased.[323]

Within six weeks, the Wehrmacht had reached a goal that had eluded the armies of Kaiser Wilhelm II through four years of bloody warfare from 1914 to 1918. The German victory was complete, and Adolf Hitler stood at the apex of his power and popularity. He had ascended to the pinnacle of greatness. Those doubters who had questioned the Führer's "genius" – especially those within the military establishment – were viewed as "whiners and defeatists."[324] The ever-obsequious Wilhelm Keitel proclaimed Hitler Größter Feldherr aller Zeiten (greatest commander of all time),[325] an appellation that few, even Hitler's enemies, would have dared to challenge in the early summer of 1940. His exploits dazzled friend and foe alike.

The mood of the German nation at this time has been described as follows:

> For perhaps the only time during the Third Reich there was genuine war-fever among the population. Incited by incessant propaganda, hatred of Britain was now widespread. People were now thirsting to see the high-and-mighty long-standing rival finally brought to its knees. But mingled with the aggression were still feelings of fear and anxiety. Whether triumphalist, or fearful, the wish to bring the war to a speedy end was almost universal.[326]

Those nagging fears would never quite go away. For the moment, however, the Third Reich was at the zenith of its popularity and would remain at that point for the next twelve months. During this golden summer of 1940, the German nation basked in the afterglow of victory and savored the literal fruits of conquest, such as French wines and Dutch cheeses, in unprecedented quantities and at unprecedented low prices. More significantly, a new era, a *neue Gründerzeit*, was dawning for Germany. The rapid defeat of France had wiped the slate clean. The disgrace of the 1918 armistice and the Diktat of Versailles were expunged from the record, and the German people were the masters of all they surveyed. National Socialism had proven its superiority over all other sociopolitical systems,[327] or so it seemed.[328]

Hitler's triumphs in the spring and early summer of 1940 devastated the resistance movement and brought virtually all anti-Nazi activity to a temporary end. The men of the resistance had expected a spirited French and British riposte that would produce a military stalemate of the type experienced in the Great War, which in turn would bring a swift collapse of Nazi rule. The reality was just the reverse. The Third Reich now was entrenched in Germany more firmly than ever, and Round II of the army's resistance movement was dead. Its last gasp came just hours before Case Yellow (Fall Gelb) – the western offensive – was launched, when Hans Oster committed one final act of treason. He sent one last warning to the Dutch government of the planned attack scheduled for May 10.

Oster had continued his contacts with his friend, the Dutch military attaché Gijsbertus Sas, throughout the remaining months of the Sitzkrieg; and each time Hitler established a date for the western offensive, Oster dutifully contacted Sas, who forwarded the information to the Dutch government. Sas also maintained contact with his counterpart in the Belgian government, Colonel Georges Goethals, who relayed Oster's warnings to his own superiors. Tragically, however, each time a postponement was made, the credibility of Oster and Sas was further undermined with both the Dutch and Belgian governments. When the final order was given on May 9 for the invasion to commence the following day, Oster contacted Sas and gave him the code word "Danzig." Sas passed the information on to Goethals. Thus, both governments were warned, and both governments ignored the warning. The boy had cried wolf once too often.[329]

The dilemma in which the resistance now found itself was partly the result of its own doing. The rationale for a coup attempt was the prospect of a major German military defeat, but Germany's unexpected, yet stunning, military victory completely undermined that rationale. Once again, the conspirators were completely undone. The foundation that they thought was solid had crumbled beneath them. Thus, "by basing their rejection of the Third Reich largely on its ineptness rather than its immorality, the leading resisters were staking everything on Germany's military defeat … [And] their subordination of moral principle to political expedience would have disastrous consequences."[330]

The scope of Hitler's accomplishments was a spellbinding experience for most of the German nation, as well as for a significant number of those within the resistance, especially the men of the OKH. Even men like Ulrich von Hassell and Carl Goerdeler "were torn between an acceptance of the regime's gains and accomplishments and a rejection of its policies and methods." Past injustices perpetrated against Germany were avenged, making the "gains in foreign affairs [appear] … legitimate and justifiable."[331] The long arm of history continued to determine the present, especially within the military establishment. Those generals who were on the fringes of the resistance could not take their eyes off the magnitude of the military victories. The men who had drunk the bitter dregs of defeat in 1918 and then had endured a humiliating peace settlement now felt vindicated.

Yet the moral cost of these victories in 1940 was not calculated in the final accounting of the western offensive. Even recent memories of the moral outrage resulting from the depraved behavior of the Nazis in Poland were forgotten in the flush of victory in the west. "The dirt blowing westward from Poland was buried under the rug."[332] Hitler explained this phenomenon with the simple statement that victory "excused everything."[333] Unfortunately his remark was correct, and those within the OKH who were on the fringes of the resistance simply faded away. Abwehr chief Admiral Wilhelm Canaris reputedly said that the numbers of those still in the resistance "had shrunk to fewer than the five fingers on one hand."[334] In the case of the Abwehr, this was almost literally true.

A question remains: Could a coup d'état based solely upon revelations of Nazi criminality have succeeded in the weeks prior to May 10? It seems doubtful. The truly dedicated resistance members retained their resolve to eradicate the Nazi cancer by the radical surgery of assassination. For others, whose commitment was less than wholehearted, it is highly probable that only a decisive military defeat in the west would have roused them to action against the Nazi leader and his regime. A coup based upon moral issues alone would have been insufficient motivation for these men located on the periphery. A successful overthrow of Nazi rule in the spring of 1940 required a calamitous defeat of Germany's armies.

* * * *

Though shattered by the success of Case Yellow, the resistance refused to die. The survivors of Rounds I and II held together.[335] Time and again, their hopes had been raised, only to have them ultimately dashed; but they persevered. These gallant men, these precious few, remained steadfast and "refused to succumb to the intoxication of success."[336] They fully comprehended the evil nature of the Nazi system, and though despondent over the totally unanticipated course of events, their resolve to exorcise the demons that were destroying the soul of their fatherland continued undiminished.

Helmuth James von Moltke commented in a letter to a friend in the spring of 1940 that the German victories in the west marked the "triumph of evil." He said that now he would "have to wade through a 'swamp of outward success, ease, and well-being.'" Military defeat "would have been far preferable to this progressive corruption of the national soul."[337] The comment of Ulrich von Hassell is instructive as well. In his diary, published after World War II, Hassell wrote of the Nazi victories in the west as follows:

"With Beck, as with Popitz and Goerdeler, I was at one that, *despite* the minimal chances, we could not for a moment give up hammering away" (italics in original).[338] And indeed, they *did* hammer away. Although ultimate failure was a virtual certainty, their moral convictions compelled them to persist in their resolve to destroy the Third Reich, even at the cost of total military defeat.

Dietrich Bonhoeffer, always the conscience of the conspirators, spoke to the moral dimension of the resistance with the following words: "If we want to be Christians, we must not permit tactical considerations to influence us. Hitler is the anti-Christ. Therefore we must continue in our work and expunge him, no matter whether he is successful or not."[339] Bonhoeffer was part of a very small, tight-knit circle of five men within the Abwehr who had been privy to the Oster–Sas connection. The others were his brother-in-law Hans von Dohnányi, Franz Liedig, Hans Berndt Gisevius, and Oster himself. Together they had shared the struggles of conscience, and together they had concluded that, as Bonhoeffer described it, the "treason" of which Oster was guilty was, in fact, "devotion to the true welfare of the country."[340] These men surrendered neither to the blandishments of military victory nor to the despair of failure. Their goal – the overthrow of Nazi rule – was simple, although extremely difficult to achieve. Their failure to reach that goal is irrelevant. Their singleness of purpose in its pursuit is very relevant.

One fact was clear in the summer of 1940. With Hitler at the high tide of his popularity, the resistance had absolutely no broad base of support. This state of affairs would continue well into the autumn of 1941. Hence, any action to bring down the Third Reich now depended exclusively upon the elimination of the Führer. But questions remained: How could this be accomplished? What was the best way to dispatch the archfiend? The subsequent history of the anti-Nazi resistance is the story of the many attempts that were made to answer this question.

As early as May 1940, two men with connections to the Kreisau Circle, the lawyer Fritz-Dietlof von der Schulenburg, now in military service, together with the clergyman Eugen Gerstenmaier, schemed to assassinate Hitler with a one-hundred-man commando unit. The plot was abandoned, however, due in part to military transfers. Plans for two additional assassination attempts were laid in the early summer of 1940 at the Paris headquarters of Erwin von Witzleben, now commander in chief of the western army groups and recently promoted to the position of field marshal, the highest rank within the army. Members of Witzleben's staff plotted to have one or more sharpshooters dispatch Hitler as he rode down the Champs-Élysées during a victory parade. However, the parade never took place, partly because Luftwaffe chief Hermann Göring was unable to guarantee protection from a possible British air raid. Still a third assassination plan called for a hand grenade assault against Hitler during an anticipated visit to Witzleben's headquarters. Once again, the conspirators were foiled when Hitler declined to visit the headquarters.[341]

Paradoxically, the summer of 1940 witnessed a revival of the civilian opposition that was centered in the Beck–Goerdeler group. These men were convinced that history would soon vindicate them. Their assessment essentially was correct. Hitler was incapable of understanding that his conquests could be "possessed" only with the exclusive and continual exercise of naked force, which eventually would exhaust his resources and fatally weaken his empire.[342] With clear insight, Carl Goerdeler fully grasped this problem and predicted that the Nazi system could not long survive. Hitler, he said, was unable to rule his empire "in such a way that the honor and freedom of the peoples living there are preserved."[343]

In stating his position, Goerdeler quoted the Prussian statesman Baron Karl vom und zum Stein, in words delivered to Prussian king Friedrich Wilhelm III in October 1808, urging the king to resist Napoleon:

> The only salvation for the honest man is the conviction that the wicked are prepared for any evil ... It is worse than blindness to trust a man who has hell in his heart and chaos in his head. If nothing awaits you but disaster and suffering, at least make a choice that is noble and honorable and that will provide some consolation and comfort if things turn out poorly.[344]

Goerdeler and his supporters realized that "Hitler had been carried away by his own success and was hopelessly overextending Germany's resources."[345] Hence, the Nazi empire was facing "imminent collapse."[346] Nemesis ultimately would replace hubris. Goerdeler's analysis was absolutely correct, but his timing was off by several years. The expected collapse did not come until 1945, and only after unspeakable horrors and millions of deaths had occurred.

Round III: Army Group Center, August 1942 to October 1943

Despite the dramatic success of the western campaign and the benefits that the Nazis accrued from the defeat of France, Adolf Hitler never lost sight of the lands to the east. If his foreign policy had a lodestar, this was it. This region was the key to the Greater Germany, the dominant world power of his febrile imagination. Now that Germany was free from the French threat in the west, he could devote his energies to achieving his goals in the east.

Even the unfinished business of Great Britain – which, thanks to its Royal Air Force, had thwarted the Nazi attempt to invade the British Isles – could be subsumed into the broader scope of the anticipated assault against the Soviet Union. Hitler viewed the Soviet Union as Great Britain's best sword in this war.[347] Therefore, the elimination of the colossus to the east was the best way to bring the Churchill government to the conference table. Even the subsequent conflicts in the Balkans and North Africa failed to deter Hitler from carrying out his plans.

* * * *

On December 18, 1940, Hitler issued his directive for the invasion of the Soviet Union to the Wehrmacht. The directive began as follows: "The German Armed Forces must be prepared to crush Soviet Russia in a quick campaign even before the conclusion of the war against England. For this purpose the Army will have to employ all available units."[348] There was a widespread belief among the generals that the estimated eight- to ten-week campaign would be "rapid and devastating."[349] The generals who dissented remained quiescent.

By June 22, 1941, more than three million Wehrmacht troops in three army groups – North, Center, and South – were deployed along the entire length of the western border of the Soviet Union, from the Baltic Sea to the Black Sea, from Finland to Romania. Soviet forces were roughly equal in numbers to the Wehrmacht.[350] This third blitzkrieg – technically the fourth, since a lightning strike against Yugoslavia in April preceded it – was the largest invasion force ever assembled up to that time, and like its predecessors, it relied upon the element of surprise and speed for success.[351]

The attack began at 3:15 a.m., June 22, 1941, with a massive artillery barrage along the entire front line. The date had historical significance, for exactly 129 years earlier, Napoleon had launched his own campaign against Imperial Russia. The ensuing struggle between Nazi Germany and the Soviet Union was not only the most titanic conflict ever fought up to that time but also perhaps the most titanic that ever will be fought.

> The front extended 1,900 miles (greater than the distance from the northern border of Maine to the southern tip of Florida), and

> German troops advanced over 1,000 miles into Soviet territory (equivalent to the distance from the East Coast to Topeka, Kansas). And they clashed in a seemingly unrelenting series of military operations of unparalleled scale; the battle of Kursk alone ... involved 3.5 million men.[352]

The first weeks of Einsatz Barbarossa (Operation Barbarossa, so named for the emperor of the Holy Roman Empire Friedrich I Barbarossa, or "Red Beard") appeared to be a replay of the previous lightning wars. The Wehrmacht enjoyed "stunning initial successes." Within three weeks, German forces were almost halfway to Moscow and Leningrad and were closing in on Kiev.[353] They had taken hundreds of thousands of Soviet soldiers prisoners of war, many of whom were deserters from the Red Army. By autumn, that figure had grown to some three million.[354] Additionally, "vast stocks" of Soviet matériel, including some twelve hundred tanks and six hundred big guns, had been captured, and the Luftwaffe had secured almost total air superiority. As early as July 4, Hitler was declaring victory. Many of his generals concurred.[355] They were supremely confident that the conflict would be over before the end of the year, and they made little or no provision for an extended military campaign.

Hitler's confidence in a quick victory was so great that on July 14 he shifted the priority for armaments production from the army to the Luftwaffe and the Kriegsmarine. The consequence was a drop of some 29 percent to 38 percent (depending on the source cited) in army weapons production during the first six months of Barbarossa. Aircraft production for the second half of the previous year declined as well. Conversely, warship production was doubled.[356] In addition, "a record five million men were recorded as having been excused from military service."[357] Hitler also refused to reallocate economic resources from "his favorite projects" – such as the Autobahnen (superhighways), private and Nazi Party buildings, and various projects for the city of Berlin – to the production of military equipment. Gambling on a short campaign in the east, he was "waging war on the cheap," even as he was planning for Barbarossa.[358]

Not everyone shared this overconfidence.[359] Even civilians had their doubts, partly because Barbarossa had come as a complete surprise. In an attempt to catch the Soviet government off guard, the Nazis had carried out a program of deception that did not include the usual propaganda barrage that normally accompanied a Nazi military campaign. Thus, the German people, totally unprepared for the events of June 22, 1941, reacted in a way that has been described as "mixed."³⁶⁰ There were expressions of satisfaction that the "unnatural" alliance between Germany and the Soviet Union had come to an end, but these feelings were shared with fears that the war would be extended indefinitely into the future. Others feared that the Führer had overreached himself and that Germany would pay a heavy price for the decision to attack the enemy in the east.³⁶¹ Words such as "anxiety," "apprehension," "dismay," "agitation," "paralysis," and "shock" appear in contemporary reports of the public mood. A staff officer who was well acquainted with the region under attack said, "Our German army is only a breath of wind on the endless Russian steppes." Hence, a "nagging sense of foreboding" began to permeate all segments of German life and society.³⁶²

Indeed, the approach of autumn revealed disturbing signs that all was not well with Operation Barbarossa. First of all, the "quick knock-out blow"³⁶³ failed to materialize, as the Soviet forces put up a stubborn and determined resistance, giving the lie to the confident belief that the Soviet system would collapse like the proverbial house of cards at the first blow. By the end of July, disquieting signs of impending trouble appeared. For example, reports from the front lines of "fanatical fighting by Soviet soldiers" were filtering back to army headquarters.³⁶⁴ Logistical problems arose as well. The rapid advance of German forces deep into the Soviet Union naturally produced extended supply lines and created serious strains on the military transport system, which reduced the ability of the Wehrmacht to provide needed matériel to the forward units. Moreover, the men of the high command fatally underestimated the vast distances involved in the pursuit of their goals. An infinite horizon greeted the German soldiers as they moved across the Russian steppes. Consequently, as early as August 6, the high command issued a report stating that the army would not be able to reach its anticipated territorial goals for 1941. Several days later, Franz Halder, chief of the general staff, wrote that the "colossus Russia" had been "underestimated."³⁶⁵

More ominously, Hitler, in a reprise of his behavior during Weserübung against Norway, began to meddle in the tactics of Barbarossa, to the dismay of the high command. The officers of the general staff were beginning to see Hitler for the rank amateur in military affairs that he was.³⁶⁶ His experience as a frontline soldier in the Great War represented the sum total of his "expertise" as a military strategist and tactician. That experience ill served him and his army in 1941, and the aura of invincibility that previously had surrounded him began to slip away.³⁶⁷ All of this became an increasing problem with the passage of time, and it contributed to the ultimate disasters of the Russian campaign. Although the generals committed their full share of errors, Hitler's persistent interference only made matters worse.[368]

Additional problems arose. The Soviet armies proved to be very resilient and, though suffering terrible losses, were able to call upon seemingly inexhaustible reserves of men and matériel. They remained a formidable force. The planned eight- to ten-week campaign now threatened to continue on into an indefinite future, and this did not augur well for Germany. Casualty figures at the end of August showed the German forces experiencing losses approaching 11 percent of the total Wehrmacht manpower in the east.[369] Weather conditions only added to their woes. By the end of the year, Einsatz Barbarossa was dead, even though the Wehrmacht had almost literally reached the gates of Moscow. An advance patrol had come within a dozen or so miles of the city center, but the invaders could go no farther.[370] The euphoria of July now gave way to the despair of December.

On December 5, 1941,[371] the Red Army, with military reserves of which the Germans had absolutely no knowledge, launched a massive counterattack against Army Group Center that was arrayed before Moscow. This attack, consisting of "100 divisions along a 200 mile stretch of the front,"[372] caught the Wehrmacht completely off guard. Two days later, Walther von Brauchitsch, a broken man in ill health, asked to be relieved of his position as commander in chief. Hitler accepted the resignation on December 19, and assumed for himself field command of the army, an action that essentially eliminated the OKH from any position of operational authority for Germany's ground forces.[373] Hitler now was Germany's warlord. At this point, conditions on the ground were deteriorating significantly as Soviet forces hammered Army Group Center mercilessly. However, Hitler adamantly refused to allow a retreat and issued "a strongly-worded directive to Army Group Center … to hold position and fight to the last man."[374] Remarkably, the front held.

As January came to an end, the immediate crisis was over. The Eastern Front had stabilized, albeit at great cost.[375] Of some 357,000 German troops killed or missing in action in 1941, over 300,000 had been lost on the Eastern Front.[376] To those who viewed the situation realistically, the tide of war definitely was beginning to turn against Germany. The month of December 1941 is now seen as "the turning point in the short life of the Third Reich."[377] Almost three and a half years of fighting remained, but from now on the prospect of ultimate victory became increasingly problematic.

Nemesis was beginning to overtake hubris. The "imminent collapse" of the Nazi system that Carl Goerdeler and his coterie of fellow resisters had predicted was still well over three years away, but it was becoming more and more inevitable. As defeat began to overtake victory, Hitler's reputation began to plummet as well, and this gave heart to the resistance. A military rationale for removing Adolf Hitler from power had resurfaced.

* * * *

In the winter months that followed, German forces "managed to hang on, but just barely, aided as much by Soviet incompetence and difficulties as by their own efforts."[378] The carnage continued and would only get worse. From the beginning of Barbarossa on June 22, 1941, to the beginning of April 1942, the German Army in the Soviet Union suffered over 1.1 million casualties, that is, men killed, wounded, or missing. Of that figure, 900,000 had fallen since the beginning of November. The replacement figures tell an even more somber story. As of May 1, 1942, the German armies in the Soviet Union, especially the combat units, were under strength by some 625,000 men. Matériel losses were severe as well, and Germany's ability to replace these losses was inadequate in relation to the needs.[379]

Nonetheless, the arrival of spring 1942 brought with it a renewal of the Drang nach Osten (drive to the east). The high command had made plans for a resumption of the offensive during the preceding winter months. The final version, given the code name Fall Blau (Case Blue), was essentially the work of Hitler. It called for a phased thrust southward toward the Caucasus and the Crimean Peninsula. It also included a drive against Stalingrad, an important industrial city located on the Volga River and a distribution center for supplies headed toward the Caucasus oil fields. For a man like Adolf Hitler, the mere name also had a special symbolic significance. Unable to destroy either Moscow or Leningrad, he decided that the city bearing Stalin's name had to be obliterated.[380] All men of the city would be put to death and the women and children would be deported, because, according to Hitler, Stalingrad's "thoroughly communist population of a million [was] especially dangerous."[381] The titanic struggle that ensued for control of Stalingrad would become a metaphor for the entire war in the east.

The directive for Case Blue was issued on April 5 and put into operation on June 28.[382] As in the previous summer, the Wehrmacht advanced rapidly, and with renewed fury. This time, however, the Red Army, instead of standing its ground and risking encirclement and capture, retreated in orderly fashion. Once more, German supply lines became overextended and the offensive bogged down. Hitler, oblivious to the realities on the ground, ordered the advance to continue without pause.

When a Soviet counterattack in August 1942 threatened Army Group Center, he angrily rejected Halder's request to allow a withdrawal to a more secure and defensible position. He accused Halder of cowardice, whereupon Halder angrily responded, "Out there, brave musketeers and lieutenants are falling in the thousands and thousands as a useless sacrifice in a hopeless situation simply because their commanders are not allowed to make the only reasonable decision and have their hands tied behind their backs."[383] Hitler flew into a characteristic rage: "Colonel-General Halder, how dare you use language like that to me! Do you think you can teach me what the man at the front is thinking? What do you know about what goes on at the front? Where were you in the First World War? And you try to pretend that I don't understand what it's like at the front. I won't stand for that! It's outrageous!"[384]

Franz Halder's days as chief of staff were numbered. The ax fell on September 24, 1942, when he was summarily dismissed.[385] Although no longer an active participant in the resistance movement, he had remained in contact with the conspirators. His departure marked the end of their "contact with the highest echelons of the military."[386] His replacement was General Kurt Zeitzler, who has been described as "a younger man without Halder's experience or authority, a fact which recommended him to Hitler."[387] For the general staff, this appointment symbolized the "final point of capitulation to the forces to which it had wedded itself in 1933."[388]

Little by little, Hitler's interference in the day-to-day operations became more intense. Regular briefings continued unabated, along with orders issued with increasing frequency and detail, all of which only made matters worse for the generals charged with the responsibility of conducting the war.[389] In the month before his dismissal, Halder had written, "One cannot speak of serious work any more. This so-called 'leadership' is characterized by pathological reaction to the impressions of the moment and a complete lack of judgment in assessing the command apparatus and its capabilities."[390] This situation would only get worse with the passage of time. The ultimate consequences of Hitler's military leadership reached fulfillment several months later at Stalingrad.

* * * *

Throughout the summer of 1942, German forces continued a steady advance toward their objectives, although increasing Soviet resistance created delays, resulting in more confrontations between Hitler and his generals as he demanded an ever-greater effort from an increasingly overextended and undersupplied army. More disturbing was the steady decline in the capture of Soviet soldiers, an indication that Soviet forces were pulling back for an eventual counteroffensive.[391] In July, Hitler, confident that the Red Army was "close to the end of its tether,"[392] altered the original directive for Case Blue. He diverted a part of the forces southward toward the Caucasus oil fields, which had the effect of weakening the thrust against Stalingrad. This revised strategy has been described as "sheer lunacy."[393] The stage was being set for a disaster of gargantuan proportions.

The attack on Stalingrad commenced on August 23 with a series of unrelenting air strikes that continued for several weeks. On September 12, advance units of the German Sixth Army, under the command of General Friedrich Paulus, entered a city that air and artillery bombardment had reduced to rubble. Ironically, the devastation resulting from this bombardment gave the city's defenders a distinct advantage, because they could hide in the ruins and strike back at the attackers from positions that were more easily concealed in the destroyed streets and buildings. Air strikes also were less effective in such conditions.

> Digging in behind heaps of rubble, living in cellars and posting snipers in the upper floors of half-demolished apartment blocks, they were able to ambush the advancing German troops, break up their mass assaults, or channel the enemy advance into avenues where they could be disposed of by concealed anti-tank guns and heavy weaponry.[394]

Hand-to-hand fighting with bayonets and daggers completed the ghastly picture of a battle degenerating into a war of attrition of the most dreadful and primitive sort. Hitler was determined to capture Stalingrad, and Stalin was determined to hold it. Once again, the Führer had risked everything – including the lives of thousands of men – in an all-or-nothing gamble. This time, the outcome was nothing. The offensive launched in June came to a dead end in the debris-filled streets of a destroyed city in September, even though German troops had captured two-thirds of that city. At this point, Hitler announced that victory was imminent.[395] Reality dictated otherwise.

He was still proclaiming imminent victory on November 9, when he stated publicly, "I wanted to get to the Volga and to do so at a particular point where stands a certain town. By chance it bears the name of Stalin himself. I wanted to take the place and, do you know, we've pulled it off, we've got it really, except for a few enemy positions still holding out."[396] Ten days later, a Soviet counterattack struck the German positions, and two days after that, the Soviets completely encircled the German Sixth Army.

The ultimate crisis at Stalingrad had arrived. The survival of the Sixth Army demanded a withdrawal, but that was the last thing that Hitler would countenance. As demonstrated earlier in the war, the concept of strategic withdrawal was completely foreign to him.[397] Hitler ordered General Paulus to stand and fight. Paulus, the good soldier, obeyed orders "to the letter" and displayed absolutely no initiative whatsoever. "Finally, when the fate of a quarter of a million men rested in his hands, he 'froze' and did little but let events take their course to the complete destruction of his army and the miserable deaths of most of his soldiers."[398]

The siege had begun in November 1942 with three hundred thousand men in the German Sixth Army. By February 1943, some ninety thousand starving German soldiers were left to surrender to the Red Army. These survivors, including General Paulus, were marched into captivity, subsequently spending ten years in Soviet labor camps. Six thousand survivors eventually returned to Germany.[399] The Battle of Stalingrad – Germany's greatest-ever military defeat in a single battle – "was the result of the deliberate and callous indifference of its ruler to the fate of its sons."[400]

As a consequence of this military catastrophe, the resistance movement began to renew efforts to depose its architect after a hiatus of nearly two and a half years. In the late summer of 1942, Colonel Henning von Tresckow, a general staff officer in the high command of Army Group Center, began to assume leadership of the army's resistance activities.[401]

* * * *

As the military catastrophe was running its terrible course across the Russian steppes, a much more diabolic catastrophe of even greater proportions was playing out in the occupied territories behind the front lines, and its implications for the resistance were monumental. There, the minions of the Nazi Party were actually implementing Adolf Hitler's gruesome racial program. Ideology had become policy. Everything that had been foreshadowed in Poland was now taking place in a far larger venue and on a much-greater scale and scope. Its evil nature was almost beyond comprehension.

Of all human activities, warfare arguably is the most prevalent and the most execrable. Too often, words such as "inhumanity," "atrocity," and "brutality" accompany the actual conduct of war. Seldom, however, do they convey a sense of "premeditated or systemic" activity as an actual part of war planning.[402] Nonetheless, as applied to the Nazi campaign against the Soviet Union, they describe conditions in Eastern Europe quite accurately. The Wehrmacht was to become an integral part of a new kind of warfare that arguably was unique in the annals of history. It embraced a gruesomely simple program of racial extermination that:

> ... grew out of the biologistic insanity of Nazi ideology, and for that reason it is completely unlike the terror of revolutions and wars of the past. Here we are faced with the completely impersonal, bureaucratic 'extermination' of a people officially classified as a species of inferior subhumans, as 'vermin,' a problem which [Reichsführer and SS chieftain] Himmler handled as though it were a biological disease.[403]

A moral issue of staggering proportions had been laid at the doorstep of the resistance movement. Now the two issues of incompetent military leadership and severe moral turpitude were conflated. How would the resistance leaders respond? More significantly, how would the generals respond? Despite postwar protestations to the contrary, "the [German] military leadership could have been in absolutely no doubt about the intended systematic murder of communists. They also knew that Hitler equated the Jews with Bolshevism."[404]

On March 30, 1941, Hitler addressed the leaders of the Wehrmacht and laid out his objectives for Barbarossa. In so doing, he gave a clear statement of his expectations regarding the army's role in the impending campaign. This would not be a "conventional military conflict"[405] but rather an "ideological crusade," a "clash of two ideologies," a "war of annihilation," and extermination against "Jewish Bolshevism," in which the normal constraints of international and military law did not apply. He emphasized that "every commander must be involved."[406] Thus, Barbarossa required active army participation in liquidating the "Jewish Bolsheviks."[407] Not one of the generals at this meeting expressed open opposition to Hitler's remarks. They accepted his plans without protest or challenge.[408]

Following the March 30 speech, Hitler issued a series of directives known to history as the Kommissar Erlass (Commissar Order) to the top military command of the Wehrmacht. In part, it read as follows:

The war against Russia cannot be fought in knightly fashion. The struggle is one of ideologies and racial differences and will have to be waged with unprecedented, unmerciful, and unrelenting hardness. All officers will have to get rid of any old-fashioned ideas they may have. I realize that the necessity for conducting such warfare is beyond the comprehension of you generals, but I must insist that my orders be followed without complaint. The commissars hold views directly opposite to those of National Socialism. Hence these commissars must be eliminated.[409]

It goes on: "Political commissars have initiated barbaric, Asiatic methods of warfare. Consequently, they will be dealt with *immediately* and with maximum severity. As a matter of principle, they will be shot at once, whether captured *during operations or otherwise showing resistance*" (italics in original).[410]

The net effect of this decree and its supplements was to officially sanction the murder of both combatants and civilians. German military forces and SS operatives were given carte blanche to carry out the mad plan to totally eradicate "Jewish Bolshevism" from the face of the earth. Thus, entire villages were subjected to reprisals if individuals perpetrating guerilla warfare against the Wehrmacht could not be apprehended immediately.[411] Furthermore, since the definition of a "political commissar" was flexible, a German soldier "could shoot everything down to a postman or a refuse-collector." The actual identification of a commissar was unnecessary, and civilians were exterminated on a "vast scale."[412] Prisoners of war were simply murdered en masse. An estimated three million Soviet prisoners of war died at the hands of the Germans. The total number of Soviet civilians and military personnel who perished in World War II is calculated at some twenty-one million.[413] These abstract figures can only give a hint of the truly monstrous nature of the war in the east.

The reaction of the generals to the Commissar Order was both interesting and disturbing. During the Polish campaign, which has been described as "an experimental training ground"[414] for what was about to occur in the Soviet Union, Generals Halder and Brauchitsch had done nothing that could be regarded as real dissent. For example, they had meekly acquiesced to Hitler's order of October 17, 1939, removing the SS and the police from military jurisdiction.[415] The announcement of the Commissar Order in March 1941 found the generals once again acting irresponsibly. Aside from voicing "feeble protests," they did nothing to resist it. They immersed themselves in strictly military matters and tried to ignore even the things "they were *forced* to see and know" (italics in original).[416] Thus, the stench arising from the moral rot that had been slowly destroying the soul of the German Army for the past ten years became increasingly intense as the Einsatzgruppen moved into the Soviet Union. The Commissar Order was merely one additional step on the path that ultimately led to the complete moral degradation of the army, because it had the effect of making the army complicit in the atrocities.

Additionally, some within the army leadership – too many, as it turned out – willingly accepted these guidelines for what essentially was criminal activity carried out in the conduct of the war.[417] Men such as these already heartily despised communism, and they considered the Soviet commissars to be little more than criminals. Doubtlessly, their prejudices had been deepened and their moral sensibilities dulled by the especially barbaric nature of the war in the east and by the steady drumbeat of Nazi propaganda. Furthermore, most of them had come of age in a late nineteenth-century racist culture that was steeped in vicious anti-Semitism and predisposed to denigrate the Slav as inferior to the Teuton. They also had absorbed the concept of a Mitteleuropa, or Middle Europe, an Eastern Europe in which Germany would become, both strategically and economically, the hegemonic power.[418] This idea had achieved considerable popularity among those Germans who were conservative expansionists in the early years of the twentieth century. This notion of a German-dominated Mitteleuropa actually became a declared war aim of the imperial government during the Great War. Consequently, many of the senior Wehrmacht officers were already conditioned to accept the implications of the Commissar Order. Anti-Semitism, alongside a long-standing fear of and hatred for the revolutionary Marxism that now controlled the government in Moscow, dominated the thinking of these men.

Colonel General Georg von Küchler, commander of the Eighteenth Army on the Eastern Front, was a typical example of such officers. Speaking to his divisional commanders about the Commissar Order, he declared, "A deep chasm separates us ideologically and racially from Russia." It was, he said, an "Asiatic state." Therefore, German armies had to "annihilate" and "dissolve" the "Russian European state."[419] Officers who held such views only too willingly cooperated with the SD (Sicherheitsdienst, or Security Service) and the SiPo (Sicherheitspolizei, or Security Police), both organs of the SS, in their attempt to thoroughly eradicate "Jewish Bolshevism."[420] Tragically, there was little of the moral outrage among these men that

General Blaskowitz had expressed at the time of the Polish campaign in 1939.

Nonetheless, many of these men were horrified once they came to understand the barbarity that was the true nature of Nazi-inspired anti-Semitism.[421] The anti-Semitism that was part of their cultural and social milieu never contemplated annihilation and extermination. This was especially true of those who held anti-Semitic beliefs but who were part of the wider resistance movement, both civilian and military. Many failed to realize until quite late in the game, however, that the logic of racism led directly to the final solution to the Jewish question. Such are the dangers of ideology.

At long last, the military issues were now linked to the broader moral issues surrounding Nazism and its leader. Only the most obtuse could fail to see that the Third Reich was an instrument of moral corruption that was destroying the soul of the German nation.

* * * *

Despite the attitude of those officers who accepted the Commissar Order without serious question, many senior members of the command structure greeted news of the order with "a storm of indignation."[422] This outrage contributed to a significant decline in "enthusiasm for the regime," especially as these men realized that the order would make the army complicit in the atrocities and crimes already being perpetrated against civilians and military personnel in the name of the German nation.[423] Additionally, the savage war already being waged against Europe's Jews deeply disturbed many officers in both the senior and junior ranks, especially those who already were part of the resistance movement.

Thus, one ultimate consequence of Hitler's Commissar Order was a revival of the resistance movement. Army units stationed both in Paris and Berlin became centers of resistance to the order and "to the regime in general."[424] In Berlin, Hans Oster was one of the first to learn of Hitler's directive, and he brought a copy to a meeting of several resistance leaders at Ludwig Beck's home. According to a participant in that meeting, "everyone's hair stood on end." They realized that compliance with the order "would systematically transform military justice for the civilian population into a caricature that mocked every concept of law." They agreed that Brauchitsch was "sacrificing the honor of the German army."[425] This conviction became more widespread among members of the general staff as the Commissar Order and its subsequent directives became known. They "were aroused to shame and anger."[426]

No member of the officer corps felt a greater sense of shame and anger than Henning von Tresckow. His unremitting hatred for the Third Reich and all it represented had long since replaced his original support for Nazism. Now, with German forces mired in an increasingly unwinnable conflict deep inside the Soviet Union, Tresckow decided that the time for action had come. Like others in the resistance, he realized that a successful coup required someone with field command of forces to cast their lot with the conspirators, and to that end he worked assiduously to enlist the support of the commander of Army Group Center, General Hans von Kluge, to whose staff he was assigned. Regrettably, he ultimately met with failure. Kluge, though very sympathetic to the cause of the resistance, could never take that ultimate step. In frustration, Tresckow began making his own plans to eliminate Hitler. As early as the summer of 1942, well before the Battle of Stalingrad, he was plotting a strike against the man.[427] Thus, the headquarters of Army Group Center deep inside the Soviet Union became the locus of resistance activity within the military establishment, and the mantle of the conspiracy's leadership was placed upon the shoulders of Colonel Henning von Tresckow. His credentials as a soldier and patriot were impeccable.

He is considered to have been one of the "most gifted staff officers in the OKH" (Oberkommando des Heeres, or Army Supreme Command).[428] Born into "an old Prussian officer family,"[429] Tresckow had served with distinction as a platoon commander in the Great War, ultimately receiving three Iron Crosses for valor, the first as a seventeen-year-old lieutenant. He remained in the postwar army, the Reichswehr, until 1920, when he resigned his commission to study law and economics. He subsequently became a world traveler working for a bank. He rejoined the army in 1924, attended Staff College, and graduated at the top of his class in 1936, becoming a member of the army's general staff that same year.[430] He was highly regarded as "an outstandingly capable officer, far above average, very hard-working and exceptionally capable of taking decisions."[431] It is also said of him that he "could not abide anything mean or unjust."[432] He is remembered as a man whose "vigorous soul, faultlessly upright, radiated from an inner peace that infused his whole way of being. The strength of his personality, imbued with an authentic and unostentatious piety, was naturally communicated to those round him."[433]

Like Oster, Tresckow had an early dalliance with Nazism. Hans Berndt Gisevius, one of the few conspirators to survive the war, said of him, "He was for many years able to see only the side of National Socialism attractive to a soldier: the assertion of discipline, the reestablishment of military primacy, and the revision of the Treaty of Versailles."[434] Ultimately, however, Tresckow became completely disillusioned with Nazism. Like Oster, he had reached a turning point when the blood purge of June 30, 1934, was carried out. The events of the next several years served to confirm his revulsion of the Nazi system and its leadership. These were the years when Hitler launched his menacing expansionist foreign policy that foreshadowed war and worse. As early as 1938, Tresckow was contemplating treason and assassination as the only way to rid Germany of the Nazi plague. "Hitler," he said, "is a whirling dervish. He must be shot down."[435] Later, as the ghastly drama of World War II began to play out in Eastern Europe, Tresckow, reflecting on the mad policy of racial extermination, declared that it one day would exact a just retribution on the German nation. The only way to bring the insanity of Nazism to an end was to decapitate the Nazi state. Hitler had to be killed.[436]

By the summer of 1941, Tresckow was serving as a general staff officer of Army Group Center at Posen in the eastern part of Germany, now Poznan, Poland.[437] Like many, his outrage over the criminal behavior of the Einsatzgruppen and other SS organizations in Poland grew more intense with the realization that their activities would be extended to the Soviet Union and – even more significantly – that the army was expected to participate in this gruesome work. He clearly understood the obvious: they all were being morally compromised as the net of complicity tightened around them. He desperately tried, without success, to induce his commander, Field Marshal Fedor von Bock, who was also his uncle, to speak with Hitler in an attempt to rescind the Commissar Order.

In a conversation with his friend Major Rudolph-Christoph von Gersdorff, Tresckow reputedly said, "If we do not succeed in persuading the Field Marshal to fly to Hitler immediately and bring about the revocation of these orders, then a burden of guilt will descend on the German nation that the world will not forget for hundreds of years." This burden would be borne by the entire German nation, "on you and me, on your wife and my wife, on your children and my children, on the old woman who is going into a store over there, on the man who is just now riding past us on his bicycle, and on the small child there playing with his ball."[438] Although these words may be more of a paraphrase than a direct quote, they are an accurate reflection of his convictions. The passage of time has confirmed the prophetic accuracy of his remarks.

The behavior of those generals who submitted to Hitler's demands without protest was a source of maddening frustration for the members of the resistance; they desperately searched for some means to rescue their army and nation from the catastrophe looming ahead, and to reset the nation's moral compass. However, the oath of allegiance that was taken in 1934 continued to cast its malevolent shadow over the German army almost a decade later. Only the assassination of Adolf Hitler could remove this shadow. To that end, Tresckow began to build a resistance group within the headquarters of Army Group Center.

In the months that followed, Tresckow filled all of the more important positions with younger like-minded men, including a number of officers of "old Prussian stock,"[439] such as his friend Major von Gersdorff, a cavalry officer whose revulsion of the Nazis would lead him to offer himself as a suicide bomber in an attempt to assassinate Hitler. These men of Army Group Center's general staff have been accurately described as "the largest and most tightly knit resistance group" to be found anywhere within the German anti-Nazi movement at this time.[440] They offered the best hope of removing the tyrant from his throne.

In sum, of all the active resistance cells, the one located in the headquarters of Army Group Center was the most important. Hence, the Commissar Order had one beneficial and unintended consequence: it became a "trigger" that galvanized Tresckow and his fellow conspirators to take action against the regime. The Commissar Order was evaded in many instances. As the eastward advance commenced in June 1941, false reports of executions were deliberately sent to the SS in order to satisfy demands for results, and several commanders issued verbal orders to field officers not to carry out the executions. Another unintended consequence was its effect upon the Soviet people themselves. It became counterproductive, serving only to strengthen "the enemy's will to fight." Its usefulness greatly diminished, the Commissar Order was officially withdrawn in the summer of 1942, by which time the damage had been done. Russian resistance, both in the army and among the civilian population, had hardened.[441]

In September 1941, Tresckow sent Fabian von Schlabrendorff – a lawyer by profession, reserve lieutenant, adjutant to Tresckow, and one of his most trusted aides – to Berlin for the first of several discussions with Ludwig Beck and his group of conspirators, in order to determine the best way to launch a coup against the Third Reich. Schlabrendorff's visit "was the first initiative to come from the [war] front and the Army" and thus presented a new and encouraging dimension to the resistance.[442] A series of consultations took place over the next fifteen months or more that included a number of various resistance groups.[443] These men completely understood the ever-present reality of Gestapo and SS surveillance. They also understood the danger of detection becoming ever greater as the resistance, of necessity, increased in numbers and in organizational complexity. Nevertheless, they were willing to risk all for the sake of rescuing their nation from the clutches of its mad leader and his satraps.[444] Their revulsion of the Nazis was absolute. This regime had violated "the norms of political morality, [and] had forfeited its legitimate claim to power."[445] This was a struggle for Germany's soul.

* * * *

By the spring of 1943, a page in the chronicles of World War II had been turned. Nazi Germany's future looked increasingly grim. Victory was now all but impossible.[446] The unrelenting retreat from Stalingrad was under way and would end only with the entry of the Red Army into a destroyed Berlin in 1945. In addition, the military situation in North Africa was deteriorating rapidly. German military action in that region of the world had been prompted by the misadventures of Benito Mussolini, whose Italian armies had suffered significant reverses in a series of engagements with British forces. Hitler was obliged to rescue his Axis partner in order to prevent a complete military collapse in North Africa. Although General Erwin Rommel and his famed Afrika Korps initially succeeded in temporarily restoring Axis fortunes, the British Army, aided by the US invasion of North Africa in November 1942, ultimately overwhelmed the Axis armies, resulting in their surrender in May 1943. In addition, the naval war in the North Atlantic was beginning to turn against the Kriegsmarine, and the suffering of the civilian population deepened with the increasing ferocity of Allied bombing of German cities.

Among the German public, a growing anxiety accompanied the all too obvious unbroken string of military defeats that followed the collapse at Stalingrad. The initial sense of foreboding that had appeared at the beginning of Barbarossa now returned. For all practical purposes, the war was already lost, and they knew it.[447] Morale plummeted in 1943, and Hitler's popularity declined significantly, both among his generals and the civilians. The "military genius" of Hitler was now seen for the myth that it was. He no longer could escape responsibility for what obviously had become the consequences of his decisions.[448] Goebbels's infamous "Total War" speech of February was a blatant attempt to quash the increasing disaffection of the German people by equating loyalty to Hitler with the pursuit of that total war, despite its rising material and human cost.[449] A popular joke then circulating in Germany gives an indication of Goebbels's success in rallying the nation to further effort: "What's the difference between Germany and India?" The answer: "In India, one person [Gandhi] starves for everybody. In Germany, everybody starves for one person [Hitler]."[450] The time for definitive action against the Führer had arrived. The compounding of one military disaster after another was the catalyst for a renewal of the resistance.

Rumors of increasing tension and dissent within army headquarters spurred Tresckow and his fellow conspirators to further action.[451] In fact, clashes between Hitler and his generals over war policy and strategy had been evident since 1942. Hitler's quarrel with his chief of staff, Franz Halder, was symptomatic of this growing problem. The progressive disintegration of the Nazi war machine only made it more acute. This "fractious dispute" has aptly been described as a contest between "one fantasy" and "one strategy," rather than a clash of two strategies. Additionally, there was a growing realization among many army leaders that "lower level authorities" had not instigated the abhorrent crimes being committed on the Eastern Front, but that Hitler alone was responsible. This realization further alienated many of the army officers from their Führer.[452]

* * * *

By the summer of 1942, months before the calamity at Stalingrad, Tresckow had made the irrevocable decision to assassinate Hitler. By this time, Field Marshal Günther von Kluge was the commander of Army Group Center. Knowing that Nazi behavior outraged and even sickened Kluge, Tresckow tried earnestly to enlist his support, but the aristocratic Prussian field marshal never was able to make a wholehearted commitment to the resistance. His continued vacillation earned for him the sobriquet "Kluge Hans," or "Clever Hans," which was a wordplay on his last name. The German word "klug" translates into English as "clever." He was one of several generals whose ambivalence ultimately brought the resistance to a catastrophic end. Others were not ambivalent but merely opportunistic. They hoped to place themselves on the winning side, wherever it was. The infamous oath of allegiance inhibited still others. In some cases, reluctance was doubtlessly a combination of both ambivalence and inhibition. Kluge possessed the ability to play both ends against the middle, but he lacked the moral courage to make an unequivocal commitment to the resistance.[453] For this reason, Tresckow could never depend completely upon him for support. To his credit, however, Kluge never betrayed the conspirators.

Despite the unreliability of his commanding officer, Tresckow pressed ahead with his plans to dispatch Hitler. The how remained the ever-present problem. Various alternatives were contemplated – "arrest, shooting by a single assailant or by a group, [or] a raid on the Führer's headquarters,"[454] – but the final choice was a bomb, because it represented the greatest hope for success.

Tresckow's friend Baron Rudolph-Christoph von Gersdorff, now a lieutenant colonel, was selected for the task of finding the suitable explosive material. This in itself was a challenge because Gersdorff had to have a credible explanation for wanting explosives in order to satisfy the curiosity of the SS. He explained that he planned to recruit Russian volunteers serving with German forces to engage in antiguerilla warfare, saying that explosives would be essential to this activity. His deception was successful. The ultimate choice was a small British bomb known as a "clam," which had been captured from British commando raids in France in the summer of 1941, as well as from parachute drops in France intended for the French Resistance fighters.[455] British fuses were chosen as well, because they were completely silent.

Tresckow also made contact with conspirators in Berlin – both civilian and military – in order to coordinate plans with three main "hubs of resistance."[456] These hubs would participate in a coup d'état once Hitler was eliminated. The first hub was the field army, specifically Army Group Center. The replacement army, also referred to as the "reserve" or "home" army, was the second hub. Its function was to protect the regime against "internal disturbances" that might arise from a breakdown of civil order due to deteriorating conditions inside Germany. An uprising of slave laborers was especially feared. The third hub consisted of the civilians who were part of the resistance, especially members of the Beck–Goerdeler group. Tresckow also worked closely with the conspirators within the Abwehr, specifically Hans Oster and Helmuth Groscurth, in order to coordinate their collective efforts. Retired general Ludwig Beck "was officially 'constituted as the headquarters'" of the resistance.[457]

Regardless of the overweening presence of the SS and Gestapo, these resistance hubs were able to establish and maintain continuous contact with one another from the summer of 1942 on. Schlabrendorff provided liaison between Army Group Center and the Beck–Goerdeler group.[458] One of the most important of these contacts occurred in March 1943, when Oster made a connection with General Friedrich Olbricht, who was stationed at army headquarters in Berlin.

Olbricht is described as "one of the most determined and resolute opponents of the regime."⁴⁵⁹ A man of deep religious conviction – it was said of him that he was "driven largely by Christian and patriotic feelings"⁴⁶⁰ – Olbricht had been an ardent anti-Nazi since 1933. Beck, Tresckow, and Olbricht formed a triumvirate that quickly became the de facto leadership of the resistance. Olbricht's responsibility was the planning for the assumption of power by the provisional government once Hitler was eliminated.⁴⁶¹ This included coordinating measures to seize power not only in Berlin but also in Vienna, Cologne, and Munich.⁴⁶² As Olbricht laid his plans for seizing control of the government, Tresckow worked on his own plans to assassinate the Führer.⁴⁶³

By March 1943, the basic plan for the coup attempt was in place. This would be no mere putsch or palace revolt. Rather, it would represent the "other," the "real" Germany that the Nazis had hijacked and had transformed into the dreadful Volksgemeinschaft. Therefore, the active participation by prominent civilians in a provisional government was vitally important to the success of their efforts. Together, the army conspirators and the civilian resistance would topple the Nazi regime and create a provisional government. An immediate seizure of power in Berlin was to follow Hitler's assassination. Carl Goerdeler, the former mayor (Bürgermeister) of Leipzig, would become chancellor, and Field Marshal Erwin von Witzleben, now retired, would take command of the Wehrmacht.⁴⁶⁴

As always, the most significant challenge was finding a way to get access to Hitler. He now was becoming more withdrawn and secretive, spending increasing amounts of time at his Wolfschanze (Wolf's Lair) at Rastenburg, East Prussia (now Kętrzyn, Poland). His public appearances became more infrequent, and he often changed his limited travel plans abruptly and on short notice. Furthermore, security around him was tightened progressively.⁴⁶⁵ The SS was not unaware of the growing disgust and despair that was festering within the officer corps of the Wehrmacht. The SS leadership knew full well that assassination plots were brewing within the army leadership, although they did not yet have adequate information for taking action against specific individuals.

By this time, military conditions on the Eastern Front had deteriorated so badly that Hitler decided to visit various military units personally and evaluate the situation for himself. This decision opened the door to several scenarios for a coup attempt. The first opportunity arose when he elected to visit Army Group B headquarters in Poltava in the Central Ukraine on February 17. There, a group of officers who had agreed "that Hitler was a criminal and must be removed" prepared to arrest and, if necessary, assassinate him.[466] In a typical last-minute decision, however, Hitler changed the destination from Poltava to Saporozhe, also in the Ukraine, because Army Group B headquarters had already left Poltava. Additionally, Hitler was furious that General Hubert Lanz, the commanding officer at Poltava, had disobeyed his specific order to hold the city of Kharkov at all costs. He therefore decided to meet Lanz's superior in Saporozhe to demand the latter's dismissal. Thus, this "Lanz Plan" came to nothing.[467] At Saporozhe, a perverse fate rescued Hitler from an even worse fate than arrest and possible assassination. As the three transport planes for his entourage prepared for takeoff from Saporozhe, Soviet tanks were approaching the eastern edge of the airfield. They were stopped from launching an attack because they had run out of fuel.[468]

An additional opportunity for an assault against Hitler arose on March 13, when he made a trip to one of the hubs of the resistance, namely, the headquarters of Army Group Center, then located at Smolensk, some 225 miles west-southwest of Moscow. Tresckow had devised several alternative assassination plans, such as shooting Hitler at lunch or during his walk back to his car that was to take him to the airfield, or attaching a bomb under his car that would explode during the short trip from the headquarters building to the airfield. The best alternative, however, was the placement of a bomb on the airplane that would take Hitler back to Rastenburg and the Wolfschanze.

The scheme for placing the bomb in the plane proved to be simplicity itself. During the luncheon, Tresckow requested one of the officers scheduled to ride on Hitler's plane to carry a package containing a "bottle of Cointreau Cognac" back to headquarters for a friend there. The "bottle" was in fact two of the British "clams" (bombs) carefully wrapped to resemble a bottle of Cointreau. As Hitler boarded his plane, the fuse was activated, and the package was given to the "courier" for the trip home. The bomb was timed to explode after thirty minutes and about 125 to 150 miles into the flight. Immediately after the three transport aircraft and their fighter escort took off, Fabian von Schlabrendorff, who was with Tresckow in Smolensk, placed a call to Abwehr headquarters in Berlin and gave the code word "flash," indicating that the assassination plot had been launched. Now the conspirators had to wait until news was received in Smolensk of the plane's destruction, whereupon Berlin would be notified and General Olbricht's carefully devised plans for the coup would be put into motion.

The Army – Four Rounds of Resistance

The news never arrived. Instead, the conspirators, waiting in Smolensk in an atmosphere charged with increasing tension and anxiety, eventually received a report that Hitler and his entourage had arrived safely in Rastenburg. Immediately, Schlabrendorff called Abwehr headquarters and gave the code word indicating that the plot had failed. Tresckow then called the "courier," a certain Colonel Brandt, and calmly told him that a mix-up had occurred, that he should hold on to the "Cointreau," and that Schlabrendorff would take a normal courier aircraft the next day from Smolensk to Rastenburg to retrieve the package.

The following hours were extremely stressful for the conspirators, partly because no one knew whether or not the bomb would detonate. Fortunately, nothing happened. Schlabrendorff arrived in Rastenburg the following day, exchanged the bomb for a real bottle of Cointreau, and went to his quarters to examine the bomb. He carefully disassembled the package and discovered that all had worked as anticipated, except for one thing. The explosive had not detonated because it was sensitive to the extreme cold of the plane's cargo compartment.[469]

The failure of Operation Flash was a terrible blow to the resistance. Of all the assassination plots against Adolf Hitler during the war years, this one had held the greatest promise. With Hitler's death occurring in such a manner and before an investigation of the episode would have begun, the army justifiably could have taken control of the government "in the interests of national security."[470] A successful coup d'état would have effectively neutered the Nazi Party and arguably altered the course of World War II. Most importantly, untold numbers of lives could have been saved and senseless destruction avoided.

Once again, the conspirators were devastated. All of their hard work under the most trying of circumstances, all of the tension and anxiety they had experienced, and all of their laboring within the suffocating and menacing atmosphere of a police state had been for naught. And yet, they persevered. The more hopeless their situation became, the more determined they were to press on toward their goal. Within a matter of days, in fact, they were plotting still another attempt on Hitler's life. The occasion was the annual celebration of Heroes' Memorial Day, which normally was held around March 15. This year, 1943, it was planned for the twenty-first. Colonel von Gersdorff was scheduled to attend the ceremony, which included an exhibit of captured Soviet war matériel. The intelligence section of Army Group Center that was under Gersdorff's personal command had prepared it, thus making him the logical person to escort Hitler through the exhibit.

The conspirators were once again presented with an opportunity to assassinate the Führer. They were in general agreement that the best means was another bomb attack – but how? The venue for the ceremony was the Old Arsenal Museum in central Berlin, and the exhibit was in one of its halls. The placement of a bomb somewhere within the exhibit was no guarantee of success, since there was no way of knowing exactly when and where Hitler would be at any given time. Besides, the conspirators had no way to plant the bomb without detection. A suicide bomber was the only way to ensure success, and Lieutenant Colonel Baron von Gersdorff was the only logical candidate. In a conversation with Tresckow, Gersdorff volunteered for the mission. He had no dependents – his wife had died in January 1942 – and he declared "that in view of the object, his own life did not seem to him too great a sacrifice."[471]

Almost immediately, however, several difficulties arose. First, there was the matter of the fuse required to detonate the explosive, the same British clam bomb that just days earlier had failed to explode on Hitler's airplane. The type of fuse used in the earlier attempt had a thirty-minute delay. Ideally the type used in this attempt should be instantaneous, but none could be found in the short time available to the conspirators. Suitable German fuses detonated within four or five seconds, but they made a noisy hiss, which would alert the security guards around Hitler. The most suitable and available fuses were silent ten-minute British-made time fuses, and this was the fuse that Gersdorff chose.

Other issues were encountered as well. For example, Hitler's chief aide, Brigadier General Rudolph Schmundt – an old friend of both Gersdorff and Tresckow, but devoted to Hitler personally – initially refused to divulge any information about Hitler's schedule or to allow Gersdorff to serve as Hitler's guide for the exhibits tour. Schmundt doubtlessly knew how his two old friends felt about Hitler, "that they did not love the Führer anything like as much as he did."[472] Only the intervention of the commander in chief of the German Ninth Army, Field Marshal Walter Model, who argued that Gersdorff's presence was essential to answer any questions that Hitler might have about the exhibit, persuaded Schmundt to allow Gersdorff to serve as Hitler's guide. Model, of course, had absolutely no knowledge of the plot.

At the appointed time, Hitler, after giving an unexpectedly short speech in the great hall of the museum, approached the exhibit. Gersdorff, with two clam bombs, one in each pocket of his greatcoat, unobtrusively, with his left hand in the left pocket, squeezed the acid capsule that armed the fuse as he gave the "Hitler salute" with his right arm. He dared not put his right hand in the other pocket to arm the other bomb, because the ever-alert SS guards could be expected to pounce on him, suspecting a pistol. In an earlier incident, an SS guard had seized an officer's arm as he reached into his pocket for a handkerchief while he was in Hitler's presence. In ten minutes, it would all be over. Both Hitler and Gersdorff, along with anyone with the misfortune to be too close to them, would be dead.

But it never happened. The bomb never was detonated, and no one was killed. To everyone's amazement, Hitler, asking no questions and scarcely casting a glance at any artifacts on display, almost literally ran through the exhibit. Within barely two minutes, he was outside the museum, where he spent a few minutes inspecting a captured Soviet tank. Gersdorff, now left in the wake of Hitler's abrupt departure from the building, had to disarm the bomb in his pocket as quickly as possible. Finding a washroom nearby, he rushed in and ripped the fuse from the bomb before it could detonate.

Once more, Hitler had cheated death. His Fingerspitzengefühl ("fingertip sensitivity," or sixth sense) appeared to be at work, warning him of the dangers inside the building.[473] The comments of historian Peter Hoffmann provide an apt summary of the episode:

> If anyone says that Hitler must have had some presentiment or "smell" of danger, this need not be brushed aside as ridiculous. Men who live so much on their emotions and so dangerously as Hitler do not possess supernatural qualities as a result but their senses are highly perceptive and sharp. The possibility that Hitler sensed Gersdorff's nervousness and took warning from it is not so far-fetched. It is sufficient, however, merely to establish the facts of what happened.[474]

The lack of an instantaneous fuse, together with Hitler's "often intentionally unpredictable behavior," were the two fatal flaws in this assassination plot.[475]

This brief examination of Gersdorff's failed assassination attempt clearly reveals the almost insuperable barriers facing the conspirators by 1943. The ever-tightening noose of SS surveillance heightened the dangers, and the setbacks mounted. Continued efforts to secure the support of top military commanders met with recurring failure. For example, Tresckow remained unable to bring Kluge into the conspiracy. The latter agreed that the only way "to save the German Reich and people from total ruin" was to eliminate Hitler, but "he could not bring himself to do it."[476] This was an attitude all too common among the generals, and it ultimately was the undoing of the resistance. The reaction of one general to a proposal that all the army field marshals should take concerted action against Hitler was: "Prussian Marshals do not mutiny."[477]

Even General Olbricht, who was an integral part of the entire resistance operation, showed hesitation. It was said of him that "he needed constant prodding to keep him up to the mark."[478] The comment of a junior officer closely connected to the resistance gives an excellent summation of the problem: "One will only take action if orders are given and the other will only give orders if action is taken."[479] Helmuth James von Moltke, the leader of the Kreisau civilian resistance group, wrote the following words to a friend at this time: "The main mistake was to leave such an attempt to the generals. It was a vain hope from the start, but it was hard to convince most people of that in time. The French generals couldn't get rid of Napoleon. It's exactly the same with the Germans today."[480]

More misfortune befell the resistance. Illness and death removed several of the most ardent and active participants at this critical moment in its history. General Kurt von Hammerstein-Equord, who had tried to assassinate Hitler at the beginning of the war, was asked early in 1943 to use his persuasive powers to induce an especially important general to support the resistance, but he declined. Hammerstein was now suffering from terminal cancer, and his deteriorating health doubtlessly was a factor in his decision. Even at this late date, however, he showed remnants of the determination that had inspired him in 1939. He responded to this last request with the comment that if he had a division at his disposal, "he would be prepared to fetch that devil (Hitler) out of hell."[481] He died in April. Longtime resistance leader Ludwig Beck, also suffering from cancer, was forced to undergo surgery in March. Another leading military figure in the resistance, General Erwin von Witzleben, was hospitalized in July with a gastric ulcer.[482] To make matters even worse, later in the year, in October, Field Marshal von Kluge, still vacillating but nonetheless sympathetic to the resistance, was seriously injured in an automobile accident. His replacement as commander of Army Group Center was a "Hitler disciple," Field Marshal Ernst Busch, an appointment that only made matters even more difficult for Tresckow.[483]

Another, much more serious blow struck the resistance on April 5, when the Reich RSHA launched a "direct assault"[484] against the Abwehr. On that date, a Nazi prosecutor appeared in the office of Abwehr chief Admiral Wilhelm Canaris to announce the beginning of an investigation of the Abwehr. Furthermore, Hans von Dohnányi, along with his brother-in-law Dietrich Bonhoeffer and others, were arrested at that same time. Shortly thereafter, Hans Oster was dismissed from his office, bringing an end to his participation in the resistance. From then on, he was under constant SS surveillance until his arrest at the time of the July 20, 1944, bomb plot.[485]

This episode was the culmination of a series of events that cast an ominous shadow over the entire resistance movement. For several months, there were indications that the police were closing in on various resistance groups, including the Abwehr. Both Ulrich von Hassell and Hans von Dohnányi were warned that they were being shadowed, and in March, Colonel Fritz Jäger, serving in the Abwehr, was arrested on the charge that he was "conspiring." Additionally, SS chief Heinrich Himmler was making statements to the effect that he was aware that certain army leaders were planning a coup against the Nazi government.[486] The appearance of the SS officers at Abwehr headquarters on April 5 resulted initially in the arrest of Hans von Dohnányi on charges of "numerous currency violations, corruption, and even treason."[487] Dohnányi had assisted some Jews to be illegally compensated in foreign currency for seizures of their property, a move officially described as a "scandal." He also had been using Jews as "agents" in foreign countries for a number of years. In so doing, he had protected them from "special treatment," meaning death.[488]

Oster demanded that he, as Dohnányi's superior, be arrested instead, but to no avail. During the episode, Oster was seen removing some incriminating papers from Dohnányi's desk and putting them into his pocket. He immediately was placed under house arrest and subsequently suspended from the Abwehr. Also arrested on that same day, April 5, 1943, were Dietrich Bonhoeffer and his sister Christine, who was Dohnányi's wife.[489] Oster's dismissal caused what fellow conspirator Hans Berndt Gisevius described as a "psychological shock," which produced a "conspiratorial vacuum" at the very center of resistance operations.[490]

The SS had delivered a devastating body blow to the resistance. For all practical purposes, the Abwehr was finished as a center of conspiratorial activity. The final blow fell a year later, when in February 1944, the RSHA abolished the Abwehr as a viable organization, and Canaris was placed under house arrest.[491]

By the summer of 1943, the resistance was in a state of near paralysis. The leadership was decimated, and a sense of resignation and despair threatened to overwhelm them all. They felt powerless against what appeared to be the forces of history, which were sweeping the Third

Reich toward its inevitably catastrophic end. Hitler, it seemed, was indeed Germany's tragic destiny.[492] Considering all that had transpired since 1938 – the many near misses and foiled plots – their fatalism is understandable. They would have been justified in believing that a malevolent power was protecting Hitler and enabling him to pursue his evil deeds. The resistance desperately needed leadership. Those who had been at the helm from the beginning were gone.

The SS had effectively isolated Oster. Olbricht "was nearer the potential centre of power but he had neither the initiative nor drive to act."[493] Besides, he commanded no troops. Hammerstein-Equord was dead. As for the others: "Canaris had always worked cleverly in the background; Beck was sick; Witzleben was a warrior, not a conspirator or politician, and also was sick; Tresckow had both the energy and determination to lead but neither the position nor influence."[494] Tresckow was further frustrated in his efforts to revive the resistance when he was transferred back to the Eastern Front after serving several months in Berlin during the late summer of 1943. Feigning battle fatigue, he had wangled a sick leave and had gone to Berlin in order to reactivate and reconstruct the resistance movement. By this time, he had become the acknowledged leader of the military conspiracy. He was, in fact, its "brain." His return to the Eastern Front effectively removed him from the center of conspiratorial activity. He was given command of an infantry regiment that was part of Army Group South. Some believed that he had been put into "cold storage."[495]

Round III thus came to an end. Yet the resistance survived. Once again, a mere handful of determined men refused to surrender to a seemingly relentless and perverse fate. By the end of the year, these men were again at work plotting assassination and a coup. The lack of a strong leader to bring all of the disparate elements of the conspiracy together in a unified plan of action remained a critical problem, however. Henning von Tresckow was the last best hope of the resistance, and with his departure to the east, a vacuum had appeared at the top.

Round IV: Operation Valkyrie, March to July 1944

The year was 1944. Germany, losing ground on all fronts, was facing total defeat, and everyone except the complete ideologues acknowledged it. Catastrophe was unfolding. The red juggernaut was moving inexorably westward, even as Britain's Royal Air Force and the US Eighth Air Force were reducing Germany's cities to rubble with their round-the-clock bombing. Events of the previous year had destroyed the prospect of ultimate victory.

Stalingrad was the most devastating military defeat, but there were others, both military and diplomatic.

Germany's forces in North Africa surrendered to the Anglo-American armies in May 1943. Sicily, invaded in July, fell to the Allies thirty-nine days later; and in that same month, Benito Mussolini, Hitler's partner in the Axis alliance, was deposed. The new Italian government subsequently signed an armistice with the Allies and declared war on its erstwhile ally to the north in October.[496] The tide of battle also had turned against Japan, the third power in the Axis alliance. By the beginning of 1944, Japan was suffering severe reverses, as the perimeter around earlier conquests on the East Asian mainland and in the islands of the western Pacific Ocean was shrinking significantly. Early in 1945, a bombing assault was launched against the home islands, which culminated in the atomic bombing of Hiroshima and Nagasaki in August. Operation Overlord, the cross-channel invasion of France on June 6, 1944, would complete the grim picture for the Third Reich.

* * * *

Time was running out for everyone in the spring of 1944, including the resistance. Before 1943, many of the conspirators had hoped that the elimination of Hitler would bring an end to hostilities and produce a peace settlement that, at a minimum, would allow Germany to preserve its territorial integrity. Others of this group had dared to hope that some of Hitler's conquests could be retained, especially Austria and the Sudetenland. By 1944, however, the illusory nature of those goals was apparent to all. There was absolutely no way that these territories could ever remain a part of the German nation, regardless of Hitler's fate. The Allied powers would never accede to this. Peace would come only with the acceptance of the Allied demand for "unconditional surrender," and this included relinquishing all the lands that Germany had acquired since 1938. A coup could no longer change the course of a war that would have to be fought to the bitter end. Nothing could be salvaged.

Why, then, did the conspirators persist? Why did they continue plotting to kill Hitler even though they knew that they could not change the course of events and that their efforts very possibly would end in failure and in their deaths? The answer is really quite simple. They were Germany's conscience, and they knew it. They had to act in the name of morality. The words of Henning von Tresckow provide an eloquent summation of their convictions. In June 1944, shortly after Operation Overlord took place,

Stauffenberg sent a message to Tresckow – who at the time was in East Prussia for a commanders' conference – asking if he thought that Operation Valkyrie should continue. Tresckow responded with the following words: "The assassination must take place *coûte que coûte* (come what may). Even if it does not succeed, the Berlin action must go forward. The point now is not whether the coup has any practical purpose, but to prove to the world and before history that [the] German resistance is ready to stake its all. Compared to this, everything is a side issue."[497]

A statement of Ludwig Beck, made about the same time, conveys the same message:

> The decisive thing is not what happens to this or that individual personally ... The decisive thing is not even the consequence for our nation. It is rather the unbearable reality that for a long time crime after crime and murder after murder have multiplied in the name of the German people, and that it is a moral duty to put a halt with all available means to these crimes committed in the usurped name of our people.[498]

An even more succinct and pointed comment made just prior to the July 20 bombing has been attributed to Berthold von Stauffenberg, brother of Claus: "The worst thing is knowing that we cannot succeed and yet that we have to do it, for our country and our children."[499] Thus, "What mattered was proving to the world that at least some Germans, acting out of conscience ... were willing to sacrifice themselves to protect humanity against a monstrous evil. The act of resistance assumed a symbolic meaning that transcended the practical outcome of an uprising."[500] The strike against Hitler was now "a source of personal redemption" and "an act of atonement [and] expiation."[501] "They carried on not in the hope of success but solely as an act of self-purification."[502]

* * * *

By early 1944, mounting pessimism, together with increasing physical and emotional exhaustion, was beginning to overwhelm many within the resistance movement. The failure to kill Hitler after coming so close so many times, the menacing and growing presence of the SS police apparatus, and the increasingly grim military situation all were taking an emotional toll on the conspirators. Some historians of the resistance believe that the failures of March 1943 signaled a turning point and that the "inner strength" of the resistance was ebbing by early 1944.[503] The arrests that had taken place the previous spring had effectively crippled the entire resistance movement. If these men hoped to accomplish anything, they needed an immediate infusion of new leadership, and they had to act quickly, before events completely overwhelmed them. Very fortuitously, a young, dynamic, charismatic leader did emerge quite late in the game. Of all the highly dedicated traitorous patriots, he came closest to eliminating Adolf Hitler. His name was Claus Schenk von Stauffenberg.[504]

Like Henning von Tresckow, Stauffenberg was the scion of a distinguished Prussian family steeped in its military traditions. A descendant on his mother's side of the great Prussian field marshal August Graf Neidhardt von Gneisenau – one of the founders of the modern Prussian Army, who also was one of the heroes of the wars of liberation against Napoleon in the early nineteenth century, Claus Philipp Maria Graf Schenk von Stauffenberg was born on the family estate at Jettingen, Swabia, in southwest Germany on November 15, 1907. His father was Lord Chamberlain to the king and queen of Württemberg (Württemburg was one of four kingdoms within the German Empire). The family's origins could be traced back to the thirteenth century; its ranks included men who had served with the Teutonic Knights and the Knights of Saint John.[505] Following in the footsteps of his ancestors, Claus also chose a military career and entered cadet school, where he displayed leadership talents of a high order. He also is described as possessing "great natural charm."[506] He received his commission as a second lieutenant on January 1, 1930, just as Germany was beginning its descent into the hell of Nazism.

According to one biographer, Stauffenberg adopted a "wait and see" attitude toward the new regime.[507] Like so many other Germans caught up in the aftermath of the Great War, he had no use for the Weimar Republic, and as a staunch nationalist, he was sympathetic to the seeming vitality and energy of the new Nazi leadership, which, it was hoped, would bring with it a revival and renewal of the nation's fortunes.[508] Disillusionment quickly followed. As early as 1934, he was expressing his doubts about the Nazis, and often made disparaging remarks about Hitler and his petit bourgeois origins, referring to him as the "wall-paper hanger."[509]

According to some sources, Stauffenberg shared the mild anti-Semitism that was characteristic of his social class and generation, although writer Anton Gill claims that Stauffenberg "seems to have been completely free of any racism whatsoever."[510] Regardless of his general views of anti-Semitism, the vicious Kristallnacht pogrom perpetrated against the Jewish community on November 9, 1938, appalled him. For many Germans, including Stauffenberg, this horrific episode was a turning point in their assessment of Nazism. After the war, two fellow officers who had known him claimed that the Nazis' murderous anti-Semitism, together with their oppression of the Christian churches (he was a devout Roman Catholic), above all else led Stauffenberg to repudiate the Nazis.[511]

He also revealed his growing fears of Hitler's increasingly bellicose and adventurous foreign policy. As the decade of the thirties approached its end, Stauffenberg declared, "The fool is heading for war."[512] Once World War II began, however, he devoted himself exclusively to military matters. His first goal was victory. After that, "the brown-shirted plague would be swept away. Until shortly before 20 July 1944 Stauffenberg invariably insisted on the necessity for a military decision."[513]

Quite early in the Russian campaign, however, he realized that the prospect of ultimate victory was fading rapidly. The blatant incompetence of both the high command and Hitler's military leadership increasingly disturbed him,[514] and he came to realize that the only way to rescue Germany from total ruin was to eliminate the Führer. The passage of time increasingly demonstrated Hitler's limitations as a military leader, and Stauffenberg, when asked how the man's method of command could be changed, answered, "Kill him."[515] As early as mid-1942, he had decided to join the resistance; and now in early 1943, the Stalingrad catastrophe confirmed his decision.[516]

In early February 1943, Stauffenberg was transferred from the organization section of the army general staff to the position of senior staff officer to the Tenth Panzer Army in North Africa.[517] Just before this transfer took place, the Sixth Army surrendered at Stalingrad. Ever the clear-eyed realist, Stauffenberg now recognized that the specter of total defeat had replaced the prospect of ultimate victory.[518]

Others within the resistance adopted the same attitude. With military defeat a certainty, the distinction between "patriotic loyalty and ethical principle" had evaporated. What had been treason "now became duty."[519] The national interest and moral values were as one. By this time, there was almost total agreement throughout the entire resistance movement that Hitler must die. Those dissenters who initially had rejected assassination now recognized that mere arrest would not do; he had to be killed. Stauffenberg agreed wholeheartedly.[520]

Like so many others within the resistance, Stauffenberg was acting from religious conviction. A devout Christian, he found inspiration in the writings of the medieval theologian Saint Thomas Aquinas, whose teachings included the moral justification of tyrannicide. The poet Stefan George also influenced him deeply. The young Stauffenberg joined a group known as the Georgekreis (George Circle) and became personally acquainted with the man who has been described as his "spiritual mentor." According to his friends, Stauffenberg often quoted one of George's poems entitled "The Antichrist," which begins with the following words: "The High Priest of Vermin extends his domain."[521] According to his biographer, Nigel Jones, Stauffenberg probably decided early on that he would have to take upon himself the mission of eliminating "the High Priest of Vermin."[522] Like others of Stauffenberg's generation, the infamous loyalty oath did not constrain him. He understood that "there are limits to loyalty and obedience."[523] He also realized that Hitler had invalidated the oath on so many occasions that now it was totally without meaning.[524] He reputedly commented to a relative, "Since the generals have failed to do anything, it's now up to the colonels."[525] His first meeting with Hitler and several other top Nazis at the Berghof in June 1944 confirmed his earlier assessment of these men. He characterized them as "psychopaths" and described the atmosphere around them as "poisonous and rotten, making it hard to breathe."[526]

Stauffenberg's posting to the Tenth Panzer Army came to an abrupt end on April 7, 1943, when a low-level air strike by Britain's Royal Air Force severely wounded him. His right hand was amputated at the field dressing station, together with the third and fourth fingers of his left hand. His left eye had to be removed as well. He subsequently was taken to a military hospital in Tunis, thence to Italy, and ultimately to Munich, where he underwent additional surgery. These grievous injuries did not deter him, however. He resumed his conspiratorial activities as early as the ensuing summer. It was said of him that from autumn 1943 to July 20, 1944, he was "the real driving force behind the attempt to assassinate Hitler."[527] After the war, his surgeon's son said that Stauffenberg had declared, "I could never look the wives and children of the fallen in the eye if I did not do something to stop this senseless slaughter."[528]

Subsequent to his recovery, Stauffenberg was appointed chief of staff to the AHA, or Allgemeines Heeresamt (General Army Office), in Berlin. He assumed his duties on October 1, 1943.[529] General Friedrich Olbricht, who – along with Tresckow and Beck – was part of the triumvirate providing de facto leadership for the resistance at this time, was also the AHA commander. The AHA was responsible for training and equipping the German Army and for personnel matters.[530] Stauffenberg met with

Tresckow, whom he had known since 1941, in mid-August, and from then on he played an increasingly pivotal role in the conspiracy to assassinate Hitler.[531] It was said of Stauffenberg that he successfully revitalized the resistance with his "infectious energy." He also combined an "exuberant idealism" with a "cool pragmatism" and was able "to encourage Olbricht's cautious deliberations and heighten Tresckow's determination. He seemed to send an electric charge through the lifeless resistance networks as he quickly and naturally assumed a leadership role."[532] He replaced Tresckow as the leader of the conspiracy after the latter was transferred to the Eastern Front. His no-nonsense approach to the resistance movement prompted him to dismiss what he considered to be secondary problems, such as foreign policy issues like dealing with the Allies and controversies over the political structure of a post-Nazi Germany. His single-minded goal was the eradication of Adolf Hitler. He was a man of action, and his weapon of choice was the army. Consequently, the civilian groups were eclipsed as the conspiracy entered its last phase. Some civilian resistance members like Carl Goerdeler resented Stauffenberg, but they could do little to challenge his leadership or his methods.

From the time that Tresckow and Stauffenberg met in August 1943 until the former was transferred to the Eastern Front the following October,[533] the two worked closely to revise and refine a plan that Olbricht's staff had developed to deal with potential disorders resulting from a breakdown of the government. The two conspirators transformed it into a plan for a coup d'état. Code-named Einsatz Walküre (Operation Valkyrie), it became the basis for the July 20, 1944, assault at the Wolfschanze.

Before this final assault, however, Stauffenberg and Tresckow plotted two earlier attempts on Hitler's life. Each attack was planned as a suicide mission, and each was aborted, although one came within a hair's breadth of success.

The first attempt was planned for either late 1943 or early 1944. The biggest challenge was finding a suicide bomber. After at least one potential candidate had been rejected, Stauffenberg was introduced to a much-decorated military officer, twenty-four-year-old Captain Axel Freiherr von dem Bussche-Streithorst. Bussche had sustained a serious lung wound in early 1942 and was reassigned to a reserve unit in the Berlin suburb of Potsdam. Later he returned to the Eastern Front, where, on October 5, he witnessed a traumatizing episode at an airfield at the Ukrainian town of Dubno. There, SS officers were supervising a group of Ukrainian auxiliaries, described as "a rag-tag assortment of ... nationalists, fanatical anti-Semites and criminal thugs,"[534] who were in the process of massacring Jews – men, women, and children – living in the vicinity. The victims were "herded along," and then were "compelled to strip and then to lie face downwards on top of the dead or still writhing Jews who had dug the pit and then been shot; the newcomers were then also killed by a shot in the nape of the neck. The SS men did all this in a calm, orderly fashion; they were clearly acting under orders." Bussche estimated that between two thousand and three thousand persons were murdered at Dubno. As he observed the horrific scene, he realized that these SS men were acting under orders that doubtlessly came from the top echelons of the government that he was serving, a government "whose orders he was carrying out, to which he had sworn an oath and which ruled his country."[535] From that time forward, Axel von dem Bussche-Streithorst, who has been described as a "committed Christian,"[536] dedicated himself to the task of doing whatever he could to destroy Hitler and all that the man represented. He reportedly reacted to the Dubno episode with the comment that an honorable military officer had one of three ways to react: "to die in battle, to desert, or to rebel."[537]

An opportunity to take direct action arose the following year. As a result of talks with Stauffenberg in October and November 1943, Bussche agreed to attempt a suicide assassination mission against Hitler. After a brief discussion about the preferred method, they concluded that a bomb was the means most likely to succeed. A bomb was more easily concealed, and a pistol shot might miss the mark or produce only a superficial wound. It also was believed that Hitler wore a bulletproof waistcoat.[538] The occasion for the planned attack was a demonstration of new equipment and winter uniforms developed for use on the Eastern Front. Bussche agreed to be a model for one of the uniforms. He was a perfect choice for such a role. He looked "Nordic," which was a highly valued quality, and he had served over the entire length of the Eastern Front. He also was a highly decorated veteran of the conflict.[539] As to the weapon of choice, Bussche settled on the German bomb with its four- to five-second fuse. He was more familiar with the German explosive than with its British counterpart, and he believed that he could mask its hissing noise by clearing his throat or feigning a coughing fit.[540] He planned to conceal the bomb in a deep pocket of the new uniform, and in the course of explaining its features, arm the bomb, begin to cough, and then jump on Hitler and throw him to the ground, holding him there for the few seconds required for the bomb to explode. The venue for the display was to be the Wolfschanze at Rastenburg.[541]

The first challenge facing Bussche was to acquire the necessary explosive materials without attracting the attention of the SS. The challenge proved to be formidable. Ultimately Stauffenberg secured the materials from trusted army accomplices stationed at a military base near Rastenburg that contained an explosives supply depot. Next, he had to get direct access to Hitler, who was becoming more and more withdrawn and reclusive. In addition, Hitler's penchant for avoiding precise schedules or commitments and for changing his plans at the last minute had to be overcome. By the end of November, however, an "approximate date" for the planned uniform demonstration had been set, and everything was in place – or so everyone thought. Bussche went to East Prussia to await final instructions. But a series of postponements by Hitler foiled the plot. Problems were compounded when, during this waiting period, an Allied air raid destroyed the railway car containing the demonstration equipment and new uniforms. The plot collapsed completely when Bussche subsequently sustained a severe leg wound that required amputation. Several other candidates for the mission were considered, including Tresckow himself, but ultimately the plan was abandoned. The long-postponed uniform demonstration finally took place without incident near Salzburg on July 7, 1944.[542]

By early 1944, the resistance was facing an SS menace that was more threatening than ever. On January 12, the Solf Circle was broken up and its members were arrested. About the same time, the Kreisau Circle received a mortal blow with the arrest of Helmuth von Moltke. Other civilians were rounded up as well. More significantly, the ring around the army conspirators continued to tighten. Admiral Wilhelm Canaris was dismissed as chief of military intelligence on February 11, despite the lack of concrete evidence of his involvement in a conspiracy to topple the Nazi state.[543] In the Third Reich, mere suspicion was adequate grounds for police action. The Abwehr itself was put under SS control and effectively destroyed.[544]

At this point, Tresckow made yet one more attempt to eradicate Hitler. It was his last effort before Stauffenberg's decision to make his own direct attempt. The volunteer for this suicide mission was a cavalry officer named Eberhard von Breitenbuch, adjutant to Field Marshal Ernst Busch, the man who had replaced Kluge as commander of Army Group Center after the latter's automobile accident. In early March, Busch was summoned to a briefing with Hitler and others at the Berghof, Hitler's mountain retreat at Berchtesgaden. Accompanying him were his operations officer, a Colonel von der Gröben, and his adjutant, Breitenbuch. Others in attendance included Wilhelm Keitel, chief of the OKW; General Alfred

Jodl, chief of the OKW Operations Office; and Propaganda Minister Joseph Paul Goebbels.[545] On the morning of March 11, they all assembled in the anteroom of the conference hall. At the appropriate time, the door to the conference hall was opened, and a man in SS uniform told the assembled group that the Führer was ready to receive them. They entered, single file, according to rank. Breitenbuch, with a loaded pistol in his pocket and carrying a briefcase, was last in line because he was lowest in rank. As he approached the doorway, however, the SS guard grasped his arm, preventing him from entering the room. No adjutants were to participate in the briefing. Busch, who of course knew nothing about the assassination plot, adamantly protested, saying that he needed his adjutant at the meeting. Nonetheless, Breitenbuch was denied entrance into the room and was forced to wait in the anteroom. After his return to Army Group Center headquarters in the Soviet Union, Breitenbuch met with Tresckow, who greeted him with the words, "Well, Breitenbuch, the thing was blown." Evidently a telephone call that Tresckow had made to the conspirators in Berlin giving them the signal for the impending assassination attempt had raised suspicions within the SS, prompting them to increase security around Hitler. Although Breitenbuch had at least one more opportunity to make another assassination attempt, he declined. "One can only do that sort of thing once," he said.[546] Other assassination plots were stillborn.

* * * *

Even though these schemes failed and even though the nervous tension and psychological strain became almost overwhelming, these men remained resolute in their determination to purge Germany and the world of the Nazi scourge. Stauffenberg continued working on Operation Valkyrie, the plan that General Olbricht's staff originally had devised. The key to its success was the replacement army, whose commander was General Friedrich Fromm, who has been described as "a man with an eye to the main chance."[547] Another writer colorfully put it, "He was a man who wanted to run with the hare and hunt with the hounds."[548] Fromm reputedly said of himself many times that he "always came down on the right side" in all situations.[549] He was one of those generals playing both ends against the middle, an opportunist willing to go with either side. Lacking moral conviction, he wanted to be with the winner. Like Kluge, however, he actually showed some sympathy for the conspirators and their goal, and he did not betray them.[550]

The personnel of the replacement army consisted of training units, soldiers on leave, and sick and wounded servicemen who had recovered but had not yet been reassigned, along with workers and employees to be drawn from private industry.[551] Initially conceived as a means of filling "gaps in the field army," the mission of these Operation "Valkyrie" units was altered by General Fromm, and approved by Hitler, to serve as a military response group to potential domestic disorder. By late 1943 and early 1944, the Reich was filled with prisoners – that is, slave laborers – brought into the country in order to replenish the nation's increasingly depleted manpower resources resulting from military losses. In addition to this potentially explosive situation, fears of foreign agents infiltrating the country for purposes of sabotage, and fears of airborne assault troops conducting raids, perhaps with the support of the Communist underground, were widespread.[552] Gossip and rumors about an assassination plot were rampant. "Rumours, allegations, denunciations, false reports and suppositions are stock-in-trade, particularly under a dictatorship and particularly in Germany's situation of 1943 and 1944."[553] Dislocations and distress resulting from the incessant bombing of the cities, along with the increasingly rapid deterioration of the military situation, only compounded a confusing and complicated scene. This, then, was the revised purpose of the replacement army: to respond to "internal disturbances"[554] that is, a rebellion. Hitler approved the plan, which was given the code name "Operation Valkyrie."

Stauffenberg, Tresckow, Olbricht, and others within the resistance had other plans for the replacement army, however. They schemed to turn Operation Valkyrie upside down. Rather than suppressing an uprising, the replacement army would become an instrument used to neutralize the Wehrmacht in a coup d'état. The idea was both simple and ingenious. The plan was to initiate the operation with a secret declaration, to be read immediately after Hitler's assassination, beginning with the following words: "The Führer Adolf Hitler is dead! A treacherous group of party leaders has attempted to exploit the situation by attacking our embattled soldiers from the rear in order to seize power for themselves."[555] This declaration was to be the signal for the replacement army to mobilize immediately and seize control of key government ministries, offices of the Nazi Party, radio stations, telephone offices, and even the concentration camps. Furthermore, the SS would be disarmed, and any SS officers refusing to obey were to be shot forthwith.[556] The plan was devised from the outset to ensure that the army units "would intervene smoothly, rapidly and by surprise."[557]

Operation Valkyrie, in the eyes of the resistance, was nothing less than a gigantic hoax, a plan of massive deception to be perpetrated against the entire Nazi apparatus, the success of which depended upon two things. First of all, Hitler had to be killed. Second, the intricate chain of command had to be followed precisely "by scores of officers and troops obliviously following orders."[558] There were no guarantees that this would happen, however. Equally important, the chain of command itself contained a significant and ultimately fatal weakness. None of the conspirators had command authority to issue the necessary orders to initiate the coup. Such orders could come only from the actual commander of the replacement army, Friedrich Fromm, who at best was unreliable.[559] In order to bypass Fromm, the conspirators tried to enlist the support of other, higher-ranking officers, including Hans von Kluge, who had recovered from his injuries sustained in the automobile accident and who on July 7, 1944 – a month after the Allies launched Operation Overlord – was appointed commander in chief of all the German armies in the west. As always, however, he remained noncommittal toward the resistance, though supportive.[560]

This scheme had been evolving for at least a year. As early as January 1943, Olbricht had agreed to organize a coup using the replacement army units located in Berlin, Munich, Cologne, and Vienna.[561] A debate over which organization – the field army or the replacement army – should be the instrument of the initial strike against the Nazi system was resolved in August in favor of the replacement army. Stauffenberg's arguments had carried the day.[562] Thus, by the spring of 1944:

> ... the conspirators had ... created, by perfectly legitimate methods, an instrument with which they could, if conditions were right, set in motion all available mobile military forces in Germany with the exception of the SS. The orders were perfectly sensible and suitable for an emergency; on the face of it they were neutral and non-political.[563]

The assassination problem remained unresolved, however. The key to the success of Valkyrie was the immediate elimination of Hitler, but the history of such efforts gave little cause for optimism. On top of this, the target was becoming more elusive, secretive, and closely guarded than ever. The immediate challenge was to find the right man for the job, someone not only with the courage and determination but also with direct access to the Führer.

Ultimately, Stauffenberg decided to make the attempt himself, despite his physical handicap. Thus, he was the assassin as well as the acknowledged leader of Operation Valkyrie, and this twofold job created still another problem for him. Essentially, he had to be in two places at once. Hitler no longer resided in Berlin but now was spending most of his time at the Wolfschanze at Rastenburg, with occasional visits to the Berghof, all under tight security.[564] Inevitably there would be a delay of up to two hours between the actual assassination and Stauffenberg's return to Berlin to assume command of Operation Valkyrie. The logical solution would have been to designate someone else, probably Olbricht, to command the operation, at least temporarily. Olbricht declined, however, admitting that he was not the man for this job; neither, apparently, was anyone else. And so the task ultimately fell to Stauffenberg. In the end, this time delay proved to be disastrous for the conspirators.[565]

The problem of access to the intended victim was conveniently resolved when, on July 1, Stauffenberg was promoted to full colonel and appointed to the position of chief of staff to General Fromm.[566] This appointment meant that from now on, he would accompany Fromm to all of the latter's meetings with Hitler. One can only speculate on Fromm's motives in choosing Stauffenberg. He knew that his chief of staff was deeply involved in anti-Hitler activity, and perhaps he wanted to "keep an eye" on him. Perhaps also he was "hedging his bets" by keeping in touch with the conspirators through Stauffenberg in case the roll of the dice would fall against Hitler and the Nazis. Or perhaps he merely wanted to have a highly talented and able chief of staff at his side. We shall never know the reason for Fromm's choice of Stauffenberg. As for Stauffenberg himself, the message was clear. According to Berthold von Stauffenberg, this appointment confirmed his brother's decision to make the assassination attempt, because now he had direct access to his target.[567]

The time was short. Soon it would be too late for a coup attempt. Operation Overlord was launched on June 6, and within ten days, British and American armies had established a secure foothold on French soil. To the east, Army Group Center had been annihilated, Soviet forces completely surrounded Army Group North, and Soviet tanks were scarcely sixty miles from the Wolfschanze.[568] Total military collapse was inevitable. The conspirators now faced yet another question. Should they continue plotting for a coup, or should they now let events unfold to their destined conclusion? Some believed that it would be best to allow Hitler to "charge on into the abyss alone," and thus demonstrate to Germany and the world that the responsibility for this cataclysm was his alone. This would be a lesson to future generations, enabling them to avoid following similar "demons of destruction."[569] In addition, the Allied invasion of Normandy finally convinced all within the resistance that there was absolutely no hope of a negotiated peace. The "last remaining strategic cards [had been] snatched from the plotters' hands."[570] Nothing less than unconditional surrender could be expected. Consequently, even with Hitler dead and a government purged of Nazis, Germany either would have to capitulate or continue to fight "a hopeless war to its inevitable conclusion."[571] Others argued that the soul of the German nation was on the line. They wanted the world to know that a determined few were willing to sacrifice everything for the sake of ridding their nation of this monstrous evil, that the nation itself had "made some visible effort to cleanse its own house."[572]

Ultimately, it all became a simple matter of conscience. It was said of Stauffenberg that his "conscience demanded every conceivable effort to save thousands, probably hundreds of thousands of human lives, to save the Reich, to purge the nation and salvage its honour."[573] Others within the conspiracy agreed completely. General Ludwig Beck, who had been an integral part of the resistance from the beginning, continued to argue that the attempt must be made regardless of the consequences.[574] Thus, even in the face of a terrible defeat for their country and the prospect of abject failure of their coup attempt, the determination of these men to go on grew more intense as the time to take action grew ever shorter, all the while knowing full well that they would be excoriated by the German people for what they hoped to accomplish. "Practical success no longer mattered most."[575] What did matter most was the attempt of these men to free Germany from a satanic regime.

Stauffenberg also fully understood another issue facing the resistance. He recognized that the German people themselves would consider him and his coconspirators to be traitors, abandoning their nation in its darkest hour and time of greatest need. But he remained undeterred. His conscience would not allow him to surrender to the rampant fatalism gripping Germany, nor to accept the needless loss of life and the destruction that would accompany a continuation of the war under Nazi rule. A few days before the final assassination attempt on July 20, he said, "It's time now for something to be done. He who has the courage to act must know that he will go down in German history as a traitor. But if he fails to act, he will be a traitor to his own conscience."[576] Conscience alone determined his actions.

Stauffenberg's first personal encounter with Hitler took place at the Berghof on June 7, the day after the Allied landing in France and a month before his promotion and appointment as chief of staff to Fromm. The occasion was a briefing on the condition and the state of readiness of the replacement army. Stauffenberg's intentions at the time remain unclear, but he is known to have had access to explosives. He attended two additional meetings at the Berghof on July 6 and 11, plus a third meeting at Rastenburg on July 15.[577] He had a bomb with him on each of these occasions, but for reasons that to this to this day are not entirely clear, attacks were never made. The generally accepted theory is that Stauffenberg was dissuaded from acting because neither Göring nor especially Himmler was present. Several conspirators, including Beck, wanted these two men dispatched along with Hitler. There also is speculation that on at least one occasion, the meeting on the fifteenth, Stauffenberg did not have time to arm the bomb. On this latter date, Operation Valkyrie actually was set into motion but had to be called off at the last minute. Olbricht was able to convince his superiors that the action already taken by the reserve army was merely an "exercise" to test its readiness.[578]

Another meeting was called for the Wolfschanze on July 20, where Stauffenberg was scheduled to give another briefing. There was general agreement among the conspirators that it was now or never.[579] The SS and Gestapo were closing in with a relentless and implacable intensity that threatened to overwhelm the entire resistance movement at any moment. Additional arrests were made between the fifteenth and the twentieth, and a warrant for Goerdeler's arrest was issued as well, forcing him to go into hiding.[580] In what had to have been an atmosphere of incredible anxiety and tension, a series of meetings was held on the nineteenth in an attempt to coordinate a very complex operation.

The barriers to success were many, the element of chance was very great, and the premonition of failure hung over the entire conspiracy.[581] Nevertheless, Henning von Tresckow, effectively isolated on the Eastern Front and no longer able to play a direct role in the conspiracy, remained convinced that the coup must proceed regardless of the cost. His message to Stauffenberg shortly after the Allies launched Operation Overlord remains the definitive statement of those who felt as he did.[582] Prospects for Operation Valkyrie's success remained minimal. Everything had to mesh perfectly. Moreover, the reliability of the various commanders, especially Fromm and Kluge, was also essential, and here there were no guarantees. During this time, rumors of an assassination plot continued to circulate throughout Berlin, which only increased the anxiety of the conspirators.[583]

* * * *

Early in the morning of the twentieth, Stauffenberg took a courier flight from Berlin to Rastenburg. He also had made arrangements to have a plane at Rastenburg at the ready for a return flight to Berlin. After his arrival at Rastenburg, Stauffenberg and his aide, Lieutenant Werner von Haeften, set about making preparations to arm the bombs – they had two – which they planned to take to the briefing. Only one bomb was armed and taken to the conference, however. Various reasons have been offered by way of explanation. The generally accepted theory is that both men – Stauffenberg and Haeften – were under severe constraints of time, because the others attending the briefing were impatiently awaiting their appearance at the meeting. Hitler was expected at any moment, and he did not like to be kept waiting.[584]

As he entered the wooden briefing hut, Stauffenberg managed to position himself close to Hitler, whereupon he slipped the briefcase containing the armed bomb under the table. After a few moments, he excused himself, saying that he had to take a telephone call from Berlin. Shortly thereafter, according to eyewitnesses, "A deafening crack shattered the midday quiet, and a bluish-yellow flame rocketed skyward … [and] a dark plume of smoke rose and hung in the air over the wreckage of the briefing barracks. Shards of glass, wood, and fiberboard swirled about, and scorched pieces of paper and insulation rained down." As Stauffenberg observed the scene, he noted a body covered with Hitler's cloak being carried out of the briefing hut on a stretcher and logically assumed that the Führer was dead. At that point, he and Haeften sped to the airfield, where they boarded the plane that flew them to Berlin.[585]

Of course, Hitler was not dead. Yet once more, the conspirators had come so close to achieving their goal but had failed. Yet once more, a malevolent force – or so it must have seemed to the resistance – was protecting Hitler and allowing him to pursue his evil work of death and destruction. Hitler literally had come within inches of losing his life. According to eyewitness testimony and a subsequent investigation by the Nazis, Stauffenberg's briefcase containing the bomb had been moved farther under the conference table in the last seconds before the explosion in order to provide additional room for the participants around the table. Consequently, the table acted as a partial shield, protecting Hitler from the full force of the blast, doubtlessly sparing him from serious injury or death.[586] Additionally, the conference was being held in a wooden-framed building with many windows that were wide open because of the stifling heat of the day. Hence, the concussion from the blast was dissipated somewhat, thereby weakening the destructive effect of the explosion. The failure to bring both bombs to the meeting proved to be disastrous. Had both been there, they doubtlessly would have exploded, even though one was not armed. The explosion of the armed bomb would have detonated the unarmed bomb, and this double explosion almost certainly would have killed everyone in the room.[587] Nevertheless, the carnage produced by the explosion was not insignificant. Of twenty-four men in attendance, one, a stenographer, died that afternoon, and three others ultimately succumbed to their wounds. Others suffered "moderate, though considerable injuries." But Hitler, along with most of the others, survived with relatively minor injuries.[588] Several officers who were a part of the conspiracy also were attached to the headquarters staff at Rastenburg. General Erich Fellgiebel, head of the Army Signal Corps, was one such man. He was responsible for the communications system at the Wolfschanze and had warned Stauffenberg that a total blackout probably was impossible. Events proved him correct.[589] An officer on the fringes of the conspiracy was Major General Helmuth Stieff, head of the Organization Department of the general staff. He had been instrumental in securing the explosives for the conspirators and initially had volunteered to be a suicide bomber against Hitler in 1943, but he'd later reneged.[590] These men realized almost immediately that Hitler had survived the blast.

Sometime between 1:00 and 1:30 p.m., General Fellgiebel put through a call to the Bendlerstraße (Bendler Street)[591] and spoke to Lieutenant General Fritz Thiele, another member of the conspiracy, sending him a cryptic message (explained below) that led to total confusion. Thiele transmitted the message to General Friedrich Olbricht, but lacking additional information about the circumstances of the episode, Olbricht and Thiele chose to do nothing for the time being. They did, however, notify General Eduard Wagner in Zossen, who also was part of the conspiracy.[592] Hitler's survival completely unnerved them, and they did not know how to react. It also helped to destroy Operation Valkyrie. For several critical hours in the early afternoon of July 20, nothing was done.[593] Even with Hitler alive, decisive action at this point might well have made the difference between success and failure for Operation Valkyrie. However, Generals Olbricht and Thiele considered the actual words of the message to be "vague [and] ambiguous,"[594] and, lacking what they considered to be definitive information, they hesitated.

The reasons for their behavior have never been adequately explained and never will be. What were they actually thinking? We can only speculate. The English translation of Fellgiebel's words is as follows: "Something terrible has happened." After a brief pause, he added, "The Führer is alive."[595] What did this mean? Had the bomb exploded or not? Had Stauffenberg been apprehended in attempting the assault?[596] Perhaps the message was incorrect; or if it was correct, it did not necessarily mean that the entire conspiracy was in jeopardy. Perhaps the Nazi leadership saw the bombing as the lone action of a single assassin. In that case, it would be best to do nothing. In this way, Operation Valkyrie could be preserved intact. Perhaps they lost their nerve. Perhaps events simply overwhelmed them and they were unable to respond to the situation. The news of Hitler's survival obviously not only discomfited them; it also paralyzed them. They were in a state of complete confusion and "saw no alternative to inactivity."[597]

Olbricht, though one of the most highly dedicated members of the resistance, was by nature a careful, cautious man who lacked the audacity of a Hans Oster, a Henning von Tresckow, or a Claus von Stauffenberg. Had Stauffenberg been at the Bendlerstraße the afternoon of July 20, the scenario very possibly would have played out very differently, but we shall never know. Regardless of the actual reason or reasons for his behavior, Olbricht "had 'played dead' on July 20 between 1:00 and 3:00 p.m., and he ... did not display any energy and determination" during these critical hours.[598]

The most calamitous flaw in Operation Valkyrie was the incredible failure to consider the possibility that Hitler might actually survive this bomb attack. "Everything had been predicated upon killing Hitler."[599] Consequently, the architects of the plot had not adopted a contingency plan should the unthinkable actually happen.[600] With Hitler alive, they now faced a situation that had been altered drastically, even fatally. No longer could they present themselves as a military force attempting to bring order and stability to "the remnants of a regime deprived of its Führer." Instead, they were now "a group of conspirators within the staff of the replacement army versus the whole of the rest of the Wehrmacht and the leadership of the Third Reich which was still completely intact."[601] Shortly before Stauffenberg's arrival at the Bendlerstraße, Olbricht, apparently believing that Hitler was dead after all, belatedly took action.[602] He went to a safe and retrieved the Operation Valkyrie order announcing Hitler's assassination, declaring that Field Marshal von Witzleben had taken command of the Wehrmacht and that Colonel General Beck had assumed leadership of the Reich.[603] Olbricht presented the document to his immediate superior, the commander of the replacement army, General Fromm, for his signature. Fromm, ever suspicious and always anxious to be on the "right" side, contacted OKW chief general Wilhelm Keitel, who was with Hitler at the Wolfschanze. Keitel assured Fromm that the Führer was indeed alive and well. Consequently, Fromm refused to sign the order. However, a second order giving instructions for implementing the first order had been issued carrying Fromm's name but without his knowledge, although countersigned by Stauffenberg.[604] Once at the Bendlerstraße, Stauffenberg confronted Fromm and stated his belief that Hitler was dead. According to eyewitness recollections of this encounter, Fromm said, "That is impossible. Keitel has assured me to the contrary." Stauffenberg replied, "Field Marshal Keitel is lying as usual. I myself saw Hitler being carried out dead."[605] He then told Fromm that he had planted the bomb himself. Fromm also learned that the second order had been issued in his name but without his direct authorization. A further exchange between the two men ensued. Suddenly, Fromm "jumped up in a rage and rushed up to [Stauffenberg] with flailing fists." Two of Stauffenberg's aides drew their pistols, and one of them "pressed the muzzle of his pistol into Fromm's stomach whereupon Fromm immediately ceased all resistance."[606] A retrospective consideration of that episode suggests that the tragic dénouement of the events of that day just might have been avoided if Fromm had been summarily shot, although this is mere speculation. Nevertheless, his life was spared; the conspirators arrested him and placed him under guard.[607]

The main challenge now facing Operation Valkyrie was to ensure that the orders issued at the Bendlerstraße were being passed seamlessly down the chain of command and were being obeyed without question. This, however, required the entire communication system – all radio and telephone contact – to be completely under the control of the conspirators. The Wolfschanze had to be totally isolated from the outside world, and all SS and Gestapo units in Berlin had to be denied information. Lastly, those directing the coup needed to act ruthlessly to suppress the men supporting the regime. In a word, they should have been killed – murdered. Two longtime members of the resistance, the lawyer Hans Berndt Gisevius and the theologian Eugen Gerstenmaier, thought the coup leaders "were being far too gentle with their opponents."[608] Gerstenmaier carried both a pistol and a Bible in his pocket. "On a day like this, [Gerstenmaier] said, and if one were proposing to revolt against people like the Nazis and the SS, there must be shooting; caution could only unnecessarily endanger both the success of the coup and the lives of the conspirators."[609] Yet, as with earlier coup attempts, the conspirators were prisoners of their conscience. In order to take such action, they would have had to violate the very principles for which they were fighting, namely, "humanity and justice."[610] Ironically, the observance of these convictions contributed to the ultimate tragedy.

By late afternoon, news was filtering back to Berlin from Rastenburg that the Führer was alive and well and that he remained completely in command of the government and its armed forces. This led to a proliferation of orders and counterorders around the offices of the various military units stationed in Berlin and across Germany, as well as the occupied countries. Confusion reigned supreme, and many conspirators began to lose their nerve. With Hitler alive, they were faced with a choice between certain torture and death were they to remain in the conspiracy should it fail – and it was faltering – or a "feeble glimmer of hope of escape" by deserting the cause. These men lacked the "steadfastness and courage" of Stauffenberg, Schulenburg, Beck, and the others who were willing to risk all for the sake of bringing an end both to Nazi rule and the wretched war now destroying their nation.[611]

The single most important member of the Nazi hierarchy in Berlin at this juncture was Joseph Paul Goebbels. Not only was he head of the Ministry of Propaganda, but also he was Nazi Party Gauleiter (district leader) of Berlin – a very powerful position – as well as Reich defense commissar.[612] Inexplicably, the telephone lines to his house had not been severed, and sometime between 5:00 and 6:00 p.m., he was able to make contact with Hitler in Rastenburg, thereby reassuring himself that the Führer had not been killed or seriously injured in the bomb attack.[613] He also learned that a coup definitely was under way across Germany.

About this same time, Albert Speer, minister of armaments and war production for the Third Reich, arrived at Goebbels's residence at the latter's request. He described the scene outside:

> The office windows looked out on the street. A few minutes after my arrival I saw fully equipped soldiers, in steel helmets, hand grenades at their belts and submachine guns in their hands, moving toward the Brandenburg Gate in small, battle ready groups. They set up machine guns at the gate and stopped all traffic. Meanwhile, two heavily armed men went up to the door

at the wall along the park and stood guard there. I summoned Goebbels. He understood the significance at once, vanished into his adjacent bedroom, took a few pills from a box, and put them into his coat pocket. "Well, just in case!" he said, with visible tension.[614]

The pills were potassium cyanide capsules.

In the meantime, late in the afternoon, around four fifteen, Lieutenant General Paul von Hase, commandant of the city of Berlin and a longtime member of the resistance, told Major Otto Ernst Remer, commander of the Großdeutschland (Greater Germany) Guard Battalion, that the army was assuming plenary powers of government, and ordered him to cordon off the government quarter of the city. Remer, a decorated war veteran and convinced Nazi, supposedly could be relied upon to carry out his orders efficiently and with dispatch. Some within the conspiracy, however, had their doubts about Remer's reliability because of his strong commitment to National Socialism. Nonetheless, Hase believed – mistakenly – that Remer would follow his orders to the letter, regardless of his Nazi convictions.[615]

Remer completed his mission as ordered. By 6:30 p.m., the entire government quarter was cordoned off and sentries were posted at Goebbels's house. However, Remer was becoming increasingly disturbed about the entire situation, and concluded that he was being drawn into subversive activity of some sort.[616] Speaking to a subordinate, he said, "Our heads are at stake. There seems to be a military putsch after all."[617] Remer was not certain where Goebbels stood in this confused situation. Did the propaganda minister support Hitler, or was he on the side of the conspirators? And where did Hase, his commanding officer, stand? Whom should he obey? Through an intermediary, a meeting was arranged between Remer and Goebbels. It took place between 6:30 and 7:00 p.m.[618] In the discussion that followed, Goebbels, seeing an opportunity to use Remer as an instrument to destroy the coup, contacted Hitler and had Remer speak to him personally.[619] Remer immediately recognized the voice and literally snapped to attention. Hitler then gave Remer his orders: "You are commissioned by me with the task of immediately restoring calm and security in the Reich capital, if necessary by force. You are under my personal command for this purpose until the Reichsführer-SS [Himmler] arrives in the capital."[620] Thus, the Nazi chain of command was restored. Remer had received direct orders from Hitler himself, and he could be relied upon to follow them to the letter.

This conversation was the coup de grâce for the resistance. Goebbels then spoke to the men of the guard battalion under Remer's command – about 150 soldiers – who had taken up positions in the garden at Goebbels's residence. He told them about the assassination attempt. Using all of his rhetorical skills, he "rapidly won them over."[621] According to Speer, his speech had a "mesmeric effect" on them. It consisted not of "commands and threats, but … a plea to their long-conditioned loyalty."[622] Several hours earlier, Goebbels had broadcast a communiqué over German radio, assuring his hearers that the Führer was alive and well and that he would speak to the nation later that evening.[623] Goebbels began the broadcast with the following words: "Today an attempt was made on the Führer's life with explosives … The Führer himself suffered no injuries beyond light burns and bruises. He resumed his work immediately."[624]

By 9:00 p.m., Operation Valkyrie was unraveling with frightening speed and was about to collapse completely. The hesitation, indecision, and uncertain loyalties that had been part of the conspiracy from the beginning were about to produce their bitter fruit. The conspirators had failed to carry out four tasks that were critical to a successful coup d'état. Specifically, they did not (1) kill Hitler; (2) act quickly to initiate Operation Valkyrie upon receipt of news that the bomb at the Wolfschanze had exploded, with the implication that Hitler had died in the blast; (3) secure immediate control of the radio and telephone communication systems; or (4) arrest Goebbels and kill him if necessary. The conspirators at the Bendlerstraße had planned to have a unit of the guard battalion arrest Goebbels, but that plan was foiled when Remer, the loyal Nazi, refused to obey his commander, General von Hase. Next to Hitler's survival, the conspirators' failure to seize control of the radio and telephone systems – especially to isolate the Wolfschanze – undoubtedly was the worst blunder of the whole operation. Detailed plans for this part of the coup had been laid weeks earlier and had included the arrest of Goebbels and the seizure of the long-distance telephone office, the main telegraph office, the radio broadcasting facilities in and around Berlin, and the central post office.[625] In his memoirs, Albert Speer wrote that "only a few soldiers would have been needed to break into Goebbels' office and arrest the minister without resistance."[626] Incomprehensibly, the conspirators did not carry out these actions with sufficient dispatch, and this produced utter and fatal confusion.

Sometime between 8:00 and 9:00 p.m., the cordon that the conspirators had established around the government quarter was lifted. The guard battalion had clearly remained loyal to the Nazi government. Other military units that initially had supported the conspirators were switching loyalties back to the Nazis.[627] Thanks to a series of radio announcements that were broadcast throughout Germany and disseminated by various means, such as the monitoring service of the BBC, knowledge of Hitler's survival of an assassination attempt quickly spread worldwide, progressively undermining the position of the conspirators and reviving the fortunes of the Hitler loyalists.[628] Operation Valkyrie was completely undone, and Germany, together with the rest of Europe, was doomed to another ten months of unremitting total war and all of its implications.

By 10:00 p.m., forces loyal to the government were able to seize control of the Bendlerstraße from the resistance leaders. Colonel General Friedrich Fromm, whom Stauffenberg and his men had taken prisoner earlier in the day, confining him to his quarters at the Bendlerstraße, was freed to resume command of the replacement army. As he confronted Stauffenberg and the handful of loyalists still with him, he reputedly said, "So gentlemen, now I'm going to do to you what you did to me this afternoon." After a drumhead court-martial, the conspirators were taken into the courtyard and shot. Those executed in addition to Stauffenberg were Lieutenant General Friedrich Olbricht and his chief of staff, Colonel Albrecht Ritter Mertz von Quirnheim, who actually had issued the Operation Valkyrie order from the Bendlerstraße and who was a close friend of Stauffenberg; and Lieutenant Werner von Haeften, Stauffenberg's aide-de-camp, who had accompanied the latter to Rastenburg and helped him to arm the bomb. Other conspirators at the Bendlerstraße included men such as Stauffenberg's brother Berthold, Graf Peter Yorck von Wartenburg, and Graf Fritz-Dietlof von der Schulenburg. They were apprehended as well, but their lives were temporarily spared. On August 8, however, they were subjected to a kangaroo court – the People's Court presided over by the notorious Judge Roland Freisler – before they were executed. Though he was at the Bendlerstraße on July 20, Hans Berndt Gisevius went underground and managed to flee to Switzerland in disguise, thanks partly to his foreign contacts, especially with Allen W. Dulles, chief of the Office of Strategic Services (the espionage agency of the US government).[629]

Yet many of the conspirators chose not to attempt flight. Instead, they remained in place, calmly awaiting arrest. Some even "turned themselves in out of a feeling that can best be described as part pride and part exhaustion. They were no longer willing or able to hide out or to continue the duplicitous life they had led for far too long, at the cost, they believed of their self respect." Ulrich von Hassell, for example, had been at his home in Bavaria on July 20. Soon thereafter, he went to Berlin "by a circuitous route, making many stops." After wandering "restlessly through the streets of the capital … he went to his desk and waited calmly for the Gestapo to arrive."[630] Field Marshal von Witzleben had gone to the Bendlerstraße on the evening of the twentieth but subsequently left, thoroughly disgusted with the ineptitude of the conspirators, and returned to his home, where he was arrested the following day.[631] Doubtlessly another motive for their behavior was the wish to spare their families the ordeal of undergoing questioning about their whereabouts by the Gestapo.

The fate of Colonel General Ludwig Beck was especially grim. He also had been with Stauffenberg at the Bendlerstraße and was marked for execution by Fromm. However, he asked the latter for permission to keep his handgun in order to commit suicide, to which Fromm gave his assent. But Beck succeeded only in severely wounding himself. Fromm thereupon ordered one of his men to deliver the fatal shot.[632]

After this bloodletting ceased, Fromm, in an obvious attempt to impress the Nazi leadership with his loyalty to Hitler, "gave an impassioned address to those assembled in the courtyard, attributing Hitler's wondrous salvation to the work of Providence. He ended with a threefold 'Sieg Heil' to the Führer."[633] Fromm doubtlessly ordered the sham court-martial and immediate execution of Stauffenberg and his coconspirators in an attempt to suppress knowledge of his early flirtations with the resistance. It has been said of him that his behavior during these critical hours "is explicable only by a desire to wait and see and cover up both ways."[634] Operation Valkyrie and the entire resistance movement had come to an end. With carte blanche to arrest and imprison anyone remotely connected with resistance activities of any sort, or anyone merely suspected of such activities, the SS and Gestapo secured a stranglehold on Germany. By late 1944, the complete SS state had become a reality.

CHAPTER 6

The Last Act

For all of their sophistication, talent, and determination, the conspirators had been remarkably amateurish and even naïve in much of their planning and actions. Simply too much was left to chance, and too little was devoted to contingency plans. For example, not everyone who was part of the chain of command essential to Operation Valkyrie's success obeyed without question. Commanders of the military districts of Hamburg, Danzig, and Dresden did not automatically follow the orders issued from the Bendlerstraße. Instead, they delayed taking action pending clarification from local Gestapo and party officials.[1] Additionally, Operation Valkyrie was entirely predicated on the assumption that Hitler would be assassinated. But what if he should survive? What then? No one knew. When the ultimate moment of truth came, too many conspirators became feckless and fainthearted. They lacked the audacity to carry out such a bold plan. It has been said of the conspiracy that it had all the earmarks of a "dilettante organization. Too many loose ends had been left dangling. Too little attention had been paid to small but important details in timing, coordination, and, not least, communications."[2] In sum, the plan as carried out was a haphazard operation.

There was one additional "failure," if indeed it can be so described, and it may well have been the most important element of all. That "failure" was the conspirators' sense of integrity and honor. They would not permit themselves to commit acts that required them to violate their moral convictions in order to take the final, brutal steps essential to the realization of their goal on July 20, 1944. Throughout the history of the resistance, these men had faced a terrible moral dilemma. They would have to resort to what they believed were immoral means in order to achieve a moral purpose. With few exceptions, the men of July 20 lacked the classic "instinct for the jugular," a regrettable but sometimes necessary quality in dealing with hoodlums such as the Nazis. They were too inhibited, cautious, and restrained. Consequently they exhibited "too much uncertainty; and too much hesitation."[3]

A review of the Oster conspiracy of 1938 is instructive. At that time, Hans Oster had at his disposal a group of men led by the amoral Captain Friedrich Wilhelm Heinz, who would have perpetrated violence and murder without compunction in order to eliminate Hitler. Unfortunately for the conspirators of July 20, there was no one with this kind of ruthlessness available to them.[4] Most of the men within the military establishment who were not an active part of the conspiracy displayed "deeply ingrained attitudes and behaviors that inhibited any kind of revolt."[5] They may have disliked or even despised Hitler and the Nazis, but the thought of open revolt was repellent to them. No officer who was not party to the conspiracy before July 20 participated in the coup attempt that day.[6]

In addition to their reluctance to countenance violence and murder in their attempt to topple the Nazis, the conspirators also displayed deplorably inept organizational skills in their planning for Operation Valkyrie. Joseph Paul Goebbels, reflecting on these events, spoke the following words to Heinrich Himmler after the latter's return to Berlin late that same day:

> If they hadn't been so clumsy! They had an enormous chance. What dolts! What childishness! When I think how I would have handled such a thing. Why didn't they occupy the radio station and spread the wildest lies? Here they put guards in front of my door. But they let me go right ahead and telephone the Führer, mobilize everything! They didn't even silence my telephone. To hold so many trumps and botch it – what beginners![7]

Ironically, Goebbels's assessment was correct. Had they followed his prescription, they just might have pulled it off, even with Hitler still alive. We will never know for certain. Nor will we ever know what the actual consequences of a successful coup would have been. Germany could have been plunged into a civil war pitting the fanatical Nazis and the SS against the resistance members, with an ultimate victory for the fanatical Nazis and the SS. Had the resistance prevailed, however, surrender to the Allies probably would have ensued, bringing an end to the carnage that ultimately was allowed to continue for another ten months.[8]

Retribution and Martyrdom

What we do know is that retribution came inevitably and swiftly. The SS and Gestapo went to work as early as the night of July 20, beginning with a series of manhunts for anyone and everyone who was suspected of having the slightest contact with known conspirators or who had displayed behavior that could be construed as questionable, such as an indiscreet comment or conduct that could be interpreted as "defeatist."[9] It was all very capricious and arbitrary.

Many who had no connection with the resistance whatsoever were apprehended, whereas others who were deeply involved in the conspiracy avoided immediate detection. A very few escaped capture altogether. One army officer was arrested and sent to the Gestapo prison in Berlin for four days simply because he had made a telephone call to his wife that night. He was subsequently released without explanation.[10] The number of arrests of those directly implicated in Operation Valkyrie is estimated at about six hundred, of whom some two hundred were executed. Ultimately, approximately a thousand people either were executed or committed suicide as a direct or indirect consequence of Operation Valkyrie.[11]

The dragnet steadily widened. Carl Goerdeler was apprehended on August 12 after hiding out for several weeks.[12] A second wave of arrests took place in mid-August and has been described as a "full-scale police operation." It was given the name Gewitteraktion (Thunderstorm). An additional five thousand known opponents of the Nazi regime who had no direct connection to Operation Valkyrie were arrested.[13] Many had been prominent figures in the Weimar Republic. Their numbers included Konrad Adenauer, former mayor (Bürgermeister) of Cologne and the first chancellor of the postwar West German Federal Republic.[14] Subsequent arrests included top army officers such as Franz Halder and Walther von Brauchitsch.[15]

Others whose only connection to the resistance was through family ties were swept into the Gestapo maelstrom of arrest and incarceration. Heinrich Himmler, the architect of this action, spoke of the "necessity" of apprehending family members in this roundup of enemies of the Third Reich.[16] It was a "kith and kin," or Blutrache (blood vengeance), approach to the roundup. Every member of a conspirator's family was automatically suspect. Claiming that he was returning to an ancient Teutonic tradition, Himmler, speaking to a group of the party faithful shortly after the coup attempt, said that he would "introduce absolute responsibility of kin … a very old custom practiced among our forefathers." The Teutonic sagas, he said, "were utterly consistent" in these matters. The conspirators had what he called "bad blood," or "traitor's blood … that must be wiped out … down to the last member."[17] This statement is an example of the bizarre and horrifying nature of Nazi ideology and "morality."

In the case of the Stauffenberg family, virtually all of them were arrested, including siblings and their spouses and children, of whom one was three years old. At the other end of the age spectrum, an eighty-five-year-old uncle was arrested. Stauffenberg's wife and mother were sent to a concentration camp. His children were placed in an orphanage and were given another surname, "Meister" (Master). It is thought that the Gestapo intended the new name to be an "ironic allusion to the Stefan George circle whose members referred to their mentor as 'master.'"[18] The families of other conspirators suffered a similar fate. Only the end of World War II brought release from the Nazi curse.[19]

In addition to the general Gestapo roundup of suspects, a military "court of honor" was set up under Hitler's orders to pass judgment on the military officers who had been part of the resistance. It was comprised of several generals of the Wehrmacht – including the ever-obsequious Wilhelm Keitel – and was convened on August 4. The results were a foregone conclusion. Some twenty-two men were expelled from the army, thus denying them the right of a formal court-martial, and therefore "depriving them of the last shreds of legal protection" from Nazi "justice."[20] Hitler was obsessed with wreaking vengeance on these men. He was determined to "wipe out and eradicate (*ausmerzen und ausrotten*)" every one of them. "They must hang immediately, without any mercy."[21] Goebbels said of Hitler, "The Führer is extraordinarily furious at the generals, especially those of the General Staff ... He is absolutely determined to set a bloody example ... The punishment which must now be meted out must have historic dimensions."[22] Other sources quote Hitler as saying that he wanted these men "to be hanged, strung up like butchered cattle."[23]

The fates of Generals Friedrich Fromm and "Clever Hans" von Kluge are especially noteworthy. Subsequent to the summary execution of Stauffenberg and his associates at the Bendlerstraße on the night of July 20–21, Fromm, convinced that he had "come down on the right side," went to see Goebbels, hoping to be the first to proclaim the end of the conspiracy and also hoping to speak directly to Hitler. Much to his surprise and dismay, he was arrested.[24] Hitler had been enraged upon learning that Fromm had executed Stauffenberg and his associates. With Goebbels's undoubted encouragement and believing – correctly – that Fromm was attempting to conceal his own complicity in the conspiracy, Hitler had him imprisoned. In a "mockery of a trial before the People's Court" – of which more will be said in the pages following – Fromm was convicted months later on a trumped-up charge of cowardice and was executed by a firing squad in March 1945.²⁵ Friedrich Fromm's opportunism ultimately exacted its highest price from him.

Kluge's dilemma has been described as a "complex combination of contempt for the regime and submissiveness to it, indecision and legalism."²⁶ The man could not make up his mind. This dilemma soon would cost him his life. He had been appointed commander in chief of all the German armies in the west on July 17 – a time when military conditions were deteriorating rapidly – and was given the unenviable task of reversing the Allied advance into France; but it was a doomed mission, and he knew it. German military resistance was crumbling under the crushing blows of the Allied offensive. Yet this man continued to vacillate between the realization that the war was all but lost and Hitler's hypnotic ability to convince him that the Allies could be repulsed.

After a tour of the front in mid-July, Kluge finally realized that Hitler "lived by wishful thinking, and when his dreams faded, searched for scapegoats."²⁷ Kluge concluded that the war in the west had to be brought to an end, but in order for that to happen, Hitler had to be eliminated. Had he made an irrevocable commitment to support Stauffenberg, Beck, and Goerdeler, hostilities in France just might have been concluded.²⁸ Nonetheless, the stumbling block remained. Hitler did not die. His survival led Kluge to still another reversal of position. During the critical hours of July 20, he wavered. Upon learning that Hitler was indeed alive, he abandoned the conspiracy and openly cast his lot with the Nazi government, stating to the resistance leaders that he had agreed to cooperate with them on condition that Hitler be assassinated.²⁹ Late in the evening of July 20, he sent a fulsome telegram to Hitler, "expressing his devotion." It read in part, "The attempt of villainous murderers to kill you, my Führer, has been foiled by the fortuitous hand of fate."³⁰ Nonetheless, his own fate was about to be sealed.

By the middle of August, Kluge's troops were in a hopeless situation. On the fifteenth, he went to the battle zone in order to assess the situation, but he lost radio contact, because enemy fire had put his communication equipment out of action. When Hitler was unable to get in touch with him, he assumed that the field marshal had gone to the Allied forces for the purpose of negotiating an armistice. German intercepts of Allied radio signals asking the whereabouts of Kluge reinforced this perception. After the war, an aide to General George Patton, commander of the US Third Army, stated that Patton had disappeared for an entire day in mid-August. Upon his return, he reported to his aide that "he had tried to make contact with a German emissary who had not turned up at the appointed place."

In a postwar interview, Dr. Udo Esche, Kluge's son-in-law, told Allied interrogators that his father-in-law had discussed with him the question of surrender. Esche also said that Kluge "went to the front lines but was unable to get in touch with the Allied commanders."[31]

On August 17, General Walter Model appeared at Kluge's headquarters with orders from Hitler to replace Kluge as commander in chief of German forces in the west. Kluge, relieved of his command, was ordered to keep Berlin "advised of where in Germany he intends to go."[32] Well aware of Hitler's suspicions of his dalliance with the resistance, he interpreted this message, probably correctly, as a preliminary to arrest, expulsion from the Wehrmacht, and trial before the People's Court. Therefore, as he and his entourage were on their way back to Germany, he stopped near Verdun, site of the blood-soaked battlefield of the Great War where he had fought as a young officer, swallowed a capsule of potassium cyanide that his son-in-law, Dr. Esche, had given to him, and was dead within seconds. Before this final act, however, he had written an effusive last letter to his Führer, declaring, "I have always admired your greatness [and] your iron will … You have fought an honorable and great fight." The letter ended with "Heil, Mein Führer!"[33]

Hans Günther von Kluge is one of the more tragic figures in the history of the resistance. Neither he nor Friedrich Fromm had the moral courage of the resistance leaders. Although Kluge apparently remained conflicted to the end, Fromm's single-minded goal was to be on the winning side, and he cared not which group it was. Sadly, they both paid the ultimate price for nothing. History has not been kind to them for good reason.

A conversation held between Kluge and Rudolph-Christoph von Gersdorff, the dedicated conspirator who had attempted to kill Hitler with a suicide bomb, reveals much about Kluge. Merely days before his death, Kluge spoke with Gersdorff, who tried to persuade him to surrender the western forces to the Allies, thereby avoiding further needless bloodshed and destruction, and then to join forces with "a few reliable units" in another attempt to overthrow Nazi rule. Kluge demurred, saying that he would be remembered as the "biggest swine in world history" should the attempt fail. Gersdorff retorted, "'Every great man in world history,' has faced a decision that would cause him to be remembered either as a criminal or as 'a savior in times of dire need.' Kluge simply laid his hand on the colonel's shoulder and remarked, 'Gersdorff, Field Marshal Kluge is no great man.'"[34] Regrettably, this is his epitaph.

* * * *

By the time these events transpired in the west, the first eight conspirators had been brought before the People's Court that had been convened on August 7. They were Field Marshal Erwin von Witzleben, Colonel General Erich Hoepner, General Helmuth Stieff, Lieutenant General Paul von Hase, Lieutenant Robert Bernardis, Captain Friedrich Klausing, Lieutenant Albrecht von Hagen, and Graf Peter Yorck von Wartenburg. Hitler had dismissed Hoepner from his command in the east for disobeying a direct order not to withdraw his troops from the battle for Moscow in 1941 and 1942. According to some accounts, he joined the conspirators as much out of "personal pique as principle."[35] He had been slated to assume command of the home army after the removal of his friend Friedrich Fromm from that position.[36] Bernardis was an Austrian whose friendship with Stauffenberg long predated the Anschluss.[37] Klausing, an aide-de-camp to Stauffenberg (Haeften was ill at the time), had been with the latter at the time of the two failed bombing attempts on July 11 and July 15.[38] Hagen was on the staff of General Helmuth Stieff, and was involved in the planning of Stieff's aborted suicide attempt against Hitler. He also had helped Axel von dem Bussche to obtain explosives for Bussche's failed suicide attack against Hitler.[39]

This People's Court was a so-called "judicial body," created in 1934 to deal with "political crimes."[40] What followed on the seventh and in succeeding months was a grotesque parody of justice. These trials had a single purpose, namely, the execution of the enemies of the Third Reich.[41] The presiding judge was Roland Freisler, an infamous and fanatical Nazi whom the Russians had captured in the Great War and who had embraced Bolshevism – the Russian version of revolutionary Marxism – while in Russia. Subsequent to his return to Germany after the war, he switched ideologies, rejecting Bolshevism and becoming instead a fervent Nazi. Perhaps as a result of this volte-face, Hitler never fully trusted him. Perhaps also Freisler attempted to prove his bona fides as a true Nazi by appearing to be more royal than the king. Whatever the reason, he became notorious for his outrageous conduct as a judge.

His behavior at these trials produced a crescendo of vituperation and vitriol that reached monstrous proportions. He subjected the defendants to his "ferocious wrath" and "scathing contempt." He was so bad that even hardened Nazis within the fraudulent justice system were thoroughly disgusted with his hideous antics.[42] His modus operandi included reprehensible and abusive language directed at the defendants, screaming at them with such epithets as "pigs," "traitors," "criminals," and "rabble."[43]

His voice became so loud that the camera crews who – under orders – were filming the "proceedings" had to inform Freisler that he was ruining their sound recordings.[44]

In addition to his execrable antics, Freisler subjected the defendants to indignities and humiliations of the worst sort. Denied even the rudiments of dignity, they were forced to dress in shabby and ill-fitting clothes and even were forbidden to wear neckties. Handcuffed as they entered the courtroom, their manacles were not removed until after they were seated. Field Marshal von Witzleben suffered additional humiliation when he was given a pair of ill-fitting trousers to wear and then was denied a belt and suspenders. He was forced to hold them up with his hands. Freisler thereupon mocked him as a "dirty old man" for "fiddling with his trousers." One account of this gruesome farce claims that he was even denied his dentures.[45] Roland Freisler was a thoroughly repulsive man. All of this demonstrates once again how the Nazis corrupted everything they touched, including in this instance the judicial system.

As anticipated, the two-day trial concluded with the conviction of all eight men. Immediately thereafter, the condemned were taken to Plötzensee Prison in Berlin and executed. Whereas death by firing squad was the customary method of execution for military officers convicted of capital crimes, civilians sentenced to death in the Third Reich were beheaded.[46] However, Hitler ordered these men to be hanged by methods that were especially inhumane, even by Nazi standards. They were led into the place of execution, which was a gaunt room with two windows at one end and a beam across the ceiling to which were attached several meat hooks. "The condemned men were led in handcuffed and wearing prison trousers. There were no last words, no comfort from a priest or pastor … The hanging was carried out within twenty seconds of the prisoner entering the room."[47]

Of all the methods of execution, death by hanging is considered to be the most agonizing, even in instances wherein suffering is not intended. The most humane method is to stand the prisoner on a trapdoor, then spring it and allow the body to drop through the opening, thus breaking the neck and bringing death swiftly, or at the very least, bringing immediate unconsciousness. An alternative is to raise the body up and then drop it as rapidly as possible, achieving the same result. Hitler, however, wanted to extend the death agonies as long as possible. Therefore, the victims were raised up and brought down very slowly, thereby prolonging their torment. The victims supposedly were strung up with piano wire, although this has been dismissed as legend. Still others say – probably correctly – that "specially thin rope" accomplished the grim deed.[48] The most grisly example of this procedure took place on April 9, 1945, with the execution of Admiral Wilhelm Canaris at Flossenbürg concentration camp in northeast Bavaria near the Czech border. According to at least one source, Canaris "was kept hanging until he was almost dead, then revived and hanged again and so on; he did not die until he was strangled six times."[49] Hans Oster and Dietrich Bonhoeffer were numbered among those also executed at Flossenbürg.[50]

A final profanity was perpetrated against the eight men who were executed at Plötzensee Prison on August 8, 1944, when, as they were slowly expiring, they were stripped of their trousers and left hanging naked in their death throes.[51] Through it all, these men, according to eyewitness accounts, displayed "steadfastness and dignity." Their deportment was in sharp contrast to the coarse behavior of their executioner, one Wilhelm Roettger, who spewed forth a "constant litany of jeers, leers and obscene jokes" during this bestial affair. Together, Roettger and his victims symbolized the contrast between "the system of nihilism and death that [the former] served, and the hope of civilisation that [the latter] represented."[52]

As a finale to this grim affair, the entire savage process, from the trials of August 7–8 to the executions, was preserved on motion picture film, presumably under orders from Goebbels at Hitler's behest. Every excruciating detail was made part of the record. Nothing was omitted. After processing, the film was immediately sent to the Führer's headquarters at Rastenburg, where it was then shown to those who were present. Whether or not Hitler actually saw the film himself remains a matter of conjecture. Some twenty-five years or so after the war, Albert Speer claimed that Hitler watched the film "over and over again." However, another member of the headquarters staff stated that Hitler showed little interest in the still photographs of this dreadful episode, thus implying that he was not interested in the motion picture film, but this seems doubtful.[53]

The court "proceedings" were filmed for propaganda purposes. Selected excerpts, as well as a so-called "documentary" entitled *Verräter vor dem Volksgericht* (Traitors before the People's Court), were to be shown in the motion picture theaters throughout Germany. Hitler got more than he bargained for, however. Throughout this atrocious charade, the defendants displayed steadfast courage and grim determination in their effort to confront abhorrent evil. Their demeanor stands as a magnificent rebuke to the loathsome antics of Roland Freisler. In sum:

> The propaganda purpose was not achieved and only excerpts from the films were later shown to the public. Even these selected extracts had the opposite effect to that intended. All the accused behaved like upright courageous men; their statements put the regime in the dock. Their quiet dignity, accentuated by their sufferings in captivity, merely underlined the contrast with the screaming, gesticulating, undignified judge.[54]

The defendants had expected to have an opportunity to speak their minds freely in their own defense at their trials, which they wanted to use as a forum to press their case against a patently criminal regime. But they were not allowed to address the court directly and were unable "to reach any sort of understanding with their attorneys, who were seated some distance away." In fact many of the defense attorneys – though not all – clearly supported the prosecution.[55] Nonetheless, many defendants were able to speak out against the Nazis despite Freisler's efforts to muzzle them. At one point during that first series of trials on August 7, Freisler mockingly asked Witzleben "whether he and Beck could have managed things better than their Führer." The old soldier responded with a defiant shout of "*Ja.*"[56]

In the second round of trials, held on August 10, Freisler told a resistance member, Josef Wirmer, that he "would soon find himself roasting in hell," to which Wirmer "bowed curtly and riposted, 'I'll look forward to your own imminent arrival, Your Honor!'" Wirmer was a lawyer and had been politically active in the left wing of the Catholic Center Party. He had formed close ties with trade union leader Jakob Kaiser, and had been an outspoken opponent of the Nazis from the beginning.[57]

Another defendant, Cäsar von Hofacker, a cousin of Stauffenberg, was a lawyer in civilian life and served on the staff of the military commander in France, General Carl Heinrich von Stülpnagel, who was part of the conspiracy. Hofacker had strongly supported a coup attempt in Paris. He served as a messenger between Stülpnagel and Stauffenberg. During the course of his trial, he interrupted one of Freisler's tirades with, "Be quiet now, Herr Freisler, because today it's my neck that's on the block. But in a year it will be yours!"[58]

Fritz-Dietlof von der Schulenburg, the lawyer who had joined the Nazi Party in 1932 but had been expelled in 1940 because of his "unreliability" and who subsequently became an active member of the resistance, made one of the most eloquent statements of any of the defendants. Speaking before the court, he said, "We resolved to take this deed upon ourselves in order to save Germany from indescribable misery. I realize that I shall be hanged for my part in it, but I do not regret what I did and only hope that someone else will succeed in luckier circumstances."[59]

Most of the defendants voiced similar convictions. All of the accused completely understood the fate that awaited them at the end of these "proceedings," but they never wavered. They showed no remorse or contrition for what they had done. The unshakable conviction that theirs was a just and moral cause sustained them throughout this dreadful time. It mattered not to them that they had failed. It did matter that they had made the attempt. Thus the assault on Hitler's life on July 20, 1944, has been accurately described as a "symbolic act … The gesture … was its own justification."[60]

These kangaroo courts were intended to serve a second purpose. Hitler wanted to show to the nation that the conspirators of July 20 were, in his words, part of a "tiny clique" of malcontents.[61] Like the show trial scheme, however, this plan also failed. As the Gestapo dragnet spread across Germany throughout August and September 1944, there was a growing realization that the "tiny clique" of which Hitler spoke was merely the tip of the proverbial iceberg. Operation Valkyrie was indeed the work of a small group of men, and the army's attempt to depose Hitler during the years of his ascendency – when in General Keitel's words, he was the "greatest commander of all time" – comprised a pitifully small group of conspirators.

Nevertheless, the Gestapo dragnet revealed an anti-Nazi opposition that was far more extensive and intense than Hitler and his henchman ever realized. Its diversity included almost every facet of German society – the youth and the elderly, rich and poor, aristocrats and commoners, liberals and conservatives, Social Democrats and authoritarians. Discontent, dissatisfaction, and disillusionment were everywhere. The Volksgemeinschaft was revealing itself for what it had been from the beginning – a gigantic lie. The resistance "extended far beyond the army to civilian circles on both sides of the political spectrum, even to groups presumed to be close to the Nazi Party."[62] Tragically, however, it remained as it had been at the beginning: unorganized and, for all practical purposes, leaderless.

Hitler had correctly assumed that it included many members of the old landed aristocracy, who as a class had always showed a disdain and contempt for the Nazis. He hated them, and the feeling was reciprocated. He had not assumed, however, that any of the old fighters – *die alten Kämpfer* – who had been part of the Nazi Party from the earliest days would ever turn against him and join the conspiracy. One man, however, had done just that. He was Wolf Heinrich Graf von Helldorf, Berlin police president and a onetime leader within the SA, the "Brownshirts." Another "old fighter" who'd turned against Hitler was the former SA soldier Friedrich Wilhelm Heinz, the leader of the assault force that was part of the failed Oster conspiracy of 1938.

Others within the armed services who were neither members of the aristocracy nor "old fighters" doubtlessly sympathized with the efforts to bring Hitler down, if for no other reason than to bring the wretched war to an end. One example of men such as these was Colonel Harald Momm, commander of a military installation near Berlin. Upon hearing the erroneous report that Stauffenberg's bomb had killed Hitler, he shouted, "Orderly! A bottle of champagne; the pig's dead."[63] One can never know how many German soldiers held feelings such as this in July 1944, but it can reasonably be assumed that the numbers were not insignificant. This suggests that, regardless of success or failure, the coup may well have had considerable potential support within the ranks of the Wehrmacht.

* * * *

As it was at the beginning of Nazi rule, so it remained throughout the life of the Third Reich to its tragic finale. Since 1933, the opposition had been very intense in many instances, but also very diffuse. For reasons that have been cited, the masses remained unorganized, also because there was no one able to create a successful opposition out of this widespread dissent. This remained especially true after the failure of Operation Valkyrie. Nazi Germany was now a complete totalitarian state ruled by a party and a secret police that were particularly merciless and effective in their ability to suppress any kind of opposition. Moreover, the German people were desperately trying to survive in a country devastated by modern total war, which included an aerial bombing campaign of horrific proportions. Most of Germany's cities were all but destroyed. Historian Richard Evans has provided a vivid picture of conditions on the ground: "Ordinary Germans, their towns and cities bombed to rubble, their gas, electricity and water services working only intermittently if at all, their factories and workplaces destroyed, their food and fuel supplies dwindling, had to concentrate on simply keeping themselves and their families alive."[64] Only the army had the organizational and leadership capability to challenge the Gestapo and the SS. To be successful, the army's resistance efforts required leadership from those few generals at the top of the chain of command. Regrettably, these few men lacked the moral courage to lead.

The discovery of papers in army headquarters at Zossen in September 1944 further confirmed the fact that the conspiracy was both widespread and long-standing. It also destroyed the "belief in the unity of Volk and Führer." Even though little in the way of new evidence was disclosed, the Zossen papers clearly showed that July 20 "was not the work of a few disgruntled, resentful, or exhausted officers, unhappy with the reversal in the tide of war." Also, the diaries of Admiral Wilhelm Canaris, discovered in April 1945, provided further confirmation of the fact that Stauffenberg and his fellow conspirators were part of an army anti-Nazi resistance movement that was much more extensive and pervasive than Nazi authorities had realized. The Gestapo report revealed that the origins of the army conspiracy could be traced at least as far back as 1938 and to the work of Hans Oster.[65] The Gestapo also learned that the conspirators had criticized and condemned Nazi attitudes and behavior over a wide range of issues such as the "'handling of the Jewish question,' the Nazis' policy toward the churches, and the generally 'harmful influence' of Himmler and the Gestapo."[66]

Hitler recognized the implications of these discoveries and was forced to rescind his decision to use the show trials for propaganda purposes. He ordered a halt to press coverage of Freisler's so-called court "proceedings" as early as August 17. He also was forced to suppress all information disclosing the widespread nature of the resistance movement. "In the end, not even the executions were publicly announced."[67] His propaganda efforts had failed. The investigations that followed the episode at the Wolfschanze clearly revealed the Nazi "people's community" for what it was, namely, a morally bankrupt fraud.[68] The facts of Operation Valkyrie not merely confirmed the existence of long-standing and pervasive anti-Nazi dissent throughout the Third Reich, both military and civilian, but also served to highlight the ultimate tragedy of the overall German anti-Nazi resistance movement, namely, that its leadership was too small in numbers and too diverse in character to mobilize the forces of opposition and to give voice to their aspirations.

One heinous consequence of these revelations was Hitler's reaction to them. Unwilling and unable to view his world realistically, he convinced himself that the conspirators were solely responsible for the destruction of his grand design for Germany. Thus, he was determined to wreak a horrible vengeance on those who had foiled him in the pursuit of his vision. Such were the workings of a disordered mind that ordered the orgy of killings to continue until the end of the war.[69] Consumed with rage, he was determined to eradicate anyone and everyone who had even the slightest connection to the July 20 conspiracy or the overall resistance movement, as well as many who had no connection whatsoever with either the resistance or the conspiracy. These victims merely were the political opponents of Adolf Hitler and the Nazis.

One such person was Ernst Thälmann, the leader of the German Communist Party. He had been incarcerated since 1933 and thus had absolutely no connection with the resistance. Nevertheless, he was executed on Hitler's orders. This wanton bloodshed revealed ever more clearly the unbelievably evil nature of Nazism and its Führer. It also is an indication of the increasingly desperate position of the crumbling Third Reich. Although Hitler professed to believe in ultimate victory, even he assuredly knew his Nazi empire was coming to an end. As the spring of 1945 approached, all that was left to him was continued mayhem and murder, which were the only things that he and his minions really knew.[70]

* * * *

Remarkably – miraculously even – a few members of the resistance survived the carnage. For most of them, it was a matter of pure chance. Some were outside the country; others successfully remained in hiding. Baron Rudolph-Christoph von Gersdorff, for example, escaped arrest because the Gestapo investigations failed to uncover his close connection to the resistance. The same was true of Baron Axel von dem Bussche, the young officer who had witnessed the massacre of the Jewish community at the Ukrainian village of Dubno, and whose plan to become a suicide bomber against Hitler was never fulfilled.

Eugen Gerstenmaier, the Protestant theologian with connections to the Kreisau Circle, was arrested and brought to the Freisler court, where he successfully portrayed himself as a "naïve theologian baffled and bewildered by the world of politics."[71] He escaped the hangman but was sentenced to seven years in prison. Men such as these undoubtedly owed their lives to the fortitude and courage of those of the resistance who had been apprehended but had refused to name their coconspirators despite being subjected to "intensified interrogation."[72] It has been said of Himmler's men that they "employed every means to extract confessions ... all forms of torture were used without hesitation."[73]

Fabian von Schlabrendorff had been captured during the second wave of Gestapo arrests in August 1944. His experience is a remarkable account of survival under the most inhuman conditions. As adjutant to Henning von Tresckow, he was well acquainted with the co-conspirators at Army Group Center headquarters, but he refused to reveal any names even though he was subjected to the most savage of tortures. The following extended quotation gives a horrifying picture of the agonies that he experienced:

> In the first stage Schlabrendorff's hands were tied behind his back and his fingers encased in a contraption in which spikes penetrated into his fingertips; with the turning of a screw they penetrated deeper. When this produced no answer the prisoner was strapped down on a sort of bedstead and his legs encased in tubes covered on the inside with sharp metal spikes; the tubes were slowly drawn tighter so that the spikes gradually penetrated deeper into the flesh. During this process his head was pushed into a sort of metal hood and covered with a blanket to muffle his screams. Meanwhile he was belaboured with bamboo canes and leather switches. In the third stage, using the same bedstead, his body was stretched either violently and in jerks or gradually. If he lost consciousness he was revived with douches of cold water. These tortures had still extracted no confession from Schlabrendorff and so another method was tried. He was trussed up, bent forwards so that he could move neither backwards nor sideways and was then beaten from behind with a heavy club; with each blow he fell forward on his face with his full weight. All these tortures were applied to Schlabrendorff on the same day but the only result was that he lost consciousness. The next day he had a heart attack and could not move for several days. As soon as he had recovered, however, the tortures were repeated. Finally Schlabrendorff decided to say something: he knew that Tresckow [who by now was dead] had frequently spoken of removing Hitler either with or without force and that he had been particularly busy just before 20 July … This seemed temporarily to satisfy the Gestapo; it was enough to prove complicity. Schlabrendorff was left in peace for a time.[74]

The endurance of these men almost defies human comprehension. Their willingness to suffer such torture solely to save the lives of their fellow conspirators who thus far had evaded the Gestapo and SS bespeaks their "sense of ethical obligation to fight injustice, crime and destruction even at the price of one's own life."[75] In the case of Schlabrendorff and others, their Christian faith sustained them throughout their horrible ordeals.[76]

Miraculously, Schlabrendorff survived the war. Along with others, he was finally brought before the People's Court on February 3, 1945. Just as the court was about to convene, however, an Allied air raid took place, and a bomb fell on the building housing the court, killing Roland Freisler. The court reconvened the following month with a new judge. Schlabrendorff, a lawyer, was able to successfully defend himself by describing the tortures he had endured and pointing out that Frederick the Great had abolished torture in Prussia two hundred years earlier. He was acquitted and released, but the Gestapo seized him once again, declaring that the court decision was wrong. He was subsequently taken to the Flossenbürg concentration camp, where Bonhoeffer, Canaris, Oster, Dohnányi, and others had been executed. Advancing US troops forced closure of the camp, however, and all the prisoners were removed, eventually arriving in the South Tyrol in Austria. Here they ultimately were liberated.[77]

After the war, Schlabrendorff resumed his legal career and eventually became a judge in the constitutional court of the West German Federal Republic. The men whose stories have been told here were among the very few who survived the inhuman Nazi vengeance. Most of the others paid the ultimate price for their opposition. Included in this latter group was former lord mayor of Leipzig and longtime activist in the resistance Carl Goerdeler. Although condemned in September 1944, he was kept alive until his execution in February 1945. This delay was in itself a form of inhuman torture.[78]

By March 1945, the once vast Nazi empire that had encompassed almost all of Europe – from Scandinavia in the north to the Mediterranean Sea in the south and from the English Channel in the west to the Russian steppes in the east – had been reduced to a few hundred square miles around the city of Berlin. Its emperor was enduring a troglodyte existence of a few thousand square yards underneath his destroyed capital city. He was a man in broken health, whose body was racked by Parkinson's disease. He also was suffering from the aftereffects of the bomb attack, which had burst his eardrums. He experienced occasional dizzy spells as well, and he "shuffled rather than walked."[79] In the words of Albert Speer, he was "shriveling up like an old man."[80] Another member of his entourage referred to his "pathological" consumption of pastry. He was a "cake-devouring wreck."[81] Yet he remained fully capable of insane ranting and paroxysms of rage.[82]

The advance of the Soviet Army had forced Hitler's return to Berlin from Rastenburg in January 1945. Once confined to the bunker, he became completely isolated from the outside world and totally detached from objective reality. In a word, he was delusional.[83] It was in this oppressively grim and fetid atmosphere, and in a "mood of apocalyptic defeatism," that he decided to perpetrate a final obscene act of retribution against the German people themselves.[84]

On March 19, Hitler issued his infamous "Nero Order" – named for the Roman emperor who supposedly was responsible for the destruction of Rome by fire – that called for the total destruction of the entire German nation, including bridges, industrial plants, the electrical grid, roads and railway lines, mines, the telecommunication system, and canals. Anything and everything vital to its survival was to be reduced to rubble – even its priceless cultural heritage. Nazi Germany was to be totally destroyed in a self-initiated immolation, a kind of Wagnerian Götterdämmerung. Just as the Germans themselves had been the first victims of Nazi brutalities, so they now were to become the last victims of Nazi madness.[85]

One day earlier, Hitler had received a message from Albert Speer that outlined procedures to be taken for the preservation of what was left of the German economic infrastructure. This would provide a foundation for the restoration of the nation in the postwar world. Hitler replied that there was no need to plan for the future. The German people had lost the Darwinian struggle for survival and did not deserve to live. The best of the racial stock had been killed in the war, and those who remained were not worthy of survival.[86] Thus, the Nero Order reflected his profound contempt for the German people. In addition, his fixation on race as the determining factor in history remained with him to the end. Central to this fixation was his anti-Semitism.

The last words of Hitler's so-called "political testament," written just hours before his suicide, read as follows: "Above all, I charge the leaders of the nation and those under them to scrupulous observance of the laws of race and to merciless opposition to the universal poisoner of all peoples, international Jewry."[87] Ever the ideologue, his commitment to Weltmacht oder Vernichtung was about to end in Vernichtung for him, for the nation, and, if he could achieve it, for its people. The "profound nihilism" of the Nazi ideology could no longer be denied, and Adolf Hitler, the Führer, the great leader of his people, had become their implacable enemy.[88]

Thanks to the herculean efforts of Albert Speer, the Nero Order was never carried out. Shortly after it was given, Speer embarked upon a tour of the battlefronts with the purpose of countermanding the order.[89] Speaking to the various commanders and Gauleitern (district party leaders), he tried to convince them that the struggle was hopeless and that they should ignore the order to destroy their nation. Fortunately, he found support among those with whom he spoke. "Few, even of [Hitler's] closest acolytes, were ready to follow this self-destructive urge to the letter."[90] What's more, the order could not be physically implemented. Military conditions were deteriorating hourly, and the resources were no longer available to carry it out. Consequently, even those few fanatics who wanted to obey their Führer to the very end could not.[91]

Nonetheless, yet one more wanton act of savagery did take place before the final curtain fell on the Third Reich, when Hitler issued what in effect was his last order, which brought about the destruction of all the remaining bridges in Berlin and the flooding of the rail tunnels that were used to house wounded German soldiers, drowning these men and all who were with them in the tunnels.[92] With this last act of hideous barbarity, Hitler brought to an end what was left of his monstrous "people's community." Finis Volksgemeinschaft.

The nightmare of the Third Reich finally came to an end with the unconditional surrender of all German forces on May 7, 1945, in the person of General Alfred Jodl (Hitler had committed suicide on April 30). The following day, May 8, US President Harry S. Truman and British Prime Minister Winston S. Churchill issued a joint statement proclaiming the end of the European war. All fighting officially ceased on May 9.[93] The physical destruction and loss of life was almost beyond comprehension. In Germany alone, Allied bombing had destroyed an estimated sixty cities, with another hundred damaged, some severely. The nation's cultural heritage had been devastated. "Well over a thousand churches and museums burned to the ground. The medieval centers of Frankfurt, Ulm, Aachen, Würzburg, Cologne and Nuremberg were simply wiped off the face of the earth. A millennium of Europe's finest architecture and culture were gone. Twenty million books had been burned."[94]

The human cost in lives for the German nation was an estimated 3,300,000 military personnel and 2,300,000 civilians. An additional 170,000 Germans of the Jewish faith had been murdered. Of Europe's total Jewish population of 8,851,800 before 1939, some 5,933,900 had been killed during the war. Thus most of the Jews murdered in the Nazi death camps in World War II were not German nationals, but rather citizens of the countries conquered by the Nazis, especially those from Eastern Europe.[95] Moreover, an estimated 5,000,000 non-Jewish victims – Jehovah's Witnesses, Gypsies, Slavs, homosexuals and lesbians, the physically or mentally handicapped, and other "asocials" who did not belong in the Volksgemeinschaft – are thought to have perished as well.[96] Although these figures vary somewhat with different sources, the message is clear: the number of those who died as a result of Adolf Hitler's madness is both astronomical and beyond belief.

Finale

The greatest tragedy of the Third Reich is the millions of deaths and the incalculable destruction suffered as the consequence of Nazi rule. A second tragedy is the burden of moral guilt the German nation and its people still bear as the result of that rule. When Germany embarked on this path, few if any could know what lay at its end. Most Germans in 1933 only saw their nation in a terrible state of disarray and distress, and they desperately sought a better future for themselves and their progeny. Beginning in 1914, Germany had experienced over a decade and a half of catastrophic war and defeat, revolution, economic disaster, social distress and upheaval, and political instability. After a five-year period of relative calm in the latter twenties, the Great Depression once again plunged the German nation into distress and privation.

In such times, people often turn to extremist politics and false messiahs who promise an earthly paradise. That promise, couched in the language of ideology, is comprised of simplistic solutions that guarantee perfection. In addition, the search for a scapegoat often accompanies a willing acceptance of violence and mayhem as part of the "perfecting" process. Such unscrupulous leaders, of whom the Nazis are prototypical examples, delude even those with strong moral and ethical values. Hitler and his henchmen debased all that they touched. They were masters of deception who had a powerful Ministry of Propaganda at their disposal that was capable of lying without compunction. With consummate skill, they twisted moral and ethical values to serve their demented purposes. Thus, they manipulated the masses with virtuosic brilliance. Many who thought of themselves as "good Germans" committed deeds of incomprehensible evil, thinking that they were serving a higher good. Others used Hitler's Aryanization program to cynically promote their own interests. For example, they welcomed the destruction of Jewish business establishments and in many cases absorbed their erstwhile competitors wholesale. Historian Richard Evans states, "By 1937, virtually every large company in Germany was joining in the division of the spoils."[97] Profiteering and self-aggrandizement took place on a massive scale at every level of society.

In sum, the Nazis corrupted the mind and soul of the German nation. Decent men and women, who under normal circumstances would have recoiled in disgust and horror at the monstrous actions of the Nazis, now not only acquiesced but also in many cases actively participated in the evil deeds of the regime. Of those who became the functionaries and apparatchiki of the Nazi apparatus, most were totally lacking in moral scruple and integrity. They easily succumbed to the siren song of Nazism. Pure opportunism and ambition motivated them as they pursued their goal of personal aggrandizement, to the exclusion of all other considerations. Such individuals tend to proliferate in any debased and corrupted society. In this instance, they provided the means whereby the Nazis could carry out their despicable work. The German experience with Nazism demonstrates how easily a people in great distress can be deceived by a demon of darkness posing as an angel of light. It is a lesson for all people in all times.

Thanks to the constant barrage of racist propaganda that the appalling conditions of total war reinforced, their consciences were further dulled and rendered insensate to the enormity of their own behavior. The German historian Koppel S. Pinson has given a superb summation of the Third Reich with the following words: "In the twelve years of Nazi rule an entire people was corrupted and poisoned and from the heart of its youth was torn all aspirations for a better, more just and nobler world, the pious reverence before the altars of humanity, the chivalrous attitude toward the weak, the suffering and the vanquished."[98]

Many who supported the Nazis in the beginning, including men and women who ultimately became active and dedicated members of the resistance, sincerely believed that Nazism was a positive and truly progressive movement, representing the best of the historic German tradition. In their eyes, the Weimar Republic was undermining it. They also believed that Hitler and his Nazis, once in power, would reclaim this tradition and restore Germany to its imperial greatness. They failed to understand, however, that the past as remembered can never be recaptured. The promised new Nazi-ruled Germany would, in truth, be a crude parody of the nation they were trying to restore.

They also failed to calculate the cost of that hoped-for recovery. They saw the violence and brutality associated with the Nazi "movement" as excesses – an aberration – that only a few "unruly" elements within the party had instigated. Ultimately, however, they came face-to-face with the ugly truth. These excesses were not an aberration, but rather at the very core of Nazism. The Nazis were purposely destroying the very "traditional values" that they allegedly espoused.

Germany's experience with Nazism provides a simple message for all people at all times. A nation that violates its own ethos, ethical principles, and moral values as a matter of policy does so at great mortal peril, especially when the issue in question is war and peace. When a government goes to war in the name of its people, the people are left to bear the moral consequences of that decision long after the war has ended. For too long, the Nazis succeeded with their deceptions. For too long, the German nation continued to follow the path the Nazis charted. For too long, too many Germans – especially the army leadership – continued to practice self-deception. They learned too late that the Nazi Volksgemeinschaft was a frightful swindle. Nazism was completely nihilistic and devoid of substance. The Third Reich took Germany on a journey that went from nothing to nothing.

* * * *

Nonetheless, Germany under Nazi rule never was the totalitarian monolith that the contemporary world believed it to be. Although many Germans became Hitler's willing executioners and eagerly participated in the hideous Nazi crimes, either out of conviction or opportunism, many others – doubtlessly most – did not. They went along because they had little choice. Isolated, powerless, and apathetic in a totalitarian police state, they unwillingly and unwittingly became associated with a monstrous machine of death simply because they were Germans. Still others – and we shall never know how many – did not merely refuse to cooperate with the regime. They actively opposed it in ways large and small.

Again, we shall never know how many Georg Elsers, Franz Jägerstätters, and Kurt Gersteins there were who participated in an unseen and unheard resistance. We shall never know of those who gave succor to their Jewish friends and neighbors, shielding them from the omnipresent Nazi Party, or who simply refused to cooperate with the authorities and defied them in various ways, such as listening to the BBC broadcasts, or who participated in some form of passive resistance in the workplace or refused to believe the lies spewing forth from the Ministry of Propaganda.

Just a hint of the extent of this unknown resistance can be found in the number and diverse nature of the many clandestine resistance groups that existed in Nazi Germany. They "came from all social backgrounds, left and right, aristocratic and civic, with Christian and Communist backgrounds.

They often did not know of each other, had to act in secret and alone, always in fear of being discovered. In the end they all failed, yet all succeeded in leaving a lasting sign of defiance in times of darkness."[99]

All of those who resisted the Nazis in whatever manner could be described as traitorous patriots. They loved their country, but they recognized the essential criminality of the regime, and they tried to resist it as best they could. However, they were impotent against the leviathan Nazi state. They had no power and no leaders. Events ultimately demonstrated that the only institution capable of taking direct action against Nazi rule was the German Army, and the story of the conspiracy against Hitler ultimately must examine the efforts of the pitifully small number of men within that institution who led the conspiracy, as well as the civilians who supported them and worked with them. This group was indeed "a tiny minority."[100]

They also were a remarkable minority. They wrestled mightily with the question of tyrannicide before concluding that desperate times required desperate measures. They risked – and lost – everything in their efforts to bring down the Nazis. They fully realized that their nation would view them as traitors. "But they faced a crisis of conscience, a spiritual dilemma that forced them to choose between national allegiance and moral imperative."[101] They were flawed individuals; many of them had flawed ideas. They carried within themselves the prejudices of their social class and era. They were children of their time. A few sincerely, if mistakenly, believed that Nazism had positive features that its leaders had corrupted.[102] They had all of the contradictions and foibles that the term "human" implies.

They have been accurately described as "fallible, gullible, [and] sometimes culpable," with "motives [that] may have been mixed, parochial and universal, expedient and selfless, patriotic and humanitarian, mean and noble."[103] But they also had an extremely acute moral sensitivity – a moral compass – directing them as they moved against a regime that was a sinister caricature of their nation. The revulsion they felt for Nazism and all it represented reached completion as they came face-to-face with palpable evil; and they were determined to resist it, regardless of the cost, even as they recognized toward the end that their efforts were doomed. Although their moral convictions may have been founded in diverse sources, they shared a common quality: they were absolute.

For many, that source was their Christian conscience and faith. It was their lodestar. This has been described as a "feature of the Resistance." Many of its members "were, or became, devout Christians." An exemplar of these people was Henning von Tresckow. The US high commissioner to West Germany after World War II, John J. McCloy, has written that subsequent to Tresckow's death, the police commissar who investigated the case told Fabian von Schlabrendorff that among Tresckow's personal effects were several theological books, including a volume on Catholic moral philosophy, one on Protestant ethics, several publications on the reconciliation between Catholics and Protestants, and a Bible.[104] These men and women practiced a prophetic religion, which, in the tradition of the great Hebrew prophets of an earlier time, dares to speak truth to power. They were fully aware of their journey's probable destination, but they remained resolute.[105]

Of those who were devout Christians, only their own words are capable of expressing their convictions and their testimonies of faith. After World War II, Fabian von Schlabrendorff spoke the following words about his horrible ordeal at the hands of the Gestapo:

> We all made the discovery that we could endure far more than we had ever believed possible. The two great polar forces of human emotions, love and hate, together formed a supporting structure on which we could rely when things became unbearable. Love, the positive force, included our faith in the moral worth of our actions, the knowledge that we had fought for humanity and decency, and the sense of having fulfilled a higher duty. Those among us who had never prayed learned to do so now, and discovered that in a situation such as ours prayer, and prayer alone, is capable of bringing comfort and lending almost superhuman strength. One also finds that love in the form of prayers by relatives and friends on the outside transmits currents of strength.
>
> Hate, the negative force, was just as important in sustaining us. The consuming, unqualified hatred, made up of equal parts of revulsion, contempt, and fury which we felt for the evil of Nazism, was so powerful a force that it helped us endure situations which otherwise would have been intolerable.[106]

Schlabrendorff also testified to the faith of his dear friend Hans Oster, proclaiming that he "was a man after God's own heart."[107] Oster himself wrote to his son while awaiting death, saying that he had always tried to be a "decent man," and concluded with the words "All we fear is the wrath of God."[108]

Heinrich Lehndorff, described as a "courageous East Prussian aristocrat and landowner," and being a convicted conspirator, wrote to his wife shortly before his death:

> I have always had the firm impression that you were walking by my side, and this feeling shall remain with me to my last hour ... The Christian faith and belief in a "Kingdom of Heaven" are the only help in distress. The road to it, however, seems to lead only to sorrow, and all our old habits must first be removed by force – only then can one become a "new being." In any case, I shall die in this faith without fear or dread.[109]

Carl Goerdeler was another man of deep and profound Christian faith. Like many of his compatriots, he was committed to the overthrow of the Third Reich as an "ethical imperative." Among his papers found after the collapse of the conspiracy was a statement of purpose that was to have been read to the nation after Hitler's overthrow. It read in part, "The nation's 'most urgent task' ... was to cleanse the 'much dishonored German name ... Let us scrupulously follow in all things God's commandments ... Let us do everything to heal wounded souls and alleviate suffering.'" Goerdeler and his compatriots were seeking "not political but moral regeneration, not a national but a spiritual rebirth."[110]

Peter Yorck von Wartenburg, a lawyer who became one of the most important members of the Kreisau Circle and who was one of the group of eight executed on August 8, 1944, wrote a farewell letter to his wife shortly before his death. It included the following words: "I hope my death will be accepted as an atonement for all my sins, and as an expiatory sacrifice ... By this sacrifice, our time's distance from God may be shortened by some small measure ... We want to kindle the torch of life; a sea of flames surrounds us."[111] Thus, for many, "the attempt to assassinate Hitler was a form of vicarious atonement for their earlier support of his regime."[112]

As noted, Dietrich Bonhoeffer spoke forcefully against Hitler and his so-called "movement" from the moment the Führer and his party first gained prominence. For him, the question of tyrannicide was never an issue. He had concluded well before the onset of Nazi rule that, if necessary, murder was an acceptable and moral means of purging Germany and the world of the terrible Nazi scourge. "Because Jesus took upon himself the guilt of all people," he said, "everyone who acts responsibly becomes guilty."[113] And he accepted the consequence of that guilt without reservation, even as he continued to minister to the condemned, of whom he was one. In 1948, Anglican bishop and former member of the House of Lords George Bell wrote in tribute to his late dear friend, "He was crystal clear in his convictions; and young as he was, and humble-minded as he was, he saw the truth and spoke it with a complete absence of fear." S. Payne Best, the British intelligence agent apprehended at the time of the Venlo incident in 1939, met Bonhoeffer in prison. The two became good friends. Writing after the war of his experiences, he said of his fellow prisoner, "His soul really shone in the dark desperation of our prison." He was in fact a source of inspiration and comfort to all, guard and prisoner alike.[114] Bonhoeffer's Christian faith sustained him to the end.

One of the most eloquent of all the statements made by the conspirators came from the lips of General Henning von Tresckow. When he learned that the assassination plot had failed and that the conspiracy had collapsed, he knew that he would be arrested because his complicity in the resistance and the conspiracy to kill Hitler was well documented. Fearing that he would reveal the names of other conspirators under torture, he told Fabian von Schlabrendorff "in a totally calm, collected way"[115] that he would have to commit suicide. As they parted, he spoke the following words to Schlabrendorff:

> Now they will heap abuse on us all. But I am convinced, now as much as ever, that we have done the right thing. I believe that Hitler is the arch-enemy, not only of Germany, but of the entire world. In a few hours' time I shall stand before God and answer both for my actions and the things I neglected to do. I think I can with a clear conscience stand by all I have done in the battle against Hitler. Just as God once promised Abraham that he would spare Sodom if only ten just men could be found in the city, I have reason to hope that, for our sake, he will not destroy Germany. No one among us can complain about his death, for whoever joined our ranks put on the poisoned shirt of Nessus [in Greek mythology, the fiery shirt the dying centaur Nessus tricked Hercules into wearing, which could not be removed until it had killed him]. A man's moral worth is established only at the point when he is prepared to give his life for his convictions.[116]

Shortly after making this statement and bidding farewell, Tresckow drove off toward the front line near Bialystock in what is now northeast Poland, put a rifle grenade against his cheek, and blew his head off.[117]

What may well be the ultimate irony of the resistance movement is found in the following observation of the historian Peter Hoffmann: "The conspirators who were ready to embark on a coup to save human life could be labeled as traitors; the general who sent millions to their death was 'doing his duty' and so was honourable."[118] This observation is an incisive commentary on the convoluted logic and morality of the times and of war in general. It has been said "that spiritual faith can at times withstand even the most intense political intimidation or psychological pressure."[119] Those who tried to rescue Germany from the deadly embrace of Nazism were their nation's conscience during those years of incredible darkness.

APPENDIX A

Glossary

Abwehr – The foreign and counterintelligence department of the Armed Forces Supreme Command.
Action Group Zossen – A resistance cell inside the army high command (OKW) headquarters at the town of Zossen near Berlin.
Allgemeines Heeresamt (AHA) – The General Army Office located in Berlin.
Anschluss (connection/union) – The term used to describe Nazi Germany's peaceful though forcible conquest of Austria in 1938.
Aryans – A group of people declared by Nazi doctrine to be "racially superior" to all other so-called "races" of the human family.
The Barmen Declaration – A statement written by the theologian Karl Barth defining the Articles of Faith for the members of the anti-Nazi Confessing Church.
The Bendlerstraße – The Berlin street where army headquarters was located. The term was used to designate army headquarters (also referred to as the Bendlerblock in some publications).
The Berghof – Hitler's mountaintop retreat at Berchtesgaden, in the Bavarian Alps.
Bewegung (movement) – The self-proclaimed description of the Nazi Party as a political and social "movement" rather than a mere political party.
blitzkrieg (lightning war) – A highly mechanized and fluid type of warfare that relies upon motorized panzer (armored) units combined with airpower to break through stationary enemy defenses and quickly surround them.
block – The smallest unit of the Nazi party's administrative structure throughout Germany, directed by the Blockleiter (block leader).
Bolshevik – The name given to the revolutionary faction of the Russian Social Democratic Labor Party. It became the nucleus of the Soviet Russian Communist Party.
Blutrache (blood feud or blood vengeance) – The action taken by the SS against innocent family members of those who were part of Operation Valkyrie.
The Brownshirts – The popular name for the Sturm Abteilung, or SA, which was the private army of the Nazi Party.
The Bürgerbräukeller – The name of the beer cellar in Munich where Hitler staged his "Beer Hall Putsch" in 1923.
Commissar Order – Hitler's order given to his military commanders in March 1941 declaring that the impending war against the Soviet Union would not "be fought in knightly fashion," but would be "waged with unprecedented, unmerciful, and unrelenting hardness." It was to be an ideological war of annihilation.

Glossary

court of honor – A special military court set up to pass judgment on military officers connected to the resistance. Its actual purpose was to sanction judicial murder.

the dual monarchy – The Austro-Hungarian Empire, 1867–1918.

Edelweiß Piraten (Edelweiss Pirates) – A group of German youth who resisted the Nazis.

Einsatz Barbarossa (Operation Barbarossa) – The code name for the attack on the Soviet Union on June 22, 1941.

Einsatz Walküre (Operation Valkyrie) – The code name for the assassination attempt against Hitler on July 20, 1944.

Einsatzgruppen (operations groups or task forces) – The name of the murder squads of the SS that were given the task of carrying out the racial extermination program of the Third Reich.

Eintopf (one-pot meal) – A single meal one Sunday a month described by the Nazis as a "meal of sacrifice" for the Third Reich.

Evolutionary Socialists – Majority Socialists (see Majority Socialists)

Fall Blau (Case Blue) – The code name for the resumed German offensive (1942) in the Soviet Union.

Fall Gelb (Case Yellow) – The code name for the German attack (1940) against Western Europe.

Fall Grün (Case Green) – The code name for the planned German attack (1938) against Czechoslovakia, which, as a result of the Munich Conference, never took place.

flash – The code word for the attempted bombing of Hitler's airplane on March 13, 1943.

Freikorps (free corps) – Groups of mercenary soldiers hired by the provisional government to suppress the left-wing Spartacist Rebellion in 1919.

Gau (district) – The highest-level territorial administrative unit of the Nazi Party, which divided the nation into forty-two such districts. Each Gau had a Gauleiter (district leader) who was responsible directly to Hitler.

German Christians – The name of a Nazi-inspired "church" with a corrupt "theology" based upon Nazi ideology. It was an utter failure.

The German Social Democratic Party (SPD, Sozialdemokratische Partei Deutschlands) – The political party of German socialism that originally comprised both the Revisionist and Orthodox factions.

Gestapo (Geheime Staatspolitzei, or Secret State Police) – The Nazi political police. Its purpose was to suppress all dissent.

Gewitteraktion (Thunderstorm) – A wholesale police roundup of anyone and everyone suspected of being in the opposition to the Nazis. It took place after the July 20, 1944, assassination attempt against Hitler.

Gleichschaltung (Coordination) – The program that subordinated every aspect of German life to the direction and control of the Nazi Party. It created a complete totalitarian state.

Graf – Title of lesser nobility, and translated into English as Count.

Habsburgs – The ruling family of Austria.

Hochverrat and Landesverrat – German law recognizes two types of treason, high treason, or Hochverrat, which is disloyalty to the government or head of state, and Landesverrat, or treason to the nation. Of the two types, Landesverrat is considered to be a much-worse crime.

Hohenzollerns – The ruling family of Prussia.

Kreis (circle or circuit) – An intermediate level of organization of the Nazi Party just below the Gau, or district, directed by a Kreisleiter (circle leader).

Kreisau Circle – The resistance group comprised of mostly civilians whose leaders were Helmuth James von Moltke and Peter Yorck von Wartenburg. It was named for the Moltke estate Kreisau, located in the German region of Silesia.

Kriegsmarine – The German Navy.

Kristallnacht (Crystal Night) – The "Night of Broken Glass," November 9, 1938, when the Nazis precipitated a vicious pogrom throughout Germany against Germans of the Jewish faith.

Landesverrat – *See* Hochverrat.

The Lanz Plan – A plan devised by General Hubert Lanz, a field commander of German troops in the Soviet Union, to arrest Hitler during a visit of the latter to the Eastern Front. It failed when Hitler changed his plans at the last moment.

Lebensraum (living space) – A term associated with Nazi ideology and with other extremist German nationalist groups. Germany, they declared, needed more territory to accommodate its expanding population.

Majority Socialists – The name given to those members of the German Social Democratic Party who rejected the belief that violent revolution was the only way to bring true social democracy to Germany. They believed the ballot box was more effective than the bullet in achieving their goals. This branch of socialism is also referred to as evolutionary or revisionist socialism.

The Nazi Labor Front (Deutsche Arbeitsfront, or DAF) – The Nazi-sanctioned organization that superseded the bona fide labor unions. Its purpose was to control the workers rather than to represent them and their interests.

The Nazi Party (Nationalsozialistische Deutsche Arbeiter Partei, or NSDAP) – The National Socialist German Workers Party. Its core beliefs were built upon a foundation of extremist nationalism, racism, and a crude form of Social Darwinism.

The Nero Order – The order given by Hitler in March 1945 that called for the complete destruction of the entire infrastructure of the German nation. It was never carried out.

Oberkommando der Wehrmacht (OKW) – The Supreme Command of the Armed Forces of the German military establishment.

Oberkommando des Heeres (OKH) – The Supreme Command of the Army. This organization was subordinate to the OKW.

Obrigkeitsstaat – An authoritarian state, as opposed to a democratic state.

Orthodox Socialists – Also called Revolutionary Socialists, these were people committed to the belief that violent revolution was essential to achieving a socialist society. This group formed the nucleus of what became the German Communist Party.

Glossary

Ortsgruppe – A lower-level territorial administrative unit or district of the Nazi Party, just below the Kreis and directed by the Ortsgruppenleiter (district group leader).

Overlord – The Allied code word for the cross-channel invasion of France on June 6, 1944.

Plötzensee Prison – The Berlin prison where victims of Nazi "justice" were executed.

The Polish Corridor – The strip of territory taken from Germany at the end of the Great War and given to the reconstituted state of Poland in order to give it access to the Baltic Sea. This action separated the territory of East Prussia from Germany proper.

Reichssicherheitshauptamt (Reich Security Head Office, or RSHA) – The top security office in the Third Reich. All police operations were under its purview.

Reichswehr – The official name of the German military establishment, 1919–1935.

replacement army – Also known as the reserve army and home army, it was created to protect the Reich against internal disorder. The anti-Nazi conspirators had hoped to use it as an instrument for their planned coup against the Third Reich.

Revisionist Socialists – Majority Socialists (see Majority Socialists)

Revolutionary Socialists – Orthodox Socialists (see Orthodox Socialists)

Rote Kapelle (Red Orchestra) – A small, loosely connected Marxist-oriented group of anti-Nazis who engaged in various resistance activities.

Schutzstaffel (protection unit/staff or SS, Security Staff) – Originally Hitler's bodyguard, the SS ultimately became a sprawling organization of great complexity. The first of its two main divisions was the Allgemeine (General) SS. It was the main SS administrative division and encompassed the entire SS police apparatus. It also became the instrument of fulfilling Nazi racial policies, including the entire concentration/death camp system. The second major division was the Waffen SS, which was its military branch, consisting of combat units that were separate from and often in competition with the regular Wehrmacht, though ostensibly under overall Wehrmacht command.

***Das Schwarze Korps* (the Black Corps)** – The official publication of the SS.

Sicherheitsdienst (security service, or SD) – The intelligence branch of the SS. Its primary function, according to Heinrich Himmler, was to "investigate crimes against Nazi ideology."[1] Hence, it essentially was a spy agency conducting surveillance activities throughout Germany and the conquered lands.

Sicherheitspolizei (SiPo, security police) – A Nazi police organization that combined the Gestapo and the Kripo (Kriminalpolitzei, or criminal police).

Sitzkrieg – The "phony war," from September 1939 to April 1940, the period between the defeat of Poland and the invasion of Norway in which no significant military activity took place.

The Social Democratic Party in Exile (Die Sozialdemokratische Partei Deutschlands im Exil, SOPADE) – A group of SPD leaders who fled Germany after the Nazis came into power. Subsequently they received secret reports from members who remained in Germany. These documents were subsequently published under the title "Reports on Germany."

Spartakus Rebellion – A completely failed uprising in early 1919 that was led by the Spartakus Bund (Spartacist League), a revolutionary socialist group.

Stahlhelm (Steel Helmet) – An organization of Great War veterans with an ultranationalist ideology.

Studie Oster – A plan developed by Hans Oster for a coup d'état at the time of the Munich Conference in 1938.

Sturm Abteilung (SA) – *See* the Brownshirts.

Sudetenland – The westernmost region of Bohemia, which had been inhabited by both Bohemians and Germans for centuries. It became the cause célèbre for Hitler's planned strike against Czechoslovakia in 1938.

The Third Reich – Nazi Germany, 1933–1945. The term came from the title of a book written by the author Arthur Moeller van den Bruck in 1923. The First Reich was the medieval Holy Roman Empire, and the second was Bismarck's Prussian-dominated Deutsches Reich, 1871–1918.

The Treaty of Versailles – The peace treaty between Germany and the Allied powers (except the United States) that officially ended the Great War.

Volksgemeinschaft (people's community) – A term that the Nazis used to denote a "national community" based upon "purity of blood and race."[2] The members of this "community" were the Volksgenossen, that is, the "racial comrades." All others were excluded from the "community."

Wehrmacht – The official name of the combined German military establishment, army, navy, and air force, from 1935 to 1945.

Weltmacht oder Vernichtung (World Power or Destruction) – The term for Hitler's worldview of Germany. Either Germany would be the dominant world power or it would suffer complete destruction.

Weserübung (Weser Exercise) – The code name for the Nazi invasion (1940) of Denmark and Norway.

Wolfschanze – The name given to Hitler's headquarters at Rastenburg in East Prussia.

Zell – The administrative territorial unit (cell) of the Nazi Party just below the Ortsgruppe, directed by the Zellenleiter (cell leader).

APPENDIX B

Dramatis Personae

KARL BARTH was a Swiss theologian and professor at Bonn University. He was active in the Confessing Church and authored the Barmen Declaration. The Nazis expelled him from Germany.

LUDWIG BECK was a career military officer and was chief of the general staff, 1935–38. He became a major figure in the resistance.

JOHANNES BLASKOWITZ commanded the German occupation forces in Poland and became a severe critic of the SS operations.

WERNER VON BLOMBERG was minister of defense in 1933 and subsequently was named minister of war and commander in chief of the Wehrmacht. He opposed Hitler's war plans, and was forced to retire in 1938. The excuse for his dismissal was his marriage to a woman of ill repute.

FEDOR VON BOCK served as a field marshal in the German Army. His relations with Hitler were stormy. Although angered and disgusted by Nazi racist policies, he never joined the resistance. Resistance leader Henning von Tresckow was his nephew.

DIETRICH BONHOEFFER was a clergyman active in the resistance. He was a founder of the Confessing Church and became a courier and double agent for the Abwehr.

WALTHER VON BRAUCHITSCH was commander in chief of the army. He was critical of Hitler but refused to participate in the resistance.

EBERHARD VON BREITENBUCH was an officer on the staff of Army Group Center and became adjutant to Field Marshal Ernst Busch. Intending to shoot Hitler while attending a conference at Hitler's mountaintop retreat in the Bavarian Alps, he was prevented from entering the conference room by an SS guard.

ERNST BUSCH was a field marshal in the Wehrmacht. He replaced Hans Günther von Kluge as commander of Army Group Center after Kluge was injured in an automobile accident. Busch was totally dedicated and committed to Hitler.

AXEL FREIHERR VON DEM BUSSCHE-STREITHORST was an army captain who initially was an enthusiastic supporter of the Nazis. He became completely disillusioned, however, and agreed to become a suicide bomber in an attempt to assassinate Hitler, but he was severely wounded before he could act.

WILHELM CANARIS was chief of the Abwehr and made it an integral part of the resistance. He was one of the most important members of the resistance.

ALFRED DELP was a Jesuit priest who was a member of the Kreisau Circle.

Traitors or Patriots?

HANS VON DOHNÁNYI was a lawyer and jurist attached to the Abwehr. He was an active anti-Nazi from the beginning of Nazi rule and played an active part in the Oster conspiracy of 1938. He was the brother-in-law of theologian Dietrich Bonhoeffer.

GEORG ELSER was a clockmaker, cabinetmaker, and carpenter. He despised the Nazis and plotted to kill Hitler with a bomb at a 1939 Nazi Party meeting in Munich. He came within a hair's breadth of success.

ERICH FELLGIEBEL was a career military officer and head of the Army Signal Corps. He was a key member of Stauffenberg's conspiracy to kill Hitler on July 20, 1944.

ROLAND FREISLER was a notorious Nazi judge of the "People's Court" who presided over the so-called "trials" of several resistance leaders. He was a thoroughly loathsome man.

WERNER VON FRITSCH, an army general, was dismissed as chief of the army command as a result of a trumped-up charge of homosexuality because he had opposed Hitler's expansionist foreign policy plans in the late 1930s.

FRIEDRICH FROMM was commander of the reserve army and a thoroughgoing opportunist. He played a duplicitous role in the resistance movement and ordered the execution of Stauffenberg, Olbricht, and others after the July 20, 1944, bomb plot. He himself was arrested and ultimately executed by the Nazis.

CLEMENS AUGUST VON GALEN was the Roman Catholic bishop of Münster. Initially a supporter of the Nazis, he ultimately became an ardent opponent.

BARON RUDOLPH-CHRISTOPH VON GERSDORFF was an intelligence officer posted to Army Group Center who made an unsuccessful attempt to assassinate Hitler as a suicide bomber.

KURT GERSTEIN tried to fight Nazism "from the inside." He joined the SS in order to expose its murderous activities, but he failed in the attempt.

EUGEN GERSTENMAIER, a Protestant theologian, was opposed to the pro-Nazi "German Christian" movement. He was active in the Kreisau Circle and served in the West German Bundestag as a member of the Christian Democratic Union after World War II.

HANS BERNDT GISEVIUS, a lawyer, played an active role in the Oster conspiracy of 1938.

JOSEPH PAUL GOEBBELS, the notorious Nazi minister of propaganda, played an important part in destroying Operation Valkyrie on July 20, 1944.

CARL GOERDELER was mayor of Leipzig and became an active member of the resistance as part of the Beck–Goerdeler group.

HERMANN GÖRING, one of the top Nazis, joined the party in the early 1920s. A flier in the Great War, he became commander of the Nazi air force, the Luftwaffe.

HELMUTH GROSCURTH, a career military officer, played a significant role in the Oster conspiracy of 1938.

HANS BERND VON HAEFTEN, a lawyer, diplomat, and member of the Confessing Church, was a member of the Kreisau Circle and an important contact person for Stauffenberg in the foreign office.

WERNER VON HAEFTEN, brother of Hans Bernd von Haeften, became aide-de-camp of Stauffenberg and accompanied him to Rastenburg on July 20, 1944.

Dramatis Personae

FRANZ HALDER was chief of the general staff, 1938–1942. He despised Hitler and the Nazis but lacked the personal qualities to lead a coup against them.

KURT VON HAMMERSTEIN-EQUORD was a career military officer and an outspoken opponent of the Nazis from the beginning of the Third Reich.

ARVID HARNACK AND MILDRED HARNACK-FISH were husband and wife members of the Marxist-oriented resistance group the Rote Kapelle.

PAUL VON HASE, army general and member of the resistance, was commander of the Berlin military district and participated in Operation Valkyrie.

ULRICH VON HASSELL, a career diplomat and ardent anti-Nazi, was an active member of the resistance, with close ties to various resistance leaders. His diaries are an important primary source of information about the resistance.

FRIEDRICH WILHELM HEINZ had been associated with various right-wing extremist groups and was an early member of the Nazi Party. He became disillusioned with the Nazis and participated in the Oster conspiracy of 1938.

WOLF HEINRICH GRAF VON HELLDORF was a former Nazi and SA (Nazi Party Army) member who became disillusioned with the Nazis and joined the resistance.

HEINRICH HIMMLER was one of the top Nazis. He was head of the SS and Gestapo and presided over the entire Nazi apparatus of death. He was a sadistic fanatic totally dedicated to the Nazi ideology.

PAUL VON HINDENBURG was a highly revered military leader of the Great War who became the second and last president of the Weimar Republic.

FRANZ JÄGERSTÄTTER was a deeply religious Austrian peasant farmer who despised the Nazis and all they stood for. He paid with his life for his refusal to serve in the German Army.

GUSTAV VON KAHR was minister-president of Bavaria at the end of the Great War; he was sympathetic to right-wing political extremism. Adolf Hitler and his storm troopers hijacked a rally that he was holding at the Bürgerbräukeller beer cellar in Munich on the night of November 8–9, 1923, that led to the Beer Hall Putsch and Hitler's arrest.

JAKOB KAISER was a Catholic trade union member and a leader of the Christian labor movement in the Weimar Republic. He became an active participant in the resistance and served as adviser to Carl Goerdeler.

WILHELM KEITEL was a career military officer and became chief of the OKW (Supreme Command of the Armed Forces). An ardent admirer of Hitler, he was completely subservient to the Führer.

EWALD VON KLEIST-SCHMENZIN was a lawyer and early opponent of the Nazis. He was a member of the Beck–Goerdeler group.

EWALD HEINRICH VON KLEIST-SCHMENZIN, the son of Ewald von Kleist-Schmenzin, agreed to become a suicide bomber in an assassination attempt against Hitler. The plot was aborted, however.

HANS GÜNTHER VON KLUGE was a field marshal in the German Army. He held an intense dislike for Hitler and was sympathetic to the resistance but could never make a commitment to join it.

Traitors or Patriots?

THEO AND ERICH KORDT were brothers. Lawyers and diplomats, they were ardent anti-Nazis and used their foreign contacts to secure support for the resistance, but they were ultimately foiled in this endeavor.

JULIUS LEBER was a politician and member of the Social Democratic Party, and was active in the resistance, especially the Kreisau Circle.

WILHELM LEUSCHNER, a union leader and member of the Social Democratic Party, was a committed anti-Nazi and an active participant in the resistance.

FRANZ MARIE LIEDIG, a career military officer, was an active member of the resistance group centered in the Abwehr. He was a close friend and associate of Hans Oster.

WALTER MODEL was a field marshal in the German Army and a Hitler loyalist from beginning to end.

HELMUTH JAMES VON MOLTKE, a lawyer, was a leader of the Kreisau Circle, which was named for his estate in Silesia, where meetings were occasionally held.

LUDWIG MÜLLER was appointed Reich bishop of the Nazi-controlled pseudoreligious group known as the German Christians.

MARTIN NIEMÖLLER was a clergyman and an outspoken opponent and critic of Hitler and the Nazis. He was a cofounder of the Confessing Church.

FRIEDRICH OLBRICHT was a career military officer. As deputy commander of the reserve army, he worked closely with Stauffenberg and Tresckow in planning Operation Valkyrie.

HANS OSTER was chief of staff of the Abwehr and the leader of the Oster conspiracy of 1938. He despised the Nazis and was a driving force in the resistance.

FRIEDRICH PAULUS was commander of the German Sixth Army, which surrendered at Stalingrad.

JOHANNES POPITZ was a jurist and Prussian minister of finance, and was active in the civilian resistance.

WALTER VON REICHENAU was often called the "Nazi general," but he became increasingly disillusioned with Hitler.

ADOLF REICHWEIN was an educator with socialist leanings. He became a member of the Kreisau Circle.

ERNST REMER was a career army officer, a dedicated Nazi, and a key figure in thwarting Operation Valkyrie on July 20, 1944.

JOACHIM VON RIBBENTROP was a Nazi diplomat. He was the coarchitect of the Molotov–Ribbentrop Treaty between Germany and the Soviet Union, which opened the door to World War II.

ALFRED ROSENBERG was the "official philosopher" of Nazism. As minister for the Eastern Occupied Territories, he was responsible for implementing Nazi racial policies.

GIJSBERTUS SAS was military attaché in the Dutch Embassy in Berlin and a close friend of Hans Oster. He was the man to whom Oster gave information of Hitler's intention to invade the Netherlands.

HJALMAR SCHACHT was a financier and economics expert. As minister of economics, he originally was a supporter of Hitler, but soon he became disillusioned with

Dramatis Personae

the Nazis. Although sympathetic to the resistance, he did not become an active participant.

FABIAN VON SCHLABRENDORFF was a lawyer and adjutant to Henning von Tresckow and a close friend of Tresckow and Hans Oster. A passionate anti-Nazi, he was deeply involved in the resistance.

HANS AND SOPHIE SCHOLL were brother and sister. As university students, they created the White Rose resistance movement, which printed and disseminated anti-Nazi literature throughout Germany and Austria.

FRITZ-DIETLOF VON DER SCHULENBURG, a lawyer, joined the Nazi Party but quickly grew disillusioned and became active in the resistance, especially the Kreisau Circle.

ERICH SCHULTZE was a close friend and associate of Hans Oster. The two were coconspirators in the Abwehr as part of the resistance.

HARRO SCHULZE-BOYSEN was a member of the Marxist-oriented anti-Nazi Rote Kapelle group.

KURT VON SCHUSCHNIGG was Austrian chancellor at the time of the Anschluss in 1938.

HANNA SOLF was the leader of the Solf Circle, a group of dissenters who opposed Nazism.

ALBERT SPEER, an architect, was a confidant of Hitler who became minister of armaments and war production in the Third Reich.

CLAUS SCHENK VON STAUFFENBERG was the leader of Operation Valkyrie. He placed the bomb at Hitler's headquarters in East Prussia.

KARL-HEINRICH VON STÜLPNAGEL, a career army officer, was military governor of occupied France and an active participant in the 1944 bomb plot (Operation Valkyrie) to kill Hitler.

GEORG THOMAS was director of the War Economy Department of the War Ministry and an early opponent of Hitler and the Nazis.

HENNING VON TRESCKOW, a career military officer, initially supported Hitler but quickly changed his mind and became one of the most determined and dedicated members of the resistance.

ADAM VON TROTT ZU SOLZ, a lawyer, career diplomat, and foreign policy expert, was closely associated with the Kreisau Circle. He tried without success to secure support for the resistance outside Germany.

PETER YORCK VON WARTENBURG, a lawyer, was one of the key figures in the Kreisau Circle. He has been described as its "heart."

ERNST VON WEIZSÄCKER, state secretary for foreign affairs, was on the fringes of the resistance movement. Though not an active member of the resistance, he was sympathetic to the movement and cooperated wherever he could.

ERWIN VON WITZLEBEN, a field marshal in the German Army, was a determined opponent of the Nazis and participated in several coup attempts. He was active in the resistance from beginning to end.

APPENDIX C

The Sources of Nazi Racism

The centerpiece of the Nazi ideology is its virulent racism, and this in turn raises the question of its source. The anti-Semitism that was a significant part of European racism of the early twentieth century was deeply embedded in the long history of Western civilization and could be found in every European nation. It certainly was not unique to Germany.

By the twentieth century, a new racial "science" had made its appearance in the Western world, based upon Charles Darwin's biological theory of evolution. Darwin himself used the phrase "natural selection" to explain his theory. Species of plant and animal life, he said, adapt to a changing environment in the natural world. Natural selection is "the survival process governing most living things in a world of limited resources and changing environments."[1]

Very quickly, this biological theory of natural selection was applied to the human social condition. Its supporters presented it as a means of curing the ills that beset society, such as poverty and crime. The remedy to these problems, it was argued, was the creation of a social organization that allows the "best" elements of society to thrive and prosper. The "undesirables" and the "unfit" should simply be left to die off. This process would allow human society to achieve ultimate perfection. The primary architect of this "Social Darwinism" was the English philosopher Herbert Spencer. He is closely associated with the term "survival of the fittest." The "fittest" will thrive and the "unfit" will be left to die. This, he said, is the only way to achieve true human progress. Thus, "in the struggle to survive in a harsh world, many humans were not only less worthy, many were actually destined to wither away as a rite of progress. To preserve the weak and the needy was, in essence, an unnatural act." On the other hand, selective breeding could produce "a superlative [human] species of grace and quality."[2]

Spencer began promulgating his work in the mid-nineteenth century. Then, in 1869, a book entitled *Hereditary Genius* was published, written by one Francis Galton, a cousin of Darwin and a mathematician. He agreed with Spencer that emotional, mental, and creative qualities were like physical features. He believed that inheritance was the sole determinant of a person's social behavior. A criminal in one's ancestry automatically predisposed that person to a life of criminality. A family living in poverty inevitably condemned its descendants to permanent penury. Galton then carried Social Darwinism one step further by mathematizing it. He and others produced genealogical statistics to support these theories, and then quantified the genetic information they contained. Thus was born the "science" of eugenics.

The Sources of Nazi Racism

Skeptics in Great Britain questioned the validity of eugenics as a legitimate science, and the movement did not yet take root in England. However, eugenics became a pervasive force in the United States in the first half of the twentieth century. Ultimately, American eugenics became grist for the Nazi death mill.

American eugenicists carried Galton's concepts far beyond anything that Galton himself had envisioned. Even he realized that his theories were subject to serious limitations, and commented that "musings about 'improved breeds' of the human race were still nothing more than 'speculations on the theoretical possibility.'"[3] Such constraints were not found in the United States. "In America, eugenics would become more than abstract philosophy; it would become an obsession for policymakers." It ultimately degenerated into "a ruthless campaign to destroy all those deemed inadequate."[4] Ultimately, the United States became the leader in a worldwide eugenic crusade to abolish all human inferiority as defined by the eugenicists.

Racism has been part of the American experience from its origins. Conflict between the European settlers and the Native Americans was soon followed by the importation of Africans as slaves for the rapidly growing European American colonies. Very quickly racial categories were established, and prohibitions against interracial marriage and sexual contact between whites and the two "lesser" groups became an integral part of the dominant culture of colonial America. All sorts of discriminatory actions were visited upon these and other ethnic groups as they settled into what soon became the United States of America. The existence of slavery only exacerbated the problem of American racism.

By the early twentieth century, eugenics had migrated to the United States, where it found very fertile soil and a very receptive audience. Several national eugenics organizations were created, including the American Eugenics Society, founded in 1922, described as "the key advocacy and propaganda wing of the [eugenics] movement."[5] Two others were the Eugenics Research Association and the Eugenics Record Office. Founded in 1913,[6] the Eugenics Research Association was dedicated to the promotion of eugenics on a broad base that included research, propaganda, and financing. The Eugenics Record Office was created in 1910 "to quietly register the genetic backgrounds of all Americans, separating the defective strains from the desired lineages."[7] The term "quietly" has significance, because many within the United States, as well as in Great Britain, were adamantly opposed to the eugenics movement. Nonetheless, the subject was discussed openly in both countries.

By 1920, the United States was the epicenter of the international eugenics movement. Moreover, American eugenicists had a particularly malign influence on the course of the eugenics movement. "In America, eugenics would become more than an abstract philosophy; it would become an obsession for policymakers [and] ... would become nothing less than a worldwide eugenic crusade to abolish all human inferiority."[8] It eventually became a spurious program of alleged scientific racial engineering through the practice of "racial hygiene."

The growth of the worldwide eugenics program coincided with another especially pernicious movement that came of age at the end of the nineteenth century; its name was nationalism. Together, eugenics and nationalism produced a particularly toxic witch's brew that became a primary source of the catastrophic twentieth-century wars. Nationalism became a religion. It elevated a political entity – the nation – to the status of a deity to be venerated and worshiped; and eugenics demanded racial purity for this new political entity. Those considered "unfit," "undesirable," or "inferior" in racial quality were to be excluded from the national community. The Nazi Volksgemeinschaft, or "people's community," remains the classic example of such a society. German eugenicists began to conflate their eugenics with nationalism, providing the groundwork for Hitler's future policies, both foreign and domestic.

Two types of eugenics were introduced into this venomous atmosphere, "negative" and "positive." The first was a program designed to eliminate the defective gene pool through the sterilization of the inferior segments of society. Initially, sterilization was the major instrument of negative eugenics. From 1900 to 1970, some seventy thousand American citizens – most of them women – were forcibly sterilized in an attempt to eventually eliminate all those deemed unfit to procreate. They were declared to be "essentially sub-human."[9] American eugenicists debated the desirability of euthanasia, possibly through the use of "lethal chambers" as a means of eliminating the unfit.[10] Later, the Nazis would declare euthanasia to be the elimination of "life unworthy of life." British eugenicists also debated this solution. The British eugenics movement reentered the picture by the second decade of the twentieth century and adopted many of the extremist views held by Americans.[11]

As the name implies, positive eugenics represented an attempt to create a superrace, or to use the Nazi term, "master race." The eugenicists from this camp – including several Americans – believed in the possibility of creating a superior race through selective breeding. It is said of the American eugenicists that they "were convinced they could forcibly reshape humanity in their own image."[12]

By the early twentieth century, eugenicists from several countries began to construct mathematical models for measuring intelligence. They produced tests for this purpose, including two that became a standard in the United States, the intelligence quotient (IQ) and the Scholastic Aptitude Test (SAT). These tests failed to distinguish between intelligence and ignorance, and discounted cultural, social, and economic differences among the test-takers. The tests were biased in favor of the white, upper-middle-class stratum of society, the same stratum from which the eugenicists themselves were drawn. Inevitably, those from the disadvantaged socioeconomic classes did very poorly on the tests. African Americans, for example, who were consistently denied even the rudiments of a basic education, could not be expected to perform well. The tests have been described as "vehicles for cultural exclusion." For these reasons, they were severely criticized by "many thinking people of the period."[13] Nonetheless, the eugenicists who administered these tests totally ignored their critics and persisted in their efforts to create a superrace.

Eugenicists considered geographical differences as well. A distinction was noted between those whose families were from the Alpine and Mediterranean regions of Europe, and the groups from the Nordic regions. One of the eugenicists responsible for this testing program said, "The conclusion is that our test results indicate a genuine intellectual superiority of the Nordic group over the Alpine and Mediterranean groups."[14] This "discovery" was well received by German eugenicists, who had become a significant part of the international eugenics community by the second decade of the twentieth century.

The key to the Nazis' obsession with race and eugenics was Adolf Hitler. His racist ideology had been formed early in his life, especially during his years as a youth in Vienna, from 1907 to 1913. While there, this impressionable and emotionally unstable young man absorbed the violent racism that was part of fin de siècle Vienna. Slavs and Jews were singled out as primary threats to the racial health of the Aryans – Hitler's term for the Nordic peoples. His ultimate goal was the creation of a master race (Herrenvolk), superior in every way to the lesser races (Untermenschen). In Hitler's world, the foundations of the master race would be the Aryans. The Untermenschen would have to be eliminated in the most expeditious manner possible.

Hitler became fixated on the idea of life as a struggle. In his political testament, *Mein Kampf*, which was published after he had achieved political notoriety, he declared, "The idea of struggle is as old as life itself, for life is only preserved because other living things perish through struggle ... It is not by the principles of humanity that man lives or is able to preserve himself above the animal world, but solely by means of the most brutal struggle ... If you do not fight for life, then life will never be won."[15] These two concepts – racism and struggle – remained at the heart of the Nazi Weltanschauung from beginning to end.

Hitler's ill-fated attempt to stage a coup d'état – or putsch – against the Weimar Republic earned him a five-year prison sentence in 1924, for which he actually served a scant nine months. He put those months to purposeful use. While incarcerated in Landsberg Prison near Munich under very amiable conditions, he dictated his political testament to his faithful lapdog Rudolf Hess. He also read voraciously, not for edification, understanding, or knowledge, but for confirmation of his own prejudices. Much of his reading was devoted to the works of the German eugenicists, who themselves had been greatly influenced by the Americans. According to Edwin Black, "The intellectual outlines of the eugenics Hitler adopted in 1924 were strictly American."[16] In fact, German eugenicists adopted the American eugenics model almost wholesale, including "biological courts, forced sterilization, detention for the socially inadequate, [and] debates on euthanasia."[17] In the early 1930s, the president of the American Eugenics Society, Leon Whitney, received a letter of commendation from Hitler, who by then had become a major figure in German domestic politics, though he was not yet in control of Germany. Hitler also wrote a fan letter to American geneticist Madison Grant, author of a book condemning what Grant called "a sentimental belief in the sanctity of human life." Hitler referred to the book as "his Bible." Additionally, he was especially attracted to the work of the American eugenicists because of their desire to create a "pure" and "superior" Nordic race, an idea that became an integral part of his Weltanschauung.[18]

American eugenicists maintained regular contact with their German counterparts, including Hitler himself, and they proudly served as mentors to the Nazis. As early as 1924, the eugenicists of the two nations came to be viewed as equal partners in their search for eugenic perfection. American eugenicists made a significant contribution to Nazi "racial science," and the American eugenics program effectively became the model for the Nazi Volksgemeinschaft, as the Nazis eventually put American theories into practice. Many American eugenicists are said to have considered Hitler as their genetic hero.[19]

The American eugenics movement received financial support from various corporate foundations. Three of the most prominent were the Rockefeller Foundation, the Carnegie Institution, and the E. H. Harriman Foundation. These institutions also were benefactors to eugenics activities abroad, including Germany. Without such funding, the eugenics movement might never have gained the prominence to thrive on American soil.[20] Additionally, public figures such as former secretary of state Elihu Root became associated with the American eugenics movement, giving it a degree of legitimacy it otherwise might not have had. Interestingly, although inventor Alexander Graham Bell's name became associated with the eugenics movement, he had significant reservations about it.[21]

Eugenics also achieved a high degree of academic respectability in the early twentieth century. Prestigious universities in the United States and Europe, together with well-regarded scholars in medicine and the sciences, were party to the burgeoning field.[22] Academic centers such as Harvard University, the University of Chicago, Stanford University, New York University, Yale University, and the University of California, Berkeley, adopted a eugenics curriculum in one form or other. "Eugenics rocketed through academia, becoming an institution virtually overnight." Northwestern University was referred to as "a hotbed of radical eugenic thought."[23] Several leaders of the American Eugenics Society, the Eugenics Research Association, and the Eugenics Record Office, persisted in their support of Nazi Germany and its racial policies,[24] even as anti-Semitic violence in Germany, and German military aggression against its neighbors, increased in ferocity in the late 1930s.

Nevertheless, opposition to eugenics within the United States remained constant and grew with time, especially as its ramifications became better understood and its dark side became more evident. As early as 1924, well before the advent of the Nazi state, some of its leaders were derided, satirized, and mocked by opinion leaders throughout the country.[25] By the late 1930s, the true nature of Nazism and its extremist racism was becoming increasingly evident, prompting more and more eugenicists to reconsider their association with the Third Reich. In addition, support from corporate philanthropic foundations withered. The Rockefeller Foundation, for example, began to reject any research projects associated with the term *eugenics*, including genealogical studies.[26] By the World War II years, American eugenicists – with some notable exceptions – began to realize the logical consequences of their dalliance with Nazi racism and were repelled and appalled by what they saw. By the end of the war, eugenics was in full retreat and ultimately became completely discredited as a science.

In the end, it all came to nothing. Eugenics was simple bigotry, masquerading as "race science," and was unmasked as such.[27] The emperor had no clothes. And the

Nazis, who were the most active perpetrators of this "science," produced a gruesome but accurate legacy of eugenics practiced on a massive scale. It must be remembered, however, that the United States of America was the prototype for the creation of the Nazi eugenics/racial system.

Thus, to a significant degree, the United States, through its own eugenics organizations and programs, together with its private financial institutions, gave substantial support and a significant degree of legitimacy to Nazi racism. American eugenicists were among the most important supporters of Nazi racist policies. They in fact aided and abetted the creation of the Nazi racist state. This suggests – indeed demonstrates – that evil has no respect for national boundaries.

Bibliographic Note: This essay is a brief summation of a brilliant and comprehensive history of the eugenics movement in the United States written by Edwin Black, an award-winning *New York Times* best-selling investigative writer. The book, entitled *War Against the Weak: Eugenics and America's Campaign to Create a Master Race*, was published by the Dialog Press, Washington, DC. The second paperback edition was printed in 2012.

Notes

Chapter 1

1. For a detailed account of this episode, see Roger Moorhouse, chapter 2, in *Killing Hitler* (New York: Bantam Dell, 2006).
2. Anton Gill wrote, in *An Honourable Defeat* (New York: Henry Holt, 1994), pp. 130–31, that Himmler tried to connect Elser with either the Black Front or the British Secret Service. Peter Hoffmann, *The History of the German Resistance* (Cambridge, MA: MIT Press, 1979), p. 30, makes a brief reference to Otto Strasser and the Black Front. He refers to Strasser as "one of Hitler's most dangerous adversaries in the 1930s."
3. Ian Kershaw, *Hitler, 1936–1945: Nemesis* (New York: W. W. Norton, 2000), pp. 271–75.
4. Jean-Denis G.G. LePage, *An Illustrated Dictionary of the Third Reich* (Jefferson, North Carolina, McFarland & Company, Inc., Publishers, 2014), p 41.
5. Claus Christian Malzahn, "A German Hero: The Carpenter Elser versus the Führer Hitler," *Spiegel Online*, November 8, 2005, http://www.spiegel.de/internationa l/a-german-hero-the-carpenter-elser-versus-the-fuehrer-hitler-a-383792.html.
6. Kershaw, p. 272.
7. Ibid., p. 129.
8. Ibid., p. 128.
9. Ibid., p. 274. For details of Elser's life during this time, see Helmut G. Haasis, *Bombing Hitler: The Story of the Man Who Almost Assassinated the Führer* (New York: Skyhorse Publishing, 2013), esp. chapter 16, "The Preparations," and esp. p. 158.
10. Mike Dash, "One Man Against Tyranny," *Smithsonian Magazine*, August 18, 2001, https://www.smithsonianmag.com/history/one-man-against-tyranny-53850110/.
11. Malzahn; Kershaw, p. 274.
12. Gill, pp. 130–31.
13. Ibid., p. 131.
14. Martin Gilbert, *The First World War: A Complete History* (New York: Henry Holt, 1994), p. xvi; Denis Dzidic, Marija Ristic, Milka Domanovic, Josip Ivanovic, Edona Peci, and Sinisa Jakov Marusic, "Gavrilo Princip: Hero or Villain?," *Guardian*, May 6, 2014, https://www.theguardian.com/world/2014/may/06/gavrilo-princip-hero-villain-first-world-war-balkan-history.
15. Ferdinand Schlingensiepen, *Dietrich Bonhoeffer, 1906–1945: Martyr, Thinker, Man of Resistance* (London: T & T Clark International, 2010), pp. 125–26, 237.

Notes

16. Theodore S. Hamerow, *On The Road to the Wolf's Lair: German Resistance to Hitler* (Cambridge, MA: Belknap Press of Harvard University Press, 1997), p. 263.
17. Schlingensiepen, p. 245.
18. Ibid., p. 50. Georg Elser shared similar convictions. He believed that by murdering Hitler, he would be "doing good." See Haasis, p. 152.
19. Gordon A. Craig, *Europe Since 1815* (New York: Holt, Rinehart, and Winston, 1961), p. 534.
20. Gordon A. Craig, *Germany, 1866–1945* (New York: Oxford University Press, 1978), p. 402.
21. H. W. Koch, *A Constitutional History of Germany* (London: Longman Group, 1984), p. 271.
22. Gordon A. Craig, *Germany, 1866–1945*, p. 450.
23. Joachim Fest, *Plotting Hitler's Death: The Story of the German Resistance, 1933–1945* (New York: Metropolitan Books, Henry Holt, 1996), p. 12.
24. Eric D. Weitz, *Weimar Germany: Promise and Tragedy* (Princeton: Princeton University Press, 2007), p. 2.
25. Ibid., p. 252.
26. Ian Kershaw, *Hitler, 1889–1936: Hubris* (New York: W. W. Norton, 1999), p. 171; also see page 138, wherein Kershaw describes Munich as "a major centre of anti-government nationalist agitation" while the war was still raging. For Kahr's relationship with Hitler, see Michael Burleigh, *The Third Reich: A New History* (New York: Hill and Wang, 2000), p. 59; Joachim Fest, *Hitler* (New York: Harcourt Brace Jovanovich, 1974), p. 175; Richard J. Evans, *The Coming of the Third Reich* (New York: Penguin, 2004), pp. 189–90; Alan Bullock, *Hitler: A Study in Tyranny*, rev. ed. (New York: Harper and Row, 1962), p. 103.
27. Bullock, p. 103; Kershaw, *Hitler, 1889–1936: Hubris*, p. 159.
28. This plan was based on the successful coup that Benito Mussolini had staged in Italy the previous year.
29. Fest, *Plotting*, p. 11.
30. Evans, p. 236.
31. Kershaw, *Hitler: 1889–1936: Hubris*, pp. 369–70, 374–75, 386–91; Koch, p. 386.
32. Claudia Koonz, *The Nazi Conscience* (Cambridge, MA: Belknap Press of Harvard University Press, 2003), p. 29.
33. Evans, p. 307.
34. Ibid., p. 308.
35. Kershaw, *Hitler, 1889–1936: Hubris*, p. 377.
36. Ibid., p. 377.
37. Hamerow, pp. 90–91.
38. Fest, *Plotting*, pp. 20–21.
39. Evans, p. 339.
40. Fest, *Plotting*, p. 20.
41. Gordon A. Craig, *Europe Since 1815*, p. 636; Fest, *Plotting*, p. 11.
42. Sebastian Haffner, *Defying Hitler: A Memoir*, rev. ed. (London: Phoenix, 2003), p. 106.

43. Ibid., p. 162.
44. Fest, *Plotting*, p. 201.
45. Paul Bonart, *But We Said "No": Voices from the German Underground* (San Francisco: Mark Backman Productions, 2007), pp. 32–33. Bonart subsequently explained that he and his friend were able to surreptitiously take two printed but unmarked ballots from a stack lying on the entrance counter. They then switched these ballots for their ostentatiously marked "yes" ballots, placed them in the envelopes provided to them, and gave them to an SA man standing nearby.
46. Koch, p. 308.

Chapter 2

1. Robert Gellately, *Backing Hitler: Consent and Coercion in Nazi Germany* (Oxford: Oxford University Press, 2001), pp. 13, 48–49.
2. The term "conspiracy" refers to activities directed to overthrowing the Nazis as well. The two terms "dissent" and "resistance" will be used interchangeably in *Traitors or Patriots?* See Detlev J. K. Peukert, *Inside Nazi Germany: Conformity, Opposition, and Racism in Everyday Life* (New Haven, CT: Yale University Press, 1987), p. 119.
3. Michael Burleigh, *The Third Reich: A New History* (New York: Hill and Wang, 2000), p. 153.
4. Gellately, p. 13.
5. Richard J. Evans, *The Coming of the Third Reich* (New York: Penguin, 2004), p. 390.
6. Rudolf Steiner, "My Life in Germany," Houghton Library, bMS Ger 91 (227), 99–101, quoted in Claudia Koonz, *The Nazi Conscience* (Cambridge, MA: Belknap Press of Harvard University Press, 2003), pp. 31, 75.
7. Koonz, pp. 74, 75.
8. Theodore S. Hamerow, *On the Road to the Wolf's Lair: German Resistance to Hitler* (Cambridge, MA: Belknap Press of Harvard University Press, 1997), p. 217.
9. Sebastian Haffner, *Defying Hitler: A Memoir*, rev. ed. (London: Phoenix, 2003), p. 165; Roger Moorhouse, *Killing Hitler* (New York: Bantam Dell, 2006), p. 57.
10. Richard J. Evans, *The Third Reich in Power* (New York: Penguin, 2005), p. 16; also see Eric D. Weitz, *Weimar Germany: Promise and Tragedy* (Princeton: Princeton University Press, 2007), pp. 194–205.
11. Evans, *The Third Reich in Power*, p. 237; Joachim Fest, *Plotting Hitler's Death: The Story of the German Resistance, 1933–1945* (New York: Metropolitan Books, Henry Holt, 1996), p. 48.
12. Burleigh, p. 665.
13. Karl Dietrich Bracher, *The German Dictatorship: The Origins, Structure, and Effects of National Socialism* (New York: Praeger, 1970), p. 253; Evans, *The Coming of the Third Reich*, p. 439. Burleigh, p. 287, gives the 1933 figure as forty thousand.
14. Fest, p. 34.
15. Ibid., p. 20.
16. Peter Hoffmann, *The History of the German Resistance, 1933–1945* (Cambridge, MA: MIT Press, 1979), p. 5.

Notes

17. Peter N. Stearns, ed., *The Encyclopedia of World History*, 6th ed. (Boston: Houghton Mifflin, 2001), p. 701; also see Gellately, p. 15.
18. Paul, Bonart, *But We Said "No": Voices from the German Underground* (San Francisco: Mark Backman Productions, 2007), pp. 36–38.
19. Peter Fritzsche, *Life and Death in the Third Reich* (Cambridge, MA: Belknap Press of Harvard University Press, 2008), p. 109.
20. Hamerow, p. 100. Nevertheless, there is evidence that "enthusiasm for Nazi rule" was waning as early as 1934; see Koonz, p. 74.
21. Quoted in Ulrich Herbert, "Good Times, Bad Times: Memories of the Third Reich," in Richard Bessel, ed., *Life in the Third Reich* (Oxford: Oxford University Press, 2001), p. 97.
22. Hamerow, pp. 167–68.
23. Gellately, p. 16.
24. George Gerbner, former head of the Annenberg School for Communication, quoted in Molly Ivins, "Rumsfeld Leads Us into Quicksand," *Democrat and Chronicle* (Rochester, NY), March 19, 2006.
25. Gellately, pp. 34–36, 44, 52, 60.
26. Ibid., pp. 60, 64.
27. Fest, pp. 21–22; Hoffmann, p. 16.
28. Hoffmann, p. 16.
29. Ibid., p. 58.
30. Richard J. Evans, *The Third Reich in History and Memory* (New York: Oxford University Press, 2015), p. 343.
31. Fritzsche, p. 111. For a discussion of the racist propaganda campaign, see Koonz, chapter 5.
32. Richard J. Evans, *The Third Reich in History and Memory*, p. 81.
33. Jost Dülffler, *Deutsche Geschichte, 1933–1945* (Stuttgart: Kohlhammer, 1992), cited in Burleigh, p. 571.
34. Fritzsche, p. 84.
35. Quoted in Fritzsche, p. 285; also see Koonz, pp. 98–99.
36. Louis L. Snyder, *Encyclopedia of the Third Reich* (New York: Paragon House, 1989), s.v. "Nuremberg Laws on Citizenship and Race," p. 252.
37. The term "Kristallnacht" is usually translated loosely into English as the "Night of Broken Glass," which is a cynical reference to the wanton destruction of property.
38. Evans, *The Third Reich in Power*, p. 580.
39. Burleigh, pp. 328–30; Nigel Jones, *Countdown to Valkyrie: The July Plot to Assassinate Hitler* (London: Frontline Books, 2008), p. 83.
40. Hamerow, p. 225.
41. Harold C. Deutsch, *The Conspiracy against Hitler in the Twilight War* (Minneapolis: University of Minnesota Press, 1968), p. 82; Hamerow, pp. 225, 382–83; Jones, pp. 42–43; Fest, pp. 157, 399.
42. Fest, pp. 157, 399.
43. Ibid., p. 68.
44. Ferdinand Schlingensiepen, *Dietrich Bonhoeffer, 1906–1945: Martyr, Thinker, Man of Resistance* (London: T & T Clark, 2010), p. 240; Jones, p. 283.

45. Hamerow, pp. 225, 376.
46. Ibid., pp. 218–19.
47. Peukert, p. 76.
48. Haffner, pp. 76, 114, 180.
49. Peukert, p. 46.
50. Ibid., pp. 46, 119.
51. Fritzsche, p. 45; Peukert, p. 240; Evans, *The Third Reich in Power*, pp. 465–76; Bracher, pp. 254–55.
52. Peukert, p. 49.
53. Ibid., p. 50.
54. Charles Ringma, *Seize the Day with Dietrich Bonhoeffer* (Colorado Springs: Pinion Press, 2000), reading for August 11.
55. Germany was a totalitarian society from 1933 to 1945, and its ideological intent, as with all totalitarian societies, was to create a new man acting out of a conviction based upon a complete acceptance of the ideology. Those persons adhering to such an ideology would be the true believers, the ideologues. There was nothing new about this phenomenon. History is replete with examples of attempts to create a new, ideologically pure society. Consider the actions of Maximilian Robespierre in the Reign of Terror during the French Revolution. More modern, twentieth-century examples can be found in the Soviet Union of the Bolsheviks and Mao Tse-tung's China. The intent in each case was the creation of a perfect society – a utopia – comprised of perfect individuals who had been transformed by the ideology of which they were a part. The abstract "citizens" of the Reign of Terror in the French Revolution and the "comrades" of the Bolshevik era in the Soviet Union had their counterpart in the "national comrades" (Volksgenossen) of Nazi Germany. Such a system is fatally flawed, however. Human nature does not change. Consequently, a "new man" who is the end product of the ideological transformation process, whatever it might be, will never appear.
56. Peukert, p. 49; *Encyclopedia of the Third Reich*, s.v. "Eintopf (one-pot meal)," pp. 82–83.
57. *Encyclopedia of the Third Reich*, s.v. "Winterhilfe (Winter Relief)," p. 381; Evans, *The Third Reich in Power*, pp. 483–86.
58. Gellately, pp. 192–94.
59. Ibid., p. 73.
60. Ibid., pp. 193–96.
61. Chris McNab, *World War II Data Book: The Third Reich, 1933–1945* (London: Amber Books, 2009), p. 43; Nizkor Project, "The Organization of the Nazi Party & State," chap. 6 in *Nazi Conspiracy & Aggression*, vol. 1, http://www.nizkor.org/hweb/imt/nca/nca-01/nca-01-06-organization.html; *Encyclopedia of the Third Reich*, s.v. "Gau (District)," pp. 109–10; Peukert, pp. 49, 52, 58–59, 73. Evidence of popular dissent from the Nazi norms of behavior survives in the "Reports on Germany" from the SOPADE archives and from secret internal situation reports of the Nazi Party and police; the "Reports on Germany" became a major source of information about everyday life in Nazi Germany.

62. Moorhouse, p. 73.
63. Ibid.
64. Peukert, pp. 49, 83, 117.
65. Ibid., p. 248.
66. Terry Parssinen, *The Oster Conspiracy of 1938* (New York: HarperCollins, 2003), p. 154; Fest, pp. 94–96; William L. Shirer, *The Rise and Fall of the Third Reich* (New York: Simon and Schuster, 1960), p. 399.
67. Shirer, p. 399; David Stone, *Shattered Genius: The Decline and Fall of the German General Staff in World War II* (Havertown, PA: Casemate Publishers, 2011), pp. 110–11.
68. Quoted in Stone, pp. 110–11; also see Klaus-Jürgen Müller, "Witzleben, Stülpnagel, and Speidel," in Corelli Barnett, ed., *Hitler's Generals* (New York: Grove Weidenfeld, 1989), pp. 43–49; and Hoffmann, p. 43.
69. William L. Shirer, *Berlin Diary* (New York: Alfred A. Knopf, 1949), p. 316, quoted in Roger Parkinson, *Summer, 1940: The Battle of Britain* (New York: David McKay, 1977), p. 21.
70. Peukert, p. 118.
71. Ibid.
72. Ibid., pp. 117–18.
73. Quoted in Peukert, p. 51.
74. Fritzsche, p. 279.
75. Ibid.
76. Ibid., pp. 279, 283.
77. Ibid., p. 283.
78. Günter Moltmann, "Goebbels' Rede zum totalen Krieg am 18. Februar 1943," *Vierteljarshefte für Zeitgeschichte* 12 (1964), p. 22, quoted in Fritzsche, p. 283.
79. Fritzsche, pp. 283–84.
80. Peukert, p. 51.
81. Fritzsche, p. 286.
82. Ibid.
83. Quoted in ibid., p. 286.
84. This was still the prevailing attitude in Germany several decades after the end of World War II. The writer Anton Gill interviewed a number of surviving relatives of the conspirators in preparation for his book *An Honourable Defeat* and comments as follows (p. 1): "Several relatives of conspirators whose names are famous told me that to carry such a name was a disadvantage in postwar Germany." Theodore Hamerow has written, "The critical attitude toward the resisters persisted long after the occupation came to an end. Surveys of public opinion in the early years of the German Federal Republic revealed little nostalgia for the Third Reich but considerable ambivalence toward those who had tried to overthrow it" (*On the Road to the Wolf's Lair*, p. 395). General Rudolph-Christoph von Gersdorff, an active member of the resistance, wrote in his memoirs of his experience as a prisoner of war in an American POW camp, where he not only was shunned but also experienced a death threat from fellow prisoners when they learned that

he had been an active conspirator against Hitler. See Rudolph-Christoph von Gersdorff, *Soldier in the Downfall: A Wehrmacht Cavalryman in Russia, Normandy, and the Plot to Kill Hitler* (Bedford, PA: Aberjona Press, 2012), pp. 154–55.
85. Fritzsche, p. 286. Official figures of deaths from the bombing raids are as follows: total deaths, 593,000, of whom 410,000 were "resident German civilians"; 32,000 were foreign civilians or prisoners of war, 23,000 were members of the German Army or police, and 128,000 were German refugees from the eastern territories. See Randall Hansen, chapter 28, in *Fire and Fury: The Allied Bombing of Germany, 1942–1945* (New York: NAL Caliber, 2008), p. 325n8.
86. Richard J. Evans, *The Third Reich at War* (New York: Penguin, 2009), p. 446.
87. Ibid., pp. 447, 450; also see Martin Middlebrook, *The Battle of Hamburg: Allied Bomber Forces against a German City in 1943* (New York: Charles Scribner's Sons, 1981), pp. 285–89.
88. Peukert, p. 63.
89. Ibid.
90. Ibid.
91. Quoted in Peukert, p. 240.
92. Ibid., p. 105; Hamerow, p. 368.
93. Fritzsche, p. 151.
94. Ibid.; also see Koonz, chapter 8.
95. Quoted in Fritzsche, p. 153.
96. Burleigh, pp. 603–4.
97. Hamerow, p. 282.
98. Ibid.
99. Ian Kershaw, *Hitler, 1936–1945: Nemesis* (New York: W. W. Norton, 2000), p. 358.
100. Ibid., p. 389.
101. Fritzsche, p. 151.
102. Ibid., p. 202. Fritzsche goes on to say of the German soldiers, "It was an ongoing struggle to assume the role of killer, since 'regular' moral and legal concepts continued to conflict with National Socialist ideology."

Chapter 3

1. *Gleichschaltung*, an electrical term that refers to one master switch capable of activating all subsidiary switches of several circuits, is an apt metaphor for Nazi rule. Richard J. Evans, *The Coming of the Third Reich* (New York: Penguin, 2004), p. 381.
2. Joachim Fest, *Plotting Hitler's Death: The Story of the German Resistance, 1933–1945* (New York: Metropolitan Books, Henry Holt, 1994), p. 22.
3. Sebastian Haffner, *Defying Hitler: A Memoir*, rev. ed. (London: Phoenix, 2003), p. 109.
4. Peter Hoffmann, *The History of the German Resistance, 1933–1945* (Cambridge, MA: MIT Press, 1979), p. 8.
5. Fest, p. 22.

Notes

6. Hoffmann, p. 192; also see Theodore S. Hamerow, *On the Road to the Wolf's Lair: German Resistance to Hitler* (Cambridge, MA: Belknap Press of Harvard University Press, 1997), pp. 11, 94, 287–88.
7. Hamerow, p. 11; also see pp. 118–19.
8. Gerhard Ritter, *The German Resistance: Carl Goerdeler's Struggle Against Tyranny*, (Pickle Partners Publishing, 2015, originally published in 1958). p. 17.
9. *Encyclopaedia Britannica*, Volume 10 Garrison-Halibut, (Chicago: University of Chicago Press, 1969). pp. 521-522.
10. H.W. Koch, Editor, *Aspects of the Third Reich*, (London: Palgrave/Macmillan Publishers Limited 1985). From an essay by Klaus-Jürgen Müller, *The Structure and Nature of the National Conservative Opposition in Germany up to 1940*, p. 148; also see Michael C. Thomsett, *The German Opposition to Hitler: The Resistance, the Underground, and Assassination Plots, 1938–1945* (Jefferson, NC: McFarland, 1997), pp. 85–86.
11. Quoted in Fest, p. 145. Historian Theodore Hamerow, pp. 183–84, argues that Goerdeler's final break with the Nazis came with the realization that "the Third Reich would not tolerate any disagreement with its policies, however cautious, however reasonable. It demanded total submission, which he was not prepared to offer." For a discussion of the Gewandhaus episode, see Evans, *The Third Reich in Power* (New York: Penguin, 2005), p. 192.
12. Hamerow, p. 368; Fest, pp. 335, 337.
13. Fest, pp. 157, 395.
14. Ibid., p. 153.
15. Karl Dietrich Bracher, *The German Dictatorship: The Origins, Structure, and Effects of National Socialism* (New York: Praeger, 1970), p. 372.
16. Larry L. Rasmussen, *Dietrich Bonhoeffer: Reality and Resistance* (Louisville, KY: Westminster John Knox Press, 2005), p. 174; Fest, p. 328.
17. Hoffmann, p. 20.
18. Bracher, p. 372.
19. Dorothee von Meding, *Mit dem Mut des Herzens: Die Frauen des 20. Juli* (Berlin: Siedler, 1992), p. 244, quoted in Fest, p. 328.
20. Evans, *The Coming of the Third Reich*, pp. 15, 379–82, 423–31; Ian Kershaw, *Hitler, 1889–1936: Hubris* (New York: W. W. Norton, 1999), p. 474.
21. Bracher, p. 253.
22. Ibid.
23. Hamerow, p. 66.
24. Ibid., p. 66.
25. Ibid., p. 228.
26. Ibid., p. 226.
27. Ibid., p. 228.
28. Hoffmann, p. 190.
29. Hamerow, p. 252.
30. Ibid., pp. 251–52.
31. Quoted in Hamerow, p. 252.

32. Ibid., p. 112.
33. Gordon A. Craig, *Europe Since 1815* (New York: Holt, Rinehart, and Winston, 1961), pp. 363–67.
34. Richard J. Evans, *The Coming of the Third Reich*, p. 31.
35. Hamerow, p. 19.
36. A. J. Ryder, *Twentieth-Century Germany: From Bismarck to Brandt* (New York: Columbia University Press, 1973), p. 423.
37. Hans-Ulrich Wehler, "Bismarck's Imperialism," in *Imperial Germany*, ed. James Sheehan (New York: New Viewpoints, 1976), p. 181.
38. Ibid., p. 23.
39. Ibid., p. 19.
40. There is evidence to support this last assertion. A study of the complex negotiations between Germany and the United States in the weeks preceding the armistice of November 11, 1918, indicates that the US government under the leadership of President Woodrow Wilson understandably was attempting to drive a wedge between the German people and their government. This approach had been clearly foreshadowed in Wilson's war message to the US Congress in April 1917, when he spoke the following words: "We have no feeling but one of sympathy and friendship" for the German people. On October 23, 1918, he refused to discuss armistice terms if the United States and Allies "must deal with the military masters and monarchical autocrats of Germany." Wilson was thus declaring that the price of peace had to be the overthrow of the imperial government. An American diplomat, the late George F. Kennan, has in fact alleged that both world wars were fought "with a view to changing Germany: to correcting her behavior, to making the Germans something different from what they were." Assuming this is true, as it appears to be, the Weimar Republic "was more or less imposed upon Germany from above; it did not spring from the soil." Thomas A. Bailey, *Woodrow Wilson and the Lost Peace* (Chicago: Encounter Paperbacks, Quadrangle Press, 1963), p. 38; also see George F. Kennan, *American Diplomacy, 1900–1950* (Chicago: University of Chicago Press, 1951), p. 55; Robert H. Ferrell, *American Diplomacy*, 3rd ed. (New York: W. W. Norton, 1975), p. 482; and Richard M. Watt, *The Kings Depart* (New York: Simon and Schuster, 1968), p. 153.
41. Hoffmann, p. 189.
42. Hamerow, p. 29.
43. Christopher Clark, *Iron Kingdom: The Rise and Downfall of Prussia, 1600–1947* (Cambridge, MA: Belknap Press of Harvard University Press, 2006), pp. 196, 215.
44. Laurence Lafore, *The Long Fuse: An Interpretation of the Origins of World War I* (Philadelphia: J. B. Lippincott, 1965), pp. 18–23; David Calleo, chapter 6, in *The German Problem Reconsidered – Germany and the World Order: 1870 to the Present* (Cambridge: Cambridge University Press, 1980), pp. 1–8, 27–29; Clark, pp. 596–611; Margaret MacMillan, *The War That Ended Peace: The Road to 1914* (New York: Random House, 2013), p. 328; James J. Sheehan, *Where Have All the Soldiers Gone?* (Boston: Houghton Mifflin, 2008), pp. xviii–xix, 12; E. J. Feuchtwanger, *Prussia: Myth and Reality* (Chicago: Henry Regnery, 1970), pp. 109, 236–37.

45. Feuchtwanger, p. 237; Richard J. Evans, *The Coming of the Third Reich*, p. 12; MacMillan, pp. 282–83.
46. G. J. Meyer, *A World Undone: The Story of the Great War, 1914 to 1918* (New York: Bantam Dell, 2006), p. 604; also see Erik Kirschbaum, *Burning Beethoven: The Eradication of German Culture in the United States during World War I* (New York: Berlinica Publishing, 2015).
47. H. W. Koch, *A History of Prussia* (New York: Dorset Press, 1978), pp. 80–81; Feuchtwanger, p. 236; Clark, pp. 134–44. This conception of commercial activity was based largely on the influence of German Pietism, an eighteenth-century reformist religious movement that had a significant impact on the evolution of the Prussian state and society.
48. Fabian von Schlabrendorff, *The Secret War against Hitler* (Boulder: Westview Press, 1944), p. 19. On Bismarck's social policy, see Gordon A. Craig, *Germany, 1866–1945* (New York: Oxford University Press, 1978), pp. 150–51; Koppel S. Pinson, *Modern Germany*, 2nd ed. (New York: Macmillan, 1966), pp. 240–41; Clark, pp. 615–18; Hamerow, p. 12; Christopher Clark, *Kaiser Wilhelm II* (New York: Routledge, 2013), pp. 38–39.
49. Haffner, p. 82; Fritz Stern, *Five Germanys I Have Known* (New York: Farrar, Straus, and Giroux, 2006), p. 35. Admittedly, two Hohenzollern kings were exceptions to this general behavior pattern. Frederick III ruled as Elector of Brandenburg and Duke of Prussia from 1688 to 1701, when he was crowned "King in Prussia." (The title "King in Prussia" was in deference to the superior position of the Holy Roman Emperor. Subsequent Hohenzollern kings ignored this distinction.) His reign as king lasted until his death in 1713 and was characterized by much ostentation and elaborate display. Subsequent Hohenzollern kings returned to the earlier tradition of simplicity, austerity, and frugality, which remained in place until the reign of the last Hohenzollern, Wilhelm II, who was both king of Prussia and kaiser (emperor) of Germany. His reign was marked by a pretentiousness that was reminiscent of Frederick I. The Hohenzollern dynasty came to an end with his abdication at the end of the Great War in 1918. See Clark, *Iron Kingdom*, p. 84, and chapter 4, "Majesty."
50. Dr. Louis L. Snyder, *Encyclopedia of the Third Reich*, (New York: Paragon House Publishers 1989); Jones, p. 291; Fest, pp. 388, 390–91; Hamerow, p. 98;
51. Hamerow, pp. 108–9.
52. Rasmussen, p. 180n10; Hamerow, pp. 107–8.
53. Larry Rasmussen, "The Steep Price of Grace," *Sojourners Magazine* 35, no. 2 (February 2006): pp. 18–23; Robert Gellately, *Backing Hitler: Consent and Coercion in Nazi Germany* (New York: Oxford University Press, 2001), p. 10.
54. Hamerow, p. 11.
55. Terry Parssinen, *The Oster Conspiracy of 1938* (New York: HarperCollins, 2003), p. 42.
56. Burleigh, p. 688.
57. Harold C. Deutsch, *The Conspiracy against Hitler in the Twilight War* (Minneapolis: University of Minnesota Press, 1968), p. 25.

58. Hamerow, pp. 331–32.
59. Rasmussen, *Dietrich Bonhoeffer*, pp. 200–202.
60. Peter Z. Malkin and Harry Stein, *Eichmann in My Hands* (New York: Warner Books, 1990); the quote is taken from a review of the book by the History Book Club.
61. Max Weber, *The Protestant Ethic and the Spirit of Capitalism*, 2nd ed. (Los Angeles: Roxbury Publishing, 1998).
62. Bracher, p. 329.
63. Rasmussen, *Dietrich Bonhoeffer*, pp. 202, 203.
64. *The Oxford Dictionary of Quotations*, 2nd ed. (London: Oxford University Press, 1953), #21, p. 248.
65. Hamerow, p. 20; also see pp. 12–14, 53–54, 62–63, 95–96, 133–38, 148, 209.
66. Hoffmann, pp. 13–14; Hamerow, p. 136.
67. Richard J. Evans, *The Coming of the Third Reich*, p. 350.
68. Kershaw, pp. 464–65, photographs between pp. 418 and 419; Evans, *The Third Reich in Power*, p. 222.
69. Hoffmann, p. 14.
70. Ibid.
71. Hamerow, p. 131.
72. Ibid., p. 162.
73. Ibid., p. 147.
74. Evans, *The Third Reich in Power*, p. 234.
75. Hamerow, p. 147.
76. Evans, *The Third Reich in Power*, pp. 14, 235.
77. Ibid., p. 238. The Rosenberg book is still in print and is available from several publishers. The complete title is *The Myth of the Twentieth Century: An Evaluation of the Spiritual-Intellectual Confrontations of Our Age*.
78. Ibid., p. 239.
79. Ibid.
80. Quoted in Evans, *The Third Reich in Power*, p. 238.
81. Evans, *The Third Reich in Power*, pp. 241–42.
82. Ibid., p. 243; also see pp. 238–48.
83. Ibid., p. 247.
84. Quoted in Ryder, p. 372.
85. Evans, *The Third Reich in Power*, p. 220.
86. Hamerow, pp. 146–47.
87. Ibid., p. 98.
88. Ibid., p. 263.
89. Evans, *The Third Reich in Power*, p. 228.
90. Hamerow, p. 161.
91. Ferdinand Schlingensiepen, *Dietrich Bonhoeffer, 1906–1945: Martyr, Thinker, Man of Resistance* (London: T & T Clark International, 2010), p. 126.
92. Ibid.
93. Quoted in ibid., p.126.
94. Quoted in Hamerow, pp. 33–34.

Notes

95. Ibid., pp. 77–79.
96. Schlingensiepen, pp. 126–27.
97. Ibid., p. 126.
98. Hamerow, pp. 33–34.
99. Quoted in Schlingensiepen, p. 70.
100. Schlingensiepen, p. 70.
101. Evans, *The Third Reich in Power*, p. 221.
102. Quoted in Evans, *The Third Reich in Power*, p. 221.
103. Evans, *The Third Reich in Power*, p. 221.
104. Dr. Louis L. Snyder, *Encyclopedia of the Third Reich,* (New York: Paragon House Publishers 1989).
105. Evans, *The Third Reich in Power*, p. 222.
106. Quoted in Hamerow, p. 153.
107. Ibid., pp. 153–54.
108. Ibid., pp. 155–56.
109. Ibid., pp. 262–63.
110. Quoted in Hamerow, p. 366.
111. German Historical Institute Bulletin, Spring 1999. Gh-dc.org. Archived from the original on 19 January 2018.
112. Quoted in Hamerow, p. 366.
113. Ibid., pp. 71, 159.
114. Quoted in Schlingensiepen, p. 136.
115. Renate Wind, *Dietrich Bonhoeffer: A Spoke in the Wheel* (Grand Rapids, MI: William B. Eerdmanns, 1990), p. 75; Evans, *The Third Reich in Power*, pp. 228–29.
116. James Bentley, *Martin Niemöller: 1892-1984,* (New York:Free Press), 1976. p. 223.
117. Leo Stein, *Hitler Came for Niemoeller: The Nazi War Against Religion,* (New York: Pelican, 2003).
118. Hamerow, pp. 263, 314.
119. Ryder, p. 373.
120. Ibid., p. 376.
121. Hoffmann, p. 13.
122. Ryder, p. 374.
123. Anton Gill, *An Honourable Defeat* (New York: Henry Holt, 1994), p. 47.
124. Ibid., p. 48.
125. Ibid., pp. 48, 49.
126. Evans, *The Third Reich in Power*, pp. 230–31.
127. Gestapo report, quoted in Evans, *The Third Reich in Power*, p. 231.
128. Schlingensiepen, p. 183.
129. Hoffmann, p. 13.
130. Schlingensiepen, p. 177.
131. Ibid., p. 209; Victoria J. Barnett., ed. (English edition), *Dietrich Bonhoeffer Works*, vol. 15, *Dietrich Bonhoeffer: Theological Education Underground: 1937–1940* (Minneapolis: Fortress Press, 2012), pp. 5–8.
132. Wind, p. 126.

133. Ibid., p. 115; Eberhard Bethge, *Dietrich Bonhoeffer: A Biography*, rev. ed., ed. Victoria J. Barnett (Minneapolis: Fortress Press, 2000), pp. 498–503; Victoria J. Barnett, *Dietrich Bonhoeffer: Theological Education Underground*, pp. 5–8.
134. Wind, p. 124.
135. Evans, *The Third Reich in Power*, p. 230.
136. Ryder, pp. 374–75; Louis L. Snyder, *Encyclopedia of the Third Reich* (New York: Paragon House, 1989), s.v. "Müller, Ludwig (1883–1945)," p. 235.
137. Richard Bessel, *Germany After the First World War* (New York: Oxford University Press, 1993), p. 252.
138. Ian McLean and Alistair McMillan, *The Oxford Concise Dictionary of Politics* (Oxford: Oxford University Press, 2003), pp. 496–97.
139. H. W. Koch, *A Constitutional History of Germany in the Nineteenth and Twentieth Centuries* (London: Longman Group, 1984), p. 145.
140. Koch, pp. 384–85; Craig, *Germany, 1866–1945*, p. 292.
141. Hoffmann, p. 21.
142. Pinson, pp. 212–13.
143. Quoted in ibid., pp. 212–13, Pinson.
144. Quoted in Pinson, p. 204.
145. An interesting sidelight to the question of German socialism was the situation in Prussia from 1919 to 1933. As noted, Prussian conservative ideals were the exact opposite of those proclaimed by the socialists. Nevertheless, Prussia had undergone a remarkable political transformation in the years immediately following the end of the Great War. Several factors contributed to this change. First of all, Germany's collapse at the war's end had thoroughly, albeit temporarily, discredited the conservative leadership. The powers of state had been dumped unceremoniously into the hands of the Majority Socialists, who played a primary role in creating the Weimar Republic. Moreover, Rhineland Prussia was perhaps the most highly industrialized region in the German nation. Consequently, there was widespread support for socialism among the members of the working class, who toiled in the factories and mines of this German state, so much so that "Red Prussia" became a center of strength for the SPD (Sozialdemokratische Partei Deutschlands). This was very important for national politics, because Prussia covered over half of the territory of the republic and over 57 percent of the German population lived in Prussia. Additionally, the SPD dominated the Prussian state government from 1919 until 1933, even though it never had a ruling majority in the national government. "Their policy was to make Prussia a bastion of Weimar democracy." Thus, a major goal of Weimar's enemies was to remove the socialists in Prussia from power. See Evans, *The Coming of the Third Reich*, p. 89.
146. Dr. Louis L. Snyder, *Encyclopedia of the Third Reich,* (New York: Paragon House Publishers 1989).
147. Hoffmann, p. 198. In fact, a portion of western Germany was occupied for a short time by Allied troops after the armistice of November 11, 1918.
148. Evans, *The Coming of the Third Reich*, p. 352.
149. Burleigh, p. 154.

Notes

150. Quoted in Evans, *The Coming of the Third Reich*, p. 352.
151. Bracher, p. 220.
152. Burleigh, p. 154.
153. Evans, *The Coming of the Third Reich*, pp. 353–54.
154. Koch, p. 309.
155. Hamerow. pp. 87–90.
156. Evans, *The Coming of the Third Reich*, pp. 357–58.
157. Ibid.
158. Burleigh, p. 156; Evans, *The Coming of the Third Reich*, pp. 359–60; also, Hoffmann, p. 12.
159. Evans, *The Third Reich in Power*, p. 57.
160. Hoffmann, p. 22.
161. Fest, p. 30.
162. Hamerow, p. 168.
163. Detlev J. K. Peukert, *Inside Nazi Germany: Conformity, Opposition, and Racism in Everyday Life* (New Haven, CT: Yale University Press, 1987), p. 118.
164. Ibid., p. 265n13.
165. Ryder, p. 422.
166. Hoffmann, pp. 128, 130–31.
167. Fest, pp. 25, 218, 391–92.
168. Fest, p. 392.
169. Ryder, p.544. For an account of the reconstitution of the German political parties after 1945, see Ryder, pp. 459–61.
170. Hoffmann, p. 30.
171. Ibid., p. 103.
172. Fest, pp. 241–42.
173. Burleigh, pp. 672–73; Watt, pp. 188, 192–93.
174. Fest, p. 5; also see Ryder, pp. 423–26.
175. Thomsett, pp. 87–88; also see Burleigh, p. 681.
176. Burleigh, p. 683.
177. Deutsch, p. 12.
178. Thomsett, p. 86.
179. Richard J. Evans, *The Third Reich at War* (New York: Penguin, 2009), p. 633.
180. Hoffmann, p. 364.
181. Fest, pp. 145, 389.
182. Hoffmann, p. 364.
183. Deutsch, p. 12n4; Hamerow, pp. 117–18; Fest, p. 153; Ryder, p. 423.
184. Robert O'Neill, "Fritsch, Beck, and the Führer," in Corelli Barnett, ed., *Hitler's Generals* (New York: Grove Weidenfeld, 1989), p. 26; Thomsett, p. 40.
185. Deutsch, p. 28.
186. Thomsett, p. 40.
187. Hamerow, p. 90.
188. Deutsch, p. 90.
189. O'Neill, p. 27.

190. Gill, p. 161.
191. Evans, *The Third Reich at War*, p. 631.
192. Fest, p. 157; Gill, pp. 160–64.
193. Ryder, p. 425.
194. Ibid., p. 425; Fest, pp. 5, 157.
195. Fest, p. 157.
196. Quoted in Evans, *The Third Reich at War*, p. 634.
197. Hans Rothfels, *The German Opposition to Hitler*, (Hinsdale, Illinois: Henry Regnery Company, 1948.) pp. 112, 114, 122.
198. Hamerow, p. 295.
199. Wengler, Wilhelm (1948). *Vorkaempfer der Voelkerverstaendigung und Voelkerrechtsgelehrte als Opfer des Nationalsozialismus, Nr. 9: H. J. Graf von Moltke (1906[sic]-1945)*. London: Die Friedens-Warte 48. pp. 297–305.
200. Hoffmann, p. 237.
201. Hamerow, p. 367.
202. Ibid.
203. Ibid.
204. Hoffmann, p. 372.
205. Ibid.
206. Ibid., p. 192.
207. Ibid., p. 33.
208. Fest, p. 159; Hoffmann, p. 361.
209. Ryder, p. 426.
210. Evans, *The Third Reich at War*, p. 633.
211. Fest, p. 158; Ian Kershaw, *Hitler, 1936–1945: Nemesis* (New York: W. W. Norton, 2000), p. 666. As we consider the history of Europe since the end of World War II, however, perhaps some of the ideas of the Kreisau Circle – especially the concept of a federated Europe or "international community of states" (see Evans, *The Third Reich at War*, p. 632) transcending national sovereignties – were merely a half century ahead of their time.
212. Fest, pp. 158–59; also see Evans, *The Third Reich at War*, p. 632.
213. Evans, *The Third Reich at War*, pp. 632–33; also see Fest, p. 159, and Burleigh p. 701.
214. Quoted in Hoffmann, p. 193.
215. Evans, *The Third Reich at War*, p. 632.
216. Burleigh, p. 701; Fest, p. 159.
217. Hoffmann, p. 237; Hamerow, pp. 366–67; Fest, pp. 239–40.
218. Hoffmann, p. 361.
219. Ibid.
220. Ibid., p. 362.
221. Ibid.
222. Evans, *The Third Reich at War*, pp. 632, 633; also see Hoffmann, p. 196.
223. Hoffmann, p. 200.
224. Hamerow, p. 157.

225. Fest, p. 232.
226. Evans, *The Third Reich at War*, p. 632.
227. Fest, p. 328.
228. Hoffmann, p. 253.
229. Ibid., p. 33.
230. Ibid., p. 34.
231. Ibid.
232. "Franz Jaegerstatter," Justpeace (website), accessed October 24, 2017, http://www.justpeace.org/franz.htm; Erna Putz, *Franz Jägerstätter, Martyr: A Shining Example in Dark Times* (Linz, Austria: Katholische Kirche in Oberösterreich [Catholic Church in Upper Austria], 2007), p. 9; Gordon Zahn, *In Solitary Witness: The Life and Death of Franz Jägerstätter*, rev. ed. (Springfield, IL: Templegate, 1986), p. 20.
234. Putz, p. 10.
235. Ibid., p. 12.
236. Ibid., p. 13; Zahn, p. 25.
237. Zahn, p. 19.
238. Ibid.
239. Ibid., p. 39.
240. Quoted in Putz, p. 22.
241. Evan Burr Bukey, *Hitler's Austria: Popular Sentiment in the Nazi Era, 1938–1945* (Chapel Hill: University of North Carolina Press, 2000), p. 32.
242. Zahn, p. 39.
243. Ibid., p. 47.
244. Ibid., pp. 47–48.
245. Ibid., p. 46.
246. Ibid., p. 20.
247. Putz, p. 48.
248. Ibid.
249. Ibid., p. 51.
250. Ibid.
251. Ibid., p. 57.
252. Zahn, p. 55.
253. Quoted in Putz, p. 84.
254. Zahn, p. 61.
255. Putz, p. 82.
256. Zahn, p. 87.
257. Quoted in Putz, p. 102.
258. Putz, p. 102.
259. Zahn, p. 89.
260. According to Gordon Zahn, p. 88, the military officers in charge of the trial "pleaded" and "begged" Jägerstätter to relent and accept noncombatant military service, but he refused. However, Putz, p. 107, states that the Military Historical Archive in Prague "records that the accused twice submitted a plea for permission to do medical service." The plea obviously was denied.

261. Zahn, p. 87.
262. Ibid.
263. Quoted in Zahn, p. 105.
264. Zahn, p. 160.
265. Quoted in Zahn, p. 126.
266. Zahn, p. 111.
267. Ibid., pp. 132, 162, 172–73. Jägerstätter was beatified on July 6, 2007, by Pope Benedict XVI; see foreword to Putz.
268. Saul Friedländer, *Counterfeit Nazi: The Ambiguity of Good* (Worthing: Littlehampton Book Services, 1969), cited in Burleigh, pp. 708, 908n126.
269. Friedländer, Saul. *Kurt Gerstein: The Ambiguity of Good.* (New York City: Alfred A Knopf. 1969). p.4.; also see Gill, pp. 151–55.
270. Burleigh, p. 708.
271. Hoffmann, p. 23; Gill, p. 151.
272. Burleigh, p. 708.
273. Gill, p. 153.
274. Gill, p. 153, and Burleigh, p. 708.
275. Hoffmann, p. 24.
276. Burleigh, p. 709; Gill, p. 155.
277. Burleigh, p. 708.
278. Peukert, pp. 78–79, 154–74, 202–3; Frank McDonough, *Opposition and Resistance in Nazi Germany* (Cambridge: Cambridge University Press, 2001), pp. 16–17; also see Detlev Peukert, "Youth in the Third Reich," in Richard Bessel, ed., *Life in the Third Reich* (Oxford: Oxford University Press, 2001), p. 36.
279. Annette Dumbach and Jud Newborn, *Sophie Scholl and the White Rose* (Oxford: Oneworld Publications, 2007), p. iii; Fest, p. 199; Kershaw, *Hitler, 1936–1945: Nemesis*, p. 552. Also see Inge Scholl, *The White Rose: Munich, 1942–1943* (Middletown, CT: Wesleyan University Press, 1983), p. 148.
280. Hoffmann, p. 32.
281. Ibid. The reason for the delay of the arrests probably was that the Gestapo had tapped the telephones of those in attendance because they wanted to widen the surveillance net in order to ensnare other opponents of the Nazis. See Gill, p. 160; Hoffmann, p. 32.
282. Evans, *The Third Reich at War*, p. 626.
283. Burleigh, p. 671.
284. Evans, *The Third Reich at War*, p. 626.
285. Ibid., p. 627.

Chapter 4

1. Gordon A. Craig, *Germany, 1866–1945* (New York: Oxford University Press, 1978), p. 586.
2. Richard J. Evans, *The Third Reich in Power* (New York: Penguin, 2005), p. 23; also see Heinz Höhne, "The Röhm Putsch," in *The Order of the Death's Head: The Story of Hitler's SS* (New York: Penguin, 2000), p. 128.

Notes

3. Evans, p. 25.
4. The two men, Röhm and Hitler, in conversation together, addressed each other with the informal *du* (you) rather than the formal *Sie*. *Du* was reserved for very intimate friends and close relatives. This was an indication of their closeness.
5. Evans, p. 36.
6. Gordon A. Craig, *The Politics of the Prussian Army, 1640–1945* (New York: Oxford University Press, 1956), p. 477; Michael Burleigh, *The Third Reich: A New History* (New York: Hill and Wang, 2000), p. 159.
7. Evans, pp. 40–41.
8. Gordon A. Craig, *Europe Since 1815* (New York: Holt, Rinehart, and Winston, 1961), p. 642.
9. Joachim Fest, *Plotting Hitler's Death: The Story of the German Resistance, 1933–1945* (New York: Metropolitan Books, Henry Holt, 1996), p. 51.
10. Evans, p. 39.
11. Höhne, p. 128.
12. Peter Hoffmann, *The History of the German Resistance, 1933–1945* (Cambridge, MA: MIT Press, 1979), p. 25.
13. Craig, *The Politics*, p. 478.
14. Stauffenberg quoted in Höhne, p. 128; Witzleben quoted in Fest, p. 51.
15. Craig, *The Politics*, p. 479.
16. Fest, p. 53; also see Craig, *Germany, 1866–1945*, p. 589.
17. Fest, p. 53.
18. Robert B. Asprey, *The German High Command at War: Hindenburg and Ludendorff Conduct World War I* (New York: William Morrow, 1991), pp. 90–91, 168, 296.
19. Evans, p. 110; H. W. Koch, *A Constitutional History of Germany in the Nineteenth and Twentieth Centuries* (London: Longman Group, 1984), p. 317.
20. Quoted in Hoffmann, p. 27.
21. Fest, p. 55.
22. A. Ganse, trans., "The Reich Constitution of August 11th 1919 (Weimar Constitution) with Modifications," ZUM, 2001, http://www.zum.de/psm/Weimar/Weimar_vve.php (translated and posted by permission of DHM, Berlin, http://www.DHM.de/lemo/); Craig, *Europe Since 1815*, p. 607.
23. Hoffmann, p. 27; also see Koch, p. 317.
24. Quoted in Matthew Cooper, *The German Army, 1933–1945* (New York: Bonanza Books, 1984), p. 30; also see Craig, *Germany, 1866–1945*, p. 589.
25. Ian Kershaw, *Hitler, 1889–1936: Hubris* (New York: W. W. Norton, 1999), p. 525.
26. Craig, *The Politics*, pp. 480–81; the English translation uses the term "Wehrmacht," even though the official name change from Reichswehr did not take place until 1935.
27. Ibid.
28. Craig, *Germany, 1866–1945*, p. 53; Craig, *Europe Since 1815*, p. 372.
29. Robert M. Citino, *The German Way of War* (Lawrence: University Press of Kansas, 2005), p. 308; David Stone, *Fighting for the Fatherland* (Washington, DC: Potomac Books, 2006), pp. 55–56.

30. Cooper, p. 31; Citino, p. 308.
31. E. J. Feuchtwanger, *Prussia: Myth and Reality* (Chicago: Henry Regnery, 1970), p. 44.
32. Christopher Clark, *Iron Kingdom: The Rise and Downfall of Prussia, 1600–1947* (Cambridge, MA: Belknap Press of Harvard University Press, 2006), pp. 516–17.
33. Koch, p. 164.
34. Cooper, p. 31.
35. Ibid.
36. Craig, *Germany, 1866–1945*, p. 590.
37. Fest, p. 56.
38. Quoted in Cooper, p. 30; also see Fest, p. 56.
39. Quoted in Fest, p. 138.
40. Fest, pp. 137–38.
41. Bodo Scheurig, *Henning von Tresckow: Eine Biographie* (Düsseldorf: Stalling, 1979), p. 70, quoted in Fest, p. 191.
42. A. J. Ryder, *Twentieth-Century Germany: From Bismarck to Brandt* (New York: Columbia University Press, 1973), p. 423.
43. Anton Gill, *An Honourable Defeat: A History of the German Resistance to Hitler, 1933–1945* (New York: Henry Holt, 1994), p. 37.
44. Craig, *The Politics*, p. 480; Hoffmann, p. 27; David Stone, *Shattered Genius: The Decline and Fall of the German General Staff in World War II* (Havertown, PA: Casemate Publishers, 2011), p. 67.
45. Hoffmann, p. 168.
46. Gill, p. 206.
47. Fest, pp. 190, 191.
48. Craig, *Germany, 1866–1945*, p. 684; Evans, p. 341.
49. Fest, p. 56; Evans, pp. 337–42.
50. Evans, p. 342.
51. Theodore S. Hamerow, *On the Road to the Wolf's Lair: German Resistance to Hitler* (Cambridge, MA: Belknap Press of Harvard University Press, 1997), p. 168.
52. G. M. Gaithorne-Hardy, *A Short History of International Affairs, 1920–1939*, 4th ed. (London: Oxford University Press, 1950), p. 396.
53. Ibid., p. 421.
54. Quoted in Kershaw, p. 586; also see p. 582.
55. Craig, *The Politics*, p. 485.
56. Craig, *The Politics*, pp. 485–86; quoted in Kershaw, p. 585; also see Kershaw, p. 584.
57. Kershaw, p. 582.
58. Ibid., p. 585.
59. Ibid., p. 588.
60. Evans, pp. 633–37; Kershaw, pp. 587–89. Craig, *Germany 1866–1945*, p. 691, gives the total figure as twenty-two thousand soldiers plus fourteen thousand police.
61. Hoffmann, p. 18.
62. Quoted in Craig, *The Politics*, p. 487; Evans, p. 637.

63. Craig, *The Politics*, p. 486.
64. Kershaw, pp. 590–91; Evans, p. 637.
65. Evans, pp. 634–35; Kershaw, pp. 590–91.
66. Walter Görlitz, "Keitel, Jodl, and Warlimont," in Corelli Barnett, ed., *Hitler's Generals* (New York: Grove Weidenfeld, 1989), p. 156.
67. Quoted in Evans, p. 635.
68. Harold C. Deutsch, *The Conspiracy against Hitler in the Twilight War* (Minneapolis: University of Minnesota Press, 1968), p. 26.
69. Ibid.
70. Ibid., pp. 25–26.
71. Ibid., p. 25.
72. Terry Parssinen, *The Oster Conspiracy of 1938* (New York: HarperCollins, 2003), p. 8.
73. Karl Dietrich Bracher, *The German Dictatorship: The Origins, Structure, and Effects of National Socialism* (New York: Praeger, 1970), p. 391.
74. Ibid., p. 392.
75. Friedrich Hossbach, *Zwischen Wehrmacht und Hitler, 1934–1938* [Between Wehrmacht and Hitler, 1934–1938], quoted in Evans, p. 359.
76. Some scholars have argued that Hitler's strategy was not as reckless as it seemed, because the European powers, that is, France and Great Britain, "sought desperately to avoid a new military conflict." See Hamerow, p. 231.
77. Ian Kershaw, *Hitler, 1936–1945: Nemesis* (New York: W. W. Norton, 2000), p. 49.
78. Stone, *Shattered Genius*, p. 71; Kershaw, *Hitler, 1936–1945: Nemesis*, pp. 51–52; Parssinen, p. 22; Nigel Jones, *Countdown to Valkyrie: The July Plot to Assassinate Hitler* (London: Frontline Books, 2008), pp. 46–50.
79. Craig, *The Politics*, p. 495.
80. Ibid., p. 495; Craig, *Germany, 1866–1945*, p. 700; Stone, *Shattered Genius*, p. 73. Evans, pp. 644–45, gives the respective numbers as fourteen dismissals and forty-six reassignments.
81. John W. Wheeler-Bennett, *The Nemesis of Power*, quoted in Craig, *The Politics*, p. 496.
82. Evans, p. 645.
83. Ibid.
84. Hamerow, p. 239.
85. Craig, *Germany, 1866–1945*, pp. 612, 618. Blomberg's title was changed from minister of defense to minister of war in March 1935. See Walter Görlitz, "Blomberg," in *Hitler's Generals*, p. 137.
86. Craig, *Germany, 1866–1945*, p. 618.
87. Deutsch, p. 5.
88. Parssinen, pp. 23, 25–26.
89. Parssinen, p. 26.
90. Evans, p. 25.
91. Robert O'Neill, "Fritsch, Beck, and the Führer," in Corelli Barnett, ed., *Hitler's Generals* (New York: Grove Weidenfeld, 1989), p. 28.
92. Hoffmann, p. 45.

93. Quoted in Stone, *Shattered Genius*, p. 73; Fest, p. 61; Hoffmann, pp. 45–46.
94. Hoffmann, p. 46.
95. Parssinen, pp. 28–29.
96. Ibid., p. 28.
97. Ibid., pp. 27–28; Hoffmann, pp. 40–42; Evans, pp. 417–18.
98. Parssinen, pp. 29–30.
99. Klaus-Jürgen Müller, "Witzleben, Stülpnagel, and Speidel," in Corelli Barnett, ed., *Hitler's Generals* (New York: Grove Weidenfeld, 1989), p. 47.
100. Wilhelm Canaris, "Politik und Weltmacht," quoted in *Wehrmacht und Partei*, ed. Richard Donnevert (Leipzig: Barth, 1938) and cited in Hamerow, p. 174.
101. Hoffmann, p. 172.
102. Larry L. Rasmussen, *Dietrich Bonhoeffer: Reality and Resistance* (Louisville, KY: Westminster John Knox Press, 2005), p. 203.
103. Quoted in Rasmussen, p. 59.
104. Rasmussen, p. 68; Renate Wind, *Dietrich Bonhoeffer: A Spoke in the Wheel* (Grand Rapids, MI: William B. Eerdmanns, 1990), p. 44.
105. G. Leibholz, "Memoir," in Dietrich Bonhoeffer, *The Cost of Discipleship*, rev. ed. (New York: Collier Books, Macmillan, 1963), p. 16.
106. Bonhoeffer, p. 99. His first sermon, which he preached in 1925, began with, "Christianity entails decision." His biographer comments on this passage as follows: "One can either be wholly Christian or not at all is what that means. And what decides whether one is or not, is whether one follows up one's confession of faith with appropriate actions, whatever that may cost." Ferdinand Schlingensiepen, *Dietrich Bonhoeffer, 1906–1945: Martyr, Thinker, Man of Resistance* (London: T & T Clark International, 2010), p. 33.
107. Hoffmann, p. 169; *The Oxford American College Dictionary* (New York: Oxford, 2002), s.v. "treason."
108. *New World Dictionary of the American Language*, 2nd college ed. (Cleveland: William Collins, 1980).
109. German Law Archive (germanlawarchive.iuscomp.org). Special Part, Chapter One, Tittle Two, Section 81 (High Treason Against the Federation).
110. Fest, p. 334.
111. Hamerow, p. 285.
112. Hoffmann, p. 132.
113. Ibid., p. 169.
114. Whether this original Anschluss could or would have been successful even if permitted by the Allies remains an issue that is still debated one hundred years later. See Gordon Brook-Shepherd, *The Austrians: A Thousand-Year Odyssey* (New York: Carroll & Graf, 1996), pp. 233–40.
115. See Brook-Shepherd, part 1, chapter 1, "A Germanic Cradle"; part 4, chapter 4, "An Empire Shatters"; and part 5, chapter 1, "What's Left Is Austria."
116. Parssinen, p. 32.
117. Hamerow, p. 237.
118. Ibid.

119. Ibid.
120. Ibid., p. 347.
121. Ibid., pp. 234–35.
122. Ibid., pp. 237–39; Hoffmann, p. 355.
123. Robert A. Kann, *A History of the Habsburg Empire, 1526–1918* (Berkeley: University of California Press, 1974), pp. 9, 18–19; Peter N. Stearns, ed., *The Encyclopedia of World History*, 6th ed. (Boston: Houghton Mifflin, 2001), p. 309; Kurt Reinhardt, *Germany, 2000 Years*, vol. 1, rev. ed. (New York: Continuum Publishing, 1989), p. 110.
124. Geoffrey Barraclough, *The Origins of Modern Germany* (New York: Capricorn Books, 1963), pp. 41–43; Hajo Holborn, *A History of Germany: The Reformation* (New York: Alfred A. Knopf, 1976), p. 11.
125. Holborn, p. 11.
126. Margaret Macmillan, *Paris, 1919* (New York: Random House, 2003), p. 238.
127. Gaithorne-Hardy, p. 464.
128. Evans, pp. 665–67; Ryder, pp. 331–32.
129. Gaithorne-Hardy, p. 466.
130. Evans, p. 664.
131. Gaithorne-Hardy, p. 466.
132. Quoted in Evans, p. 664.

Chapter 5

1. Harold C. Deutsch, *The Conspiracy against Hitler in the Twilight War* (Minneapolis: University of Minnesota Press, 1968), p. 6. The subsequent events described in *Traitors or Patriots?* are organized – with some modification – on the basis of these four rounds of resistance activity that the late Dr. Deutsch identified.
2. Quoted in Joachim Fest, *Plotting Hitler's Death* (New York: Metropolitan Books, Henry Holt, 1996), p. 213.
3. Ibid.
4. Ibid.
5. Deutsch, pp. 15–16.
6. Quoted in Fest, p. 396; also see pp. 72–73, 77–79, 390; Theodore S. Hamerow, *On the Road to the Wolf's Lair: German Resistance to Hitler* (Cambridge, MA: Belknap Press of Harvard University Press, 1997), pp. 238–40; Richard J. Evans, *The Third Reich in Power* (New York: Penguin, 2005), pp. 669–70.
7. Deutsch, p. 61; Fest, p. 327. Richard J. Evans, *The Third Reich in History and Memory* (New York: Oxford University Press, 2015), p. 280.
8. Evans, *The Third Reich in Power*, p. 43. The Troop Office was renamed the Army General Staff in 1935.
9. Hamerow, pp. 10, 28, 90–91.
10. Gordon A. Craig, *The Politics of the Prussian Army, 1640–1945* (New York: Oxford University Press, 1956), p. 486.
11. Deutsch, p. 31.
12. Quoted in Deutsch, p. 30.

13. Deutsch, p. 28.
14. Ibid., pp. 309–31; Terry Parssinen, *The Oster Conspiracy of 1938* (New York: HarperCollins, 2003), pp. 68, 77–78; Evans, *The Third Reich in Power*, pp. 669–70.
15. Fest, p. 68; Hamerow, p. 186; Parssinen, p. 33.
16. Fest, p. 66.
17. Deutsch, p. 12.
18. Ibid., pp. 28–30.
19. Quoted in Telford Taylor, *Munich: The Price of Peace* (New York: Vintage Books, 1980), p. 8.
20. Hamerow, p. 234; A. J. Ryder, *Twentieth-Century Germany: From Bismarck to Brandt* (New York: Columbia University Press, 1973), pp. 332–33; G. M. Gaithorne-Hardy, *A Short History of International Affairs, 1920–1939*, 4th ed. (London: Oxford University Press, 1950), pp. 466–68.
21. Deutsch, p. 31; Evans, *The Third Reich in Power*, p. 669; Parssinen, p. 43.
22. Hamerow, pp. 238–39.
23. Ibid., p. 239.
24. Ibid., pp. 238–39; also see Evans, *The Third Reich in Power*, p. 670.
25. Evans, *The Third Reich in Power*, p. 670.
26. Deutsch, p. 36.
27. Parssinen, p. 79.
28. Deutsch, p. 54.
29. Hamerow, p. 20.
30. Ibid.
31. Parssinen, p. 5; quoted in Hamerow, pp. 20–21.
32. Parssinen, p. 5.
33. Ibid., p. 6.
34. Deutsch, p. 53.
35. Ibid., p. 62.
36. Parssinen, p. 7.
37. Fest, p. 138.
38. Quoted in Parssinnen, p. 7.
39. Parssinen, p. 7.
40. Ibid.
41. Ibid., pp. 6, 25, 249; Deutsch, pp. 60, 64.
42. Taylor, p. 715.
43. Parssinen, p. 6.
44. Deutsch, pp. 60–61; Parssinen, p. 25.
45. Quoted in Parssinen, p. 25.
46. Parssinen, p. xv; Deutsch, pp. 41–42. Hamerow, pp. 242–43, challenges the belief that the resistance could have succeeded in 1938. Parssinen rejects this view – successfully, in this writer's opinion. Additionally, in the words of Terry Parssinen, both Joachim Fest (*Plotting Hitler's Death*) and Peter Hoffmann (*The History of the German Resistance, 1933–1945*) "have written cogent defenses of the resistance."

See the preface to *The Oster Conspiracy of 1938*. Harold Deutsch declares, "The wisdom of hindsight gives much support to the thesis that never again in the history of the German Opposition did circumstances so favor it as in September 1938" (*The Conspiracy against Hitler in the Twilight War*, p. 41).

47. Deutsch, p. 199.
48. Ibid., p. 201; also see Peter Hoffmann, *The History of the German Resistance, 1933–1945* (Cambridge, MA: MIT Press, 1979), p. 129.
49. Taylor, pp. 692, 716–18, 866–67, 894–96.
50. Parssinen, pp. 161–62.
51. Taylor, p. 716.
52. Brian Bond, "Brauchitsch," in Corelli Barnett, ed., *Hitler's Generals* (New York: Grove Weidenfeld, 1989), p. 75.
53. Ibid., p. 75; Deutsch, p. 34.
54. Taylor, pp. 692, 714.
55. Bond, p. 79; also see p. 76.
56. Quoted in Deutsch, p. 34.
57. Deutsch, p. 34.
58. Ian Kershaw, *Hitler, 1936–1945: Nemesis* (New York: W. W. Norton, 2000), pp. 99–100.
59. Fest, pp. 68–69; Parssinen, p. 61.
60. Klaus-Jürgen Müller, "Witzleben, Stülpnagel, and Speidel," in Corelli Barnett, ed., *Hitler's Generals* (New York: Grove Weidenfeld, 1989), p. 51.
61. Deutsch, p. 33.
62. Fest, p. 86.
63. Quoted in Hamerow, p. 257.
64. Hamerow, p. 255.
65. Deutsch, p. 102.
66. Fest, p. 69; Parssinen, p. 87.
67. Deutsch, pp. 37, 70.
68. Quoted in Parssinen, p. 70.
69. Parssinen, pp. 70–71.
70. Ibid., p. 62.
71. Ibid., p. 71.
72. Ibid., pp. 71–72.
73. Ibid., p. 71.
74. Ibid., p. 72.
75. Ibid.
76. Quoted in Hoffmann, p. 61.
77. Parssinen, p. 74.
78. Fest, pp. 72–73; Hoffmann, pp. 61–62; Parssinen, pp. 70–77.
79. Fest, p. 75.
80. Parssinnen, pp. 72–73.
81. Hoffmann, p. 66.
82. Ibid.

83. Parssinen, pp. 1–2.
84. Hoffmann, p. 66.
85. Ibid., pp. 66–67.
86. Ibid., p. 67.
87. Quoted in Hoffmann, p. 67.
88. Taylor, p. 265; also see Hoffmann, p. 67; Parssinen, pp. 106–7.
89. Taylor, pp. 393, 650; Parssinen, pp. 36–39; Kershaw, pp. 100–101.
90. Taylor, p. 393.
91. Ibid., pp. 552–53; also see Evans, *The Third Reich in History and Memory*, p. 253.
92. Gordon A. Craig, *Europe Since 1815* (New York: Holt, Rinehart, and Winston, 1961), p. 697.
93. Parssinen, p. 84.
94. Ibid., pp. 74–75.
95. Fest, pp. 78–79.
96. Parssinen, pp. 74–78.
97. Ibid., p. 76.
98. Craig, *Europe Since 1815*, p. 703.
99. Fest, p. 69; Parssinen, pp. 84–87.
100. Ibid., p. 78.
101. Kershaw, p. 109.
102. Parssinen, p. 134.
103. Ibid., p. 87.
104. Ibid., p. 112.
105. Fest, p. 86.
106. Quoted in Parssinen, p. 123.
107. Fest, p. 93.
108. Taylor, p. 7.
109. Peter N. Stearns, ed., *The Encyclopedia of World History*, 6th ed. (Boston: Houghton Mifflin, 2001), p. 678.
110. Fest, p. 89; Parssinen, p. 132.
111. Fest, p. 89; Hoffmann, p. 92.
112. Hoffmann, p. 92; Fest, pp. 89–90; Parssinen, pp. 132–35.
113. Hoffmann, pp. 92, 255.
114. Parssinen, p. 134.
115. Ibid., pp. 134–35.
116. Fest, p. 91.
117. Deutsch, p. 36; also see Parssinen, p. 133.
118. Fest, p. 94.
119. Parssinen, p. 154; Fest, pp. 94–96.
120. Hoffmann, p. 93; also see pp. 88, 95; Fest, p. 95; Parssinen, p. 139; Deutsch, p. 28; Hoffmann, pp. 88, 95.
121. Parssinen, pp. 108, 161.
122. Fest, p. 91; Parssinen, p. 134; Hoffmann, pp. 92–93.
123. Fest, p. 89.

Notes

124. Parssinen, pp. 161–64; also see Fest, pp. 195–97; Hoffmann, pp. 93–96.
125. Gordon A. Craig, *Germany, 1866–1945* (New York: Oxford University Press, 1978), p. 707; Stearns, p. 678. Telford Taylor, p. 73, gives the population figure for the German population of the Sudetenland in 1919 as "some three million Germans." There may have been an exodus of Germans subsequent to the signing of the Treaty of Saint Germain between the Allied powers and Austria. This treaty separated Bohemia from Austria and led to the creation of the Czechoslovakian state.
126. Deutsch, p. 38.
127. Ibid.
128. Fest, p. 98.
129. Quoted in Fest, p. 98.
130. Fest, pp. 97–98; Parssinen, pp. 166–72.
131. Fest, pp. 92–98.
132. Ibid., p. 98.
133. Ibid., pp. 98–100.
134. Deutsch, pp. 37, 41.
135. Quoted in Parssinen, p. 172.
136. Ibid.
137. Quoted in Parssinen, pp. 166–67.
138. Hoffmann, pp. 100–101; also see Fest, pp. 102–3.
139. Craig, *The Politics*, p. 500; Hoffmann, p. 101.
140. Fest, p. 103.
141. Ibid.
142. Hoffmann, p. 101.
143. Fest, p. 103.
144. Hoffmann, p. 101.
145. Joachim von Ribbentrop, quoted in Craig, *Europe Since 1815*, p. 705.
146. Hamerow, p. 234.
147. Quoted in Karl Dietrich Bracher, *The German Dictatorship: The Origins, Structure, and Effects of National Socialism* (New York: Praeger, 1970), p. 315.
148. Quoted in Craig, *Europe Since 1815*, p. 706; also see Evans, *The Third Reich in Power*, pp. 689–90; Stearns, p. 720.
149. Craig, *Europe Since 1815*, pp. 715–16.
150. Evans, *The Third Reich in Power*, p. 704.
151. Cited in Evans, *The Third Reich in Power*, p. 704.
152. William L. Shirer, *The Rise and Fall of the Third Reich* (New York: Simon and Schuster, 1960), p. 615.
153. Quoted in Evans, *The Third Reich in Power*, p. 704.
154. Evans, *The Third Reich in Power*, p. 704.
155. Quoted in Deutsch, p. 42.
156. Deutsch, p. 38.
157. Ibid.
158. Fest, p. 112.

159. Ibid., pp. 112–13.
160. Quoted in Christopher R. Browning, *The Origins of the Final Solution: The Evolution of Nazi Jewish Policy, September 1939–March 1942* (Lincoln: University of Nebraska Press, 2004), p. 17.
161. Bracher, p. 352; also see Richard J. Evans, *The Third Reich at War* (New York: Penguin, 2009), p. 15.
162. Bracher, p. 354.
163. Ibid.
164. Fest, p. 114.
165. Browning, p. 27.
166. Ibid., p. 28.
167. Ibid., pp. 99, 286, 296.
168. Bracher, p. 369.
169. Browning, p. 20.
170. Bracher, p. 431.
171. Browning, p. 20.
172. Ibid.
173. Ibid.
174. Hoffmann, p. 263.
175. Ibid., p. 264.
176. Ibid.
177. Fest, p. 112.
178. Hoffmann, p. 114.
179. Hamerow, p. 267.
180. Ibid., p. 250.
181. Fest, pp. 119, 121.
182. Kershaw, p. 247.
183. Quoted in Kershaw, p. 247.
184. Quoted in Fest, p. 118.
185. Fest, p. 119.
186. Ibid., p. 121.
187. Hoffmann, p. 101.
188. Ibid.
189. Deutsch, p. 40.
190. Ibid., p. 82.
191. Fest, p. 122.
192. Deutsch, p. 82.
193. Ibid., p. 88.
194. Ibid., p. 89.
195. Hoffmann, p. 91.
196. Deutsch, p. 90; Fest, p. 68.
197. Fest, p. 122.
198. Hoffmann, p. 120; Fest, p. 121.
199. Fest, p. 12.
200. Deutsch, p. 69.

201. Ibid., p. 72.
202. Ibid., p. 73.
203. Walter Görlitz, "Reichenau," in Corelli Barnett, ed., *Hitler's Generals* (New York: Grove Weidenfeld, 1989), p. 216.
204. Deutsch, p. 77.
205. Ibid., pp. 78, 79.
206. Fest, p. 124.
207. Ibid., p. 122.
208. Ibid., p. 121; Hamerow, p. 274.
209. Fest, p. 121.
210. Hamerow, p. 273.
211. Deutsch, p. 49; also see Walter Görlitz, *History of the German General Staff, 1657–1945* (New York: Frederick A. Praeger, 1954), p. 256; Fest, p. 126.
212. Matthew Cooper, *The German Army, 1933–1945: Its Political and Military Failure* (New York: Bonanza Books, 1984), p. 185.
213. Görlitz, *History*, p. 282; also see Hamerow, p. 255.
214. Deutsch, p. 49.
215. Quoted in Hamerow, p. 255.
216. Ibid.; Deutsch, p. 49.
217. Cooper, p. 185.
218. John W. Wheeler-Bennett, *The Nemesis of Power*, p. 459, quoted in Cooper, p. 185.
219. Görlitz, *History*, p. 362.
220. Deutsch, p. 51.
221. John W. Wheeler-Bennett, quoted in Deutsch, p. 51.
222. Kershaw, p. 263.
223. Hoffmann, p. 128.
224. Deutsch, p. 189.
225. Ibid.
226. Hoffmann, p. 128.
227. Ibid., p. 129.
228. Ibid.
229. Quoted in Hoffmann, p. 129.
230. Hoffmann, p. 129.
231. Deutsch, p. 197.
232. Hoffmann, p. 166.
233. Ibid.
234. Ibid., p. 146.
235. Deutsch, p. 43.
236. Ibid., p. 44.
237. Hamerow, p. 267.
238. Hoffmann, p. 63.
239. Ibid., p. 81.
240. Dr. Louis L. Snyder, *Encyclopedia of the Third Reich,* (New York: Paragon House Publishers 1989).
241. Deutsch, pp. 43–44.

242. Ibid.
243. Ibid., pp. 45–46.
244. Hoffmann, p. 128; Deutsch, p. 46.
245. Quoted in Hoffmann, p. 128.
246. Deutsch, pp. 46–47; Fest, pp. 108–9.
247. Hoffmann, p. 128.
248. Ibid., p. 119.
249. Hamerow, pp. 124–25, 193–94.
250. Deutsch, p. 153.
251. Ibid., p. 151; also see Hoffmann, p. 114.
252. Deutsch, pp. 152–53.
253. Ibid., p. 154.
254. Quoted in Hoffmann, pp. 116–17; also see Hoffmann, pp. 114–15, 118–19, Deutsch, pp. 150–57, and Fest, p. 157.
255. Subsequent to interrogation, Best and Stevens were sent to the Sachsenhausen concentration camp. Both survived the war. During his incarceration, Best met Dietrich Bonhoeffer, and they became friends. See Ferdinand Schlingensiepen, *Dietrich Bonhoeffer, 1906–1945: Martyr, Thinker, Man of Resistance* (London: T & T Clark International, 2010), pp. 370, 372, 378, 380.
256. Despite circumstantial evidence to the contrary, subsequent historical research has proven conclusively that the Elser plot had absolutely no connection to the Venlo incident. Georg Elser acted entirely alone. Deutsch, pp. 136–38; Hoffmann, p. 121; Anton Gill, *An Honourable Defeat: A History of the German Resistance to Hitler, 1933–1945* (New York: Henry Holt, 1994), p. 132.
257. See Deutsch, chapter 4, "The Vatican Exchanges."
258. Roger Moorhouse, *Killing Hitler* (New York: Bantam Dell), p. 72.
259. Quoted in Hamerow, p. 270.
260. Ibid., p. 268.
261. Hamerow, pp. 268–72.
262. Hoffmann, p. 128; also see p. 172.
263. Ibid., p. 129.
264. Müller, p. 54; Fest, pp. 124–25. Hoffmann, p. 129, places the date between October 31 and November 2.
265. Fest, p. 124; also see Hoffmann, p. 129, and Deutsch, p. 199.
266. Deutsch, pp. 199–201; Hoffmann, pp. 129–30; Fest, pp. 123–26.
267. Deutsch, p. 226; Fest, pp. 126–27.
268. Deutsch, p. 226.
269. Ibid., p. 228.
270. Ibid.
271. Ibid.
272. Quoted in Deutsch, p. 229, and Fest, p. 127.
273. Fest, p. 127.
274. Deutsch, p. 230.
275. Hoffmann, pp. 136–37; Deutsch, pp. 226–30; Fest, pp. 126–27.

Notes

276. Quoted in Hoffmann, pp. 137–38.
277. Hoffmann, p. 138.
278. Deutsch, p. 236.
279. Hoffmann, pp. 137, 139.
280. Quoted in Deutsch, p. 233.
281. Hoffmann, p. 138.
282. Deutsch, pp. 236–42, 245–46, 249–50; Fest, pp. 128–30; Hoffmann, pp. 136, 138–40.
283. Hoffmann, p. 143.
284. Bond, p. 75.
285. Barry A. Leach, "Halder," in Corelli Barnett, ed., *Hitler's Generals* (New York: Grove Weidenfeld, 1989), p. 122.
286. Fest, p. 132.
287. Ibid., pp. 128, 133.
288. Ibid., p. 136.
289. Ibid., p. 134.
290. Hoffmann, p. 141; Deutsch, p. 277.
291. Quoted in Hoffmann, p. 145.
292. Hoffmann, p. 146.
293. See Deutsch, chapter 7, "Fading Opposition Hopes," and Hoffmann, pp. 147–52.
294. Hoffmann, p. 169.
295. Parssinen, p. 173.
296. Ibid.
297. Hoffmann, p. 171.
298. Ibid.
299. Ibid., pp. 171–72.
300. Hamerow, p. 274.
301. Hoffmann, p. 172.
302. Quoted in Deutsch, p. 100.
303. Deutsch, p. 99.
304. Ibid., p. 272.
305. Ibid., pp. 270–71.
306. Ibid., p. 271.
307. Kershaw, p. 286.
308. Deutsch, p. 315.
309. Ibid., p. 316.
310. Görlitz, "Reichenau," in *History*, p. 215; Fest, p. 354n5.
311. Hoffmann, pp. 127, 140, 170.
312. Deutsch, p. 316.
313. Ibid., pp. 316–17.
314. Evans, *The Third Reich at War*, p. 119; Kershaw, p. 228; Deutsch, p. 316.
315. Stearns, p. 800.
316. Deutsch, p. 316.
317. Evans, *The Third Reich at War*, p. 119; Kershaw, pp. 288–89.

318. Geoffrey P. Megargee, *Inside Hitler's High Command* (Lawrence: University of Kansas Press, 2000), p. 79.
319. Kershaw, p. 289; Megargee, p. 79.
320. Kershaw, p. 289.
321. Cajus Bekker, *The Luftwaffe War Diaries* (New York: Ballantine Books, 1966), p. 152.
322. Craig, *Europe Since 1815*, p. 721.
323. Cooper, p. 217.
324. Hamerow, p. 278.
325. Craig, *Germany, 1866–1945*, p. 714.
326. Kershaw, pp. 300–301.
327. Peter Fritzsche, *Life and Death in the Third Reich* (Cambridge, MA: Belknap Press of Harvard University Press, 2008), pp. 177–79.
328. One problem remained, however. Hitler expected that subsequent to the French surrender, the British would quickly withdraw from the war in order to preserve their empire. The newly appointed prime minister, Winston Churchill, failed to follow this scenario, however. He had other ideas. He fully realized that Hitler's ambitions were without limit. For Hitler it was all or nothing, world power or destruction (Weltmacht oder Vernichtung). For this reason alone, Churchill would never condescend to an accommodation with Adolf Hitler. Great Britain blocked Hitler's path to total victory, and the war was doomed to continue. Therefore, on July 16, Hitler signed Directive No. 16, for Preparations of a Landing Operation against England. However, a successful invasion required command of the air. Hence, the Luftwaffe launched the air assault known to history as the Battle of Britain, in an attempt to secure air supremacy over the British Isles. This contest with the Royal Air Force raged throughout the summer and early fall of 1940 and ended with the first German defeat since the beginning of the war a year earlier. These events would have far-reaching consequences for the course of World War II and ultimately for the resistance. See Kershaw, pp. 293–94, 300, 302.
329. Hoffmann, p. 171; Stearns, p. 685.
330. Hamerow, p. 278.
331. Ibid., pp. 280–81.
332. Deutsch, p. 324.
333. Ibid., pp. 324–25.
334. Quoted in Fest, p. 143.
335. Deutsch, p. 324.
336. Hamerow, p. 279.
337. Quoted in Hamerow, p. 279.
338. Quoted in Deutsch, p. 324.
339. Quoted in Deutsch, p. 355.
340. Deutsch, p. 326.
341. Fest, pp. 143–44.
342. The great Irish statesman and philosopher Edmund Burke eloquently spoke to this issue with the following words: "The use of force alone is but temporary. It may subdue for a moment; but it does not remove the necessity of subduing again;

Notes

and a nation is not governed, which is perpetually to be conquered" (*The Oxford Dictionary of Quotations*, 2nd ed. [London: Oxford University Press, 1953], s.v. #26, p. 1009.

343. Quoted in Fest, p. 145.
344. Ibid.
345. Fest, p. 145.
346. Ibid., pp. 144–45.
347. Kershaw, p. 385; Craig, *Germany: 1866–1945*, p. 722.
348. Quoted in Craig, *Europe Since 1815*, p. 733.
349. Michael Burleigh, *The Third Reich: A New History* (New York: Hill and Wang, 2000), pp. 490–91.
350. Kershaw, p. 393.
351. Evans, *The Third Reich at War*, pp. 178–79; Kershaw, p. 393.
352. Benjamin Schwarz, "Job for Rewrite: Stalin's War," *The New York Times*, February 21, 2004.
353. Megargee, p. 132.
354. Evans, *The Third Reich at War*, p. 181; Kershaw, p. 394.
355. Megargee, p. 132; Craig, *Europe Since 1815*, p. 734; Evans, *The Third Reich at War*, pp. 187–88; Burleigh, pp. 490–91.
356. Craig, *Germany, 1866–1945*, pp. 733–34, cites the drop in production at 38 percent (p. 734); Burleigh, pp. 490–92, lists the figure at 29 percent (p. 492); also see Kershaw, p. 399, and Joachim Fest, *Hitler* (New York: Harcourt Brace Jovanovich, 1974), p. 651.
357. Burleigh, p. 492.
358. Craig, *Germany, 1866–1945*, p. 733; also see Albert Speer, *Inside the Third Reich* (New York: Macmillan, 1970), p. 180.
359. Evans, *The Third Reich at War*, pp. 189–90.
360. Ibid., p. 189; Kershaw, pp. 398–99. Stalin, though forewarned by the British government, failed to take appropriate action.
361. Evans, *The Third Reich at War*, pp. 189–90.
362. Fest, *Plotting*, p. 179.
363. Kershaw, p. 417.
364. Ibid., p. 398.
365. Megargee, p. 133.
366. Fest, *Plotting*, p. 181.
367. Ibid., p. 184.
368. Megargee, pp. 133–34; Kershaw, pp. 407–9, 417–19.
369. Kershaw, p. 417.
370. Ibid., p. 442.
371. Megargee, p. 137, gives the date as December 4.
372. Kershaw, pp. 441–42; also see Megargee, p. 137; Craig, *Germany: 1866–1945*, p. 730; Evans, *The Third Reich at War*, p. 207.
373. Alan Bullock, *Hitler: A Study in Tyranny*, rev. ed. (New York: Harper and Row, 1962), p. 667; Megargee, pp. 138, 160–61, 276n90; Kershaw, p. 452.
374. Kershaw, p. 453.

375. Ibid., p. 455.
376. Evans, *The Third Reich at War*, p. 214.
377. Bracher, p. 403.
378. Megargee, p. 172.
379. Ibid., p. 174.
380. Kershaw, p. 531.
381. Quoted in Kershaw, p. 534; also see Burleigh, pp. 503–4; Evans, *The Third Reich at War*, p. 409.
382. Evans, *The Third Reich at War*, pp. 408–9; Megargee, pp. 176–77; Kershaw, p. The complexity of a military operation such as this required significant lead time for adequate preparation.
383. Quoted in Kershaw, pp. 531–32.
384. Quoted in Burleigh, p. 503; also see Kershaw, pp. 531–32, and Megargee, pp. 180–81.
385. Evans, *The Third Reich at War*, p. 407.
386. Fest, *Plotting*, p. 187.
387. Bullock, p. 686.
388. Kershaw, p. 534.
389. Megargee, p. 178.
390. Quoted in Megargee, p. 178.
391. Kershaw, pp. 525–28; also see Megargee, pp. 177–78.
392. Kershaw, pp. 528–29.
393. Ibid., p. 529; also see Megargee, pp. 177–78.
394. Evans, *The Third Reich at War*, pp. 409–11.
395. Ibid., p. 410.
396. Craig, *Europe Since 1815*, p. 475; also see Kershaw, p. 540.
397. Hitler's all-or-nothing mentality, together with his limited perspective from his experience as a frontline dispatch runner in the Great War and with no command experience, served to reinforce his belief that one should never give ground to the enemy. This conviction was simply a restatement of a basic concept that both sides had adopted in that earlier conflict, and which Erich von Falkenhayn, chief of the Prussian General Staff, had succinctly stated during the Battle of Verdun in 1916 with the words "*Halten was zu halten ist*" (Hold on to whatever can be held). Although the tactic may have had validity in the trench warfare of those earlier days, it made absolutely no sense at Stalingrad in 1942–1943. See Gary Sheffield, *The Somme* (London: Cassell Military Paperbacks, 2003), p. 88.
398. Martin Middlebrook, "Paulus," in Corelli Barnett, ed., *Hitler's Generals* (New York: Grove Weidenfeld, 1989), p. 372.
399. Burleigh, pp. 504–8.
400. Craig, *Europe Since 1815*, p. 746. General Franz Halder, writing several years after the war, describes Hitler as follows: "Even at the height of his power there was for him no Germany, there were no German troops for whom he felt himself responsible; for him there was – at first subconsciously, but in his last years fully consciously – only one greatness, a greatness which dominated his life and to

Notes

which his evil genius sacrificed everything – his own Ego." Quoted in Bullock, p. 775.

401. Hoffmann, pp. 269–80.
402. Burleigh, p. 512.
403. Bracher, p. 430. Speaking to a group of SS officers in Poland in 1943, Himmler said, "The SS man is to be guided by one principle alone: honesty, decency, loyalty, and friendship to those of our blood and to no one else." Quoted in Bracher, p. 422.
404. Browning, p. 217.
405. Burleigh, p. 517.
406. Ibid. "The elimination of communist leaders and officials would be in their hands [*i.e.,* those of the military commanders] as much as those of Himmler and the police." Quoted in Bond, p. 89; also see Kershaw, p. 356.
407. Browning, p. 217.
408. According to testimony given after the war, several generals in attendance expressed outrage over the speech, although others who were there disputed this. See Kershaw, p. 356.
409. Quoted in Louis L. Snyder, ed., *Encyclopedia of the Third Reich* (New York: Paragon House, 1989), p. 199.
410. Kershaw, p. 358; also see Hoffmann, p. 263.
411. Kershaw, p. 357.
412. Bond, p. 91.
413. Robert Goralski, *World War II Almanac, 1931–1945: A Political and Military Record* (New York: Bonanza Books, 1981), p. 428. Presumably, this figure represents deaths resulting from the Russo-German war, 1941–1945. More recent research places the figure at 26.6 million. See Michael Ellman and S. Maksudov, "Soviet Deaths in the Great Patriotic War: A Note," in *Europe-Asia Studies* 46, no. 4 (1994), published on behalf of Central and East European Studies, University of Glasgow, by Routledge.
414. Kershaw, p. 355.
415. Hoffmann, p. 263; Kershaw, pp. 247–48.
416. Hoffmann, p. 263.
417. Kershaw, p. 358.
418. Ryder, pp. 134, 140, 152; Kershaw, pp. 359–60. For an extended discussion of anti-Semitism in Imperial Germany, see Jonathan Steinberg, chapter 10, in *Bismarck: A Life* (New York: Oxford University Press, 2011), esp. pp. 388–96.
419. Kershaw, p. 359; also see Kershaw, p. 389, and Browning, pp. 245–49.
420. Kershaw, p. 465.
421. Hamerow, pp. 178, 290–92, 316–17; Fest, *Plotting*, pp. 66–67.
422. Hoffmann, p. 267.
423. Ibid., p. 264.
424. Ibid.
425. Quoted in Fest, *Plotting*, p. 172.
426. Leach, p. 117.

427. Fest, *Plotting*, pp. 188–91; Moorhouse, pp. 238–41.
428. Leach, p. 116.
429. Hoffmann, p. 265.
430. Moorhouse, p. 237.
431. Hoffmann, p. 265.
432. Ibid.
433. Phillip Freiherr von Boeselager, *Valkyrie: The Story of the Plot to Kill Hitler, by Its Last Member* (New York: Alfred A. Knopf, 2009), p. 95.
434. Quoted in Hamerow, p. 11.
435. Quoted in Moorhouse, p. 237.
436. Hamerow, p. 316.
437. Fest, *Plotting*, p. 172.
438. Hamerow, p. 292; also see Fest, *Plotting*, pp. 174–75.
439. Fest, *Plotting*, p. 175.
440. Ibid.
441. Ibid., p. 356n11; Hoffmann, p. 268.
442. Hoffmann, p. 270.
443. Fest, *Plotting*, p. 181; Hoffmann, pp. 269–70.
444. Fest, *Plotting*, p. 187.
445. Hamerow, p. 313.
446. Megargee, p. 191.
447. Kershaw, p. 541; Fest, *Plotting*, p. 198; Hamerow, pp. 300–301.
448. Evans, *The Third Reich at War*, p. 467; Fest, *Plotting*, p. 198.
449. Evans, *The Third Reich at War*, p. 424.
450. Ibid., pp. 428–29.
451. Fest, *Plotting*, p. 181.
452. Ibid., p. 180.
453. Richard Lamb, "Kluge," in Corelli Barnett, ed., *Hitler's Generals* (New York: Grove Weidenfeld, 1989), pp. 395–96, 403, 404, 405.
454. Hoffmann, p. 272.
455. Ibid., p. 273.
456. Fest, *Plotting*, p. 187.
457. Hoffmann, pp. 271, 302; also see Fest, *Plotting*, pp. 187, 219.
458. Hoffmann, pp. 271, 302; Fest, *Plotting*, pp. 187–88; Hans Mommsen, *Germans against Hitler: The Stauffenberg Plot and Resistance Under the Third Reich* (London: I. B. Tauris, 2009), p. x.
459. Fest, *Plotting*, p. 187.
460. Kershaw, p. 659.
461. Fest, *Plotting*, p. 188.
462. Hoffmann, p. 275.
463. Fest, *Plotting*, p. 192.
464. Ibid., pp. 192, 380, 386; Hoffmann, pp. 356–60.
465. Fest, *Plotting*, pp. 192–93; Kershaw, p. 395.
466. Hoffmann, p. 280.

467. Nigel Jones, *Countdown to Valkyrie: The July Plot to Assassinate Hitler* (London: Frontline Books, 2008), pp. 135–37.
468. Hoffmann, p. 280.
469. Ibid., pp. 281–83; Fest, *Plotting*, pp. 193–95.
470. Gill, p. 209.
471. Hoffmann, p. 283.
472. Ibid., p. 152.
473. Ibid., pp. 283–89; Fest, *Plotting*, pp. 195–96; Gill, pp. 210–12; Kershaw, p. 663.
474. Hoffmann, p. 288.
475. Ibid., p. 289.
476. Ibid., p. 291.
477. Quoted in Hoffmann, p. 290.
478. Gill, p. 206.
479. Quoted in Fest, *Plotting*, p. 198.
480. Quoted in Gill, p. 213.
481. Quoted in Hoffmann, p. 291.
482. Gill, p. 213.
483. Hoffmann, p. 300; also see Gill, p. 214.
484. Hoffmann, p. 293.
485. Gill, pp. 213–16; Hoffmann, pp. 293–94.
486. Fest, *Plotting*, p. 202.
487. Ibid., p. 203.
488. Hoffmann, p. 293.
489. Ibid., pp. 292–95; Fest, *Plotting*, pp. 202–4; Gill, pp. 215–17.
490. Quoted in Fest, *Plotting*, p. 203.
491. Hoffmann, pp. 294–95.
492. Fest, *Plotting*, p. 213.
493. Hoffmann, p. 297.
494. Ibid., p. 296.
495. Fest, *Plotting*, pp. 214, 222; also see Hoffmann, p. 298, and Gill, p. 214.
496. Craig, *Europe Since 1815*, pp. 741–44; R. R. Palmer, *A History of the Modern World*, 2nd ed. (New York: Alfred A. Knopf, 1964), p. 840; Robert Goralski, *World War II Almanac 1931–1945: A Political and Military Record* (New York: Bonanza Books, 1981), pp. 273–81.
497. Quoted in Hoffmann, p. 375.
498. Quoted in Hamerow, p. 6.
499. Quoted in Hoffmann, p. 374.
500. Hamerow, p. 349.
501. Ibid.
502. Fest, *Plotting*, p. 211.
503. Ibid., pp. 226–27.
504. The account of Stauffenberg's life is based largely on Nigel Jones, *Countdown to Valkyrie*, pp. 11–15; Anton Gill, *An Honourable Defeat*, pp. 227–33; and Hoffmann, pp. 315–21.

505. Jones, pp. 11, 12; Gill, p. 227.
506. Gill, p. 228.
507. Jones, p. 27.
508. Hamerow, pp. 92–93; Hoffmann, pp. 315–17.
509. Hoffmann, p. 318.
510. Gill, p. 230; also see Hoffmann, p. 318.
511. Hamerow, pp. 224–25.
512. Hoffmann, p. 318.
513. Ibid., p. 319.
514. Ibid., p. 319; Fest, *Plotting*, pp. 217–18.
515. Hoffmann, p. 320.
516. Jones, pp. 147–48; Hamerow, p. 311–12.
517. Jones, pp. 148–49; Hoffmann, p. 320.
518. Hamerow, p. 312.
519. Ibid., p. 311.
520. Jones, p. 133; Fest, *Plotting*, pp. 180, 239–40, 325–26.
521. Quoted in Jones, p. 133; also see Hoffmann, p. 318, for a brief discussion of Stefan George and his controversial ideas.
522. Jones, pp. 19, 133; Fest, *Plotting*, p. 240.
523. Fest, *Plotting*, p. 215.
524. Ibid., p. 240.
525. Ibid., p. 215. Gill, p. 233, attributes the quote to Henning von Tresckow.
526. Jones, p. 174.
527. Hoffmann, p. 320; Gill, p. 232.
528. Quoted in Hoffmann, p. 321.
529. Hoffmann, p. 298; Gill, p. 232.
530. Hoffmann, "AHA," p. 769.
531. Hoffmann, p. 309; also see Fest, *Plotting*, p. 215.
532. Fest, *Plotting*, p. 215.
533. Hoffmann, p. 322; Fest, *Plotting*, p. 222.
534. Jones, pp. 162–63.
535. Hoffmann, p. 324.
536. Jones, p. 164.
537. Quoted in Fest, *Plotting*, p. 224; also see Hoffmann, p. 325.
538. Hoffmann, p. 325.
539. Ibid.
540. Ibid., pp. 326–27.
541. Ibid., p. 327; *Plotting*, Fest, pp. 224–25.
542. Fest, *Plotting*, pp. 224–25; Hoffmann, pp. 326–29.
543. Hoffmann, p. 513.
544. Fest, *Plotting*, pp. 227–28; Hoffmann, pp. 294–95.
545. Hoffmann, pp. 331–32. According to Jones, p. 167, Göring was in attendance as well.
546. Quoted in Hoffmann, p. 332; also see Fest, *Plotting*, pp. 225–26.

Notes

547. Evans, *The Third Reich at War*, pp. 636–37.
548. Gill, p. 239.
549. Fest, *Plotting*, p. 221.
550. Hoffmann, pp. 376–77.
551. Ibid., p. 302.
552. Ibid.
553. Ibid., p. 378.
554. Ibid., p. 302.
555. Quoted in Fest, *Plotting*, p. 219.
556. Fest, *Plotting*, p. 219.
557. Hoffmann, p. 301.
558. Fest, *Plotting*, p. 219; also see Hoffmann, p. 301.
559. Fest, *Plotting*, p. 220; Hoffmann, p. 297.
560. Hoffmann, pp. 298–99.
561. Ibid., p. 271.
562. Ibid., p. 272.
563. Ibid., p. 305.
564. Ibid., p. 374.
565. Ibid., p. 374; Evans, *The Third Reich at War*, p. 637.
566. Hoffmann, p. 374; Evans, *The Third Reich at War*, p. 637.
567. Hoffmann, p. 375.
568. Ibid., p. 373.
569. Ibid.
570. Jones, p. 171.
571. Ibid.
572. Hoffmann, p. 373.
573. Ibid., p. 373.
574. Ibid., pp. 374–76.
575. Hamerow, p. 349; also see Kershaw, pp. 698–700.
576. Quoted in Fest, *Plotting*, pp. 240–41, and Hoffmann, p. 374.
577. Hoffmann, pp. 380–82.
578. Gill, pp. 243–44; Jones, pp. 175–77, 181–82; Hoffmann, pp. 381–88.
579. Hoffmann, p. 397; Jones, p. 182; Fest, *Plotting*, p. 253.
580. Jones, pp. 182–83.
581. Hoffmann, p. 394; Fest, *Plotting*, pp. 253–54.
582. Quoted in Evans, *The Third Reich at War*, p. 638.
583. Hoffmann, p. 392; Fest, *Plotting*, p. 253.
584. Hoffmann, pp. 397–98; Gill, pp. 244–45; Jones, pp. 186–88.
585. Fest, *Plotting*, pp. 258–60; also see Jones, pp. 192–95, and Gill, pp. 245–46.
586. Hoffmann, pp. 399–401, note #25, pp. 667–68; Jones, pp. 189–92; Gill, pp. 245–46.
587. Hoffmann, pp. 397–404, note #25, pp. 667–68; Gill, pp. 245–46.
588. Hoffmann, pp. 404–5; Jones, p. 193; Fest, *Plotting, p.* 258.
589. Hoffmann, p. 411; Fest, *Plotting*, p. 243.

590. Hoffmann, pp. 300, 326, 335.
591. Army headquarters was referred to as the Bendlerstraße, and that term is used in *Patriots or Traitors?*
592. Jones, p. 197.
593. Hoffmann, pp. 411–13; Gill, pp. 246–47; Fest, *Plotting*, pp. 260–61.
594. Hoffmann, p. 413.
595. Jones, p. 197.
596. Kershaw, p. 675.
597. Hoffmann, pp. 413, 416.
598. Ibid., p. 416.
599. Kershaw, p. 677.
600. Hoffmann, p. 412.
601. Ibid., p. 456.
602. Jones, p. 199.
603. Hoffmann, p. 417.
604. Ibid., p. 420.
605. Quoted in ibid., p. 422; Gill, p. 247.
606. Hoffmann, pp. 422–23.
607. Gill, pp. 247–48.
608. Hoffmann, p. 426.
609. Ibid.
610. Ibid.
611. Ibid., p. 495.
612. Ibid., p. 480.
613. Ibid., p. 481; Fest, *Plotting*, p. 288; Kershaw p. 679; Speer, p. 383.
614. Speer, p. 383; also see p. 384, and Hoffmann, p. 481.
615. Jones, pp. 183–84; Hoffmann, pp. 390, 428, 430.
616. Hoffmann, pp. 429–30; Fest, *Plotting*, pp. 269–71.
617. Quoted in Jones, p. 216.
618. Hoffmann, pp. 430, 481–82.
619. Gill, p. 249.
620. Quoted in Kershaw, p. 680.
621. Kershaw, p. 681.
622. Speer, p. 387.
623. Jones, p. 214; Kershaw, p. 681. The precise time of Goebbels's radio address varies according to the source consulted. See Kershaw, p. 1004n112.
624. Quoted in Michel C. Thomsett, *The German Opposition to Hitler: The Resistance, the Underground, and Assassination Plots, 1938–1945* (Jefferson, NC: McFarland, 1997), p. 218; also see Jones, p. 219.
625. Speer, p. 384.
626. Ibid., p. 384; also see Hoffmann, pp. 480–81.
627. Kershaw, p. 681; Fest, *Plotting*, pp. 274, 275.
628. Hoffmann. p. 439.
629. Ibid., pp. 502–3, 507–9, 526; Kershaw, pp. 682–83; Jones, p. 254.

Notes

630. Fest, *Plotting*, p. 294.
631. Ibid., p. 294; Jones, pp. 283, 284, 286, 291.
632. Fest, *Plotting*, pp. 276–77, 279; Hoffmann, pp. 507–8.
633. Kershaw, p. 683.
634. Hoffmann, p. 377.

Chapter 6

1. Joachim Fest, *Plotting Hitler's Death: The Story of the German Resistance, 1933–1945* (New York: Metropolitan Books, Henry Holt, 1996), p. 289.
2. Ian Kershaw, *Hitler, 1936–1945: Nemesis* (New York: W. W. Norton, 2000), p. 677.
3. Ibid.
4. An interesting postscript to the assassination question is a comment made by Hjalmar Schacht, the former minister of economics, who declared after the war that the resistance had reached a turning point in the autumn of 1938. Before Munich, he believed that legal action and a coup d'état could have brought Hitler down; after Munich, however, he believed that the "only recourse" was assassination. See Theodore S. Hamerow, *On the Road to the Wolf's Lair: German Resistance to Hitler* (Cambridge, MA: Belknap Press of Harvard University Press, 1997), p. 242.
5. Fest, p. 288. Heinz commanded the Wehrmacht Patrol Service in Berlin, which had assembled two raiding parties for the purpose of arresting Goebbels. But the attempt failed when the troops that were assembled for the raid "placed themselves under the command of Major Remer." See Peter Hoffmann, *The History of the German Resistance, 1933–1945* (Cambridge, MA: MIT Press, 1979), p. 438.
6. Fest, p. 288.
7. Quoted in Albert Speer, *Inside the Third Reich* (New York: Macmillan, 1970), p. 388.
8. Richard J. Evans, *The Third Reich at War* (New York: Penguin, 2009), pp. 645–46.
9. Fest, pp. 292–93.
10. Hoffmann, p. 511.
11. Evans, p. 644; Hoffmann, pp. 512, 529, 712–13n21; Kershaw, p. 693; Fest, pp. 294–95.
12. Hoffmann, p. 516.
13. Kershaw, p. 691; Fest, pp. 294–95; Evans, p. 642; Hoffmann, p. 516.
14. Fest, p. 295; Hoffmann, p. 516.
15. Evans, p. 642.
16. Fest, pp. 303–4; Hoffmann, pp. 519–20.
17. Quoted in Fest, pp. 303–4; Kershaw, p. 691; Hoffmann, pp. 519–20.
18. Fest, p. 304.
19. See Nigel Jones, "Afterward," in *Countdown to Valkyrie: The July Plot to Assassinate Hitler* (London: Frontline Books, 2008), pp. 273–80.
20. Ibid., p. 249.
21. Quoted in Kershaw, p. 688.

22. Ibid.
23. Quoted in Fest, p. 297.
24. Fest, p. 279.
25. Kershaw, p. 689.
26. Fest, p. 289.
27. Richard Lamb, "Kluge," in Corelli Barnett, ed., *Hitler's Generals* (New York: Grove Weidenfeld, 1989), p. 406.
28. Ibid., pp. 406–7; Anton Gill, *An Honourable Defeat: A History of the German Resistance to Hitler, 1933–1945* (New York: Henry Holt, 1994), p. 254.
29. Hoffmann, pp. 470–78; Lamb, p. 407.
30. Quoted in Fest, p. 290.
31. Quoted in Lamb, p. 407; also see Lamb, pp. 406, 408. General Rudolph-Christoph von Gersdorff states categorically in his memoirs, originally published in 1976, "Unquestionably, [Kluge] had made no attempt to get into radio contact with the western Allies." On the basis of what is now known about this episode, this seems doubtful. See Baron Rudolph-Christoph von Gersdorff. *A Soldier in the Downfall: A Wehrmacht Cavalryman in Russia, Normandy, and the Plot to Kill Hitler* (Bedford, PA: Aberjona Press, 2012), p. 119.
32. Quoted in Fest, p. 290; also see Kershaw, pp. 721–22.
33. Quoted in Jones, p. 260.
34. Fest, p. 291; also see Gersdorff, p. 115.
35. Jones, p. 285.
36. Ibid.
37. Ibid., p. 237.
38. Fest, pp. 246–47, 264–66; Jones, pp. 177, 181, 283; Gill, p. 243.
39. Hoffmann, pp. 327, 334, 335; Fest, pp. 222, 224, 297.
40. Fest, p. 297; Hoffmann, p. 524.
41. Bracher, *The German Dictatorship: The Origins, Structure, and Effects of National Socialism* (New York: Praeger, 1970), p. 459.
42. Kershaw, p. 692.
43. Jones, p. 250; Fest, p. 299.
44. Kershaw, p. 692.
45. Quoted in Jones, p. 250; also see Fest, p. 297.
46. Kershaw, p. 693.
47. Ibid.
48. Evans, p. 643; Jones, pp. 251–52; Hoffmann, p. 528.
49. Hoffmann, pp. 529–30, 721n42.
50. Evans, p. 688.
51. Fest, p. 303; Jones, p. 253; Evans, p. 643.
52. Jones, p. 253; also see Kershaw, p. 693.
53. Kershaw, p. 1006n43; also see Fest, p. 303; Jones, pp. 251–53.
54. Hoffmann, p. 526.
55. Fest, pp. 294, 299–300.
56. Jones, p. 250.

57. Quoted in Fest, p. 301; also see p. 399.
58. Ibid., p. 301.
59. Quoted in ibid., p. 295.
60. Ibid., p. 340; also see pp. 341–43.
61. Evans, p. 641.
62. Fest, p. 293.
63. Quoted in Hoffmann, p. 435; Fest, pp. 269, 327, 329, 388.
64. Fest, pp. 309–10; Richard J. Evans, *The Third Reich in History and Memory* (New York: Oxford University Press, 2015), p. 350.
65. Fest, pp. 309–10; Hoffmann, p. 513.
66. Fest, pp. 309–10.
67. Ibid., p. 295.
68. Ibid., p. 310.
69. Hoffmann, p. 527; Fest, p. 319.
70. Kershaw, p. 691; Evans, *The Third Reich at War*, pp. 689–90.
71. Fest, p. 319.
72. Hoffmann, p. 521.
73. Ibid., p. 519.
74. Ibid., pp. 521, 522; also see Jones, pp. 257–59; Fest, pp. 295–96.
75. Hoffmann, p. 523.
76. On Schlabrendorff's religious convictions, see Jones, pp. x–xi, 257.
77. Hoffmann, p. 527.
78. Jones, p. 289; Fest, p. 308.
79. Evans, *The Third Reich at War*, pp. 718–20.
80. Speer, p. 472.
81. Joachim Fest, *Inside Hitler's Bunker: The Last Days of the Third Reich* (New York: Farrar, Strauss, and Giroux, 2002), pp. 22–23, 131.
82. Fest, *Inside Hitler's Bunker*, pp. 17–23, 131–32; Joachim Fest, *Hitler* (New York: Harcourt Brace Jovanovich, 1974), pp. 726–28.
83. For a detailed discussion of Hitler's last days, see Fest, *Hitler*, Book VIII, "Catastrophe," esp. chapter 2, "Götterämmerung"; Fest, *Inside Hitler's Bunker*, offers a thorough examination of this topic.
84. Evans, p. 716; Fest, *Inside Hitler's Bunker*, p. 131; Alan Bullock, *Hitler: A Study in Tyranny*, rev. ed. (New York: Harper and Row, 1962), pp. 774–75.
85. Speer, p. 442; Fest, *Inside Hitler's Bunker*, pp. 124–25; Fest, *Hitler*, p. 725.
86. Evans, *The Third Reich at War*, p. 716; see Speer, p. 440, and Bullock, pp. 774–75, for the direct quote.
87. Quoted in Bullock, p. 795.
88. Fest, *Inside Hitler's Bunker*, pp. 131, 171.
89. Fest, *Hitler*, pp. 732–33; Evans, *The Third Reich at War*, pp. 716–17. See Speer, pp. 440–43, and chapter 30, for a description of these travels.
90. Kershaw, p. 784.
91. Ibid., p. 786.
92. Michael Burleigh, *The Third Reich: A New History* (New York: Hill and Wang, 2000), p. 791.

93. Robert Goralski, *World War II Almanac 1931–1945: A Political and Military Record* (New York: Bonanza Books, 1981), pp. 404–6.
94. Randall Hansen, *Fire and Fury: The Allied Bombing of Germany, 1942–1945* (New York: NAL Caliber, 2008), p. 277.
95. Goralski, pp. 426, 428. According to Richard Evans, *The Third Reich at War*, p. 67, the total number of Germans officially classified as Jews numbered 207,000 in September 1939. They were mostly middle-aged or elderly. Of that number, approximately 15,000 escaped to a neutral country by the end of 1940. Consequently, the number of Germans of the Jewish faith probably numbered about 192,000 by the time that the final solution to the Jewish question was initiated in January 1942. If the 170,000 figure cited in the text is correct, then the Jewish population in Germany who survived the war is approximately 22,000.
96. Terese Pencak Schwartz, "The Holocaust: Non-Jewish Victims," Jewish Virtual Library, accessed October 24, 2017, www.jewishvirtuallibrary.org/non-jewish-victims-of-the-holocaust; also Terese Pencak Schwartz, *Holocaust Forgotten: Five Million Non-Jewish Victims*, vol. 1. (self-pub., CreateSpace, 2012).
97. These opportunists as described by Ian Kershaw were "individuals seeking career advancement in party or state bureaucracy, the small business man aiming to destroy a competitor though a slur on his 'Aryan' credentials, or ordinary citizens settling scores with neighbors by denouncing them to the Gestapo … doctors rushing to nominate patients of asylums for the 'euthanasia programme' in the interests of a eugenically 'healthier' people; lawyers and judges zealous to co-operate in the dismantling of legal safeguards in order to cleanse society of 'criminal elements' and undesirables; business leaders anxious to profit from preparations for war and, once in war, by grabbing of booty and exploitation of foreign slave labor; thrusting technocrats and scientists seeking to extend power and influence through jumping on the bandwagon of technological experimentation and modernization; non-Nazi military leaders keen to build up a modern army and restore Germany's hegemony in Central Europe; and old-fashioned conservatives with a distaste for the Nazis but with an even greater fear and dislike for the Bolsheviks." Ian Kershaw, *Hitler, the Germans, and the Final Solution* (New Haven, CT: Yale University Press, 2008), p. 42; Richard J. Evans, *The Third Reich in Power, 1933–1939* (New York: Penguin, 2005), pp. 393–95, 404–5.
98. Koppel S. Pinson, *Modern Germany*, 2nd ed. (New York: Macmillan, 1966), pp. 548–49.
99. "Resistance to Hitler," *The Atlantic Times, A Monthly Newspaper from Germany*, February 2009, pp. 20–21.
100. Fest, *Plotting*, p. 321.
101. Hamerow, p. 286.
102. Ibid., pp. 14–15.
103. Ibid., p. 405.
104. Gill, p. 45; Fabian von Schlabrendorff, *The Secret War against Hitler* (Boulder: Westview Press, 1944), p. xix.
105. The opposite of prophetic religion is civic religion, which serves the interests of the state. It is a creature of the state, and its object of worship is the state. It is a religion

that, in fact, is no religion at all. It totally lacks moral and ethical foundations, and its primary feature is pure opportunism. Although civic religion has varying degrees of intensity, and regrettably has been practiced on occasion by established Christian denominations to their discredit, its most extreme version appeared in the Third Reich in the form of the Reich Church and its bishop, Ludwig Müller. As noted, it had only a minimal following, and the Nazis themselves ultimately abandoned it.

106. Quoted in Jones, pp. x–xi.
107. Quoted in Fest, *Plotting*, p. 99.
108. Ibid.
109. Quoted in Jones, p. 257.
110. Hamerow, pp. 350–51.
111. Quoted in Jones, p. 272.
112. Hamerow, p. 351.
113. Dietrich Bonhoeffer, *I Want to Live These Days with You: A Year of Daily Devotions*, "Becoming Guilty," the reading for March 30 (Louisville, KY: Westminster John Knox Press, 2007), p. 93.
114. Quoted in Ferdinand Schlingensiepen, *Dietrich Bonhoeffer, 1906–1945: Martyr, Thinker, Man of Resistance* (London: T & T Clark International, 2010), pp. 153, 370.
115. Fest, *Plotting*, p. 289.
116. Quoted in Jones, p. 242; also see Hamerow, p. 369.
117. Jones, p. 242.
118. Hoffmann, p. 168.
119. Hamerow, p. 311.

Appendix A

1. Chris McNab, *World War II Data Book: The SS, 1923–1945* (London: Amber Books, 2009), p. 159.
2. Ian Kershaw, *Hitler, 1889–1936: Hubris* (New York: W. W. Norton, 1999), p. 136.

Appendix C

1. Edwin Black, *War Against the Weak: Eugenics and America's Campaign to Create a Master Race*, 2nd ed. (Washington, DC: Dialog Press, 2012), p. 12.
2. Ibid., pp. 12–13, 15.
3. Quoted in ibid., p. 18.
4. Black, p. 19.
5. Ibid., p. 137.
6. Ibid., p. 90.
7. Ibid., pp. 45, 90.
8. Black, p. 19.
9. Ibid., pp. 21, 398.
10. Ibid., pp. 249–52.
11. Ibid., p. 207.
12. Ibid., p. 21.

13. Ibid., p. 83.
14. Quoted in Black, pp. 82–83.
15. Quoted in Alan Bullock, *Hitler: A Study in Tyranny*, rev. ed. (New York: Harper and Row), 1962.
16. Black, p. 270.
17. Ibid., p. 258.
18. Ibid., pp. 259, 266, 297.
19. Ibid., pp. 277, 280, 313–14, 316.
20. Ibid., pp. 94–95, 296–97, 298, 364, 31, 46–47.
21. Ibid., pp. 31, 89–90, 104–5, 94–95.
22. Ibid., p. 89.
23. Ibid., p. 75.
24. Ibid., p. 313.
25. Ibid., pp. 199–201.
26. Ibid., p. 313.
27. Ibid., p. 31, 401.

Bibliography

Books

Asprey, Robert B. *The German High Command at War: Hindenburg and Ludendorff Conduct World War I.* New York: William Morrow, 1991.

Bailey, Thomas A. *Woodrow Wilson and the Lost Peace.* Chicago: Encounter Paperbacks, Quadrangle Press, 1963.

Barnett, Corelli, ed. *Hitler's Generals.* New York: Grove Weidenfeld, 1989.

Barnett, Victoria J., ed. (English Edition), *Dietrich Bonhoeffer Works.* vol. 15, *Dietrich Bonhoeffer: Theological Education Underground: 1935-1937.* Minneapolis: Fortress Press, 2012.

Barraclough, Geoffrey. *The Origins of Modern Germany.* New York: Capricorn Books, 1963.

Bekker, Cajus. *The Luftwaffe War Diaries.* New York: Ballantine Books, 1964.

Bessel, Richard. *Germany after the First World War.* New York: Oxford University Press, 1993.

Bethge, Eberhard. *Dietrich Bonhoeffer: A Biography*, rev. ed., ed. Victoria J Barnett. Minneapolis: Fortress Press, 2000.

Black, Edwin. *War against the Weak: Eugenics and America's Campaign to Create a Master Race.* 2nd edition. Washington, DC: Dialog Press, 2012.

Boeselager, Philipp Freiherr von. *Valkyrie: The Story of the Plot to Kill Hitler, by Its Last Member.* New York: Alfred A. Knopf, 2009.

Bonart, Paul. *But We Said "No": Voices from the German Underground.* San Francisco: Mark Backman Productions, 2007.

Bond, Brian. "Brauchitsch." In *Hitler's Generals*, edited by Corelli Barnett. New York: Grove Weidenfeld, 1989.

Bonhoeffer, Dietrich. *I Want to Live These Days with You: A Year of Daily Devotions.* Louisville, KY: Westminster John Knox Press, 2007.

Bonhoeffer, Dietrich. *The Cost of Discipleship.* Rev. ed. New York: Collier Books, 1963.

Bracher, Karl Dietrich. *The German Dictatorship: The Origins, Structure, and Effects of National Socialism.* New York: Praeger, 1970.

Brook-Shepherd, Gordon. *The Austrians: A Thousand-Year Odyssey.* New York: Carroll & Graf, 1996.

Browning, Christopher R. *The Origins of the Final Solution: The Evolution of Nazi Jewish Policy, September 1939–March 1942.* Lincoln: University of Nebraska Press, 2004.

Bukey, Evan Burr. *Hitler's Austria: Popular Sentiment in the Nazi Era, 1938–1945.* Chapel Hill: University of North Carolina Press, 2000.

Bullock, Alan. *Hitler: A Study in Tyranny.* Rev. ed. New York: Harper and Row, 1962.
Burleigh, Michael. *The Third Reich: A New History.* New York: Hill and Wang, 2000.
Calleo, David. *The German Problem Reconsidered – Germany and the World Order: 1870 to the Present.* Cambridge: Cambridge University Press, 1980.
Citino, Robert M. *The German Way of War.* Lawrence: University Press of Kansas, 2005.
Clark, Christopher. *Kaiser Wilhelm II.* London: Routledge, 2013.
Clark, Christopher. *Iron Kingdom: The Rise and Downfall of Prussia, 1600–1947.* Cambridge, MA: Belknap Press of Harvard University Press, 2006.
Cooper, Matthew. *The German Army, 1933–1945: Its Political and Military Failure.* New York: Bonanza Books, 1984.
Craig, Gordon A. *Germany, 1866–1945.* New York: Oxford University Press, 1978.
Craig, Gordon A. *Europe Since 1815.* New York: Holt, Rinehart, and Winston, 1961.
Craig, Gordon A. *The Politics of the Prussian Army, 1640–1945.* New York: Oxford University Press, 1956.
Deutsch, Harold C. *The Conspiracy against Hitler in the Twilight War.* Minneapolis: University of Minnesota Press, 1968.
Dumbach, Annette, and Jud Newborn. *Sophie Scholl and the White Rose.* Oxford: Oneworld Publications, 2007.
Evans, Richard J. *The Third Reich in History and Memory.* New York: Oxford University Press, 2015.
Evans, Richard J. *The Third Reich at War.* New York: Penguin, 2009.
Evans, Richard J. *The Third Reich in Power.* New York: Penguin, 2005.
Evans, Richard J. *The Coming of the Third Reich.* New York: Penguin, 2004.
Ferrell, Robert H. *American Diplomacy.* 3rd ed. New York: W. W. Norton, 1975.
Fest, Joachim. *Inside Hitler's Bunker: The Last Days of the Third Reich.* New York: Farrar, Strauss, and Giroux, 2002.
Fest, Joachim. *Plotting Hitler's Death: The Story of the German Resistance, 1933–1945.* New York: Metropolitan Books, Henry Holt, 1996.
Fest, Joachim. *Hitler.* New York: Harcourt Brace Jovanovich, 1974.
Feuchtwanger, E. J. *Prussia: Myth and Reality.* Chicago: Henry Regnery, 1970.
Fritzsche, Peter. *Life and Death in the Third Reich.* Cambridge, MA: Belknap Press of Harvard University Press, 2008.
Gaithorne-Hardy, G. M. *A Short History of International Affairs, 1920–1939.* 4th ed. London: Oxford University Press, 1950.
Gellately, Robert. *Backing Hitler: Consent and Coercion in Nazi Germany.* Oxford: Oxford University Press, 2001.
Gersdorff, Rudolph-Christoph. *Soldier in the Downfall.* Bedford, PA: Aberjona Press, 2012.
Gilbert, Martin. *The First World War: A Complete History.* New York: Henry Holt, 1994.
Gill, Anton. *An Honourable Defeat: A History of German Resistance to Hitler, 1933–1945.* New York: Henry Holt, 1994.
Goralski, Robert. *World War II Almanac 1931–1945: A Political and Military Record.* New York: Bonanza Books, 1981.
Görlitz, Walter. "Blomberg." In *Hitler's Generals*, edited by Corelli Barnett. New York: Grove Weidenfeld, 1989.

Bibliography

Görlitz, Walter. "Keitel, Jodl, and Warlimont." In *Hitler's Generals*, edited by Corelli Barnett. New York: Grove Weidenfeld, 1989.

Görlitz, Walter. "Reichenau." In *Hitler's Generals*, edited by Corelli Barnett. New York: Grove Weidenfeld, 1989.

Görlitz, Walter. *History of the German General Staff, 1657–1945*. New York: Frederick A. Praeger, 1954.

Haasis, Helmut. *Bombing Hitler: The Story of the Man Who Almost Assassinated the Führer*. New York: Skyhorse Publishing, 2013.

Haffner, Sebastian. *Defying Hitler: A Memoir*. Rev. ed. London: Phoenix, 2003.

Hamerow, Theodore S. *On the Road to the Wolf's Lair: German Resistance to Hitler*. Cambridge, MA: Belknap Press of Harvard University Press, 1997.

Hansen, Randall. *Fire and Fury: The Allied Bombing of Germany, 1942–1945*. New York: NAL Caliber, 2008.

Haasis, Hellmut G. *Bombing Hitler*. New York: Skyhorse Publishing, 2013. (Originally published in Germany in 2001 – English language translation 2011 copyright by William Odom).

Herbert, Ulrich. "Good Times, Bad Times: Memories of the Third Reich." In *Life in the Third Reich*, edited by Richard Bessel. Oxford: Oxford University Press, 2001.

Hoffmann, Peter. *The History of the German Resistance, 1933–1945*. Cambridge, MA: MIT Press, 1979.

Höhne, Heinz. *The Order of the Death's Head: The Story of Hitler's SS*. New York: Penguin, 2000.

Holborn, Hajo. *A History of Germany: The Reformation*. New York: Alfred A. Knopf, 1976.

Hossbach, Friedrich. *Zwischen Wehrmacht und Hitler, 1934–1938* [Between Wehrmacht and Hitler, 1934–1938]. Quoted in Evans, Richard D. *The Third Reich in Power*. New York: Penguin, 2005.

Jones, Nigel. *Countdown to Valkyrie: The July Plot to Assassinate Hitler*. London: Frontline Books, 2008.

Kann, Robert. *A History of the Habsburg Empire, 1526–1918*. Berkeley: University of California Press, 1974.

Kennan, George F. *American Diplomacy, 1900–1950*. Chicago: University of Chicago Press, 1951.

Kershaw, Ian. *Hitler, the Germans, and the Final Solution*. New Haven, CT: Yale University Press, 2008.

Kershaw, Ian. *Hitler, 1936–1945: Nemesis*. New York: W. W. Norton, 2000.

Kershaw, Ian. *Hitler, 1889–1936: Hubris*. New York: W. W. Norton, 1999.

Kirschbaum, Erik. *Burning Beethoven: The Eradication of German Culture in the United States during World War I*. New York: Berlinica Publishing, 2015.

Koch, H. W. *A Constitutional History of Germany in the Nineteenth and Twentieth Centuries*. London: Longman Group, 1984.

Koonz, Claudia. *The Nazi Conscience*. Cambridge, MA: Belknap Press of Harvard University Press, 2003.

Lafore, Laurence. *The Long Fuse: An Interpretation of the Origins of World War I*. Philadelphia: J. B. Lippincott, 1965.

Lamb, Richard. "Kluge." In *Hitler's Generals*, edited by Corelli Barnett. New York: Grove Weidenfeld, 1989.

Leach, Barry A. "Halder." In *Hitler's Generals*, edited by Corelli Barnett. New York: Grove Weidenfeld, 1989.

MacMillan, Margaret. *The War That Ended Peace*. New York: Random House, 2013.

MacMillan, Margaret. *Paris, 1919*. New York: Random House, 2003.

Malkin, Peter Z., and Harry Stein. *Eichmann in My Hands*. New York: Warner Books, 1990.

Manvell, Roger. *The Conspirators: 20 July 1944*. New York: Ballantine Books, 1971.

McDonough, Frank. *Opposition and Resistance in Nazi Germany*. Cambridge: Cambridge University Press, 2001.

McLean, Ian, and Alistair McMillan. *The Oxford Concise Dictionary of Politics*. Oxford: Oxford University Press, 2003.

McNab, Chris. *World War II Data Book: The SS, 1923–1945*. London: Amber Books, 2009.

Meyer, G. J. *A World Undone: The Story of the Great War, 1914 to 1918*. New York: Delacourt, 2006.

Megargee, Geoffrey P. *Inside Hitler's High Command*. Lawrence: University of Kansas Press, 2000.

Middlebrook, Martin. "Paulus." In *Hitler's Generals*, edited by Corelli Barnett. New York: Grove Weidenfeld, 1989.

Middlebrook, Martin. *The Battle of Hamburg: Allied Bomber Forces Against a German City in 1943*. New York: Charles Scribner's Sons, 1981.

Mommsen, Hans. *Germans against Hitler: The Stauffenberg Plot and Resistance under the Third Reich*. London: I. B. Tauris, 2009.

Moorhouse, Roger. *Killing Hitler*. New York: Bantam Dell, 2006.

Müller, Klaus-Jürgen. "Witzleben, Stülpnagel, and Speidel." In *Hitler's Generals*, edited by Corelli Barnett. New York: Grove Weidenfeld, 1989.

New World Dictionary of the American Language. 2nd college ed. Cleveland: William Collins, 1980.

O'Neill, Robert. "Fritsch, Beck, and the Führer." In *Hitler's Generals*, edited by Corelli Barnett. New York: Grove Weidenfeld, 1989.

The Oxford American College Dictionary. New York: Oxford University Press, 2002.

The Oxford Dictionary of Quotations. 2nd ed. London: Oxford University Press, 1953.

Palmer, R. R. *A History of the Modern World*. 2nd ed. New York: Alfred A. Knopf, 1964.

Parkinson, Roger. *Summer, 1940: The Battle of Britain*. New York: David McKay, 1977.

Parssinen, Terry. *The Oster Conspiracy of 1938*. New York: HarperCollins, 2003.

Peukert, Detlev. "Youth in the Third Reich." In *Life in the Third Reich*, edited by Richard Bessel. Oxford: Oxford University Press, 2001.

Peukert, Detlev. *Inside Nazi Germany: Conformity, Opposition, and Racism in Everyday Life*. New Haven, CT: Yale University Press, 1987.

Pinson, Koppel S. *Modern Germany*. 2nd ed. New York: Macmillan, 1966.

Putz, Erna. *Franz Jägerstätter, Martyr: A Shining Example in Dark Times*. Linz, Austria: Katholische Kirche in Oberösterreich [Catholic Church in Upper Austria], 2007.

Bibliography

Rasmussen, Larry L. *Dietrich Bonhoeffer: Reality and Resistance.* Louisville, KY: Westminster John Knox Press, 2005.

Reinhardt, Kurt. *Germany, 2000 Years.* Vol. 1, rev. ed. New York: Continuum, 1989.

Ringma, Charles. *Seize the Day with Dietrich Bonhoeffer.* Colorado Springs: Pinion Press, 2000.

Ryder, A. J. *Twentieth-Century Germany: From Bismarck to Brandt.* New York: Columbia University Press, 1973.

Scheurig, Bodo. *Henning von Tresckow: Eine Biographie.* Düsseldorf: Stalling, 1979. Quoted in Fest, Joachim. *Plotting Hitler's Death: The Story of the German Resistance, 1933–1945.* New York: Metropolitan Books, Henry Holt, 1996.

Schlabrendorff, Fabian von. *The Secret War against Hitler.* Boulder: Westview Press, 1994.

Schlingensiepen, Ferdinand. *Dietrich Bonhoeffer, 1906–1945: Martyr, Thinker, Man of Resistance.* London: T & T Clark International, 2010.

Scholl, Inge. *The White Rose: Munich, 1942–1943.* Middletown, CT: Wesleyan University Press, 1983.

Schwartz, Terese Pencak. *Holocaust Forgotten: Five Million Non-Jewish Victims.* Vol. 1. Self-published, CreateSpace, 2012.

Sheehan, James J. *Where Have All the Soldiers Gone?* Boston: Houghton Mifflin, 2008.

Sheehan, James J, ed. *Imperial Germany.* New York: New Viewpoints, 1976.

Sheffield, Gary. *The Somme.* London: Cassell Military Paperbacks, 2003.

Shirer, William L. *Berlin Diary.* Quoted in Parkinson, Roger. *Summer, 1940: The Battle of Britain.* New York: David McKay, 1977.

Shirer, William L. *The Rise and Fall of the Third Reich.* New York: Simon and Schuster, 1960.

Snyder, Dr. Louis L. *Encyclopedia of the Third Reich.* New York: Paragon House, 1989.

Speer, Albert. *Inside the Third Reich.* New York: Macmillan, 1970.

Stearns, Peter N., ed. *The Encyclopedia of World History.* 6th ed. Boston: Houghton Mifflin, 2001.

Stern, Fritz. *Five Germanys I Have Known.* New York: Farrar, Straus, and Giroux, 2006.

Steinberg, Jonathan. *Bismarck: A Life.* New York: Oxford University Press, 2011.

Stone, David. *Shattered Genius: The Decline and Fall of the German General Staff in World War II.* Havertown, PA: Casemate Publishers, 2011.

Stone, David. *Fighting for the Fatherland.* Washington, DC: Potomac Books, 2006.

Taylor, Telford. *Munich: The Price of Peace.* New York: Vintage Books, 1980.

Thomsett, Michael C. *The German Opposition to Hitler: The Resistance, the Underground, and Assassination Plots, 1938–1945.* Jefferson, NC: McFarland, 1997.

Watt, Richard M. *The Kings Depart.* New York: Simon and Schuster, 1968.

Weber, Max. *The Protestant Ethic and the Spirit of Capitalism.* 2nd ed. Los Angeles: Roxbury, 1998.

Wehler, Hans-Ulrich. "Bismarck's Imperialism." In *Imperial Germany*, edited by James Sheehan. New York: New Viewpoints, 1976.

Weitz, Eric D. *Weimar Germany: Promise and Tragedy.* Princeton: Princeton University Press, 2007.

Wheeler-Bennett, John W. *The Nemesis of Power.* Quoted in Cooper and in Craig, *The Politics of the Prussian Army, 1640–1945.*

Wind, Renate. *Dietrich Bonhoeffer: A Spoke in the Wheel*. Grand Rapids, MI: William B. Eerdmanns, 1990.

Zahn, Gordon. *In Solitary Witness: The Life and Death of Franz Jägerstätter*. Rev. ed. Springfield, IL: Templegate, 1986.

Magazine, Periodical, and Newspaper Articles

Ellman, Michael, and S. Maksudov. "Soviet Deaths in the Great Patriotic War: A Note." *Europe-Asia Studies* 46, no. 4 (1994), published on behalf of Central and East European Studies, University of Glasgow, by Routledge.

Ivins, Molly. "Rumsfeld Leads Us into Quicksand." *Democrat and Chronicle* (Rochester, NY). March 19, 2006.

Rasmussen, Larry. "The Steep Price of Grace." *Sojourners Magazine* 35, no. 2 (February 2006).

"Resistance to Hitler." *Atlantic Times, a Monthly Newspaper from Germany*. February 2009: pp. 20–21.

Schwarz, Benjamin. "Job for Rewrite: Stalin's War," *New York Times*. February 21, 2004.

Online References

Angel, Pierre Robert. "Eduard Bernstein." *Encyclopaedia Britannica Online*. Last modified July 28, 2016. https://www.britannica.com/biography/Eduard-Bernstein.

Dash, Mike. "One Man against Tyranny." *Smithsonian Magazine*, August 18, 2011. http://blogs.smithsonianmag.com/history/2011/08/one-man-against-tyranny/.

Dzidic, Denis, Marija Ristic, Milka Domanovic, Josip Ivanovic, Edona Peci, and Sinisa Jakov Marusic. "Gavrilo Princip: Hero or Villain?" *Guardian*, May 6, 2014. https://www.theguardian.com/world/2014/may/06/gavrilo-princip-hero-villain-first-world-war-balkan-history.

"Franz Jaegerstaetter." Just Peace. Accessed March 19, 2018. http://justpeace.org/franz.htm.

Ganse, A., trans. "The Reich Constitution of August 11th 1919 (Weimar Constitution) with Modifications." ZUM. 2001. http://www.zum.de/psm/Weimar/Weimar_vve.php (translated and posted by permission of DHM, Berlin, http://www.DHM.de/lemo/).

Malzahn, Claus Christian. "The Carpenter Elser versus the Führer Hitler." *Spiegel Online*, November 8, 2005. http://www.spiegel.de/international/0,1518,druck-383792,00.html.

Nizkor Project. "The Organization of the Nazi Party & State." Chap. 6 in *Nazi Conspiracy & Aggression*. Vol. 1. http://www.nizkor.org/hweb/imt/nca/nca-01/nca-01-06-organization.html.

Schwartz, Terese Pencak. "The Holocaust: Non-Jewish Victims." Jewish Virtual Library. Accessed October 24, 2017. www.jewishvirtuallibrary.org/non-jewish-victims-of-the-holocaust.

Index

Abwehr, 30, 63, 85, 101, 134–135, 148, 152, 154, 157, 175, 185–187, 198, 203, 212, 233, 238–239, 248
Act for the Reconstruction of the Reich, 119
Action Group Zossen, 198
Adenauer, Konrad, 266
air force (Luftwaffe), 56–57, 125, 129, 176, 216
Allgemeines Heeresamt (AHA, General Army Office), 245
American Eugenics Society, 301
Anschluss (connection/union), 107–108, 133, 141–147, 171,
anti–Nazi activity
  as existing from beginning of Nazi rule, 17
  options for anti-Nazi Germans, 23–24
anti–Semitism, 23, 31, 52–54, 76, 155, 225, 243, 280, 300
Aquinas, Saint Thomas, 245
Army Group Center, 148, 151, 214, 218, 227–229, 232, 235, 278
Aryan Paragraph, 80
Aryanization program, 283
Aryans, defined, 290
assassination
  attempts on Hitler, 4–5
  as immoral act, 6
  as justified, 6, 228
  moral issues surrounding, 2, 4
atomization of society, under Nazi rule, xiii, 32, 42
Auschwitz concentration camp, 29
Austria, incorporation of, 144

Austro–Prussian War (1866), 142
authoritarian state (Obrigkeitsstaat), 60

Barmen Declaration, 83, 290
Barth, Karl, 83, 290
Bavaria, as boiling cauldron of racist (völkisch) extremism, 11
BBC (British Broadcasting Corporation), 19
Beck, Ludwig, 15, 49, 58, 66, 96–97, 116–117, 123, 127, 134–135, 143, 158, 175, 188, 193, 203, 205, 229, 232, 238, 242, 253, 263, 295
Beecham, Thomas, 47
"Beefsteak Nazis," 20
Beer Hall Putsch, 1, 12, 14
Bell, Alexander Graham, 304
Bell, George, 288
Bendlerstraße, 256–258, 261–264, 290
Berghof, 168, 245, 248, 252, 254, 290
Bernardis, Robert, 270
Bernstein, Eduard, 88
Bernstorff, Albrecht Graf von, 114
Bessel, Richard, 86
Best, S. Payne, 196
Bethge, Eberhard, vi
Bewegung (movement), 12, 290
Bismarck, Otto von, 61
Black, Edwin, 303
Black Front, 4
Blaskowitz, Johannes, 184, 226, 295
blitzkrieg (lightning war), 176, 179, 183, 205, 209, 215, 290
block (Block), 34, 290

357

block leader (Blockleiter)/block leaders (Blockleitern), 33, 290
Blomberg, Werner von, 116, 119, 127, 132, 151, 295
blood purge, 115–118, 125. *See also* Night of the Long Knives
Blutrache (blood vengeance), 266, 290
Bock, Fedor von, 228, 296
"Bolshevik menace," 26
Bolshevik/Bolshevism, 39, 89, 223, 290. *See also* Jewish Bolshevism
Bonart, Paul, 24
Bonhoeffer, Dietrich, 5–6, 31, 58, 68, 75, 77, 100, 138, 213, 272, 287, 295
Bonhoeffer, Klaus, 58
Bormann, Martin, 158
Bosch, Robert, 96, 152
Brandt, Colonel, 235
Brauchitsch, Walther von, 92, 136, 158, 167, 170, 182, 187–188, 190–191, 199–203, 218, 226, 295
Brecht, Bertolt, 21
Bredow, Kurt von, 118
Breitenbuch, Eberhard von, 248–249, 295
British Broadcasting Corporation (BBC), 19
Brockdorff–Ahlefeldt, Walter Graf von, 158
Brownshirts, 73, 84, 90, 290. *See also* SA (Sturm Abteilung)
Brüning, Heinrich, 22, 188, 194
Buchenwald concentration camp, 35
Bürgerbräukeller
  bombing of (November 8, 1939), 1–4, 105, 196
  Hitler's speech at (1923), 1–3, 11
Busch, Ernst, 238, 248–249, 295
Bussche–Streithorst, Axel Freiherr von dem, 246–248, 270, 277, 295

Canaris, Wilhelm, 63, 134, 152, 156–157, 185, 187, 193, 212, 238, 248, 272, 276, 295

Carl Zeiss optical company, 17
Carnegie Institution, 304
Casablanca Conference (1943), 194
Catholic Center Party, 94
Catholic Church, 68, 72–74, 109
cell (Zell), 34, 294
cell leader (Zellenleiter), 294
Chamberlain, Neville, 162–168, 175, 197
Christian Democratic Union, 94
churches. *See also* Catholic Church; Confessing Church; Evangelical Church; Reich Church; Roman Catholic Church
  as first of German institutions to openly confront Third Reich, 68
Churchill, Winston, 163, 281
circuit or circle (Kreis), 34, 99, 292
climate of resignation, as option for anti–Nazi Germans, 41
Colvin, Ian, 161
Commissar Order (Kommissar Erlass), 224–226, 229, 290
"Communist threat," 16
concentration camps
  Auschwitz concentration camp, 29
  Buchenwald concentration camp, 35
  Dachau concentration camp, 4
  as fixture in Nazi state, 27
  Flossenbürg concentration camp, 272
  public description of, 27
  Sachsenhausen concentration camp, 4, 79, 83
Confessing Church, 77, 80, 83–84, 111
coordination (Gleichschaltung), 3, 33, 45, 71, 132, 291
Craig, Gordon A., 117
"Crystal Night" (Kristallnacht), 3, 33, 45, 71, 132, 291
"cultural revolution," 51
Curtis, Lionel, 100

Dachau concentration camp, 4
Darwin, Charles, 300

Index

Das Schwarze Korps (the Black Corps), 206, 293
"Day of the Awakening Nation," 15
Delp, Alfred, 99, 295
Denmark, military action in, 207
Deutsch, Harold, 96, 156, 179, 185, 188
Deutsche Arbeitsfront (DAF, Nazi Labor Front), 91, 292
Dibelius, Otto, 74
Dietrich, Marlene, 10, 21
Diktat of Versailles, 128, 210
dissent, in Nazi lexicon, 19
district (Gau), 34, 291
district leader (Gauleiter), 280, 291
Do You Want Total War? 39
Dohnányi, Christine (neé Bonhoeffer), 239
Dohnányi, Hans von, 169, 185, 213, 239, 296
dramatis personae, 295–299
Drang nach Osten (drive to the east), 219
Dreyfus, Alfred, 54
dual monarchy, 142, 291
Dulles, Allen W., 262

E. H. Harriman Foundation, 304
Ebert, Friedrich, 89, 118
Edelweiss Pirates (Edelweiß Piraten), 113, 291
Ehrhardt, Hermann, 169
Ehrhardt Freikorps, 169
Eichmann, Adolf, 67, 182
Einsatz Barbarossa (Operation Barbarossa), 43, 216, 223, 291
Einsatz Walküre (Operation Valkyrie), 240–263, 275–276, 291
Einsatzgruppen (operations groups or task forces), 29, 180–183, 206, 228, 291
Einstein, Albert, 21
Eintopf (one–pot meal), 33, 291
Elser, Georg, 2–5, 23, 35, 105–108, 111, 189, 196, 201, 296
Enabling Act (Ermächtigungsgesetz), 89

Esche, Udo, 269
eugenics, 300–302, 304–305
Eugenics Record Office, 301, 204
Eugenics Research Association, 301, 304
Evangelical Church, 68, 84
Evans, Richard, 54, 90, 275, 282
Evolutionary Socialists, 292

Fall Blau (Case Blue), 219, 291
Fall Gelb (Case Yellow), 211, 291
Fall Grün (Case Green), 159, 291
false messiah, xiii, xiv
Fellgiebel, General, 256, 296
Fest, Joachim, 202
Fingerspitzengefühl ("fingertip sensitivity," or sixth sense), 237
Finkenwalde, 84–85
flash, 234–235, 291
Flossenbürg concentration camp, 272, 279
Foreign Ministry, 127, 150, 154, 192
Frankfurter, Felix, 195
Franz Ferdinand, assassination of, 4
Frederick the Great (Friedrich der Grosse), 48, 59, 70, 122, 279
Freikorps (free corps), 169, 291
Freisler, Roland, 262, 270–273, 279, 296
Friedländer, Saul, 111
Friedrich Wilhelm III (king), 214
Fritsch, Werner von, 116, 127, 131, 134–136, 143, 186, 296
From U–Boat to Pulpit (Niemöller), 78
Fromm, Friedrich, 249, 251–252, 258, 262–263, 267, 269, 296

Galen, Clemens August von, 72, 296
Galton, Francis, 300
Gau (district), 34, 291
Gauleiter (district leader), 280, 291
Geheime Staatspolizei (Gestapo, or Secret State Police), 30, 34, 50, 73, 84, 92, 99, 135, 196, 230, 232, 254, 263–266, 276, 286, 291
General Army Office (Allgemeines Heeresamt, AHA), 245, 290

George, Stefan, 245
German Christian Movement, 82, 85
German cinema, 10
German Communist Party, 87, 91, 277
German National People's Party, 14, 18
"German revolution," beginning of, 11
German Social Democratic Party in Exile (Die Sozialdemokratische Partei Deutschlands im Exil, or SOPADE), 22, 42, 293
German Social Democratic Party (SPD, Sozialdemokratische Partei Deutschlands), 22, 291
German Workers Party, 11
Gersdorff, Rudolph–Christoph von, 123, 228–229, 232, 235–237, 269, 277, 296
Gerstein, Kurt, 111–112, 296
Gerstenmaier, Eugen, 213, 258, 277, 296
Gestapo (Geheime Staatspolitzei, or Secret State Police), 30, 34, 50, 73, 84, 92, 99, 135, 196, 230, 232, 254, 263–266, 276, 286, 291
Gewitteraktion (Thunderstorm), 266, 291
Gill, Anton, 243
Gisevius, Hans Berndt, 135, 154, 160, 173, 201, 213, 227,
Gleichschaltung (coordination), 3, 33, 45, 71, 132, 291
glossary, 290–294
Goebbels, Joseph Paul, 3, 15, 25, 30, 37, 40, 73, 158, 230, 249, 259–261, 265, 267, 296
Goerdeler, Carl, 46, 49, 52, 56, 58, 81, 93–94, 96–97, 99, 105, 130, 136, 143, 149, 152, 175, 193, 214, 233, 246, 266, 279, 287, 296
Goethals, Georges, 211
Göring, Hermann, 3, 29, 56, 133, 180, 214, 296
Grant, Madison, 303
Great Depression, 12, 26, 89, 145, 282
Gropius, Walter, 21

Groppe, Theodor, 206
Groscurth, Helmuth, 30, 68, 152, 173, 180, 185, 188, 190, 192, 198, 299, 232, 296
Gruhn, Eva (a.k.a. Marguerite or Erna), 132

Habsburg family, 142, 292
Haeften, Hans Bernd von, 30–31, 154, 296
Haeften, Werner von, 255, 262, 296
Haffner, Sebastian, 21, 45
Hagen, Albrecht von, 270
Halder, Franz, 92, 124, 151, 158, 160, 167, 174, 178, 180, 182, 190–192, 198, 22–203, 217, 220, 224, 297
Halifax, Lord, 164–165
Hamburg, destruction of, 40
Hamerow, Theodore, 138
Hammerstein–Equord, Kurt von, 58, 68, 77, 188–189, 191–192, 238, 240, 297
Harnack, Arvid, 114, 297
Harnack, Ernst von, 94
Harnack–Fish, Mildred, 114, 297
Hase, Paul von, 260, 270, 297
Hassell, Ulrich von, 30, 53, 56, 62, 104, 211–212, 239, 262, 297
Heinz, Friedrich Wilhelm, 168–170, 265, 275, 297
Helldorf, Wolf Heinrich Graf von, 158, 275, 297
Henderson, Neville, 164
Hereditary Genius (Spencer), 300
Herrenvolk (master race), 28, 303
Hess, Rudolf, 158, 303
Himmler, Heinrich, 4, 134, 158, 180, 206, 239, 265–266, 276, 293, 297
Hindemith, Paul, 21
Hindenburg, Paul von, 13–14, 16, 69–70, 118–119, 297
Hitler, Adolf
  ability of to dominate public life, 18
  as anti–Christ, 245

Index

as becoming more withdrawn and secretive, 251
as chancellor, 13–14, 18, 69, 89, 118
clashes of with generals over war policy and strategy, 231
conspiracy against, 37
decline in popularity of, 230
as delusional, 279
as epicenter of National Socialism, 134
as false messiah, xiii, xiv
favorite projects of, 216
first electoral attempt of, 13
as Führer und Reichskanzler, 118–119
as Germany's tragic destiny, 239
last order of, 209
as manipulator of modern media, 14
"military genius" of as myth, 230
military rationale for removal of, 219
as perverting and corrupting noble and honored traditions of the nation he ruled, 122
plummeting of reputation of, 219
"political testament" of, 303
as puppet who became puppeteer, 13–14
sixth sense of, 237
speech by at Bürgerbräukeller, 1
suicide of, 280
weapons of, xiv
Hitler Youth, 113
Hobbes, Thomas, 68
Hochverrat (high treason), 11, 140–141, 204, 292
Hoegner, Wilhelm, 90
Hoepner, Erich, 270
Hofacker, Cäsar von, 273
Hoffmann, Peter, 103, 140, 191, 237, 289
Hohenzollern, Fritz von (Great Elector), 58
Hohenzollern kings, 315
home army, 270, 293
An Honourable Defeat (Gill), 306
Hugenberg, Alfred, 14–18
Hull, Cordell, 194

ideology
  dangers of, 226
  as policy, 222
intelligence quotient (IQ), 302
internal exile, as option for anti–Nazi Germans, 24, 41, 150
"international Communist conspiracy," 26

Jäger, Fritz, 239
Jägerstätter, Franz, 106–110, 284, 297
Jägerstätter, Franziska, 108, 110
Jewish Bolshevism, plan for eradication of, 223–225
Jewish question, 54, 67, 76, 226, 276
Jews
  campaign against, 23, 29, 51
  disappearance of, 29
  as equated with Bolshevism by Hitler, 223
  exodus of from Germany, 22
  and Nuremberg Laws, 29, 52
  Oster conspiracy and, 149
  resettlement of, 181
  as Untermenschen, 29, 179–180
  waging of war against, 227
Jodl, Alfred, 128, 174, 249, 281
Jones, Nigel, 245
Judenreservat (Jewish reservation), 181

Kahr, Gustav von, 11, 115–116, 297
Kaiser, Jakob, 49, 93–95, 97, 99, 193, 297
Kandinsky, Wassily, 21
Keitel, Wilhelm, 109, 132, 174, 182, 197, 210, 258, 274, 297
Kerrl, Hans, 85
Kershaw, Ian, 119, 128
Klausing, Friedrich, 270
Klee, Paul, 21
Kleist–Schmenzin, Ewald Heinrich von, 297
Kleist–Schmenzin, Ewald von, 62, 68, 77, 149, 161–163, 297
Klemperer, Otto, 21

Kluge, Günther von, 124, 231, 238, 251, 267–169, 297
Kommissar Erlass (Commissar Order), 223–226, 228–229, 290
Kordt, Erich, 150, 164, 167, 173, 192, 201, 298
Kordt, Theo, 150, 164, 193
Kraft durch Freude (Strength through Joy) program, 32
Kreis (circuit or circle), 30, 292
Kreisau Circle, 49, 93, 99, 101–104, 154, 213, 248, 277, 287, 292
Kriegsmarine (navy), 129, 207–208, 216, 230, 292
Kristallnacht ("Crystal Night"), 3, 33, 45, 71, 132, 291
Küchler, Georg von, 225

Landesverrat, 140, 204, 292
Lang, Fritz, 10
Lanz, Hubert, 234
Lanz Plan, 234, 292
law and order
  in Nazi lexicon, 19
League of Nations, 24, 79
Lebensraum (living space), 131, 146, 176, 180, 292
Leber, Julius, 93, 99, 104, 144, 298
left-wing extremism, suppression of, 9
Lehndorff, Heinrich, 287
Lenya, Lotte, 21
Leuschner, Wilhelm, 49, 92–95, 97, 144, 188, 193, 298
Liedig, Franz Marie, 157, 168, 204, 298
Lippmann, Walter, 194
List, Wilhelm, 136
living space (Lebensraum), 131, 146, 176, 180, 292
Lloyd, Lord, 162
local group (Ortsgruppe), 34, 293
Lorre, Peter, 10
Lubbe, Marius van der, 16
Ludendorff, Erich, 14, 118
Luftwaffe (air force), 3, 56–57, 125, 129, 176, 209, 216

lumpenproletariat (dregs of German society), 66
Luther, Martin, 6, 74

Machtergreifung (seizure of power), 13, 16
Majority Socialists, 88–89, 291
Mann, Thomas, 21
Markwitz Circle, 94
Marx, Karl, 87
mass mobilization, history of, 49
master race (Herrenvolk), 28, 303
McCloy, John J., 286
Mein Kampf (Hitler), 305
Mendelssohn, Felix, 47
military adventurism, 126
Ministry of Propaganda, 25, 32, 39, 73, 259, 282, 284
Mit brennender Sorge (With Burning Concern), 74
Mitteleuropa (Middle Europe), 225
Model, Walter, 236, 269, 298
Moltke, Dorothy (née Rose–Innes), 100
Moltke, Helmut von the Elder, 100
Moltke, Helmut von the Younger, 100
Moltke, Helmuth James von, 96, 99, 100–101, 212, 238, 248, 298
Momm, Harald, 275
movement (Bewegung), 12, 290
Müller, Ludwig, 82, 85, 298
Munich, as safe haven for Hitler to build his "movement," 11
Munich Conference, 164, 167, 171–173
Mussolini, Benito, 230, 241
The Myth of the Twentieth Century (Rosenberg), 72

national comrades (Volksgenossen), 31–32, 38, 310
National Socialism, 21–22, 24, 33, 36, 50, 53, 74, 109, 114, 123, 134, 156–157, 227
National Socialist German Workers Party, 11

Index

National Socialist People's Welfare Organization, 34
navy (Kriegsmarine), 129, 207–208, 216, 230, 292
Nazi Labor Front (Deutsche Arbeitsfront, or DAF), 91, 292
Nazi Party (Nationalsozialistsche Deutsche Arbeiter Partei)
    accession to power by, 15–16, 19, 21–22
    choices of opponents of, 21–22
    as combining terror and repression with conciliatory gestures, declarations of moral purpose, and concessions, 32
    as committed to overthrow of Weimar Republic, 11
    as corrupting mind and soul of German nation, 282–283
    essential ingredient for success of, 12
    "high noon" of, 26, 47, 91, 105, 126
    Hitler as leader (Führer) of, 11
    ideological foundation of, 43
    as "movement" (Bewegung), 12, 290
    in Reichstag elections (1932), 12–14
    in Reichstag elections (1936), 73
    in Reichstag elections (1938), 73
    in Reichstag elections (March 5, 1933), 15–18, 24
    in Reichstag elections (November 12, 1933), 24
Nazism
    belief of some as positive and truly progressive movement, 283
    churches reaction to, 68–84
    as completely nihilistic and devoid of substance, 284
    as corrupting terms "treason" and "patriotism," 139
    ideological foundation of, 28
    ironies of, 32–33
    as making illegality "legal," 141
    Oster's and Tresckow's early dalliance with, 227

Nazi–Soviet Nonaggression Pact, 176
Nero Order, 280, 292
Neurath, Konstantin von, 131
Niebuhr, Reinhold, 139
Niemöller, Martin, 77–81, 83–84, 98, 298
Night of the Long Knives, 22, 115, 155
Not Nazis but Germans (Tosevic), xii
Nuremberg Laws, 29, 52

Oath Act, 124
oath of allegiance, 118–125, 134, 136, 149, 151, 160, 201
Oberkommando der Wehrmacht (OKW), 6, 109, 132, 136, 151, 174, 208, 292
Oberkommando des Heeres (OKH), 129, 151, 174, 185, 188, 198, 208, 211, 292
Obrigkeitsstaat (authoritarian state), 60, 292
Olbricht, Friedrich, 232–234, 238, 245–246, 250–252, 256–258, 298
Operation Barbarossa (Einsatz Barbarossa), 43, 216, 223, 291
Operation Flash, 234–235, 291
Operation Overlord, 241, 251–252, 254, 293
Operation Valkyrie (Einsatz Walküre), 240–263, 275–276, 291
operations groups or task forces (Einsatzgruppen), 29, 180–183, 206, 228, 291
Orthodox Socialists, 292
Ortsgruppe (local group), 292
Ortsgruppenleiter (district group leader), 293
Oster, Hans, 5, 15, 30, 68, 117, 123, 130, 134, 137–138, 148–175, 185, 193, 195, 201, 204–206, 211, 226, 232, 239, 257, 265, 272, 276, 286, 294, 298
Oster conspiracy, 149–175, 182, 265
Oster Study (Studie Oster), 157, 198

Papen, Franz von, 13–14, 46, 118
Paris Peace Conference (1919), 147
Parssinen, Terry, 66, 204
Pastors' Emergency League, 83
Patton, George, 268
Paulus, Friedrich, 221–222, 298
People's Court, 113, 262, 267, 269–270, 272, 279
personal isolation, as option for anti–Nazi Germans, 24
Peukert, Detlev, 37
"phony war" (Sitzkrieg), 186, 192, 197, 206, 211, 293
Pinson, Koppel S., 283
Pius XI (pope), 73
Plötzensee Prison, 271–272
Polish Corridor, 181, 184, 193, 293
political crimes, 27, 270
Popitz, Johannes, 97, 213, 298
Princip, Gavrilo, 4
Protestant Evangelical (state) Church, 68–84
The Protestant Ethic and the Spirit of Capitalism (Weber), 67
public opinion, manipulation of by Nazism, 33
Putz, Erna, 110

Quirnheim, Albrecht Ritter Mertz von, 262

racial extermination, 29, 223, 228
racial hygiene, 28, 301
racial program, 75, 222
racial purity, 28–29, 302
racial science, 304
racial violence/warfare, 53, 55
racism
  as ideological foundation of Nazism, 28
  as not exclusively a German phenomenon, 53–54
  sources of Nazi racism, 300–305
Raeder, Erich, 57, 207
rearmament, and Rhineland, 125–132

Red Front Fighters' League (Roter Frontkämpferbund), 2–3
Red Orchestra (Rote Kapelle), 114, 293
Reich Church, 69, 72, 82–84
Reich Security Head (RSHA, Reichssicherheitshauptamt), 180, 293
Reichenau, Walter von, 119, 128, 187, 207, 298
Reichswehr, 98, 116–121, 125, 134, 155, 188, 227, 293
Reichwein, Adolf, 49, 298
Reinhardt, Max, 10
Remer, Otto Ernst, 260–261, 298
replacement army, 148, 232, 249–251, 254, 257, 293
reserve army, 232, 254
resistance, in Nazi lexicon, 19
resistance movement
  active civilian opposition as futile, 130
  beginnings of true resistance movement, 135
  Chamberlain government as totally misreading, 165
  Christian conscience and faith as feature of, 286–287
  churches as first of German institutions to openly confront Third Reich, 71
  clandestine resistance groups, 284
  coup de grâce for, 261
  early history of, xiii, 51–54
  ebbing of "inner strength" of, 243
  Elser as personifying, 4
  fatal weakness of, 42
  four rounds of resistance, 148–263
  Kreisau Circle. *See* Kreisau Circle
  members who survived carnage of, 277–280
  moral dilemma of, 264–265
  as more extensive and pervasive than Nazi authorities had realized, 276
  as never having public behind it, 47
  1938 as pivotal year in history of, 133–136

Index

no secret national resistance movement as developing within Germany, 38
rallying points for, 184
response of conflation of incompetent military leadership and severe moral turpitude, 223
retribution and martyrdom of, 265–281
revival of after Commissar Order, 227
Round II, Part 1, the Abwehr, September to November 5, 1939, 175–203
Round II, Part 2, the Abwehr, November 6, 1939 to May 1940, 203–214
Round III, Army Group Center, August 1942 to October 1943, 214–240
Round I, Oster conspiracy, July to September 1938, 149–175
Round IV, Operation Valkyrie, March to July 1944, 240–264
socialists in, 94–95
in state of near paralysis, 239
as unorganized and leaderless, 274
widespread character of, 112
workers as forming most significant component of, 37
Revisionist Socialists, 293
Revolutionary Socialists, 87, 293
Ribbentrop, Joachim von, 163, 178, 298
right–wing extremism
active support of, 10
influence of, 10–12
source of, 11
Ritter, Gerhard, 46
Rockefeller Foundation, 304
Roettger, Wilhelm, 272
Röhm, Ernst, 115–117
Roman Catholic Church, 71, 109
Root, Elihu, 304
Rose–Innes, James, 100
Rosenberg, Alfred, 40, 72–73, 298

Rote Kapelle (Red Orchestra), 114, 293
RSHA (Reichssicherheitshauptamt, Reich Security Head), 180, 293

SA (Sturm Abteilung), 23, 30, 51, 90, 115, 275, 294
Sachsenhausen concentration camp, 4, 79, 83
SAP (Socialist Workers' Party), 87
Sas, Gijsbertus, 204–205, 211, 298
Schacht, Hjalmar, 126, 129–130, 135, 154, 298
Scheffer, Paul, 194
Scheidemann, Phillip, 8
Schlabrendorff, Fabian von, 229, 232, 234–235, 278–279, 268, 288, 297
schlafwandlerische Sicherheit (sleepwalker's assurance), 127
Schleichler, Kurt von, 13–14, 46, 115–116, 118
Schlingensiepen, Ferdinand, 6, 75, 77, 84
Schmundt, Rudolph, 236
Scholl, Hans, 113, 299
Scholl, Sophie, 113, 299
Schulenburg, Fritz–Dietlof von der, 149, 154, 174, 213, 259, 262, 273, 299
Schultze, Erich, 156, 299
Schulze–Boysen, Harro, 114, 299
Schuschnigg, Kurt von, 141, 299
Schutzstaffel (SS, or Security Staff), 28–29, 43, 180–181, 232–234
Schwaninger, Franziska, 107
SD (Sicherheitsdienst, or Security Service of the SS), 38, 196, 225, 293
"second revolution," 116
Secret State Police (Geheime Staatspolitzei, Gestapo), 30, 34, 50, 73, 84, 92, 99, 135, 196, 230, 232, 254, 263–266, 276, 286, 291
seizure of power (Machtergreifung), 13, 116
Shirer, William, 36–37, 177
Simonis, Susanne, 164

SiPo (Sicherheitspolizei, or Security Police), 225, 293
Sitzkrieg ("phony war"), 186, 192, 197, 206, 211, 293
Social Darwinism, 59, 300
social democratic movement, 87, 193
Social Democrats/Social Democratic Party (SPD), 9, 22–23, 48, 87–92, 94, 99, 118, 291. *See also* German Social Democratic Party in Exile (Die Sozialdemokratische Partei Deutschlands im Exil, or SOPADE); German Social Democratic Party (SPD, Sozialdemokratische Partei Deutschlands)
social exclusion, as option for anti–Nazi Germans, 24
socialist movement, 49, 60, 85, 87–89
Socialist Workers' Party (SAP), 87
Sodenstern, Georg von, 179
Solf, Hanna, 113, 299
Solf, Wilhelm, 113
Solf Circle, 113, 248
Sozialdemokratische Partei Deutschlands (SPD), 22–24. *See also* Social Democrats/Social Democratic Party (SPD)
Spartacist Rebellion, 26
Spartakus Rebellion, 293
Speer, Albert, 259, 261, 272, 279–280, 299
Spencer, Herbert, 300
"spirit of Zossen," 200
SS (Schutzstaffel, or Security Staff), 28, 30, 43, 180–181, 184, 206, 232–233, 293
Stauffenberg family, 267
Stauffenberg, Berthold von, 242, 252, 262
Stauffenberg, Claus Schenk von, 5, 15, 30, 93, 103, 117, 137, 140, 144, 148–149, 173, 242–243, 257, 299
Steel Helmet (Stahlhelm), 84, 169, 293
Stefan George circle, 267

Stein, Karl vom und zum, 214
Steiner, Rudolf, 20
Stevens, R. H., 196, 334
Stieff, Helmuth, 256, 270
storm troopers (SA, Sturm Abteilung), 11, 23, 30, 51–52, 84, 115, 294
Strasser, Otto, 2
Strength through Joy (Kraft durch Freude) program, 32
Stroheim, Erich von, 10
Studie Oster (Oster Study), 157, 198, 294
Stülpnagel, Carl Heinrich von/ Stülpnagel, Karl–Heinrich von, 198, 273, 299
"The Stuttgart Declaration of Guilt," 80
Sudetenland, 102, 141–148, 151, 153, 157, 161, 165, 168, 175, 193, 294
Supreme Command of the Army (Oberkommando des Heeres, or OKH), 129, 151–152, 174, 188, 198, 207–208, 211, 292. *See also* Oberkommando des Heeres (OKH)
swastika (Hakenkreuz), 20, 31

Thälmann, Ernst, 277
Thiele, Fritz, 256
Third Reich
  as absolute police state, 24
  acceptance of, 26
  as bringing sense of purpose and direction and new feeling of hopefulness and confidence, 25
  defined, 294
  disappearance of distinction between politics and private life in, 31
  goal of, 20
  "good times" of, 25–26
  Jews as not welcome in, 22–23
terror machine of, 24, 27, 32, 38
"veneer of legality" of, 19
Thomas, Georg, 129, 160, 299
Thunderstorm (Gewitteraktion), 266, 291
Tillich, Paul, 21

Index

To the Obscurantists of Our Day (Rosenberg), 73
Tosevic, Dimitri J., xi–xii
"Total War" speech (Goebbels), 230
treason, 19, 136–141
Treaty of Versailles, 8–9, 64, 74, 77, 79, 98, 125–126, 128, 151, 166, 194, 228, 294
Tresckow, Henning von, 5, 15, 62, 118, 123, 148, 179, 184, 222, 227–229, 231–236, 240–243, 245–246, 248–249, 254, 257, 278, 286, 288, 299
Trott zu Solz, Adam von, 123, 154, 193–195, 299
Truman, Harry S., 281
Truppenamt (Troop Office), 98, 116, 151

Übermenschen (superior peoples), 179
United States, loans from to Germany, 9
Untermenschen (lesser peoples), 29, 179–180, 303

Vansittart, Robert, 162–163
Venlo incident, 196, 288
Verbindungsmann (V–Mann), 6
Verräter vor dem Volksgericht (Traitors before the People's Court) (film), 272
Volksgemeinschaft (people's community), xiii, 28–29, 32–34, 41–42, 55, 61, 67, 70, 91, 95, 102, 274, 281–282, 284, 294 392
Volksgenossen (national comrades), 31–32, 38, 294

Wagner, Eduard, 182, 256
Walter, Bruno, 21
"war guilt clause" (Article 231), 8
War Ministry, 129
Warlimont, Walter, 187
Wartenburg, Peter Yorck von, 30–31, 99, 154, 262, 287, 299

Weber, Max, 67
Wehrmacht, 30, 38, 43, 56–57, 108–109, 120, 125, 153, 180, 184, 187, 191, 198, 223–225, 233, 250, 257, 275, 294
Weill, Kurt, 21
Weimar Constitution, 16, 119, 121, 124
Weimar Republic, 2, 8–13, 22, 26, 43, 45, 58, 62, 64, 89–90
Weiße Rose (White Rose), 113
Weizsäcker, Ernst von, 150, 152, 178, 192, 299
Wels, Otto, 90
Weltanschauung, 77, 80, 131, 303
Weltmacht oder Vernichtung (World Power or Destruction), 177, 280, 294, 336
Weserübung (Weser Exercise), 208–209, 217, 294
Wheeler–Bennett, John W., 189
White Rose (Weiße Rose), 113
Wilder, Billy, 10
Wilhelm II (emperor kaiser), 60–61
Wilson, Horace, 164
Wilson, Woodrow, 147, 314
Winter Help (Winterhilfe) program, 34
Wirmer, Josef, 273
Witzleben, Erwin von, 37, 62, 117, 135–136, 154, 157–158, 167–170, 173, 175, 178, 192, 201, 213–214, 233, 238, 240, 258, 263, 270–271, 273, 299
Wolfschanze (Wolf's Lair), 233–234, 246–247, 252, 254, 256, 258, 261, 276, 294
World Power or Destruction (Weltmacht oder Vernichtung), 177, 280, 294

Zahn, Gordon, 107, 110
Zeitzler, Kurt, 220
Zell (cell), 34, 294
Zellenleiter (cell leader), 294